DARK DAYS and BRIGHTER DAYS

FOR NORTHERN IRELAND RAILWAYS

Edwin McMillan

COLOURPOINT

Published 2016 by Colourpoint Books
an imprint of Colourpoint Creative Ltd
Colourpoint House, Jubilee Business Park
21 Jubilee Road, Newtownards, BT23 4YH
Tel: 028 9182 6339
Fax: 028 9182 1900
E-mail: sales@colourpoint.co.uk
Web: www.colourpoint.co.uk

First Edition
First Impression

A catalogue record for this book is available from the British Library.

Designed by April Sky Design, Newtownards
Tel: 028 9182 7195
Web: www.aprilsky.co.uk

Printed by W&G Baird Ltd, Antrim

ISBN 978-1-78073-094-3

Front cover: (top left) Devastation from a 1000 lb bomb driven onto the line adjacent to an Army road checkpoint,
near to Cloghogue Chapel, Newry on 1 May 1992. The explosion killed one soldier, demolished the checkpoint facility and completely
destroyed both up and down lines, leaving a large crater. *(Author)*
(top right) Damaged coaches at York Road after a six car 80 Class service from Belfast Central to Portadown was hijacked
and set on fire at Bells Row level crossing, Lurgan, 6 July 1997. *(Author)*
(bottom) CAF Class 4000 No 4001, arriving at Belfast York Road, Monday, 14 March 2011. *(Author)*

Rear cover: (left) MED No 18 in middle road, and another set at Platform One at Bangor station, 17 August 1971. *(Author)*
(right) Hunslet No 102 *Falcon*, being prepared at Belfast York Road for a special on the occasion of the official opening of the new station at
Larne on Wednesday, 3 July 1974. *(Author)*

CONTENTS

This book is dedicated to Lucinda, my wife,
who put up with me for a whole year
while I compiled the data and wrote this book.

FOREWORD

M y primary school in Bangor, County Down, was situated right beside the main station. Every day I was able to observe trains coming and going, and steam trains still frequented the station. A young railway enthusiast was now on the scene! As I transferred to the local secondary school, I cycled from home to the Brunswick Road bridge at Bangor several times a week after school to observe the trains.

I knew that I just wanted a job with Northern Ireland Railways (NIR) and during my last six months of technical college I pestered the NIR personnel office asking for a job. They gave in and I started in the headquarters offices at York Road, Belfast, in July 1973. Not only was it great to be paid but I was given a railway pass to travel on the network, which was invaluable.

I began collecting newspaper cuttings relating to railways and filled scrapbooks; I took photographs; kept personal diaries for 43 years; and saved posters and documents produced at work that would have been disposed of. Railway enthusiasts do collect many railway artefacts and I am no exception. The extent of my own personal records was one of the reasons that I was able to compile this book.

All through my 40 years with NIR, the company was affected one way or another by "the Troubles". There were many dark days. To hear that passengers had been killed or injured by terrorism was a real disaster for the many families and railway staff involved. When no warnings were given by the terrorists, this was just despicable. Stations and infrastructure were also attacked which was especially disheartening for the staff who had built the structures and those who worked there.

A lot of the incidents were set up to target the security forces but railway staff and passengers bore the brunt of most of them. My many personal experiences of this during my time with NIR included: being shot at and petrol bombed; being at locations as bombs exploded; and standing within short distances of land mines and bombs on the track.

On the brighter side, the Belfast Central Railway was re-opened; the Cross-Harbour rail link was constructed; railway routes and stations were re-opened; relaying of the track continued; new stations were built; and all of the old trains were replaced.

Writing this book has been a great experience and I hope you enjoy reading it, even through the sad parts.

Edwin C McMillan
March 2016

Key to Abbreviations

AEC	Associated Equipment Company
BCDR	Belfast & County Down Railway
BCR	Belfast Central Railway
BREL	British Rail Engineering Limited
BTP	British Transport Police
BUT	British United Traction
CCTV	Closed Circuit Television
CIÉ	Córas Iompair Éireann
CWR	Continuously welded rail
DH	Diesel hydraulic locomotive
DoE	Department of the Environment for Northern Ireland
DRD	Department of Regional Development for Northern Ireland
GNR (I)	Great Northern Railway of Ireland
IÉ	Iarnród Éireann – Irish Rail
IRRS	Irish Railway Record Society
LMSNCC	London Midland & Scottish Railway (Northern Counties Committee)
LP&HC	Londonderry Port and Harbour Commissioners
MED	Multi-engined diesel unit
MPD	Multi-purpose diesel unit
MRSI	Modern Railway Society of Ireland
NIR	Northern Ireland Railways Company Limited
NITHC	Northern Ireland Transport Holding Company
NUPE	National Union of Public Employees
PIRA	Provisional Irish Republican Army
PSNI	Police Service of Northern Ireland
PSV	Public Service Vehicle
RPSI	Railway Preservation Society of Ireland
RUC	Royal Ulster Constabulary
SLW	Single line working
TSSA	Transport Salaried Staffs' Association
UDA	Ulster Defence Association
UTA	Ulster Transport Authority
UWC	Ulster Workers' Council

NIR IN ITS INFANCY:
1966–1973

When Northern Ireland Railways (NIR) came into existence in 1967, I was only twelve years old, so I do not have many recollections of the very early days of the company. However, for the young railway enthusiast that I already was, my first school in Bangor was very well placed. I attended Trinity Primary on Brunswick Road, and in my last two years there, our classes were held in a portable building adjacent to the Bangor station railway path, and only a few feet from the signal box and tracks. I remember always trying to get a seat near the classroom windows, so that I could watch the trains coming and going.

Once I transferred to Bangor Secondary School, I didn't lose touch with the railway by any means. After school, I used to cycle from my house to the Brunswick Road bridge (otherwise known as the "Boyne Bridge"), and watch the trains there from late afternoon and into the evening rush hour. In 1970, I even cycled from Bangor to Belfast to see several of the stations there, including Queen's Quay and Adelaide Yard. As I got older and a bit more adventurous, I went by train to Belfast's Queen's Quay, and to faraway places like Jordanstown and Carrickfergus, as well as Coleraine and Portrush. Unfortunately I did not possess a camera until 1971, so my railway photographic archive before then is a bit sparse. However I was very much into tape recordings, and I still have a few audio recordings of MED (Multi-Engined Diesel) trains in operation at Bangor and Carnalea.

I suppose I inherited the interest in transport from my dad, Norman. He joined the Northern Ireland Road Transport Board as a bus driver in 1947, and went on to work for the Ulster Transport Authority and Ulsterbus; he completed a short spell with Flexibus before retiring after 47 years' service. Dad was pleased that I had joined the transport industry too, albeit in a different guise.

In spite of my lack of personal involvement in the industry at the time, I have been able to piece together – from my personal diaries, railway scrapbooks, photographs and various other items of memorabilia I uncovered – the following brief history of the railways in Northern Ireland for the period 1962 to 1973. Some of the incidents and developments I highlight in this chapter will be looked at in greater depth later in the book.

The Benson Report

Large-scale line closures had occurred throughout Northern Ireland during the 1950s and even into the early 1960s. By 1962, the outlook for the remaining railways in Northern Ireland seemed bleak. The Northern Ireland government decided to commission one last-ditch in-depth investigation into the problems of the railways, and for this purpose they engaged Sir Henry Benson CBE, a prominent London accountant.

Presented to Parliament in July 1963, the Benson Report was the last major public enquiry into transport matters in Northern Ireland. Its recommendations were drastic, but stopped short of complete closure of the whole system. Lines to be closed included both routes to Londonderry – the one from Bleach Green, and the other from Portadown. Five branch lines were also recommended for closure: Goraghwood to Newry; Newry to Warrenpoint; Dungannon to Coalisland; Knockmore Junction to Antrim; and Coleraine to Portrush. It was proposed that the lines from Belfast to Larne Harbour, Belfast to Portadown and Belfast to Bangor should be operated as commuter-only routes, although the carriage of mail including parcels would also be provided for on these. Otherwise, the transportation of freight and merchandise was to be generally discontinued. Finally, it was recommended that the line from Portadown to the Border would be retained as part of the Belfast to Dublin service, but that this should be reduced to single track – something which was strenuously opposed by Córas Iompair Éireann (CIÉ), the Republic's rail operator.

An advertisement in the *News Letter*, reminding the public of where they could travel to by train in Northern Ireland at the time. It is a stark reminder of what was left after the further cutbacks to the rail network in the mid-1960s. *(Author's collection)*

Most of the closures came into effect in 1965. The shutting down of the Londonderry line caused great dissatisfaction in the west of the Province. The two lines to Londonderry served totally different parts of the country, and it was felt that closing both would isolate those living there. It was therefore decided by the Northern Ireland government to retain the line from Coleraine (i.e. the Bleach Green line).

The Birth of Northern Ireland Railways

Transport acts in 1967 split the existing company, the Ulster Transport Authority, into two separate operations, one for road and one for rail. The first meeting of the Board of what was to become NIR, but which for the time being had been given the temporary name of Ulster Transport Railways, was held in the railway offices at York Road, Belfast on 9 June 1967, with the new general manager in place – Mr Hugh Waring. The first timetable for the new railway system came into operation on 26 June 1967.

Another key item on the agenda at that first meeting was the naming of the new railway company. One suggestion was "Ulster-rail", given that the newly-formed bus operations company had just been christened "Ulsterbus"; however, nothing was decided upon on that day. After a few more meetings, the name finally agreed upon was Northern Ireland Railways. The Company was incorporated on 21 April 1967 and, again under the provisions of the Transport Act (NI) 1967, was charged with the duty to provide, or to secure the provision of, railway services in Northern Ireland, with effect from 1 April 1968. On the same day, and also according to the terms of the Act, the Northern Ireland Transport Holding Company (NITHC) officially came into being, taking over from its previous incarnation under the 1948 (NI) Transport Act, the Ulster Transport Authority.

When NIR took over, assuming responsibility for all assets and liabilities, the company owned over 203 miles of railway, and exercised continuous running powers over an additional 62 miles in the Republic of Ireland, in the joint operation of cross-border services with CIÉ. They had seven locomotives, eight diesel electric motor coaches (70 Class), 159 diesel railcars and trailers, 17 carriages and 30 other coaching vehicles. The new railway system was to be operated in four regions – Southern, Down, Midland and North Western.

New Stations: Belfast

In the late 1960s there were three main stations in Belfast, each built by different railway companies in days gone by. These were: the Great Northern Railway station at Great Victoria Street, opened in 1839; the London Midland and Scottish Railway station at York Road, opened in 1848; and the Belfast and County Down Railway station at Queen's Quay, opened in 1848.

By April 1969 however, the NI Ministry of Development was carrying out a study into the proposal that there should be major changes to railway stations in Belfast. Of several possible scenarios being looked into, the most favoured seemed to be a plan to close the station at Great Victoria Street and divert incoming trains on the Portadown line along the old, disused Central Railway to a new station at May's Market. This new station, it was proposed, could also be used by passengers from the Bangor line, with the construction of new bridges bringing this line over from Queen's Quay.

Old station buildings in Belfast at (l-r) Great Victoria Street, York Road and Queen's Quay, circa 1970. *(Author)*

Mr Hugh Waring, the general manager of NIR, commented in April 1969 that the plan to move out of Queen's Quay had been mooted for over a year and that he, "would like to see a more compact, bright and hygienic terminal to replace the archaic, inconvenient and draughty station at Queen's Quay". The sale of the Queen's Quay site, a portion of the station frontage of Great Victoria Street station and some of the land to its rear would be an important source of finance for the project. In May 1969 the Ministry called for an in-depth report on the costs and savings such a scheme could bring. NIR appointed a firm of consultants to carry out the necessary detailed investigations.

Roy Bradford, the Minister of Development, reported in June 1971 that a move to renew the Belfast Central Railway would cost at least £1 million. The issue of the proposed re-opening and renewal was raised at Stormont and, in the ensuing discussion, concerns were also raised regarding the current state of the disused railway, due to dumping, rat infestation and vandalism. A report on the financial feasibility of the project was ordered for November 1971.

Europa Hotel

As mentioned above, by the end of the 1960s, the original large station at Great Victoria Street in Belfast had outgrown its use and a large proportion of the site was no longer required. A sizable section of the old station building was demolished to allow for the construction of an important new hotel. Due for completion in May 1971, the Europa Hotel would have 220 bedrooms and was being built for the Grand Metropolitan Hotel group. A smaller railway station frontage remained in place and the concourse and platforms were all retained for some time, however: the railway station did not finally close until 1976.

Panoramic view of the demolition work at Great Victoria Street station as featured in the *Belfast Telegraph* on 31 October 1968.

Good News for Belfast Central Project

At Stormont on 11 February 1972, Minister Roy Bradford announced that government approval had been given for the much-discussed project to renew Belfast's Central station and the associated lines, in what would represent a major facelift for Northern Ireland's railway system. A large injection of finance would fund the reopening of the

the 2.5 mile Belfast Central Railway at an estimated cost of £1.2 million, and the purchase of ten new diesel-electric trains at an estimated cost of £1.5 million. The new line, with a proposed completion date of mid-1974, would have a major station at Maysfield (which would be known as Belfast Central), as well as in the Shaftesbury Square area (which would be known as Botanic station). The line would allow trains to operate between Bangor and Craigavon, and onwards to Dublin. With the reopening of the Lisburn to Antrim railway, which at that time had no passenger services but could be ready for use within twelve months, trains from the Londonderry direction would also be able to run direct to Maysfield. It was hoped that ultimately a link would be built into Aldergrove Airport. The Belfast railway stations at Great Victoria Street and Queen's Quay would be shut down as planned, and the land redeveloped in keeping with the Belfast Urban Area Plan. Belfast's York Road station would remain in place, but to primarily serve the Larne line.

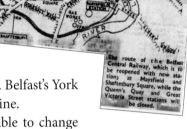

Newspaper cuttings featuring Belfast Central Railway, February 1972. *(Author's collection)*

Not least, the new system would mean that travellers would be able to change trains at the new Maysfield station, without having to labour the whole way across the city centre. The new station would be bright and modern, with shopping, restaurant, waiting room and Customs facilities for the cross-border Belfast to Dublin service.

Tendering for Belfast Central Railway Projects

On Thursday, 22 March 1973, advertisements appeared in the press for "Contract No 3" and "Contract No 4", in relation to the recommissioning of the Belfast Central Railway. Contract No 3 was for civil engineering work and included: site clearance and demolition; the laying of approximately 4.3 km of double-line railway track; the construction of five bridges including one over the River Lagan; the provision of an additional bridge – a footbridge; the reconfiguration of the Queen's Quay maintenance yard; the construction of station platforms, car parks, drainage and so on for the new Central Station; and the building of the new Shaftesbury Square/Botanic Station. Contract No 4 entailed the construction of the new Central Station building and facilities, and included site clearance, landscaping, the installation of drainage and services with the building, and pile driving. The deadline for the completion of both contract applications from contractors was 2 April 1973.

While the applications were being reviewed, another contract – for the supply of 1,000 tons of bridge steel – was placed with Braithwaite and Co of West Bromwich in July 1973. The steel would be used for the reconstruction of four bridges, including a 112-metre span of the River Lagan and the partial reconstruction of the East Bridge Street over-bridge at Belfast Central station.

On Wednesday, 3 October 1973, a press conference was held by NIR to announce that a Belfast construction company, PJ Walls and Bros, had been awarded the contract for building the new station at Belfast Central, which was valued at about £2.9 million. It was expected that the building work would take about 18 months to complete, and that the new station should be in operation from May 1975.

Contract documents were also signed with a well-known construction company, Graham, based in Dromore for Contract No 3, covering the civil engineering work required for the new Belfast Central and Shaftesbury Square/Botanic railway stations, and also including the laying of track and signalling along the routes. The consulting engineers for the entire project would be the internationally known firm, Rendel, Palmer and Tritton.

More New Stations: Portrush, Portadown and the Goodyear halt

The New University of Ulster at Coleraine had first opened its doors in 1968, and from the end of that summer the Portrush railway branch reopened for daily services. A new station was built for the University, the old Portstewart station was renamed the Cromore halt, and another new halt was opened at Dhu Varren, less than a mile from Portrush.

On 31 August 1970, a new station, the Goodyear halt, was opened one mile west of Lurgan to serve the new tyre factory. This wooden platform station was built exclusively for Goodyear employees and visitors to the large factory, which was only a few hundred yards away, built on a green field site. Unfortunately the tyre factory closed some years later, and on 30 October 1983, the station was also decommissioned: with no local housing in the area, there were not enough potential passengers to justify its continued operation.

Just a few months later, on 5 October 1970, a new railway station was opened in Portadown at a cost of around £140,000. Known as Portadown/Craigavon West, it was built on almost exactly the same site as a previous station dating back to 1848, but which had only been in active use for 15 years. The new Portadown/Craigavon West station would replace the old station in Watson Street, which was on the Belfast side of the River Bann: one of the platforms of this old station can still be seen today, within the civil engineering yard.

Advertising leaflet containing the timetable and fares, commencing 5 October 1970, for the new station at Portadown. *(Author's collection)*

A New Freight Yard

In April 1971, NIR awarded a £350,000 contract to AJ Clancy of Mallusk for a new road-rail freight yard at Adelaide in Belfast, to replace the existing yard at the city's Grosvenor Road. The nine-acre site would have 12 tracks for freight trains linking with the main Belfast to Dublin line. The depot opened in June 1972 and the first customer was the Guinness Brewery Company.

A decade previously in 1962, the railways had been in serious decline but from about 1969, NIR had been able to halt the downward trend, and by 1972, they were able to reports gains of about three per cent a year. Opening new stations and reviving old lines was a crucial part of this process of regeneration, as was the refurbishment of key existing stations.

Station Refurbishments: Bangor and Antrim

As early as February 1971, Bangor Rotary Club had formalised a call for the restoration of the town's rail link to the Belfast Central Railway, to enable direct trains to run from Dublin and the west of the Northern Ireland into Bangor. They pointed out that within one week of the demolition in 1965 of Middlepath Street bridge in Belfast (which had effectively severed the line to Bangor), a party of 2,000 Sunday School children and their parents had been lost to the resort town. One Bangor trader stated that over a five-year period, his revenue from that source alone had fallen by £5,000. Another immediate loss had been a special train to Bangor for 2,000 passengers from the Jacob's factory, travelling from Dublin. It was further suggested that the reinstatement of the link could allow the train journey from Dublin to Bangor to be achieved within two-and-a-half hours!

In the light of all of this, the Club had agreed that collective pressure should be put on the Minister of Development to move the Belfast Central line restoration project forward. There must have been considerable relief all round when the news came in February 1972 that the grand scheme was to go ahead.

As part the ongoing programme in the early 1970s to modernise Northern Ireland's railways, Bangor station received a major facelift and refurbishment, and was reopened to the public on 29 June 1971. The photograph here shows the smart and attractive new frontage of the station. However, the local press seemed more concerned about the loss of the station clock from the front of the building, than about the investment which had been poured into the revamp, about which they said very little. When NIR were asked about the absence of a clock at Bangor station, they responded by saying that the local Council had been involved in the plans for the new frontage, and that if they, the Council, had felt very strongly

Bangor Station refurbishment as featured in the *Bangor Spectator*, 29 June 1971.

about having the clock as a public amenity, they could have mentioned it at that point and that NIR would have happily incorporated it in the design, on the understanding that the Council provide the clock. The Council had however not raised the issue, it seemed, and it had therefore been deemed that they had declined the offer!

However in October 1971 Bangor Rotary Club raised the subject again. Since both NIR and the Council were unwilling to pay for a new clock, the Club discussed the issuing of a public appeal for funds. The idea was temporarily put on hold until the cost of a new clock could be ascertained. Time moved on, and before too long NIR proposed that the clock tower should be given a facelift. There was still no money available for a clock, however. The then Chief Executive of NIR, Hugh Waring decided to have a word on the matter with the Company's bank manager – and hey presto, the Northern Bank donated a clock for the clock tower!

On Tuesday, 9 February 1973, the episode of the clock was nicely rounded off, when members of the NIR Board travelled to Bangor on a lunch-hour train to inspect the newly installed three-faced clock and unveil a plaque recording the generosity of the Northern Bank in making the gift to the town.

Out with the Old: Tunnels and Stations

An unusual notice appeared in the local press in July 1969: an advertisement for the sale of an old railway tunnel at Drummilt, Loughgilly in County Armagh. The old tunnel had formed part of the railway line from Markethill to Armagh. The advert detailed that the tunnel was approximately 1,000 feet long and was dry – apart from a small section at either end. It was in fact the longest dry tunnel in Ireland! It was also noted that 200 feet of the dry part had been concreted, with electric underfloor heating, and that electricity and water supplies were on site. It seemed that the property had been used for growing mushrooms but, according to the ad, it would be ideal for warehousing or storage purposes, or, Mr Humphreys the estate agent suggested slightly more fancifully, it "could make a marvellous night club, as there is a concrete forecourt at one end of the tunnel which would make a car park – and think of the wonderful long bar you could have!" The asking price was thought to be in the region of £8,000 (the equivalent in today's terms of about £120,000). There is unfortunately no record of what the tunnel was eventually sold for and for what purpose it was used.

Portrush

From July 1972, a storm was brewing in Portrush over the future of the large original station building. The Ulster Architectural Heritage Society said that the 80-year-old station was of outstanding merit and importance, and unique to North Antrim. NIR however had submitted to the local Council plans which would entail the old station being completely demolished and replaced with a modern, single-storey shopping complex, comprising a supermarket, three shops and a site to rehouse the existing public house. The new Portrush station would be built behind the old station, and further down the line. Mr Waring, the NIR general manager, argued that the station building was much too large and out-of-date, meaning that it was impossible to keep it tidy and in proper repair.

NIR's plans were however ultimately refused by the Council, who were in favour of the preservation of the old station building. An appeal by NIR against the decision was unsuccessful, and as a result, the old station still proudly stands on its original site. Later in 1973, the new station was approved, and it was opened in due course, with the old station building being listed for preservation as an historic building.

Conductors, Customers and Fares

Conductorisation on trains in Northern Ireland came into effect from 9 June 1969, meaning that from this date train guards would be responsible for the issuing of tickets, except on the Belfast–Dublin service. Ticket offices would however still be operating at certain stations. Off-peak day returns, from 9.30 am, were introduced to attract more passengers.

From Monday, 28 June 1971, first-class travel facilities were withdrawn on the Belfast–Portadown, Belfast–Larne Harbour and Coleraine–Portrush services. From that date, such services would only be available on the Belfast–Londonderry and Belfast–Dublin routes.

Another initiative from NIR in 1971 was the introduction of free travel or concessionary fares for senior citizens. This is something which is very much taken for granted now, but it began as a pilot scheme for a trial period, when, on 11 December 1971, rail travel for senior citizens was offered at half-fare rates after 9.30 am each morning. There was no requirement for form filling: the passenger simply had to present their Pension Book to the booking clerk or the conductor on the train. The scheme was well-publicised, popular and a real benefit for those older people travelling in the run-up to Christmas.

On 19 May 1969, NIR implemented its first increase in fares since 1963. This was not too drastic, and meant a just small rise in fares for some passengers. There was a further increase in May 1971. Here are some examples I have found of representative fares at the time: a weekly return ticket from Bangor to Belfast was £1.55; a monthly ticket from Bangor to Belfast was £6.00. A day return from Belfast to Portrush was 75 pence; a day return from Belfast to Bangor was 35 pence.

Railway Timetables

The earliest copy of an NIR timetable in my archives is dated 29 June 1970; the front cover was a maroon colour. The train timetable was priced at 3 pence (6d), and detailed all local train services, as well as the cross-border service between Belfast and Dublin. It also featured the cross-channel service between Belfast and Glasgow and to London, with details of all connecting services; the ships were operated by British Rail. The Stranraer–London route was a sleeper train service. Other services included in the same train timetable were connecting Ulsterbus services from places like Donaghadee, Omagh, Cushendun and Islandmagee, and bus services operated by the Londonderry and Lough Swilly railway (buses only at this stage). Holiday timetables would also have been produced for Easter, the July holidays and Christmas.

1970 NIR timetable cover, and 1971 NIR holiday timetable. (Author's collection)

Major Upgrading: Level Crossings, Rolling Stock and New Tracks

The most dangerous part of an operational railway is where the railway lines and roads meet at level crossings. In the early days of NIR there were more than 400 level crossings on the network, consisting in the main of intersections with public roads and footpaths, as well as "occupation" and "accommodation" crossings (terms which denote level crossings where there is a dwelling house on the land and the crossing gates are operated by the authorised users). There were several hundred level crossings alone on the lines from Belfast to Londonderry and Portrush. In 1971 approximately 80 of the over 400 level crossings in Northern Ireland were classed as public roads, and these were controlled by either signallers or crossing keepers.

In the rest of the UK by this time, a new system of automatic half-barrier level crossings had been introduced, as an efficient means of controlling of road and pedestrian traffic at key intersections. It was decided by NIR to commence a renewal programme of level crossings here too, whereby existing crossing gates would be replaced by automatic lifting half-barriers. Lissue level crossing near Lisburn had been modernised in January 1967, and the next four crossings to be updated were installed at Trooperslane and Trummery on 20 June 1971, followed by Drumbane on 4 July 1971 and Kilmakee on 22 August the same year. The upgrading of level crossings across the network would continue, bringing the two-fold benefit of reducing the costs of railway operations (by dispensing with the need for crossing keepers), and minimising delays to road traffic.

The first accident at a level crossing that is noted in my own records was on Saturday, 20 March 1971, when a Belfast–Londonderry train struck a cattle lorry at Lock's accommodation crossing at Campsie, Londonderry. A dairy farmer and his son narrowly escaped death, but three cows were killed as they were thrown 30 feet into a field. The 40-year-old farmer sustained head injuries. The crossing in question was not automated, and would have been operated by the authorised users.

One of the recently acquired Hunslet locomotives being prepared at Great Victoria Street, in 1970, for the new cross-border service – No 101 *Eagle*. (*Author*)

New Rolling Stock and Track Renewal

On 1 July 1970, the Belfast to Dublin route received a major boost, with the introduction of a new NIR train formation consisting of new Hunslet locomotives and British Rail Mark 2 carriages. Rolling stock features in general are further documented in Chapter Seven.

One of the most costly items to replace was of course the railway tracks. Given the ongoing challenge of attracting investment to NIR, it was decided that track refurbishment would be done according to a rolling programme of track renewal, as and when funds became available. I have noted, for example, that on Sunday, 10 January 1971 that relaying of the track between Crawfordsburn and Carnalea on the Bangor line was taking place, and was to extend towards Helen's Bay. By Monday, 10 December 1973 the track relay had reached Holywood, and the next proposed section for relay was Holywood to Knocknagoney (towards Sydenham). A new temporary Monday/ Friday timetable was introduced for three weeks at this time, to allow for the relay of three miles of track in each direction.

Challenges to NIR: Money Matters

As has been noted, securing funds for the development and refurbishing of Northern Ireland's railway system was a perennial problem for NIR, and at the beginning of the 1970s, there were constant challenges to the feasibility of the network as a public service. One of these challenges came very publicly in January 1970 from Mr Werner Heubeck, the head of Ulsterbus, who stated that he personally could not see how the railways were making a real contribution to the economic life of the community. Heubeck went on to say that if the railways were closed, Ulsterbus would benefit by being in an even sounder economic position, with the result that there could be a general reduction in fares for public transport. Hugh Waring of NIR countered by stating that on most railway routes on the network, there had been a substantial increase in passenger numbers, in addition to which the government had been putting forward capital money for new projects. Waring's claims were vindicated a few months later in March 1970, when the Minister disclosed that NIR had recorded a £50,000 profit in the year 1969/70: by anyone's standards, a very fine achievement.

By 1972, however, things were not looking so financially rosy for the Company. On 25 May that year, published accounts revealed that more than £146,000 had been lost in the year 1971/72. However, NIR reported, the deficit was actually less than had been anticipated, and the losses were principally due to the continuing civil disturbances of "the Troubles", meaning that weekend and cross-border traffic in particular had suffered. Taking into account other factors, such as pay increases and high maintenance costs for old rolling stock still in use, the situation was not as bleak as might have first appeared.

Roads and the Railways: The M2 and the M5

I wonder how many people in Northern Ireland remember the time, pre-1970, when there was no motorway along the coastline of Belfast Lough between Belfast and Glengormley, and towards Whiteabbey? The foreshore motorway took seven years to create and cost £7 million. It was built mainly on reclaimed land from the shore of Belfast Lough.

Not long after its formation as a company, NIR won a contract to carry the spoil from the Associated Portland Cement Magheramorne Quarry to the foreshore in Belfast. In order to ensure the completion of this massive task, the Ministry of Development, in conjunction with NIR, purchased 70 special wagons to carry 30 tons each; these would be hauled by two locomotives. By the time the contract ended, on 2 May 1970, an astounding 7,600 spoil runs had been made, carrying 4,000,000 tons of rock and

The last working steam train in the UK, 2 May 1970.

spoil from Magheramorne. Of the two trains operating on the job, one was the last working steam train in the United Kingdom, and as such, it would be the subject of a television programme screened by Ulster Television on 23 July 1971.

The three-mile motorway running from the Duncrue Street area to Greencastle was opened on Wednesday, 23 May 1973 by the Minister of State, Lord Windlesham.

The new motorways would run between the lines of the railway and the centralised workshops in Duncrue Street, which had been built by the UTA in the 1950s. Since the alignment of the new roads would go straight through the railway yard at York Road, the railway part of the workshops from Duncrue Street to York Road was removed. The site at Duncrue Street would be retained by Ulsterbus and Northern Ireland Carriers.

The Holywood Bypass

NIR helped out the Northern Irish motoring public again in the early 1970s, this time in North Down, by moving part of the railway line between Holywood and Marino to a slightly different location. A new bypass was to be constructed, mostly on the foundation of the railway. The total cost of the entire operation was estimated to be in the region of £530,000. The present Holywood railway curve opened on Monday, 29 March 1971; parts of the original formation had been used for the new road. A new sea wall and footpath were also constructed by the Roads Service, but unfortunately the maintenance of these has remained with NIR, something which will surely be a financial burden in the future, as the constant wearing down of the sea wall takes its toll.

Getting Away from it all: Holidays

In the Northern Ireland of the late 1960s and early 1970s, foreign holidays were not the run-of-the-mill part of life that they are for many people now. For this reason, public transport, and the railways in particular provided an important means of travel to holiday destinations within the country, and beyond it too. My first holiday out of Northern Ireland, in August 1971, was to Ayr in Scotland. We took the boat train from Belfast York Road to Larne Harbour; from there, we walked the very short distance onto the British Rail ship. Once in Stranraer, we had another short walk from the ship to the train which would take us to Ayr. This was at a time when all forms of transport usually connected seamlessly, and there was not much effort needed to transfer between train, ship and train again.

The Larne to Stranraer route was operated by British Rail and was marketed as "the Princess Route", after the names of the ships. In July 1971, the new, £2.75 million *Ailsa Princess* had just begun operating on the route. An overnight sleeper train also ran from Stranraer to London at the time.

While on holiday in Ayr, I managed to obtain a railway yard pass from British Rail for the Newton-on-Ayr site and, after being given the nod by the foreman there, I was able to walk around and explore the area. I am including a photograph here for interest.

Accidents and Natural Disasters

The first railway collision since NIR's inception of which I have a note in my records took place on Wednesday, 7 July 1971. It involved the evening Enterprise from Dublin to Belfast, which crashed into the back of a mail train on the approach to Portadown station. (Incidentally, the "Enterprise" name had been used to refer to the cross-border service since 1947). A number of passengers and a railway guard were injured. I will be discussing this incident in more detail in Chapter Seven.

Newton-on-Ayr diesel shed, with Diesel Hydraulic 0-6-0 No 3561 awaiting a shunt. *(Author)*

Train Derailment

Wednesday, 4 August 1971 saw approximately six hours of continuous torrential rain in Londonderry from late afternoon onwards. Some streets in the city were flooded with two to three feet of water. The rear two coaches of a five-coach train travelling from Portrush to Londonderry derailed at St Columb's Park, about one mile from Londonderry station, as a result of the embankment being washed away. Passengers had no choice but to wade from the derailed train along the track to the station. One passenger sustained a broken leg in the accident, and several others had minor injuries. A stretch of 20 to 30 feet of the embankment had been affected, and over the next couple of days, passengers were taken by bus from Waterside to Culmore station to board the train there.

Byelaws and a New Rulebook

New NIR Byelaws came into operation on 15 July 1971, and these replaced the former railway company's Byelaws. Sheet copies were posted at stations but individual copies could also be purchased by the public for 15 pence. Such Byelaws serve to regulate passenger travel and the operation of the railways, including the maintenance of order on or in connection with the railway and the conduct of all persons on railway property. In particular, designated offences cover ticketing issues, intoxicated persons, disorderly and offensive behaviour, smoking, damage to equipment, the throwing of stones or other objects, and the misuse of level crossings by pedestrians or motorists.

One of the major changes which had been instituted by the new Transport Act of 1967 was the decommissioning of railway police constables (a particularly bad move, in my opinion). As a result, the enforcement of any new railway Byelaws in relation to incidents on the railway was entirely the responsibility of railway staff or, in extreme cases, police from the Royal Ulster Constabulary.

It is worth noting that, on 1 January 1973, a new NIR rule book came into operation. This was the first of its kind specific to NIR, as up until this date, the guidelines from the former railway companies had simply been retained. The new document brought together a more uniform set of rules, meaning that all NIR staff were now using the same guidelines. The NIR rule book covered all operational issues and procedures in relation to the railway, including: the duties of train drivers, conductors, guards and other grades; the operation of trains; what protocol to follow when trains broke down and for their recovery; rules governing the running of trains in difficult weather conditions such as fog or snowfall, and during track relay or other infrastructure work, and so on.

The Troubles

Most readers will, sadly, be familiar with "the Troubles", Northern Ireland's most recent period of serious civil unrest. Since the Troubles are widely acknowledged to have begun in earnest in 1969, it is clear that the early years of NIR in the period under review in this chapter, 1967 to 1973, were dominated by the shadow of the violence of the terrorist campaigns of the IRA and their Protestant counterparts. The impact on our railways and all those who worked on them was of course very great, and in fact devastating – first and foremost, in terms of the loss of life and injury to staff and passengers, but also in terms of the damage to trains, stations and other NIR assets. The financial fortunes of the company were of course affected too, and the development and expansion of services and general success of the enterprise were severely limited by what was happening on the streets of Northern Ireland.

In a historical context, the railways in Ireland as a whole had been targeted by terrorists in previous campaigns, at least as far back as the Irish Civil War in the 1920s. During the IRA's 1950s campaign, two railway bridges were blown up near Carrickmore on the line between Omagh and Pomeroy on 17 February 1957. In March 1958, a freight train was hijacked, sent on its way with no crew, and as a result, it crashed into the railway station at Foyle Road in Londonderry. In the late 1960s and early 1970s, as in earlier times of civil strife, public transport was often on the frontline and staff were placed in very difficult situations, subjected to intimidation by paramilitaries and forced to deal with anti-social behaviour, such as the stoning of trains and escalating vandalism.

In Chapters Five and Six, I will deal in detail with the impact of the Troubles on the railways in Northern Ireland and on the fortunes of NIR, by cataloguing some of the key incidents affecting the services and the system. Suffice to say for now that the early years of our railway company, during some of the most violent years of the conflict, were fraught with death, danger and difficulty for all concerned.

MY TIME AT NIR, PART ONE:
1973–1986

As mentioned in the previous chapter, I was interested in trains and the railways from early childhood. This enthusiasm didn't decline once I became a teenager – quite the opposite, in fact. Looking back at the diaries which I kept for many years, it can be seen that I made contact with Northern Ireland Railways on a number of occasions long before I was employed by them. For instance, on 16 October 1970, when I was 15 years old, I wrote to ask if there was any possibility of the Belfast Central Railway being reopened; in the same letter, I was also keen for the two excursion platforms at Bangor station to be reinstated. I have a record too of having written to NIR on 9 September 1972 about the prevalence of stone-throwing at trains in the Ballymacarrett area of the city: to this letter, I received a response from the then Managing Director, Hugh Waring, explaining what the company was doing about this problem. My interest in anti-social behaviour on the railways, and how it could be tackled, way back then in the early 1970s would, as we will see, later be revived and put to good use during my employment with NIR.

Job Vacancies in NIR

As 1973 dawned, I noticed, in the Job Vacancies section of the Belfast *News Letter*, an advertisement from NIR: they were looking for clerks (male and female), to be based at NIR Headquarters on York Road, Belfast. This is what I had been hoping to see for some time, as all I wanted was to join the railway – however I was not due to leave Bangor Technical College until the end of June that year. So I had no choice but to wait and hope that vacancies would still be on offer then.

It was difficult to wait, however, and just a few months later, in March 1973, I sent my first job-related letter to NIR, saying that I was interested in a clerk's position. I did get a response from the Company, but it was just to ask me to advise them of my exam results once they became available. Yet again, in early June 1973, a notice appeared in the Belfast *News Letter* advertising vacancies for clerks at NIR. I was still waiting for my exam results, but I was feeling more and more impatient, as I didn't want to lose out.

Working for the Railway

Summer 1973, and my exam results were in. I immediately wrote to NIR once more, asking for a job. The first-class stamp on my letter did its job, and the next afternoon I got a phone call from the company, requesting that I come for an interview the following day – Friday, 6 July.

Needless to say, it was with great excitement that I travelled to the NIR headquarters offices at York Road for my interview at 10.30 am. To my delight, after the interview, I was offered a job there and then, based in the Insurance Department at York Road. I was to be paid £11.50 per week, and would be entitled to free travel, which was a big bonus and, for me as a railway enthusiast, a huge incentive. My hours of work would be Monday to Friday, from 9.00 am to 5.20 pm. And I was starting on the following Monday!

Up bright and early the morning of 9 July 1973, I caught the 08.20 hrs service from Bangor to Belfast Queen's Quay: six-car MED set (in my excitement, I forgot to take the numbers). I returned home on the 17.45 hrs express service. This would be my usual travelling pattern while working at headquarters, and getting from Queen's Quay to York Road was a real challenge at times. In good weather, you could walk it, but on the way you had to pass through depressing scenes of demolition and clearance around Corporation Street and up through York Street. It could also be a dangerous route to take at times, with various bomb scares and security incidents along the way. From time to time, I would try several different routes by bus, but these could be hit-and-miss, with possible delays also caused by civil disturbances in the city. Although by May 1974, I had passed my driving test, I had no intention of using my dad's car to go to work. The thought of driving from Bangor to Belfast York Road was not appealing, especially with all the police checkpoints and bomb scares within Belfast. No, even though the journey from Queen's Quay to York Road at the time was not the best, I preferred to just adjust my walking routes to and from work as circumstances required.

One abiding memory of my first day is the moment when someone from Personnel came to my desk and placed in front of me two forms for signature. It wasn't a matter of deciding whether I should sign or not – I was simply advised that both documents should be signed by the end of the day. One was for the NIR pension scheme, and the other one was for membership of the clerical union, the Transport Salaried Staffs' Association. As instructed, I put my signature to both. At only 18 years old, I wondered that day why on earth I would want to sign a pension form, however when it came to my retirement, I was very glad that I had done so, and that I had stayed in the company scheme throughout my entire career there.

I didn't stay long in the Insurance Department, as I was then chosen to work in the Company Secretary's office, along with Messrs Gibson and Carson. The day I started there – Thursday, 19 July 1973 – I got my first weekly pay packet, containing £10.47 net, in cash. Looking back over my 40 years at NIR, it can be seen that my work was based mainly in two departments: the Company Secretary's department (or the equivalent, with a slightly different departmental title), and Railway Operations. In this chapter I will look at the early part of my career, from 1973 to 1986.

Belfast Central Station Model

I wonder how many of readers will remember the large-scale replica of the proposed new Belfast Central station that was put together by an expert model-maker as part of the recommissioning project? I reckon I must have been one of NIR's first railway staff to see it, as I went with the Chief Executive's chauffeur to Stormont Castle to pick it up and bring it back to his office at headquarters in York Road on Tuesday, 24 July 1973.

The model cost £1,100 to commission, and was displayed at various venues, including the Balmoral Show. I always recall that the model featured three passenger ramps leading down from the station building on to the island platforms: one to Platforms One and Two; one leading to Platforms Three and Four; and a third ramp leading down to where the parcels or beach platform was located, as this was possibly going to be a new platform for Dublin line services. In reality, the third ramp never materialised, which is a shame, as it would have been a great asset, leaving the other four platforms for through working instead of one platform being blocked for periods of time while an Enterprise train sat there waiting its next service.

I understand that the model eventually found a new home at the Bangor Model Railway Club.

Operations Department

In an unexpected development I was advised by the Chief Executive, Hugh Waring, on Thursday, 4 October 1973 that I was to be promoted to the Operations Department in York Road, from the next day. My pay would be accordingly increased to £16.29 per week, corresponding to Grade 2 (the grading system for most NIR staff was linked to similar grading systems within British Rail). I would find this work really interesting, as it included the drawing up of timetables and rolling stock schedules. I also assisted in the production of three weekly operating notices. Computers hadn't arrived in the early 1970s, so every week all these documents all had to be handwritten, then typed, run off on a Gestetner duplicating machine, bundled up, and sent out to around 700 staff.

Unofficial Strike Action

On Friday, 22 February 1974, around 80 NIR employees, all members of the National Union of Public Employees (NUPE), went on unofficial strike over pay and union recognition. Mostly from the conductors' and signalmen's grades, they were lobbying for the application of British Rail rates of pay for rail workers in NIR, and negotiating rights for NUPE. Train services were halted between Belfast and Coleraine, Crumlin and Antrim and Belfast and Greenisland.

There was an immediate stalemate. NIR said the situation was outside the company's control, given that the men had not communicated with NIR management. The NUPE representative responded however, by saying that the reason for this failure to communicate was that NUPE was not recognised by NIR, and that therefore there was no communication channel in place. The strike carried on over the weekend of 23–24 February.

There was to be no quick fix to the dispute, and further strikes followed on Monday, 8 April 1974, continuing until Friday, 12 April. The Londonderry and Larne lines continued to feel the effects of the action. Buses were not readily available as an alternative for rail passengers, since talks aimed at settling a week-old strike by 300 Ulsterbus maintenance staff had ended without agreement too. The NIR staff's action continued, with a 24-hour unofficial strike on Thursday, 26 September, affecting the same routes as previously. Parity with British Rail was an even more worthwhile objective for the strikers now, since in July that year, BR staff had received pay awards of between 10 and 29 per cent.

The following month, things took a turn for the worse, when the railway maintenance staff decided to hold a two-day strike, from Tuesday, 8 October 1974. As a direct result of this action, six trains were cancelled on the Larne and Portadown lines during the evening rush-hour period. The strike soon extended to Larne Harbour, where railway electricians, also NIR employees, were refusing to operate the ramp leading to the ships. One cargo vessel, the *Dalriada*, had to return to Stranraer. Cars on the 07.00 hrs ferry sailing also had to be taken back to Stranraer, but foot passengers were able to disembark. The dispute was eventually resolved in mid-October 1974, with new pay rates being agreed.

Timetables and Departure Boards

As I have said, one of my key tasks during this period was the drawing up and production of public timetables, which required on my part quite a bit of local travel back and forth. For example, on Thursday, 27 June 1974, I went to the NIR printers in Newry by bus with a colleague in tow, to read the final draft of the new public timetable, due to commencing on Monday, 1 July 1974. Once the printing was done, we then parcelled up the 14,000 copies. (I presume we had to do this as the printers would have charged us a lot more money to do it for us!) Then, at the end of the month, we were off to Newry again, this time to parcel up another 10,000 copies of the timetable, as well as 9,000 July holiday fortnight booklets. We certainly got the chance to perfect our parcelling and lifting skills!

Another one of my new duties was keeping the manually adjusted departure boards up-to-date. I remember the first time I went in to work with a colleague – it was Sunday, 30 June 1974, to be precise – to change the departure boards at Belfast York station. There were quite a few different boards to be made up: we needed separate ones for Monday to Fridays, for Saturdays and for Sundays.

New Spoil Contract

In the summer of 1974, NIR was awarded a new contract for carrying spoil between Magheramorne Quarry sidings and Cloghan Point. The spoil was to be used to create a new site for the building of large oil storage tanks, which would supply the power station at Ballylumford; a new jetty would also be built for oil tankers to berth at. A Hunslet locomotive was assigned for the hauling of spoil wagons to and from the site. To accommodate this additional traffic, a revised Larne line timetable was brought into operation from Monday, 7 October 1974, introducing single-line working between Cloghan Point and Whitehead. The very last spoil train on this job – the 13.32 hrs Cloghan Point to Magheramorne Loop, was formed by Hunslet locomotive No 102 and 13 empty hoppers, and is shown in the photograph opposite passing through Whitehead on Friday, 22 August 1975. Double-track working between Cloghan Point and Whitehead was restored on Saturday, 8 November 1975.

Far left: Spoil loop at Whitehead, October 1974. *(Author)*

Left: Motor points at Cloghan Point, October 1974. *(Author)*

Signal box Exercise

The Railway Operations department threw up many interesting jobs, and another new one for me was working on the regrading of a signal box. The first time I did this was at Whitehead station on Monday, 3 February 1975. The signal box at Whitehead, like many others on the national railway, used a lever-frame system of controlling points and signals. So, each time a train approached the station, a set of points and a series of signals had to be operated. Bell signals

Last spoil train, the 13.32 hrs from Cloghan Point to Magheramorne Loop, passes Whitehead on 22 August 1975. *(Author)*

were used for communications with other signal boxes on the line, as well as phone calls. The regrading of a signal box wasn't generally undertaken unless the signalmen at the box concerned requested it – mainly because it was regarded as such an onerous and time-consuming task. From the first thing in the morning to the last thing at night, every task undertaken at the box had to be recorded by the inspecting person – often someone else would take over to complete the job as the hours involved were so long. Every time a signaller did something in relation to the operation of the railway, a point would be allocated. When the total points were added up, then the grading of the box could be determined within an agreed set of rules.

A Difficult Time for the Railways

In a public statement in February 1975, NIR's Managing Director, Hugh Waring, reminded passengers and staff alike that the past couple of years had in many ways been a heartbreaking time for railway transport in Northern Ireland, with the widespread civil disorder resulting in frequent delays and the ongoing interruption of services, as well as damage to vehicles, sometimes to an extent that they had to be withdrawn from use. Despite such handicaps however, Mr Waring continued, the company's many good members of staff had worked hard to overcome the problems, and, although passengers had had to put up with many delays, in practically every case, NIR still had the satisfaction of knowing that they had managed to deliver the vast majority of customers to their intended destinations. The policy of the company despite all of the setbacks, he asserted, would continue to be the provision of the best possible transport services to the whole community. Ending on an upbeat note, Mr Waring assured the public that, "the work of improving the standard, punctuality and smooth running of the service continues unabated" (*News Letter*, 10 February 1975).

Massive Fares Increase

Perhaps the February statement had been a way of preparing the public for the bad news which was to follow, just a short month or so later, when it was announced that from Sunday, 30 March 1975 (Easter Sunday), rail fares within Northern Ireland would be increasing by a massive 30 per cent. The full increase would apply to single and return journeys, while the cost of weekly tickets would go up by 15 per cent only: this was intended to cushion the blow for regular travellers. An NIR spokesman said that the heavy additional costs that the company had had to carry during recent months – including wages and the cost of fuel oil – had been unavoidable, reminding the public too that the last fare increases had been a full 18 months previously, and that, in a period of considerable national inflation, this stability was a clear indication of the company's policy to do its best for its customers. Another commentator at the time however remarked that this fares increase was a body blow to the fabric of life in Northern Ireland, and that it was a "suicidal" course of action for the company to take.

It is hard to believe therefore that a further substantial rise in fares was imposed by NIR on Monday, 8 September the same year. This time, the increase averaged out at around 20 per cent, and regular travellers were hit with another 15 per cent rise in the cost of their weekly season tickets. An NIR spokesman again tried to provide an explanation of sorts, commenting that the continuing cost of national inflation had put a heavy burden on company's finances. In any case, the proposed increases had the approval of the Prices Commission, and were actually below the level which could have been permitted according to their stipulations. It should also be noted that fare increases were also applied to Ulsterbus and Citybus fares around the same times, in both March and September 1975, although not at the same high levels as for train travel.

British Rail Ferry Withdrawal

The British Rail Belfast to Heysham ferry service ended its 70-year run on Sunday, 6 April 1975, in spite of continued efforts on the part of various interest groups in Northern Ireland to keep it going.

Rumours of the closure of the route had abounded since July 1974, when the possibility that the ferry could run to Holyhead instead of Heysham was mooted. Then, on 24 July that year, a public notice appeared in the press, announcing "the withdrawal of the shipping service from Belfast to Heysham on 27 October 1974".

A month later, however, came the news that as a result of intervention of the Central Transport Consultative Committee, the planned withdrawal had been postponed, and a new date set for 1 February 1975. Following a public hearing, and pending consideration by the Committee, the British Railways Board finally announced, on 18 December 1974, that the route would close on 6 April 1975. Meanwhile, it was reported that the Merchant Navy and Airline Officers' Association had blacklisted both of the ships which had been used for the run – the *Duke of Argyll* and the *Duke of Lancaster* – for use on any other Sealink routes, as a mark of protest at the closure of the Heysham route.

British Rail ferry, *The Duke of Argyll*, in Belfast. *(Author)*

Line Closed for Football Final

A strange story unfolded in April 1975, when the Irish Cup Football Final was to be played at Ballymena Showgrounds, between Linfield and Coleraine. The match had been scheduled for Saturday, 19 April. Two days beforehand however, NIR decided that essential engineering bridge works would have to be carried out in the Springfarm area of Antrim on the day of the match – and so the company closed the line between Antrim and Ballymena between 8.45 am and 2.45 pm that day, to facilitate the work. This meant of course that Linfield fans would have to travel by bus to the venue.

At the time it was rumoured that the decision to close the line on such a crucial day for local football fans was a consequence of the recent vandalism which occurred on NIR's Portrush trains on Easter Monday – 31 March – that year. This was denied by the company; however local eyewitnesses observing "the work on the railway" that day reported that apparently the extent of the activity on the track was simply two men moving around ballast for a few hours!

If this really had been a scheme to deter Linfield supporters from travelling by rail, it could have been said to have backfired on NIR, since that day's match ended in a one-all draw. A replay was scheduled for Wednesday, 23 April and, as this was an ordinary weekday, the company couldn't come up with more "essential work" necessitating the closure of the line, unless they were going to disrupt commuter traffic.

As it turned out, on the day itself the company decided to make available a "mini-special", capable of transporting 150 supporters. The special left Belfast York Road for Ballymena at 17.10 hrs – with police travelling on board – and returned to Belfast at 20.55 hrs. NIR also restricted fans' access to regular services, stating that, because of rolling stock shortages and the fact that the match clashed with commuter trains, only season ticket holders and passengers with return tickets issued outside Belfast would be able to travel on the Belfast to Coleraine line from 4.00 pm and beyond. The only snag was that the result at the match at the end of the night was yet another draw, at nil-all each! The issue would finally be resolved on Tuesday, 29 April, when the final result was Linfield, 0 and Coleraine, 1.

New Rolling Stock Order

At a press conference on Monday, 12 May 1975, the government announced that they had approved a new order for rolling stock for NIR. The additional twelve 80 Class trains would be composed of nine × three cars and three × two cars, plus one extra motor coach, at a total cost of £3.9 million. Each motor coach would seat 45 passengers; the intermediate trailer would have 87 seats, and the driving trailer would accommodate 81 people. The trains would be built by BREL (British Rail Engineering Limited) in York and Derby. Delivery of the trailer cars was planned for the middle of 1977, and the whole contract was due for completion by February 1978. At the same press conference, the date for the opening of the Belfast Central Railway was confirmed as Monday, 6 October 1975.

Hugh Waring Retires

In mid-May 1975, the Chief Executive of NIR announced his retirement on health grounds. He planned to leave his post at the end of 1975, which was to be a few months after the opening of the new Belfast Central Railway. Hugh Waring started his career as a porter boy on the Belfast and County Down Railway in 1929, when he was 14 years old. He later became a trade union leader, and then a personnel officer, in the Ulster Transport Authority. What may surprise some readers is that at one point he became Central Area Manager of Ulsterbus, before moving on to become Chief Executive of NIR in 1967.

Unofficial Industrial Action

On Monday, 30 June 1975, a go-slow and overtime ban by signalmen and conductors disrupted NIR services across the network. Coincidentally, a new railway timetable had been scheduled to come into operation on the same day, which in a sense meant more confusion for passengers. A member of staff was suspended, with the result that all staff at Belfast York Road walked out. The Larne line closed at 12.40 hrs that day, followed by the Londonderry line, which ceased services at 16.00 hrs. The Bangor line ran as normal.

The dispute centred on alleged management delays in addressing employees' demands for increased pay and improved conditions of service. Railway employees in the conciliation grade had been called upon to facilitate the negotiations. On the Thursday evening of that week, 3 July, NIR employees were handed a final warning notice about the possibility of all staff being laid off if signalmen and conductors did not return to work. It was reported in the media that not all employees on strike had the support of their unions. As part of an appeal to staff, Mr Waring commented that if the conductors refused to collect money from passengers, then the company would simply not have the means to pay them (the conductors). Fortunately, further negotiations eventually resolved matters, and normal working was resumed by all from Monday, 7 July 1975.

Financial Results: A Difficult Year

NIR's financial results for 1974/75 made for grim reading, and were issued along with a warning that either another increase in transport fares, or a severe cut in services, would be inevitable – regardless of the two huge fare increases during 1975. NIR's losses stood at £750,000. At £1.2 million, Citybus losses were even worse, this being attributed mainly to the introduction of black taxi services in Belfast. Meanwhile, Ulsterbus had posted a small profit for the year of £90,000.

Walking Permit

I was getting a bit more ambitious now in my explorations of the railways, and on Thursday, 15 August 1975, I was delighted to be given my first Walking Permit for all lines and stations on the NI network. Then, it was simply a matter of applying for specific dates, reading the accompanied rules and regulations, and I was ready to go!

Customer Concerns: The Ballymena Line

As 1975 drew to a close and the prospect of the reopening of the Belfast Central line loomed on the horizon, commuters from Ballymena and Antrim were starting to think – and worry – about the implications. It seemed highly likely that their train journey would be noticeably longer whenever services were redirected via the Antrim branch to the new station at Belfast Central. In October 1975, concerns were voiced in local newspapers that the journey would take as much as another 30 minutes. In an article in the *Ballymena Observer*, journalist Des Glynn commented that in the days of steam travel, it had only taken a little over half an hour to get from Ballymena to Belfast, whereas now, in 1975, and with the town's population topping the 30,000 mark, the journey to the city was to be undertaken via a route "which might shortly resemble the Ho Chi Minh Trail". Another local commentator summed up the feelings of many on the matter: "Seventy-five minutes to travel 28 miles by train in 1975 seems ludicrous in the extreme!" A petition signed by 61 commuters was sent to NIR.

New Chief Executive of NIR

Roy Beattie was to take over from Hugh Waring as Chief Executive of NIR, and he began in his new role on 1 January 1976. Having gained an engineering degree in Belfast, he had started his career in the Nigerian Railway Corporation in 1956, where he worked for ten years. He returned to his homeland in 1966, and joined NIR as a civil engineer, moving up the ranks to become Chief Executive Designate in 1975. As such, he had been fully involved in many NIR projects from their inception, including the proposed Belfast Central Railway.

In a press interview in January 1976, Mr Beattie set out his stall as the new Chief Executive of the company on a number of matters. He declared that his hopes were high that public interest in railway travel would increase dramatically once the new Belfast Central Railway opened in the spring of that year – although no definitive date of opening was referred to. He recounted that the last seven years had been spent rebuilding Northern Ireland's railway system, by putting in new signalling systems, relaying track and focusing on the proposed development of the Belfast Central Railway. In the immediate future, as well as continuing with all of this, he stated that NIR would be developing two new areas of activity. The first of these was the expansion of freight services from the Republic to Belfast, and to Londonderry. Secondly, the company would be looking to develop the provision of travel services for organised groups, including excursions for Sunday school parties to such destinations as Bangor and Portrush, which were already very popular. In fact demand in this area had been so high that Sunday schools were now booking travel for large groups from one year to the next, with some parties having to be turned away because of insufficient rolling stock capacity for the volume of passengers wishing to travel on Saturdays.

The new Chief Executive took the opportunity to announce several other developments. Local rail services linking Bangor, Portadown and Ballymena would have a new brand name: "Citytrack". A link, provided by Citybus, would also be available from the new Belfast Central station to the city centre. Four buses in total had been allocated to Belfast Central, and they would also be identified with the same Citytrack livery as the trains they served. Rail services north of Ballymena and south of Portadown would be designated with another new name: "Inter City". Also under consideration by NIR was the provision of a new station at Craigavon Central, and a new station between Ballymacarrett and Belfast Central. A previous proposal to run a commuter service from Ballymena to Belfast York Road had been quashed, since it would be not an economically viable proposition once the service was redirected via the Antrim branch to Belfast Central.

Opening of the Belfast Central Railway

After a few false start dates, the public were at last advised of the definitive opening dates of the Belfast Central Railway by way of an advertisement in the local press. The Bangor line would be the first beneficiary, with the new service commencing on Monday, 12 April 1976. The Portadown and Dublin lines would be next, as of Monday, 26 April 1976. This topic is covered in depth in Chapter Eight.

I had been producing the weekly operating notices for some time, but with the opening of the Belfast Central Railway, a change was coming. We took the opportunity to combine the notices, and so from Tuesday, 27 April, the Londonderry and Larne line were joined and a new notice was produced for the Bangor and Southern lines to the Border.

Office Move to Belfast Central

We had been told previously that the Headquarters office staff at Belfast York Road would be relocated to Belfast Central when the new station was ready. This was something I and some of my colleagues were looking forward to, due to the long daily trek that had to be made at the time from Queen's Quay to York Road. So we were very pleased to get confirmation that our office move would take place on Sunday, 9 May 1976. Now, instead of having to trudge from Belfast Queen's Quay each morning, I would be able to get off the Bangor train and walk up the ramp straight into the offices within about three minutes. It would also be great in the evening, when I could leave the office just five minutes before the train was due to depart.

The Railway Operations team, to which I was belonged, all moved in to the top floor of Belfast Central in an open plan set-up, except for the senior manager. From an office with a view over the four tracks and platforms, I would undertake my first control duties at lunchtime on Thursday, 22 July 1976. Further moves took place on Sunday, 20 June, when the Revenue and Wages department moved to Belfast Central also, followed by the Marketing department on the following Tuesday. A small bonus of £46.80 appeared in our pay packets around this time, as we were entitled to a "disturbance allowance" due to the move.

We didn't know at the time, but the open-plan layout of our new environment, along with the very high ceiling was a recipe for fluctuating extremes of temperatures. On 23 June that first summer, we thought it was bad enough when the mercury rose to record 93° Fahrenheit. But five days later, that was surpassed by a temperature of 104 °F!

Now if the offices were absolutely sweltering in the summer, guess what happened in the winter? In our first year there, the temperature on Wednesday, 1 December was just above freezing, at 46 °F. Personnel were sent up with chicken or vegetable soup for those of us on the top floor. Some staff simply went home, as they just couldn't stick the cold. I remember sitting in that office, along with other colleagues: we were wrapped up in our coats and scarves, and could only watch as the rainwater trickled down the pillars of the building. As a matter of interest, the electricity bill for Belfast Central (the whole building) for the month of November 1976 was £3,232 (the equivalent value in 2016 would be approximately £21,000)!

Understandably, management were concerned at this expense. Part of the problem was that on the administration floor, the electric heaters were at ground level and no more than one foot from floor-to-ceiling glass panels, so the heat was effectively going out through the windows. As the ceiling was about 30 feet above our heads, the heat was also rising into the roof of the building, which was constructed partly of glass and partly of plastic sheeting. After the first winter, it was decided that a lowered ceiling should be installed over the entire length of the administration floor, and fortunately, this did help to keep the heat in.

Group Travel: Special Trains

Meanwhile, some of the other developments mooted by the new Chief Executive in his January interview continued apace. On an annual basis and for a number of years prior to the opening of the Belfast Central Railway, thousands of Sunday school students, teachers and friends would, every Saturday from mid-May to the beginning of July, take the train in large groups for day trips to the seaside (mainly to Portrush). Once the new Belfast Central Railway was operational in 1976, NIR put on a number of special trains to Bangor, specifically to cater for such groups. Every Saturday that summer, around 2,100 seats were allocated for these specials, and almost every time the allocation was taken up and the organisers would be on the phone the following Monday morning, wanting to book the train for the next year's travel!

A lot of planning was involved in marshalling these trains and finding available paths in the timetable to allow them to run. At this stage, I was in charge of preparing the Operating Weekly Notices, and found that during this time of the year, the notices could run to 20 pages or more. Everything had to be handwritten to start with of course, and then every page typed up. The process would begin every Monday morning, when the locomotive and traffic Inspectors came in for the Operations meeting, which covered special trains and so on for the following Saturday and until the next Friday. On Tuesdays and Wednesdays, the handwritten pages would be handed over to the typist; by the Thursday, the typed-up sheets were usually available to be run off on a Gestetner printer to upwards of 700 copies. On Fridays, these would be sent out for distribution throughout the network. It was generally a very tight process, and on some occasions the notices would not be out for delivery until late on the Friday evening.

NIR Float at the Lord Mayor's Show in Belfast, Saturday, 22 June 1976. *(Author)*

To give an example, a big day for the Sunday school specials that first year of 1976, was Saturday, 29 May. Due to travel that day, along with others, was the Drumcree United Sunday schools party, the largest Sunday school group: they would usually take well over 1,200 passengers from Portadown to Portrush. Of the special trains on the Saturday in question, the allocation to the Drumcree party was as follows: at 09.00 hrs from Portadown, a Hunslet No 102 and nine BUT coaches, and, at 08.40 hrs from Portadown, a four-car 80 Class set, hauling five Enterprise coaches and a separate three-car MED (Nos 26, 509, 35).

Alongside all of this, the NIR Marketing Department had been working hard to put together other organised party travel packages and accompanying brochures for destinations within Northern Ireland, the Republic of Ireland and the rest of the United Kingdom. The brochures gave details of the reduced fare travel packages which, for schools parties, included meals and overnight stays. The most popular package for schools at the time was Tour No 8: a Dublin/Shannon two-day rail/air Tour, which included, "the thrill of a half-hour flight – perhaps in a Jumbo Jet – between Dublin Airport and Shannon Airport". Bookings were of course subject to the availability of flights and accommodation, and the weather conditions.

Another key marketing initiative aimed at promoting NIR's services to the public was a brand new float, which was a gift from British Rail to its Northern Ireland counterpart. The 30-foot long lorry's theme was summer travel, and it bore a huge image of the sun beaming down on a cheeky-looking carousel. A large pair of sunglasses straddling the cab of the lorry was an added eye-catching gimmick. The float made its debut appearance at the Lord Mayor's Show in Belfast on Saturday, 22 June 1976.

Financial Results 1975/76

It had been another bleak year in the financial fortunes of the company. A published review of the accounts for 1975/76 showed that the deficit had soared to approximately £1.4 million – almost double that of the previous year.

A statement from the NIR Chairman, Myles Humphreys, followed in June 1976. On behalf of NIR, he warned that the twin effects of terrorist activity and inflation might curtail train services, particularly at off-peak periods and on Sundays. Evening travel by the public for pleasure, he said, had virtually ceased and would likely not come back into vogue again until civil unrest had died down, and until the larger towns and cities could once more became a central magnet for entertainment, rather than for trouble and uncertainty. Similarly, Sunday services, for which the company had to pay its staff high rates of overtime, had attracted virtually no demand on a broad front, and therefore no commercial case could be made for their universal retention throughout the NIR system.

Shortly thereafter, NIR announced that a review of services was now being undertaken and that within a few months, decisions would need to be taken, some of which might not be welcomed by certain sectors of the public. The Citylink bus service from Belfast Central station to the city centre was also under review and in danger of being withdrawn. Only 5,000 passengers each week were using the cheap service (with a fare of just 5 pence per journey), and it seemed that Citybus felt that unless the service gained greater support, it would be uneconomical to keep it running in its current form. Although Ulsterbus had fared relatively well again for the financial year, producing a pre-tax profit of £697,000, Citybus had incurred a hefty loss of £927,000.

Belfast Central Railway Costs

Yet more financial bad news was to come. It was revealed in August 1976 that the costs of the new Belfast Central Railway scheme had been seriously underestimated, and were now running at £3.7 million more than had been originally expected. The massive overspend was brought to light during the review of information given to the UK Commons Public Accounts Committee by Ulster civil servants. The Committee were highly critical of the Department of the Environment for its failure to exercise sufficient control over the plan, particularly in its early stages.

As mentioned in Chapter One, in 1969 a firm of railway consultants – Rendel, Palmer and Tritton – had carried out a feasibility study for the new BCR: in 1970 they had confirmed that the capital cost would be £1.03 million. Management consultants, McKinsey & Co were then asked to examine the scheme in a wider context and in 1971 gave a revised estimate of capital costs of £1.2 million. However, by 1973 the consulting engineers had increased their proposed budget to £1.9 million, and tenders later that year came in at £2.91 million. By the time the project was completed and the new scheme became operational, in April 1976, the total outlay was in the region of £4.8 million.

In January 1977 Mr John Coulthard of NUPE revealed that he was going to have the issue of the overspend of nearly £4 million raised in Parliament by union-sponsored MPs. (Many NIR staff were members of NUPE, hence the union's focus on this matter.) Coulthard launched a scathing attack on senior civil servants in the Northern Ireland Department of the Environment, for allegedly "bungling" the management of the final costs of the new Belfast Central Railway; he wanted to know where the public money had gone, and asked why so many specialist consultant firms had been engaged to look into the new system. He concluded by saying that the eagerness within the civil service to pass the buck seemed to be systemic, in a set-up where anybody could take a decision – while at the same time, no one was willing to take responsibility for any of these decisions.

Belfast Transport Plans

Unsurprisingly perhaps, there was greater mainland involvement and attention paid to subsequent plans to further address Belfast's transport problems, which were unveiled by the government on 5 April 1977. These included an M1 to M2 link-up, and the building of another motorway bridge over the River Lagan in the Customs House area, in order to join the Sydenham Bypass with the other motorways. However, previously mooted plans to build a rail link between York Street and Belfast Central – for which several routes had been proposed, as shown in the plan opposite – were now rejected. External consultants had ruled out the rail link because, in their view, the benefit to the public would be limited, while the potential costs could come in at between £3 million and £7.5 million at 1974 prices (the year in which feasibility studies had first been done).

In July 1977 however, NIR's Chief Executive, Roy Beattie told a new public inquiry into Belfast's urban transport plan that a link between York Street and Belfast Central would undoubtedly improve the economic health of the country's railways. Such link would mean that passengers travelling into Central would not have to hop onto a bus to get to York Road station, if they wanted to travel to the North West or to Larne. Beattie also warned that failure to complete the link could lead to the decline, and possibly even the closure, of the Larne line. Added support for NIR's stance came from other associations, including the Transport Users' Committee, the Foyle Tourism Association and the Royal Society of Ulster Architects. Mr Michael Lavery QC, Inspector at the public inquiry, listened intently to the arguments being made.

When the findings of the inquiry were made public on 28 April 1978, NIR executives and staff alike were delighted with the verdict, and Mr Mason, the then Secretary of State, announced that the construction of a rail link between York Street and Belfast Central was to go ahead, at an estimated cost of more than £6 million. The new line would cross the River Lagan, either on a separate rail bridge or on a combined road and rail flyover. It was expected that the design work for the cross-harbour bridges would take at least two years to complete. In the same announcement, Mr Mason

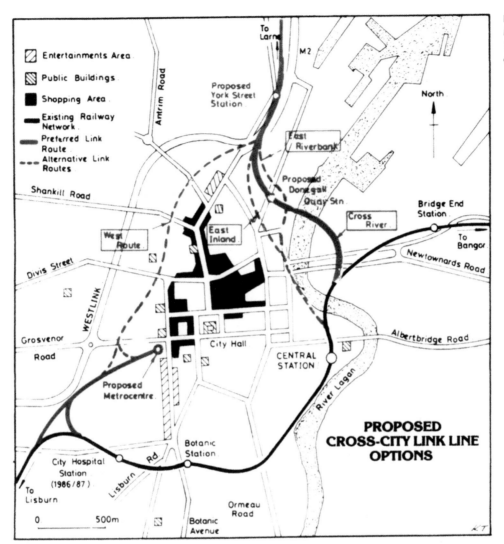

Proposed Railway Map for Belfast, 1977. *(Author's collection)*

revealed that a new central bus station would be built for Ulsterbus, although a site for this purpose had not yet been found. As expected, he also confirmed that the bulk of the funding would be going to the creation of the motorway extensions, the M1 link to the M2, and a cross-harbour link from the M2 to the Sydenham Bypass.

NIR Queen's Silver Jubilee Tickets

In the summer of 1977, 5,000 special tickets were produced to mark the occasion of the Queen's Silver Jubilee. The tickets were for a limited special offer on Sunday, 5 June 1977, entitling the bearer for a fare of 25 pence to travel anywhere by rail within Northern Ireland on that day.

The tickets went on sale on Wednesday, 1 June and were sold out by the next day. In terms of the special fare, the best bargain was for passengers travelling from the Belfast direction to Portrush or Londonderry – normal prices for such travel being £2.00 or £2.60. NIR advised that extra carriages would be added to trains on the day.

During the Queen's celebratory visit to Northern Ireland that summer, on 10–11

H.M. The Queen's Silver Jubilee
Commemorative Rail Ticket
Sunday, 5th June, 1977
Go as you please ——— 25p

Commemorative
Rail Ticket for the
Queen's Silver
Jubilee – Sunday,
5 June 1977.
(Author's collection)

August, the Chairman of the company, Myles Humphreys, was conferred with the honour of Knight Bachelor, and was thereafter to be known as Sir Myles. The Queen met him at his investiture at Hillsborough Castle on 10 August. Other NIR staff members were invited to various events scheduled for the royal visit. Norman Topley, the NIR Chief Controller, attended a reception on board the Royal Yacht Britannia in Bangor Bay; Sammy Cooke from the Belfast York Road workshops was among the guests at the Garden Party at Hillsborough Castle; George Hanthorn and John Moore attended another Garden Party at the New University of Ulster at Coleraine. There was disruption to train services on Thursday, 11 August when bomb scares closed the railway at Kilnasaggart bridge at the Border; there were further alerts at Lurgan, Cullybackey and on the Moira to Lurgan line, which was closed on the morning of 12 August. Fortunately all of these involved hoax devices.

Financial Results 1976/77

NIR were reportedly delighted with the financial results for the year 1976/77, as the deficit was over £100,000 less than the previous year. Nevertheless the balance sheet for the year recorded an overall loss of £1,282,000. In his subsequent remarks, the Chairman felt however that there were grounds to be upbeat, commenting that the reduced loss represented a significant achievement when viewed against the context of consistently unfavourable market conditions, and an annual inflation rate in excess of 20 per cent, a severe deficit trend which had persisted since 1968. Meanwhile Ulsterbus had recorded a pre-tax profit of £1,982,000, and Citybus had come out of the doldrums at last, with a pre-tax profit of £562,000.

As a matter of record, I have a note of the recorded losses for CIÉ, the Republic's state-backed transport company, for the same year as plummeting to an all-time deficit low of £33,500,000. The main reason for these catastrophic results was that CIÉ were still living in the past regarding a number of work practices, with a lot of jobs still having to be being carried out by personnel due to a lack of investment. Many staff were still employed at signal boxes and as crossing keepers at level crossings, as the cost of upgrading these infrastructures was prohibitive. Rolling stock was also old and slow, and this did nothing to entice the travelling public. In Northern Ireland on the other hand, modernisation had commenced with the arrival of new rolling stock, the construction of new station buildings, and the modernisation of level crossings and signal boxes: the resulting savings in manpower were considerable.

New Staff Magazine

In June 1977, the first issue of a new NIR staff magazine, *Signal*, was published, to be released on a quarterly basis. The first edition was a relatively simple production, just four pages in length, in A4 format; the bulk of the text was printed in black and white, with a few headings set in red. At the launch of the new publication, Sir Myles Humphreys gave an opening address, introducing the new magazine as a means of advanced communications. *Signal* proved to be a long-running success, and its publication continued until January 1991, when its last issue was produced. In the summer of that year, the first edition of its successor appeared: the new magazine was entitled *Staff Lines*, with its first issue dated June 1991.

Another Warm Year

The second summer in the offices at Belfast Central was no different from the first, in terms of the extreme heat. On Thursday, 7 July 1977 the temperature recorded at my desk was 100 °F, and 104 °F in the Marketing office. Some of the NIR Controllers decided to grow tomatoes in their office, and they were successful! It was a particularly hot summer generally that year, and the scorching weather was causing problems elsewhere too: there were two buckled rails on the track at the Dunminning curve, north of Cullybackey, and one buckled rail at Aldergrove on the Antrim branch. However, even in more temperate summers, this type of problem can still arise in any period in which there are several warm sunny days in succession, with the sun beaming down on a stretch of track from early morning to late at night.

Tour of Northern Ireland by Train

Knowing about the possible withdrawal of services from the Belfast York Road to Antrim line in the near future, I decided to take a day's annual leave to travel around the whole NIR network by train, accompanied by one of my colleagues. We set the date of our one-day trip for Thursday, 29 September 1977, and we covered the 462 miles without incident. We started with the 07.15 hrs service from Bangor to Belfast Central; then onwards to Dundalk and from there to Portrush via Lisburn. After this, we travelled back to Antrim and onwards to Londonderry; then back to Belfast York Road and onwards to Larne Harbour. Returning to York Road, we finally made our way home on the 22.20 hrs service from Belfast Central to Bangor.

It was a thoroughly enjoyable trip. Although the NIR network is relatively small, it was great to be able to start at one point – Bangor – and travel around every single mile of track in the space of one day, ending up back at our starting point without a hitch. All the trains we took were on time or near enough, and the speed of the old 70 Class trains on the Londonderry line was impressive. And of course, being members of staff, our tour had cost us nothing!

Off-Peak Fares Cut

From Monday, 7 November 1977 off-peak day return train fares throughout the entire network were cut by up to 28 per cent. The reduced rates applied to weekday services, from 10.00 hrs, and at any time on Saturday and Sunday services. The offer, which was intended as a boost to Christmas shoppers, would extend until further notice. Examples of the new fares were as follows: Bangor to Belfast, 65 pence; Holywood to Belfast, 35 pence. The special fares were discontinued after Sunday, 26 February 1978.

Maysfield Leisure Centre

The opening, on Monday, 5 December 1977, of the new Maysfield Leisure Centre, just adjacent to the station, would be another welcome perk for those of us working at Belfast Central. A good number of staff, including me, started booking slots for football, squash, badminton, table tennis or swimming during our lunch period, which was between 13.00 and 13.30 hrs. The new centre was officially opened on Monday, 19 December.

Bleach Green Junction to Antrim Line Closure

As part of the proposed plan to centralise rail services in Northern Ireland, trains between Belfast York Road and Londonderry ran for the last time on Sunday, 22 January 1978, and the line between Bleach Green Junction and Antrim was closed to passenger traffic. From Monday, 23 January, services on the Londonderry line would run from Antrim along the branch line to Lisburn, and onwards to Belfast Central station. However, due to terrorist threats that day, the first trains on the new route did not materialise in Belfast until mid-afternoon. This item is covered fully in Chapter Five.

High-Speed Plan for the Belfast–Dublin Line

The blueprint for a major upgrading of rail services in both parts of Ireland, commissioned jointly by authorities in Belfast and Dublin, was due to be delivered to British and Éire Ministers before the end of March 1978. Included in the proposal were plans for a 90 mph service, running at a frequency of up to ten trains a day each way. If the plan was accepted, it was expected to qualify for substantial EEC cash aid from Brussels. Increasing the speed of travel from 70 mph to 90 mph would require more powerful locomotives; new, heavier rails and concrete sleepers would also have to be laid.

Financial Results

It was a very welcome change when, for the financial year 1977/78, NIR was able to report an operating surplus before tax of £484,386, and that turnover had increased by 62 per cent. Chairman Sir Myles Humphreys said the main reason for this turnaround was the impact of various grants being made available through EEC legislation.

Senior Citizens' Free Travel Day

On Saturday, 2 September 1978, NIR gave senior citizens the chance to travel free on any train service within Northern Ireland. To obtain a free ticket, all the passenger had to do was present his or her NIR or bus concessionary travel pass at the ticket office or to the conductor. Big reductions were available for cross-border travel also that day.

It was estimated that somewhere between 10,000 and 15,000 senior citizens took to the trains on the day, using normal services and a few special trains. This was a huge increase on the usual daily numbers for this type of traveller at this time of year, which would have stood at around 2,000 per day. The Bangor and Portrush lines were

A three-car MED set at Belfast Central on its last day in operation – Saturday, 2 September 1978. *(Author)*

the most favoured routes. The 10.10 hrs service from Belfast Central to Portrush, for example, was formed by a five-car 70 Class hauling five BUT carriages. As it turned out, the train was full leaving Belfast Central, meaning that 300 passengers were left behind at Botanic station. To add to the excitement of the day, an RPSI (Railway Preservation Society of Ireland) steam train ran from Whitehead to Bangor (departing at 07.40 hrs), via Belfast York Road and Antrim, and was formed by Locomotive No 171 and six coaches.

This was also the last day for an MED (Multi-Engined Diesel) set to run on special workings in Northern Ireland. It was formed by Nos 32, 509 and 21. Special runs included an 11.25 hrs "special" from Lisburn to Bangor; a 12.37 hrs empty from Bangor to Belfast Central; a 16.30 hrs empty from Belfast Central to Bangor, and a 17.10 hrs football special for Glentoran supporters, running from Bangor to Belfast Central.

On-Call Railway Controller
By this time, I had had a number of responsibilities added to my clerical role in the company, and so I was now a "Scale 3". I had also recently passed my tests as temporary railway controller, and accordingly I was to be placed on the on-call rota, starting on Sunday, 29 October 1978.

In a normally functioning society and on an ordinary, run-of-the-mill transport system, the job of a railway controller will entail keeping a watching brief on all train services within his or her area – in this case, the whole of Northern Ireland and including the Border – to monitor how the cross-border service is operating, as well as other linking transport services such as the British Rail ferries coming in from Stranraer. An increase in boat passenger numbers will mean adjustments at times on other services. As well as all of this, the train crew picture has to be constantly monitored with a view to anticipating possible shortages of staff due to sickness or annual leave. There isn't much point in having two trains sitting somewhere, but having no train crew to operate them! Trespassing by individuals and also farm animals, as well as anti-social behaviour on the part of passengers could also potentially cause difficulties and need to be watched out for.

As I have said, all of this was part of a controller's remit in normal circumstances – but of course in Northern Ireland in the 1970s and beyond, there was the added difficulty of working in a "war" situation. Bomb scares were an everyday occurrence and of course, far worse were the bombs which actually exploded on the lines or on trains: all of this caused great stress to railway staff, especially those on the front line. No other railway controller, certainly in the British Isles and in most of Europe, would ever have had to deal with all of the horrific things that affected the Northern Ireland railway over the years.

The autumn of 1978 was a pretty difficult time, as terrorism attacks on the railway continued to intensify. My duties as controller included contacting the RUC Headquarters at Knock in the morning before services commenced, and calling in again before services ended at the close of day. Accordingly my work pattern now involved starting at 09.00 hrs in my office operations job and heading home from that at 18.00 hrs. I was due back in for 19.00 hrs and then acted as duty railway controller, quite often until midnight or possibly earlier, depending on the circumstances. On my very first day on the job, I received a call from the RUC, to say that seven bombs had been placed on the line between Belfast and Portadown.

Thankfully, the call ended up being confirmed by the security forces as a hoax, but during the wait for such confirmation, the tension in the control office was very high: trains were stopped, and passengers and train crew were all on tenterhooks to see what was going to happen next. Depending on the length of the closure, one of the many problems in the aftermath was trying to get things back to normal again. Trains and train crews would invariably end up in the wrong place and on occasions there were even such issues to consider as there being insufficient fuel on trains to get them back on track. The final decision to reopen a section of the line would be taken by the police, based on their own intelligence or that of the military. There are always formal protocols in place in such situations but, due to the ongoing threat of security-related incidents on the railway, even to this day, I will not go into any further detail on these here.

Fuel Shortage, Snow and Further Strikes

The winter of 1978/79 was not an easy one. A reduced train service came into effect on Wednesday, 10 January 1979, as a result of a fuel tanker drivers' strike in the United Kingdom which had been going on for several days.

During this time, there were no trains running between the hours of 10.00 am and 3.00 pm, then the normal timetable would resume until an early closure of services, at around 6.30 pm. Trains in the rush hours were said to be carrying 50 per cent more passengers than normally. To help with the fuel shortage situation, a locomotive and three oil tankers were sent from Dublin to the Central Service Depot in Belfast, carrying approximately 12,000 gallons of diesel. Imagine if the IRA had got to hear about that particular special train! During the next three days of reduced service, snow and fog came along to disrupt the network further. At one stage, temperatures as low as minus 15 °C were recorded in Lisburn. The first train out of the Central Service Depot on 11 January was at 09.35 hrs, as all of the crossovers and turnouts had frozen: not a normal service train, this one had been sent out to rescue weary, stranded passengers along the route.

To everyone's relief, the tanker drivers' strike ended on 13 January 1979.

Just a few short weeks later however, NIR's own workers were on strike too. A work-to-rule and overtime ban by conductors and signalmen began on Monday, 22 January. The first train out of Bangor that day was not until 15.35 hrs. On the same day, the signal box at Lisburn closed down for two hours from midday, which brought services there to a stop. This pattern continued until Thursday, 25 January, when the workers suspended their action for three weeks. Fortunately, by that stage, the dispute had been resolved.

Financial Results 1978/79

For the second year running, when it came to the publication of the company's annual accounts, the NIR Chairman was able to announce an operating surplus for the previous twelve months – this time, of £447,169. Total turnover was £5,344,084, which was a 9.4 per cent increase on the previous year. Passenger numbers had also risen, from 5.4 million to 5.6 million, even in spite of ongoing terrorist activity, which had led to unprecedented levels of line closures. Proposed developments in the year ahead included the building of new stations at Ballymena, Londonderry and Lurgan.

Another Change of Direction for me

In the autumn of 1979, things changed again for me on the career front, and I began working in the Company Secretary's office on 1 October (at Grade 3). Just a short year or so later, a reorganisation was carried out in the office, following which my duties were expanded, and I was promoted to management level (Management Grade 1), with the designation of Office Supervisor. I was to begin in this new role from 1 December 1980. My responsibilities now included: supervising three clerical officers in their duties relating to company secretary work; criminal damage claims; insurance matters; routine pension work; property matters; and the prosecution of offenders under railway legislation. I was still on the on-call rota for Railway Control, and this could entail overnight shifts from 11.00 pm to 7.00 am.

The night-shift rota generally was on-call at home or, if the security situation at large was not great, then you were based in the control office in Belfast. If you were at home, this meant that you could get a phone call at any time from Police Headquarters in Knock, Belfast, requesting information or advising you of a security alert affecting the railway or in its vicinity. So sleeping patterns were disrupted on more than a few occasions. Depending on the situation, you might have to then go in to the control office to sort it out. However, like many railway staff at the time, I didn't really mind, since, like my colleagues, I was keen to keep the train services operating for the public, who were our bread-and-butter after all. It also gave me great pleasure to be able to support the rest of our staff on the ground.

More Fare Increases and Financial Results 1979/80

Just before Christmas 1979, NIR were not in festive mood when they announced that big fare increases would take effect from Monday, 7 January 1980. The increase was the equivalent of around 20 per cent across the whole fare structure. An NIR spokesperson at the time said that thankfully passenger numbers had been growing, since, but for this support from the public, the projected rise in fares would have been greater. Inflation was however a fact of life in most sectors during this era: British Rail fares were being increased on the same day and Sealink, British Rail's ferry company, was also putting up its fares by an average of 15 per cent.

In spite of the difficult economy, another good set of financial results was disclosed later in the year by the Chairman, with the company accounts recording a surplus after interest of £507,000. Sir Myles however commented that the past year had been a grim one, due to the uncertainty arising from the Government's attitude to public expenditure and, especially to its future plans for investment in the railways.

Trial Opening of Belfast–Antrim Line

Following some pressure from the travelling public and from local representatives, the Belfast York Road to Antrim line was reopened for a trial period in 1980, to assess the number of passengers likely to use the route. The temporary service commenced on Monday, 16 June that year. During the trial period, a timber platform was constructed at Templepatrick and it opened as a temporary station on Monday, 1 September 1980. The new extended service encompassed stations at Whiteabbey, Monkstown, Mossley and Templepatrick. A copy of the timetable is shown.

A few months later, on 29 October, a public notice appeared in the press, giving formal notice that the train service between Belfast York Road and Antrim would be terminated on 20 December 1980. The deadline passed due to a number of objections being received, but unfortunately the reality was that the service had not attracted sufficient numbers to make it viable, and the line and intermediate stations were closed on 23 February 1981.

New timetable for Belfast York Road to Antrim local service, from Monday, 1 September 1980. *(Author's collection)*

TABLE 3   **MONDAYS TO SATURDAYS**

BELFAST (York Road) – WHITEABBEY – ANTRIM

(With connections to and from Ballymena/Londonderry)

Commencing Monday, 1st September 1980 until further notice

						A	
BELFAST (York Road)	dep.	08.30	11.15	14.10	15.50	17.20	–
Whiteabbey	„	08.37	11.22	14.17	15.57	17.27	–
Monkstown	„	08.42	11.27	14.22	16.02	17.32	–
Mossley	„	08.45	11.30	14.25	16.05	17.35	–
Templepatrick	„	08.56	11.41	14.36	16.16	17.46	–
ANTRIM	arr.	09.04	11.49	14.44	16.24	17.54	–
Antrim	dep.	09.07	11.57	14.52	16.28	**17.55**	–
Ballymena	arr.	09.19	12.09	15.04	16.40	**18.07**	–
Londonderry	„	10.30	13.20	16.15	18.10	–	–
Londonderry	dep.	06.30	08.00	10.50	–	14.40	–
Ballymena	„	07.46	09.15	12.03	14.45	15.54	–
Antrim	arr.	07.59	09.27	12.15	14.57	16.06	–
ANTRIM	dep.	08.03	09.30	12.20	15.08	16.32	–
Templepatrick	„	08.12	09.39	12.29	15.17	16.41	–
Mossley	„	08.22	09.49	12.39	15.27	16.51	–
Monkstown	„	08.25	09.52	12.42	15.30	16.54	–
Whiteabbey	„	08.28	09.55	12.45	15.33	16.57	–
BELFAST (York Road)	arr.	08.35	10.02	12.52	15.40	17.04	–

A–Through train Belfast (York Road) to Ballymena.

CITY LINK BUS SERVICE AVAILABLE BETWEEN YORK ROAD STATION AND CENTRAL STATION VIA CITY CENTRE

NO SUNDAY SERVICE BETWEEN BELFAST (York Road) AND ANTRIM

Parcels Service: Centralisation and Expansion

As part of a plan to streamline parcels handling in Belfast and to improve and extend the existing services, NIR centralised its Belfast parcels services, basing all operations in a new, purpose-designed warehouse under the road bridge at Belfast Central station, from Saturday, 19 June 1982.

Further developments would come in September 1984, with the launch of a new parcel service at Belfast Central station. The new "Night Star" parcels service was an extension into Northern Ireland of a service already operating throughout England, Scotland and Wales. A parcel brought to any manned railway station in Northern Ireland could now be delivered, through NIR and British Rail, to any destination in the United Kingdom. Night Star was more than just a guaranteed, next-day delivery service to another railway station: parcels could be delivered to the doorstep of the premises of the addressee. In a clever stroke of marketing, the new service was launched by Cliff Michelmore, a well-known TV personality at the time, who presented the BBC's *Holiday* programme, and whose name was of course synonymous with packages of a different kind – holiday packages.

Northern Ireland Assembly Debates the Future of the Railways

In March 1983, a full debate was carried out in the chamber of the recently established Northern Ireland Assembly regarding the future of the railways in Northern Ireland. Mr Roy Beggs, Chairman of the Assembly's Economic Development Committee, moved a motion demanding immediate clarification from the Minister responsible, as to whether the necessary improvements to the existing Belfast to Larne line, and the proposed construction of the cross-city link from Belfast York Road to Belfast, would proceed. Among other proposed developments discussed were a new station to be created near Belfast's High Street at the old site of the Heysham ferry building, and a new passenger terminal for Larne Harbour. Mr Beggs voiced his support for the latter measure in particular, saying that the modernisation and expansion of passenger facilities would enhance the welcome afforded to visitors arriving in Northern Ireland. He added that he hoped the April 1983 start date for this project could be kept to.

Another Assembly man, Mr Will Glendinning suggested that the proposed new rail link between Belfast York Road station and Belfast Central station be built along the Lagan and into Belfast Central without crossing the river. This, he said, would allow a station to be built at the bottom of High Street, at the back of the present Customs House where the old Heysham building was. In other matters, Lord Dunleath called for a through service from Belfast to Aldergrove Airport off the Antrim branch.

New Rolling Stock Order

In November 1983, NIR awarded a contract worth £2,500,000 to BREL, for the supply of three 3-car diesel electric multiple units. The contract also included an option for the order of a further six 3-car car sets, pending Government approval. The deal was signed amid tight security at Belfast York Road workshops by NIR Chairman, Sir Myles Humphreys and BREL Chairman, James Urquhart.

The new trains, which were intended for use on the Larne line, were based on the 455 Class electric units currently being delivered in the Southern Region of British Rail. They would be built at York, and Derby would supply the bogies (the steel frames which support the two wheel sets below a carriage or locomotive). A few months later, BREL landed a big order from CIÉ (the Irish transport authority) worth £25 million, for the supply of 124 coaches based on the British Rail MK III design.

The Railway Security Patrol

Around this time, my role in the company began to develop in another new direction, due to my interest in trying to stem anti-social behaviour on the railways. From November 1983, I decided to take the lead on this, and organised patrols tasked with detecting trespassers and stone throwers around the network. On these patrols, we would be accompanied by contracted private security personnel, usually with an Alsatian dog. I will look at this aspect of my work and the whole area of antisocial behaviour on the railway in more detail in Chapter Nine.

In July 1985, as part of a further reorganisation of the Company Secretariat, my job title was changed to Administrative Officer (Secretariat). A considerable number of changes were made to my remit at this time, including added responsibilities relating to the enforcement of the Company's Byelaws and other legislation, and the apprehension and subsequent prosecution of offenders through work of the Railway Patrol. My new job description was eventually forwarded to the Job Evaluation panel but the process took so long that, by the time it was looked at, a further job description had been put forward and approved. In February 1987, I was given the new job title of Safety/Security Manager, and was marked up to Management Grade 2.

MY TIME AT NIR, PART TWO:
1986–1995

Future of NIR Once More in Doubt

In the mid-1980s, as an input to the Belfast Transportation Strategy Review, the Department of the Environment (Northern Ireland) requested a high-level appraisal of Northern Ireland Railways by way of a Cost Benefit Analysis. The report was prepared by Steer Davies Gleave, in association with Halcrow Fox & Associates, and was submitted to the Department in July 1986. Thankfully, at the time this report was seen only by those at executive level and above within NIR, since the picture it painted was a gloomy one.

Regarding the future of Northern Ireland's railway system, seven options were proposed in the detail of the report. These were as follows:

1. The base system to be kept as today, but with the addition of the Londonderry line via the Antrim branch;
2. Complete closure of the NIR system;
3. The base system to be maintained, but with the withdrawal of all freight traffic;
4. The withdrawal of long-distance services, i.e., no services north of Ballymena or south of Newry;
5. Focus only on sub-regional (local) services – similar to option 4, but with no services south of Portadown;
6. Keep cross-border main line, only between Belfast towards Dundalk (and drop all other local routes);
7. The rationalisation of services

Fortunately however, after further reviews by Transecon International and other consultants, along with government input, within one year the Cross-Harbour Rail Link was approved (see later in this chapter for more details) – i.e., Option 1 above was adopted.

British Transport Police

As mentioned in the previous chapter, the success of the NIR Railway Patrol over several years had brought into focus the extent of anti-social behaviour that was happening around the network. Railway police had been on the ground in Northern Ireland previously, something which was sanctioned under Section 66 of the Transport Act (NI) 1948. This gave the former Ulster Transport Authority – and any other railway organisation – the powers to have railway police officers in their employ, but this provision had been repealed by the Transport Act (NI) 1967. Now again, in the mid-1980s, a plan was hatched at Executive level, to assess whether NIR could once more come under the remit of the mainland police force, the British Transport Police.

On Friday, 26 September 1986 my line manager and I met with British Transport Police, along with the Chief Constable and his assistant, in their Euston Headquarters. The purpose of the meeting was to discuss if it might be possible to extend the area covered by the BTP to include Northern Ireland. As a follow-up visit, on Wednesday, 15 October 1986, a BTP Inspector from the West Midlands came on a fact-finding visit to NIR.

Now that the issue was being discussed at senior management level in NIR, and in government circles, it was decided that I should participate in the training programme for new recruits at the British Transport Police College in Tadworth, near London. On the mainland at the time, transport police recruits would undertake the same initial training as any other police officer, and then finish by attending an intensive two-week course at Tadworth, specialising in railway operations.

On Monday, 5 January 1987, I travelled to Tadworth for the two-week duration of the course. I was met by the Chief Inspector from the college, and was then introduced to the 13 male police officers and two women officers participating in the course. These officers, having completed their 14-week police training at the national force college, were now to undertaking their final two weeks covering railway procedures and railway law, before they would be appointed to their new posts.

I attended the training classes each day along with the recruits. Thankfully I was a bit younger then, because on the Thursday of the first week, I joined the class for 50 minutes of circuit training and later, 50 minutes of football. The next day, Friday, I travelled with the Inspector to Liverpool and joined in with the evening patrols on the Southport line. This included having to escort 200 boisterous and slightly intoxicated passengers on the 23.05 hrs service from Southport to Liverpool. Up to 90 of them detrained at Formby, where they were met by a police unit of around ten officers, as well as travelling ticket inspectors. Most of these passengers didn't have tickets, but all paid up without too much protest before they were allowed to leave the station.

On Saturday, 10 January, we travelled to Chester to assist a good number of British Transport Police officers aboard a six-car DMU football special from Chester to Wrexham for an FA Cup match. There were 400 supporters on board the train, and a few flares had been set off by fans outside the station. (By the way, Chester won the match.)

The following Monday, we arrived back at Tadworth College. The weather had turned a bit on us by now, with snow delaying our journey. It was minus 11 °C at the college. By Wednesday 14 January, the Tadworth branch line was closed at 09.30 hrs due to snow blizzards, so on the following day, an escape plan was implemented for us, and, once we eventually got a minibus dug out of the snow, we headed back to London and then on to Belfast. I felt that it had been a really worthwhile trip, not least in highlighting the differences between what I was able to do with the Railway Patrol, and the capabilities of a fully-equipped police force for dealing with similar situations.

The possibility of railway police being introduced in Northern Ireland was mentioned in a press report in April 1988, after a worrying increase in the incidence of anti-social behaviour in general on the railways. NIR was in favour of having something like the British Transport Police, and such a possibility was discussed on many occasions at this point and in years to come. However, ultimately the idea was not taken forward, the main reasons relating to financial constraints, and an unwillingness on the part of the Department to contemplate having another police force in operation in Northern Ireland.

Also relating this aspect of my work, a new set of NIR Byelaws came into operation on 18 December 1986. This comprehensive set of regulations made provision for NIR to prosecute for virtually any offence, and a few new ones had been added from other operators. This subject is covered in more depth in Chapter Nine. One of the new offence categories introduced into the regulations at this point related to the taking, or the attempted taking, of intoxicating liquor aboard trains. The power to prohibit alcohol was crucial for NIR, as on certain days of the year in particular, alcohol-related offences were difficult to deal with. Following the introduction of the related regulations, NIR were able to ban alcohol on trains on specific days, such as Easter Monday and Tuesday, for the duration of the annual North West 200 motorcycle race and the Portrush raft race, on loyal order parade days and on the dates of certain football matches.

In the meantime, my work with the Railway Security Patrol at NIR continued apace. When I had first put forward the idea of the patrol in November 1983, I had been advised that there was at that stage no mechanism for additional payments to compensate my out-of-hours work on the project, but time off in lieu was permitted through flexible working. However, some recognition of my additional work was made in January 1987, when my position was upgraded. I was in any case dedicated to this work and at that stage would have continued with it regardless. Then, in June 1988, a system of payment was brought into NIR, which was geared specifically for staff like me, who worked regularly on an out-of-hours basis. It was the same system used by British Rail in such cases, whereby an hourly rate would be paid. However, as within British Rail, but the first 20 hours' overtime in each quarter were to be worked with no payment – which basically meant that I worked three evening security duty shifts without payment. If I had been doing my ordinary day-time job according to this overtime rule, I wouldn't have minded so much, but the evening security patrols were quite dangerous, as we were operating without any security back-up. Certainly, when the police were called, they turned up pretty quickly in most instances, but there were occasions when we were left on our own for quite some time with a number of unruly people. The patrol was also operating in a background of a "war" situation, and certain areas of the network were totally out of bounds to us unless we had guaranteed police back-up.

As I have said however, I was committed to the work, and pleased to be able to make a difference on this front. On Monday, 25 July 1988, I was privileged to be asked to travel on a special train from Belfast Central to Bangor with the then Minister of State, Richard Needham. I was introduced to the Minister by NIR executives and during our journey, we talked about the possibility of working with the British Transport Police and about my work with the Railway Security Patrol.

This important aspect of my job would continue until October 1994, when, sadly, it came to an abrupt end. One day I presented my overtime return for signature as usual, and it was simply refused. I knew I would be unable to sustain the level of my involvement in the patrol without some kind of remuneration – so I had to accept, with a great deal of regret and some anger, that the work could no longer be done. I did get some consolation however from the fact that members of the train crews and other staff on the ground thanked and acknowledged me for what I had done. These staff also complained to operational management about the Security Patrol coming to an end, but, sadly, to no avail. I will look in more detail at this episode in Chapter Nine.

More Job Title Changes

As I have mentioned previously, from the beginning of 1987, my job title was changed to Safety/Security Manager. I was now in charge of the private security company contract, NIR Revenue Inspectors (of which we had three), the Health and Safety Advisor and the clerical staff, as well as the management of criminal damage and injury claims against the company. Eight months later, with the supervision of the Health and Safety Advisor moving to a different line manager, my job title was again changed, this time to Claims/Security Manager.

From March 1987, I attended and recorded the Minutes at a newly instigated bi-monthly NIR Security Meeting, which was chaired by the Deputy Chief Executive. The purpose of these meetings was to discuss such matters as the current security situation within the country as a whole, and the possible knock-on effects for the railway, as well as any special public events on the horizon which might affect the railway, and the general levels of crime and anti-social behaviour on our transport system. Senior officials from NIR and a member of the private security contractor attended; as time went on, a representative from the RUC was also a regular participant. The meetings would continue until August 1995, just before the merger of the bus and rail companies.

New Ticketing Machines

On 30 March 1987, NIR signed a contract for £750,000 with Thorn EMI Electronics of Somerset for the supply of an advanced ticket-issuing and revenue accounting system. The PORTIS portable ticket machines would be similar to those being used by British Rail. Gone would be the old Almex paper tickets, which meant nothing to passengers, as the print was all in codes; in their place, customers would be given a more durable, detailed ticket showing their station of origin and destination, the fare paid and the dates of validity. It was anticipated that the new machines would be up and running by the autumn of 1988.

NIR Leasing Limited

Around this time too, a new limited company, NIR Leasing Limited, was formed, with the chief shareholder being NIR. This company would specialise in the leasing to other companies of equipment and vehicles, including rolling stock.

A selection of
tickets used by NIR.
(Author's collection)

In 1987, NIR was able to come to the aid of Irish Rail, when a number of their trains had to be withdrawn from service after an engineering inspection condemned them. After an absence of local rail services which lasted several weeks, and during which time buses provided a stopgap for rail travellers, a three-car 80 Class set was sent to undertake the Bray to Greystones service for Irish Rail. Two other 80 Class sets had been called for, to cover train services between Dublin Connolly and Maynooth, and services between Cork and Cobh. The three 80 Class sets retained their NIR livery and numbers, but Irish Rail put their own logos on them. At that stage it was anticipated the trains would remain with Irish Rail for two years until new railcar sets were provided, and this is indeed what happened, with the 80 Class sets being returned to NIR in due course.

Cross-Harbour Link Approved

There was great news for NIR on Wednesday, 6 May 1987, when the government gave the green light for a £60 million cross-harbour road and rail link for the centre of Belfast. The ambitious new plan would link the Larne railway at Belfast York Road with Belfast Central station, at a cost of £15 million; the cross-harbour road link would also be built, at a cost of £45 million.

The news was announced at a press conference by the then Environment Minister, Richard Needham. He went on to say that the reporting consultants, Halcrow Fox & Associates, had firmly endorsed the importance of the rail and road bridges as key transport investments for Northern Ireland. He also emphasised however that the plans for the new bridges depended on the necessary finance being secured. Subject to the availability of finance, it was thought that construction on the bridges' project could start in 1990 and be completed by 1993.

The consultants' recommendations also included: the construction of a single-track, cross-river rail link, with a new station at York Street; the closure of York Road station and Queen's Quay Depot; and the provision of additional unmanned halts at Skegoneill, Whitehouse and Monkstown in North Belfast and Newtownabbey.

The report had also advised that most of the Ulsterbus services which terminated at Oxford Street bus station should be redirected instead to a new, modernised bus station at Great Victoria Street, which would allow for the containment of passengers and buses in an enclosed concourse area. The brand new "Europa Buscentre" opened in May 1991, and by then was the busiest bus station in Northern Ireland. An estimated 46,000 passengers per week were using the new station, with 388 bus departures every weekday.

By January 1993, the estimated cost of this ambitious railway project had risen to £24 million.

InterCity Buses

Ongoing terrorist attacks, on the Belfast to Dublin line in particular, had caused many problems, not only for staff but also of course for many passengers, who at the very least suffered disruptions to their travel, and sometimes much worse. Due to the unpredictable nature of these incidents, it was often difficult to obtain back-up buses at short notice. In 1989, to overcome some of these issues, NIR's Inter City division purchased five modern coaches. These would be kept by Ulsterbus on a stand-by basis in order to respond to emergency situations. The coaches were 1984 Leyland Tigers, with 53-seat Van Hool Alizee coachwork. Their high-floor design offered a superior standard of comfort for passengers. The coaches had previously been operated by Smiths Shearings of Wigan, but, in their new incarnation, were painted in NIR livery.

Performance-Related Pay

In 1989, following the issue of a revised Management Staff Terms and Conditions document, a new system of pay was introduced at NIR. Under this system, managers were issued with a set of objectives for the year ahead, and these would be reviewed at the end of the year at an appraisal meeting, for which each manager would have to also submit a self-appraisal form. Depending on how the company had performed during the previous year and depending on how the individual had performed, a bonus would be paid at a rate decided by the company.

The first bonus to those entitled (of which, thankfully, I was one) was paid in July 1989. This system continued, with reasonable bonuses being paid, until 1995, when a measly £100 was offered to staff as a one-off gratia payment, due to the poor performance of NIR in the previous financial year. However, things would improve in the newly merged company set-up thereafter, with most of managers being awarded enhanced-performance payments under Translink.

150 Years of the Railway

On Saturday, 12 August 1989, the 150th anniversary of the first railway to run in the northern part of Ireland was celebrated. The Ulster Railway had originally been opened in 1839 and ran from Belfast Great Victoria Street to Lisburn, with one intermediate stop at Dunmurry. Up to seven trains ran each way per day, including Sundays; there was no difference in the fare for those travelling from Dunmurry.

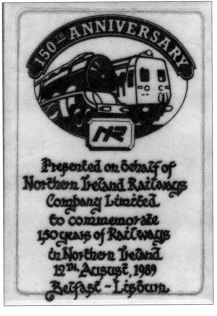

Far left: Ticket issued for the 150th Anniversary of the Ulster Railway – Saturday, 12 August 1989. *(Author's collection)*

Left: The 150th Anniversary ceramic plaque inscription: 12 August 1989. *(Author's collection)*

Special tickets were printed for the event in Lisburn, but they were not free issue. For example, the adult return fare from Belfast to Lisburn was £2.50, and the Concessionary fare was £1.25. Anniversary events were held at Lisburn station throughout the day on Saturday, 12 August; a full programme of events had also been planned from 8 July to 20 August 1989. The RPSI ran a number of special trains during this period.

Before the anniversary year was out, members of staff were presented with mementoes of the day, including a ceramic plaque. The men were given cufflinks and women, lovely trinket boxes. I was one of a group of staff to be presented with these gifts on 4 December 1989.

New Container Crane

At the end of September 1989, a new 35-tonne gantry crane was commissioned at Adelaide Freight Yard in Belfast. The existing crane was no longer fit for purpose, and only able to lift containers in the 20-tonne range. The new crane, built in West Germany, was officially handed over at a prestigious ceremony on 20 October 1989, when NIR Chairman Sir Myles Humphreys received the key from Herr Franz Aumund of the Aumund Group in Germany.

Another Job Change

As a result of a job evaluation exercise carried out on all management positions in 1989–90 by Hay Management Consultants, I was promoted to Management Grade 3. I was given the grand job title of Assistant Company Secretary, which I felt as a great privilege. My new nameplate looked well on my office door!

One of my first tasks in my new role was recording the Minutes at the NIR Board meeting on Thursday, 5 July 1990: something which was to become a regular part of my duties. One of the key items on the agenda at that first meeting was the appointment, from 1 July 1990, of Mr William H de Forde Smyth as Chairman of

NIR: he would be taking over from Sir Myles Humphreys, who had been reappointed Chairman of the Northern Ireland Transport Holding Company.

One of the highlights of my first months in my new job was being invited to a meeting with the Army in their Lisburn Headquarters, on Tuesday, 9 October 1990, in order to review security for the NIR system. I was privileged to be asked on a return visit the following Monday, when I would escort the General Officer Commanding for Northern Ireland and other military officers around a number of depots and locations. This inspection was followed by lunch with the NIR Board in Belfast.

Cross-Border High Speed Train Service

In the spring of 1991, NIR's proposals for a high-speed train service between Belfast and Dublin, involving nine trains a day in each direction operating at 90 mph, were submitted to the Northern Ireland Office and the government of the Republic of Ireland for study and confirmation. The subsequent consultants' report suggested that the £52 million project would include the acquisition of new passenger rolling stock and the relay of the remaining track to the Border, as well as re-signalling. It was estimated that 75 per cent of the costs could be provided for by European grants.

Included in the various options for consideration outlined in the report, there was even a proposal to provide a possible diversionary route on the cross-border line: some 11 miles long, this would take the track from Moira to Tandragee via Waringstown. It was also highlighted that if the overall project received approval, the question of whether or not the track between Portadown and the Border should be singled could be put aside permanently. Everyone involved was delighted when, 18 months later, the project was approved.

Big Jobs Shake-Up All Round

On 31 March 1992, after 16 years as Chief Executive of NIR, Roy Beattie retired. A new position of Managing Director was to be advertised; in the meantime, Mr Jim Aiken took up the acting role. In August 1992, Mr Don Price was appointed as the new Managing Director.

At this juncture, NIR's complete management structure was put under review. As a result, by October 1992, several senior executives in the company had been made redundant; a month later, 11 management posts had been dispensed with. Things were being approached in a bit of a cloak-and-dagger way around this time. Managers were asked to attend interviews with just a few hours' notice: at these interviews, some of them were simply told that they were no longer required, and that they could leave there and then. On Tuesday, 10 November, when it came to my turn, I was advised by Jim Aiken that I was being offered the post of Train Control Manager – which, at Management Grade 4, represented a promotion for me. I accepted the new position right away, as it meant that I would be back in the frontline of railway operations again, and that, in some ways, I had always considered my "real" railway job. My last day at Belfast Central as Assistant Company Secretary was on Friday, 27 November 1992.

The following Monday, 30 November, I returned to Railway Operations again, this time at Belfast York Road. I was now directly responsible for two Traffic Inspectors, four controllers and five LLPA (Long Line Public Address) announcers, who were tasked with announcing train arrivals and departures within most of the Citytrack area. I was also indirectly responsible for 25 signalpersons, nine crossing keepers, the Bann Bridge operator (at Coleraine), and the private security contract. My updated contract of employment was issued in April 1993.

My first two visits to all of the signal boxes and crossing keepers' huts were on Wednesday 10 and Thursday 11 February 1993. Some of the staff were glad to see me: they hadn't had a visit from management for a long time, and basic amenities for them, such as cookers, had been forgotten about. After my visits, eight cookers were ordered for signal boxes and huts without delay.

On Thursday, 27 January 1994, Railway Control moved from Belfast York Road back to Belfast Central, where it had been based when I first started in this department in 1976. Our offices would be where they had originally been when the station had opened – looking over the tracks and the platforms. However a big new control desk, which had been built by the NIR joiner, Sammy Norton, was installed into the Control area on Thursday, 20 January. A fine piece of work! After an extension was built on the roof of Central Station, the rest of the Operations team and the Safety division, which also included the Secretariat, also moved from York Road to Central.

Family Railway Enthusiasts

Thankfully for me, right from the time we first met, my wife Lucinda had been interested in railways also. Over the years, we have travelled many thousands of miles by rail together. We got to know each other in 1979 in Bangor, and we started off just travelling locally in Northern Ireland and then cross-border to Dublin. After getting married in 1981, we travelled extensively around the United Kingdom and also in France, Germany, Austria, Italy, Holland, as well as other countries. In terms of railway travel, our favourite location in Europe is Switzerland. The railway system there is very

The author's wife, Lucinda and daughter, Ruth at Coleraine railway station on a day trip to Portrush on 6 August 1989. *(Author)*

The author with his daughters, Ruth and Sharon, at Amiens railway station in France, 27 July 2002. *(Author)*

McMillan family railway enthusiasts at Belfast Yorkgate station, Saturday, 17 October 1992. *(Author)*

close to perfect: train punctuality is second to none, and the cleanliness of trains and the stations has to be seen to be believed. Switzerland is a wonderful country generally, and I would recommend anyone to make a point of travelling there.

Our first daughter, Ruth, was born in 1986 and our second daughter, Sharon, in 1990. The girls have travelled with us on some of our railway journeys in the United Kingdom and in Europe. Although both of them enjoyed these trips, Ruth would have been more of a railway enthusiast, and she remains so to this day. The photograph above shows Lucinda with Ruth and Sharon at the new station at Yorkgate in Belfast on its opening day, 17 October 1992.

Cross-Border Railway Development Project

All the while, monthly bulletins were being issued to keep passengers up-to-date on developments on the cross-border line project, giving details also of any anticipated travel delays or rescheduling of trains, and so on. The bulletins of April and July 1993 confirmed that NIR and CIÉ were carrying out a £88 million Cross-Border Railway Development Project. The investment would enable the creation of a 90 mph train service with significantly reduced journey times, increased frequency and new rolling stock; the projected completion date was given as some time in 1996.

By summer 1995, 18 miles of continuously welded relay had been completed. A further 19 miles was due for completion by that September. A number of bridges had already been replaced, and two more were scheduled for construction in the autumn.

Reopening of Belfast Station

On Wednesday, 27 January 1993 the government announced plans to reopen Belfast Great Victoria Street station, which had been closed since 1976. A plan which was first drawn up in 1982 had finally been given the green light by the Department of the Environment! Thankfully, plans proposed in the late 1970s for an elevated ring road, which would run through the same site, never materialised.

It was estimated that Great Victoria Street station would be back in business by April 1995. The new station would however be a much more modest affair than the original one. It would form an integral part of the successful Europa Bus Centre, so that passengers would easily be able to switch between train and bus. Closer integration of bus and rail services in this way was a key part of a new government strategy to give public transport a higher profile.

The new train station would have four platforms, two of which would extend beneath the Boyne Bridge and would be long enough to accommodate six-coach trains. The single-storey station would be geared to commuter trains, and passengers would reach the Great Victoria Street frontage by means of a covered walkway and the shopping mall in the new Great Northern Centre tower block. It was expected that the Great Northern shopping mall would also receive a boost from the new station. Opened in the summer of 1993, 45,000 bus passengers a week were currently passing through this mall; by February 1995, seven of the 16 units had tenants. It was estimated that an additional 30,000 transport users a week would be passing through it once the railway station was in operation, making it likely that the remaining empty retail units would quickly attract new businesses.

Another key to the future would be the opening of the Cross-Harbour Rail Link, due for completion in October 1994, which would for the first time give trains from the Larne line direct access to Belfast Central station. Crucial to the scheme was a new spur of railway line in a 200-metre tunnel in the Donegall Road area, designed to allow trains to travel direct from Great Victoria Street to Belfast Central. One of the difficult works to be undertaken was the diversion and replacement of a Victorian brick arch sewer, which crossed the site of the platforms and station building.

The cost of the entire Belfast Great Victoria Street project was estimated to be £6.8 million. Because of its importance to Northern Ireland's transport infrastructure – market research indicated that the new station would potentially attract 800,000 additional passenger journeys a year – the project secured a 75 per cent grant from the European Regional Development Fund.

By February 1995 the construction of the new station and track layout was well underway. The then Environment Minister, Malcolm Moss visited the site that month, along with NIR Chairman, Bill Smyth. On 24 July 1995 the Minister made another visit to the site to check on progress. On this occasion, he was able to take a short ride up the track on a tamping and lining machine which was working on the site at the time.

The scheme was completed within budget and almost exactly on schedule. However, coming in on budget meant that the platforms to accommodate longer trains like the Enterprise had not been built as yet; however the foundations had been laid for such platforms and their extended canopies. The new station at Belfast Great Victoria Street opened informally on Saturday, 30 September 1995, with the official opening on Tuesday, 7 November 1995. More details on this, and associated initiatives, are given in Chapter Eight.

Government Approves Antrim Line Relay

On the day that the Cross-Harbour link between Belfast York Road and Belfast Central opened – Monday, 28 November 1994 – the government announced the approval of the relay of the line between Bleach Green Junction and Antrim. This would allow train services from Londonderry and Portrush to revert to their original routes, and save passengers approximately 20 minutes along the way. The scheme would cost £8 million and entail track upgrading to provide line speed of 70 mph, the automation of five level crossings, re-signalling, and the construction on the single-line section of "passing loops" (i.e. double-track sections of railway where two trains coming in opposite direction towards each other can pass). It was estimated that the new line would be ready for operation in mid-1997. However, the word on the ground at the time was that these changes could in turn see the end of services on the Antrim branch between Antrim and Lisburn: the feeling was that the Department didn't think that NIR needed two railway routes from Belfast to Antrim, even though these served different communities.

The estimated deadline for opening soon passed, however. Delays in the procurement processes continued for a long time, so much so that the relaying of the track did not commence until 29 November 1999, by which stage the estimated cost had risen to £14.4 million. It would be almost 2001 before passenger services made an appearance. More details about this project are recorded in Chapter Eight of the book.

Conclusion

In the period from the mid-1980s to the mid-1990s, the Troubles certainly took a toll on NIR in terms of passenger numbers. A good many of our regular customers stuck with us through thick and thin, but others left, choosing to travel by bus or car instead, since the frequent bomb scares on the railway could last for hours and maybe even for an entire day, and often involved passengers being bussed for parts of their journey anyway. The cross-border route suffered badly, with passengers leaving in large numbers during this period.

Although NIR did not have any other rail companies as direct competitors, Ulsterbus certainly represented a rival in terms of passenger numbers. The most difficult route for the railway to compete on was the line from Belfast to Londonderry, since this was 102 miles by rail, but only 75 miles by road. Ulsterbus's "Maiden City Flyer" service was a really good Goldline route which took only an hour and 40 minutes, whereas the train generally took around two hours and 20 minutes.

However by 1995, change was afoot, with the merger of the bus and rail companies in the offing. For the travelling public and in transportation terms, this would be good news, leading to the creation of more bus and rail connections, and new timetables which offered more services between bus and rail. However, for NIR's workforce, things were a bit more hit-and-miss. Since both bus and rail companies had similar departments within their distinct structures, there would now be a threat to jobs for some staff, including me. There followed quite a protracted period of uncertainty, during which a number of members of staff left NIR, one way or the other. I would count myself very lucky that I was one of those allocated a job within the new organisation.

MY TIME AT NIR, PART THREE:
1995–2013

Merger of Transport Companies

On Tuesday, 17 January 1995, the Government announced that comprehensive changes were to be made to the provision of public transport in Northern Ireland, and that a new company would be formed to incorporate NIR, Ulsterbus and Citybus. Soon the brand name for the new, integrated public transport service was also announced: "Translink". In terms of operational structure, the new company would be similar to the former Ulster Transport Authority. Unlike in the rest of the United Kingdom, public transport in Northern Ireland was to be ultimately retained under state control.

The existing boards of NIR and Ulsterbus/Citybus would be replaced with boards having a common membership, and comprising largely of senior executives answerable to the NITHC. Translink would have a unified managerial structure, with one Managing Director. Accordingly, in May 1995, the then Managing Director of NIR, Don Price, left the company to return to the private sector. Jim Aiken took on the role of Acting Chief Executive until the new position of Managing Director, Group Operations was appointed. At the beginning of August 1995, Ted Hesketh was appointed the new Managing Director, Group Operations. Mr Hesketh had started his career in 1971, when he joined Ulsterbus in 1971 as assistant accountant; in 1988, he had become the Managing Director of Ulsterbus and Citybus.

A booklet was produced by Translink for its staff, setting out key targets for the new organisation. *Moving Forward on Public Transport* revealed that a number of integrated bus and rail terminals would be set up, with very much the same concept in mind as the existing Europa Bus Centre and railway station at Great Victoria Street. The first of these planned integrated centres would be at Bangor and Coleraine. New ticketing systems would be introduced and a common corporate identity was to be established, with the new brand name prominently displayed on all vehicles and publications.

Understandably, staff at NIR and the bus companies were concerned about their jobs and the future of the organisation as a whole. It wasn't too long before a meeting for managers was held, with the subject for discussion being the future of public transport. The first of two such meetings took place at the Europa Hotel on Friday, 22 September 1995; the second at the Glenavna Hotel at Whiteabbey on Tuesday, 19 December.

Staff Magazines

The last edition of the NIR staff magazine, *Staff Lines*, was published in the autumn of

1995, with the last edition of the Ulsterbus/Citybus staff magazine *The Express* being issued around the same time. A competition was organised to give a new title to a combined staff magazine from Christmas 1995. The name for the new magazine was eventually confirmed as *Express Lines*, which came from a combination of the two former titles.

New Structure, New Job

From January 1996, it was for many of us a matter of watching and waiting for new jobs to appear on the staff noticeboards. Very few jobs retained their original titles, so the majority of posts had to be applied for again. I put myself forward for a number of railway operations positions, but was unsuccessful. This is when in some senses the clock was turned back for me, as I ended up carrying on with my company secretarial duties along with prosecution work in my new position of Corporate Services Manager. During the six-month period from January to June 1996, a total of 18 managerial positions were discontinued. Also lost were 14 supervisory and over 25 clerical positions. A voluntary early retirement scheme had been also offered by the company.

On Monday, 10 June that year, I started in my new role, based at Milewater Road in Belfast under the Translink Financial Executive. If I had thought in earlier years that the journey from Queen's Quay to York Road in Belfast was bad, then this new journey – from Belfast Central to Milewater Road – was on a par, or even worse. However, at least I was now able to finish work at 2.00 pm on a Friday.

My usual travel pattern to work was now to take a train from Seahill to Belfast Central, a train from Central to Yorkgate, and then I had a ten-minute walk up the road (it was awful in the rain!). In the evenings, it would be the same pattern in reverse. On really bad weather days, there was the option of catching the staff bus from Great Victoria Street. The Milewater Road offices were certainly remote, and it was more or less like working in the shipyard: any type of shop was at least ten minutes' journey away. After a short period of time, however, management put on a staff bus, which ran on Thursday lunchtimes to the city centre and back. It was known as the "Happy Bus", and certainly was a great morale booster when Thursdays came along!

More Fares Increases

On Monday, 1 April 1996 the Group Managing Director of NIR, Ulsterbus and Citybus felt compelled to publicly defend a decision to increase fares for the second time within 12 months. Ted Hesketh also said that the move towards an integrated public transport system meant it would be sensible henceforth to have a common date for fare revisions. Bus fares were usually revised in April, while rail fares were normally reviewed in August. Mr Hesketh pointed out that the level of increases reflected the fact that railway fares had been raised in August 1995: NIR fares were being increased by 2.2 per cent, Ulsterbus fares by 3.6 per cent, and the cash cost of a Citybus ticket had risen by 6.8 per cent. He also mentioned that a new Belfast central zone fare was being introduced for train services, and would include the area from Yorkgate to Great

Victoria Street stations. This was good news for passengers from the Larne line, who would see their fares reduced when travelling through the central zone.

New Centrelink Bus Service

A new bus service linking the three transport centres now in Belfast commenced on 9 December 1996. This new "Centrelink" bus service was supported by the Department of the Environment Transport Policy Branch and Marks & Spencer, and it would replace the Rail Link bus service. The 15-minute frequency service ran from Belfast Central station to the Europa Bus Centre and Great Victoria Street station, and on to the Laganside Bus Centre via the city centre, before returning to Belfast Central Station. It was free to holders of valid bus and rail tickets. This was incidentally the first scheduled service in Northern Ireland to attract independent funding from the private sector.

Upgrading the Cross-Border Route

The next major project to look forward to in early 1996 was the £115 million upgrade of the Belfast to Dublin route, which was due for completion by the end of 1996, as mentioned in the previous chapter. Work had begun in October 1992, and was continuing apace. The work to be done included raising bridges, track relaying in certain areas, the easing of curves, carrying out station improvements and installing new signalling. All of this would facilitate the increasing of train speeds from 70 to 90 mph, and cut 25 minutes off the end-to-end journey times.

Even before the upgrade was due to be completed, passenger figures on the route were already soaring. Statistics showed that, in the year up to April 1996, some 810,000 passengers had travelled on the Belfast to Dublin line. The figure set a new record, representing a 16 per cent increase on the 1994–95 numbers, and more than double the 372,000 tally for 1990–91.

The new trains, comprising French-built TGV style carriages (De Dietrich) and General Motors 3,200 hp locomotives, promised to transform travel on the line. Train frequency was to increase from six to nine departures each way per day, and each train would carry up to 360 passengers. The journey time would be 1 hour and 50 minutes, but this would be reduced to 1 hour and 40 minutes after the track was relaid between Belfast and Lisburn (which was due to commence in November 1996).

On 20 August 1996, however, Ted Hesketh revealed that the start date for the upgraded Belfast to Dublin rail service had been put back from December 1996 to March 1997. NIR blamed the postponement on delays in the carriages being delivered from France: some of these were not expected to arrive until the New Year. Mr Hesketh advised that the delivery programme with the French had slipped three times, and that there was provision in the contract for liquidated damages in the event of an excessively delayed delivery.

Delays led to further delays however, and the new trains did not enter service until 1 September 1997. Unfortunately, due to a serious back injury at the time, I missed the big day! I did manage though to get my hands on one of the Commemorative Tickets: No B 1199, as shown overleaf.

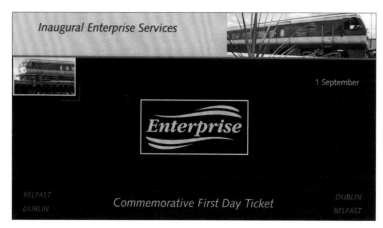

Commemorative First Day Ticket of the new Enterprise, 1 September 1997. *(Author's collection)*

The introduction of the luxury high-speed Enterprise train service between Belfast and Dublin was, as we have seen, the culmination of a project that had begun in 1992, and came in at a final cost of £120 million. The launch took place on 1 September 1997 in Dundalk, and Lord Dubs, the Northern Ireland Environment Minister, and Mary O'Rourke TD, Minister for Public Enterprise in the Republic of Ireland, were both present to officiate. Commemorative plaques were also unveiled in Belfast, Portadown, Drogheda and Dublin. The locomotives that would be used to operate the Enterprise services for the foreseeable future were named, and the Irish Traction Group presented the brass plaques. The NIR locomotives would be known as *River Lagan* (No 208) and *River Foyle* (No 209); the Irish Rail locomotives, as *River Liffey* (No 206) and *River Boyne* (No 207). Hence was honoured the railway tradition of carrying forward historic engine names to the next generation.

However the full benefits of the speed of the service could not be experienced until the relaying of the track between Central Junction and Lisburn was completed. This was also delayed for various reasons, but was finally completed in December 1998.

Further Duties for Me

At the beginning of 1997, my duties as Corporate Services Manager at Translink were extended slightly, as I was called upon to record the Minutes at the senior management team meetings, which were generally held at Belfast Central station. On Monday, 13 January 1997 I was introduced to the team and from then on for a number of years, I recorded the Minutes at their meetings. Then, on 18 March that year, a directive from Ted Hesketh advised the Translink Board that I would be taking on the duties of Assistant to the Company Secretary, which would include the production of Board minutes and action lists. I attended at the Translink Board meeting for the first time in this role on Tuesday, 8 April 1997. I regarded this as a great privilege and of course my lips remain sealed as to what was discussed during the meetings! These meetings became even more interesting for me when the Board went on on-site visits around the network. I thought this was a great idea, as the Board members had the opportunity to spend part of the time at the depots, speaking to the staff on the ground, and listening to their concerns and ideas.

After only 18 months in this role, things changed again for me. A reorganisation within the Finance department saw three job adverts being placed on the staff noticeboard: in fact, these were intended in principle for three managers currently in post. From 1 April 1998, my new title was Secretariat Manager, and this job was basically a realignment of my existing duties. When I started at Milewater Road in 1996, I had a pokey office on the ground floor – but now I was on the up and up! A year later I had an office on the first floor, and in August 1999 I moved to an office on the second floor, two doors from the Director of Finance.

In the meantime, Mrs Joan Smyth CBE (who was from Bangor) became the new NITHC Chairman, from 1 July 1999. Candidates for the roles of Chairman and the directors of the Holding Company were chosen by Government Department officials. Mrs Smyth had previously chaired the Equal Opportunities Commission for Northern Ireland. She was well-liked during her time at NIR, and she regularly travelled by train from Bangor to Belfast, which gave the staff a chance to get to know her. She also made sure to travel to other locations by rail and to use such opportunities to talk with the staff, which is very important for this kind of role, in my view.

Service Badges

In early 1994, it was suggested by a member of staff that NIR should issue lapel badges for 15, 20 or 25 years' service in the company. Two designs were commissioned – a round version, and a square version. Staff were asked to pick a version, to see if there was a preference. The result was announced in the summer of 1994: the vast majority those who responded had opted for the round version. The first issue to all eligible staff took place in 1995 at Easter time.

Unfortunately, the issuing of the service badges was something Translink/NIR didn't do very well. After I had completed my 25 years' service at the company, on 9 July 1998, my badge arrived in the post, along with a very standard typed letter: not very personal, I thought. Apart from that, the letter was dated 13 October 1998! Five years later, my 30 years' service badge was issued on 1 April 2004, which was nine months behind time. At least on that occasion, it was handed to me by the Director of Finance, and we were later treated to a cup of tea and a bun!

On a much more positive note, a perk which many Translink employees looked forward to and greatly enjoyed, was the "Fun Days" organised by the company for all bus staff and their families. The first of these Days were held in 1999, on Saturday 18 and Sunday 19 September. The venue was the Ulster Folk and Transport Museum: on the Saturday, the Fun Day was attended by 2,500 staff and family members, while 4,500 came along on the Sunday. A sit-down lunch was provided for all in a marquee in the grounds. The Fun Days were a great success, back in the days when the company could afford such things!

Bridge Bashing

In 1999, a new bridge map for all road and rail bridges in Northern Ireland was produced by the NIR infrastructure department in association with the Department of the Environment Roads Service and Ordnance Survey, highlighting all low bridges which pass over public roads (under Department regulations, a "low" bridge was deemed as being one under 16 feet 6 inches). The aim was to reduce the number of bridges damaged as a result of careless driving.

Although the bridges were painted and signed by the DoE, the railway network had a number of bridges which were lower than 16 feet 6 inches. Bridge No 282 at

Lisburn, for example – a railway bridge – was hit more frequently than any other, despite the signage being in place. Even after a number of years, when very large warnings had been painted in yellow on the walls, motorists still ran into the steel bridge. The culprits were in the main lorry drivers, who were either preoccupied with what they were doing, or just didn't know the height of their vehicles (even though the height will always displayed somewhere on a lorry). Colliding with any bridge is serious, but striking a steel bridge is extremely hazardous to the railway, as the bridge could move out of place if struck hard enough. In most severe cases, an out-of-line railway bridge will lead to a train derailment.

On this issue of damage to bridges, a monthly meeting was held with all of the interested agencies attending, including myself. My role there was to give updates on enforcement issues and the prosecution of offenders. Eventually bridge protection beams were installed at bridge No 282, and indeed a number of other bridges.

Railways Task Force

As the new Millennium dawned, once more the future of the railways in Northern Ireland seemed under threat. On 28 March 2000, a grim warning was issued by the then Regional Development Minister, Adam Ingram, after the publication of a new safety review which claimed that an investment of £183 million was needed for NIR over the next ten years. In the review, which had been commissioned by Translink, Cambridge-based international consultants, Arthur D Little called for funding for new trains, track upgrades and train safety equipment, so that the network would be able to keep abreast with future safety requirements – although they did stress that at present NIR was operating a safe railway. Mr Ingram admitted that the picture revealed by the report was one of a rail system which had suffered from years of underinvestment.

There was however a real question mark over the priority which expenditure on this scale should be given over the many other pressing demands on the public purse. A number of difficult options needed to be carefully considered, including whether new sources could be found for funding aspects of transportation, and whether ultimately it was the case that the government could simply not continue to support a rail network of the present extent in Northern Ireland. The publication of the safety report at this juncture brought to a head a growing campaign by the Northern Ireland Transport Holding Company for more funding for public transport. The Department of Regional Development's response however was to declare that such a large sum of money was not available.

According to the report, the specific funding requirements at the time were:
- £72 million for 19 new three-car train sets to replace NIR's oldest trains;
- £67 million for relaying 123 of its 290 miles of track, replacing six bridges and fortifying coastal defences on the Larne and Londonderry lines;
- £25.5 million for an upgrading of on-train safety systems, including a Train Protection Warning System, as well as the completion of signalling improvements at Castlerock and Portrush.

Mr Ingram announced that a Railways Task Force was to be set up, comprising six high-level civil servants, who would produce an options paper on the future of railways in Northern Ireland. The Task Force was expected to report back by the summer of 2000. It was understood that the worst case scenario could entail the closure of every line, apart from the link between Belfast and the Border. Short of that, the lines most at risk in any pruning of the system would be the Coleraine to Londonderry line and that from Whitehead to Larne Harbour.

The Chairman of the Holding Company, Joan Smyth, called for the government to implement the recommendations of the report, and to make the funding available. A similar call was made by the NI General Consumer Council's Maeve Bell, who said that the government had to come up with the money without delay.

In March 2000 also, Translink were waiting for Government approval to proceed with two schemes for which European Union funding had already been secured. The EU was putting up 75 per cent of the cost of a scheme to relay the Belfast to Bangor railway line, priced at £14 million; 75 per cent funding had also been secured for work to upgrade Belfast Central station, priced at £4 million. However, the terms of the EU grants were that all of the work had to be completed, and all the bills paid for, by the end of 2001. Ultimately, the delay caused by the Government meant that there would not be sufficient time for the relay of the Belfast to Bangor railway line. However, tendering systems proceeded regardless, with the government pushing for the scheme to be completed on time.

When it comes to relaying a railway, the common misconception seems to be that you can just arrive with sleepers and rails, and simply throw them down on the previous alignment. Unfortunately, the process involves a lot more than this – the existing alignment has to be surveyed, and realigned if necessary; new drainage must be installed; platform heights must be adjusted; and you have to focus too on somehow maintaining a train service on part of the line as the relaying is in process. In this instance, the project went over budget and did not meet its deadline, and ended up being raised at the Commons Select Committee, as mentioned previously. Sadly, the upgrade at Belfast Central station would run into similar difficulties.

The *Belfast Telegraph* newspaper started up a campaign based on the slogan, "Save Our Railways", and this phrase, combined with a distinctive circular logo, was used when any story about the railways was in the news. NIR picked up on the media campaign, and the same large circular logos were placed on the front of each train set.

At the end of June 2000, three public consultation meetings took place in Belfast,

"Save Our Railways" campaign – stickers and bookmark. *(Author's collection)*

Londonderry and Ballymena; a further three were scheduled for Bangor, Larne and Craigavon in July 2000. The Chair of these meetings was Paul Sweeney, the Deputy Secretary of the Department of Regional Development. There were good attendances at each meeting, and this too helped to raise awareness of the plight of the railways in the Northern Ireland.

On Tuesday, 17 October 2000, Northern Ireland Finance Minister, Mark Durkan announced plans for the inclusion of additional funding for railways in his draft budget proposals. If the budget was approved, this funding could be used to immediately begin the track relay programmed for the Bangor line, and to order 23 new trains (which included four additional trains to allow for enhancement of services, as well as the 19 needed to replace existing units).

The draft budget was confirmed on 18 December 2000, and the two projects above mentioned were to proceed. The Assembly also announced their "Programme of Government" initiative, which confirmed an additional £105 million investment in NIR over the next three years. The acquisition and implementation of new rolling stock was a complex matter, and a full consultation process with staff, users and interested parties was begun at once. A detailed questionnaire was mailed to 5,000 people, including staff, and was also available at main bus and rail stations and on the Translink website. The tendering process for the new trains opened in August 2001, and tender documents were to be returned by 16 November that year. On 19 February 2002, an announcement was made that the contract to provide 23 new trains had been awarded to the Spanish company, CAF, and would be built in their factories in Zaragoza in northern Spain.

The first of the 23 new trains from CAF would arrive on Tuesday 20 April 2004, when Train No 3001 was unloaded at Belfast docks. The ship returned to Spain the same day. The new trains were built to NIR's specification, meeting the highest standards in terms of safety, accessibility and comfort. Compliant with all relevant UK standards, they would be capable of travelling at speeds of up to 90 mph, with seating in each three-car train for 200 passengers. Further details are recorded in Chapter Seven.

At this time also, as well as the new trains, an innovative and groundbreaking staff development programme was being undertaken at NIR, delivered by Power Train UK Ltd. Comprising 73 separate training events, the large-scale "Corporate Culture Change" training programme would run until November 2005. This fresh approach was to be of benefit to all staff. As the new corporate slogan at the time went, "Getting there is getting better".

Threat to Lisburn to Antrim Branch

The threat to the Lisburn to Antrim branch, which was rumoured back in 1994 when the announcement to reopen the line between Bleach Green and Antrim was debated, became reality when a public notice appeared in the press on 4 March 2001, stating that services would be withdrawn when the new Bleach Green line imminently opened. The announcement was later withdrawn for a period of time.

However, further public announcements were published in due course, and on

Sunday, 29 June 2003, the Antrim branch was finally closed after the last scheduled services that day. A number of railway enthusiasts (including myself) travelled on the two final services, which were the 17.20 hrs, Bangor to Antrim, and the 18.10 hrs, Portrush to Belfast Central (from Antrim). Incidentally, both trains were 13 minutes late. The RPSI also ran services on the Branch that day to mark the occasion: over 600 passengers on two fully-booked trains enjoyed the sense of the occasion, with many more turning out to wave from stations and bridges as spectators. The following day, Monday, 30 June, a new NIR timetable commenced – one which of course excluded services on the now-defunct route.

The line was to remain intact however, as a diversionary route and also for special and engineering trains. After the closure, a new enhanced bus service for the Antrim branch route was provided by Ulsterbus. The long-term possibility of services being reinstated was envisaged in the Regional Development Strategy for Northern Ireland 2025 plan, and in 2016, the long-term plan for reopening remains in place.

An Additional Member of Staff: Maureen Jefferson

For a number of years, I had been dealing with my workload on my own, apart from getting a helping hand from the internal typing pool when possible. Due to the sheer volume of work I had to manage, this had been a struggle on many occasions. Then in late 2001 came great news that assistance was to be given to me and the Director of Finance, with the recruitment of a senior clerical officer to work for us. Maureen Jefferson started with us on 2 January 2002, and the flexible arrangement was that she was to have a shared workload between the Finance Director and myself. At that stage, Maureen already had almost 20 years' service with Ulsterbus, and she was a great asset, right from the start.

For some time, I had had been investigating the possibility of dealing with prosecutions for the bus companies also, and in relation to this, a preliminary meeting with the Department of the Environment at River House, Belfast had been held on Thursday, 16 September 1999. At this meeting, we had begun to explore the possibility of new legislation which would allow prosecutions to be pursued by the bus companies. This subject is covered in more depth in Chapter Nine.

Now, with Maureen to assist me, I was at last able to start work on the proposed prosecution procedures for the bus companies. This meant quite a bit of research for both of us, including a visit to Dublin on Thursday, 14 February 2002 to meet with Dublin Bus officials and then with CIÉ solicitors. Dublin Bus where far ahead of us, as they already had bus Byelaws in place.

As a result of this work, a set of prosecution guidelines for bus staff was prepared and tabled at the Executive Group meeting on 31 May 2002. The guidelines were approved and, following a few more internal procedures, the booklets were printed and the new system came into operation on 17 February 2003.

Future of Public Transport

It wasn't long before public transport system in Northern Ireland was up for review again. On 17 September 2002, the then Minister for Regional Development, Peter

Robinson announced the findings of a consultation looking at possible changes to the future governance, planning and delivery of public transport services in Northern Ireland. The paper was entitled, "A New Start for Public Transport in Northern Ireland".

A statement from Translink, addressing the report's exploration of the potential for private sector involvement in public transport, stressed that as far as they were concerned, there were no plans to privatise Translink. The paper also suggested the possible amalgamation of NITHC and Translink into a single body, which could be called "Transport Northern Ireland" and would focus on operations, while a separate public transport regulator could be established, as was common with the utilities sector on the mainland. Translink, the NITHC and members of the public were invited to submit their responses to these proposals to the Department. Although NITHC did not respond to the proposals, in the meantime, Transport Northern Ireland has been formed and exists as a business unit within the Department of Regional Development. As of 2016, a separate public transport regulator has yet to be established.

Freight Traffic

The beginning of the end for railway freight traffic in Northern Ireland was on New Year's Eve, 31 December 2002, when container traffic on some Irish Rail routes ceased, including such traffic between Dublin and Belfast's Adelaide Yard. Up until this point, all of the freight arriving into Belfast by rail had been from the Republic of Ireland, but now Irish Rail decided that any freight route would have to pay for itself and that no further subsidies could be provided by them. This would ultimately be the death toll for most freight movements in the Republic. A few trains were reformed for use by private freight operators, but none of these have ventured to cross the Border into Northern Ireland. NIR did attempt to sell the freight crane to Irish Rail, but they did not have any need for it.

By New Year's Eve, 31 December 2003, Irish Rail had pulled out of more freight traffic routes, and the yard at Adelaide was virtually empty, apart from Guinness trains running through it to their private siding further up the third line in Belfast. Cross-border freight traffic ceased completely on 27 February 2004, with the withdrawal of the Guinness trains. The freight crane in Adelaide Yard was dismantled and eventually scrapped in January 2010.

The TravelSafe Conference

The inaugural TravelSafe Conference was organised by NIR in 2004. Up to 100 members of the PSNI, participants from the Community Safety Unit (Northern Ireland Office), and Translink staff attended the one-day event at Cultra Manor on Thursday, 27 March 2004, which was chaired by former Acting Assistant Chief Constable of the British Transport Police, Peter Whent. The purpose of the conference was to bring together the different agencies, and give them the opportunity to plan and work together to provide better, safer public transport services. A number of speakers gave reports on their different areas of work; I gave a presentation on railway and bus prosecutions.

At the conference, it was highlighted that in 2003 Translink had suffered over 7,000 incidents across the Northern Ireland bus and rail network, including assaults on staff and passengers, vandalism, stone-throwing and general civil unrest. These incidents had cost the company over £7 million in damage repairs, revenue loss, insurance claims and additional staff cover.

Local Community Safety Coordinators, who were also well represented at the event, were tasked with reviewing and presenting the outcomes of the conference; they were then to develop individual audits for their areas, aimed at producing local action plans. The conference, and what came out of it, proved to be extremely valuable for all concerned.

More Staff Changes

On 31 March 2003, the Managing Director of Translink, Ted Hesketh retired. A celebration of his career was held at a function on Thursday, 27 March at Belfast Castle. From 1 April, Jim Aiken from the NITHC took over as Acting Chief Executive while the recruitment process was being carried out. The position of Chief Executive was taken up on 1 October 2003 by Keith Moffett, who had previously been involved in bus and rail companies on the mainland and in Europe.

Approval for More Clerical Support

Although Maureen was invaluable in assisting me with the workload, the increasing numbers of prosecution court cases and the implementation of impending changes through legal procedures were such that there was a need for more, full-time support for us. To this end, I had been putting in applications for more clerical support over a period of time, and was very glad when this was finally approved, in June 2004. On Monday, 1 November 2004, following the recruitment process, Karen Hutchinson started in her new position in our office. Karen had joined Translink in 2002 and had experience working within the engineering and administration divisions.

It wasn't long before Karen, by chasing up reports from staff and the police, had put into operation new processes relating to the early stages of prosecution work. She had also made new and additional contacts within each police division, which proved invaluable in clearing our office log-jam, which had chiefly been caused by delays in obtaining information and documentation. To ease the burden on Maureen in terms of frequently attending court, Karen was trained in this aspect of the work too, meaning that the number of outings could be shared around. There were occasions of course when both were out of the office at the same time, due the number of court cases happening around the country.

Railway Routes Saved

On Monday, 20 December 2004, the Government Finance Minister, Ian Pearson announced additional investment funding of £23.6 million for NIR, which would secure the future of the railway routes north of Ballymena and Whitehead, until now termed as "non-core routes". A question mark had been hanging over the future of these routes for 18 months, so the announcement was very welcome news for NIR and of course its passengers.

New Railway Timetable

My prior expertise in railways operations was called upon in September 2004, when I was asked to assist with the drawing up and producing of a timetable which would be based on a new, frequent rush-hour service to be provided by the newly acquired CAF trains. This was a priority job, so most of my work was to be put to the side for Maureen and Karen to review if necessary.

Once I had been given the parameters, I basically set to work with pen and paper; I also worked from home on a number of days, while keeping in close contact with the member of staff from Operations whom I was assisting. Not only was the train timetable to be drawn up, but a complete train set working diagram was also to be prepared. Drawing up a train set working diagram involves calculating how many trains are needed to operate the entire train service each day, all the while ensuring that the correct number of trains are in position at each depot at the relevant times. Such a diagram does not work on the assumption that all trains will be in service at any one time, as each train has to be maintained: accordingly, a proportion of the total number will be marked off for servicing. Additionally, since trains of course must be fuelled, the total mileage each train will run per day must be calculated, so that each can be fuelled at the correct time and at the correct depot. So it is quite a complex procedure!

On Tuesday, 26 October 2004, I attended the Railway Operations timetable meeting, and handed over my work. When the new timetable was brought into operation on 6 June 2005, I was pleased that a certain amount of my work had been taken on board. The June 2005 timetable introduced a new 20-minute stopping frequency between Bangor and Portadown on the Belfast to Dublin line, with express services on the Bangor and Lisburn lines during rush hours. It was developed around a "central corridor" service between Portadown and Bangor, which would operate the showcase service and work on a simple, customer-friendly, regular "clock-face" basis. Passenger rail journey figures released in the spring of 2006 showed an increase of 28 per cent on the Portadown–Bangor central corridor for the first part of that year, compared to the same period in 2004.

Unfortunately the new timetable brought an end to the catering trolley service on the Londonderry line from 27 May 2005: surely this was a mistake? Trolleys had been purchased for the job, a special compartment had been constructed to keep them secure in each train – however, as the concession was losing money, it was decided to withdraw this service. Sadly it was not a mistake which was to be soon rectified by NIR, even though track improvements were imminent and passenger numbers were very much on the increase.

Order for New Trains and Further Investment

By the summer of 2006, the preparation of a proposal for another order of new trains had begun. The first step was to prepare a detailed Business Case, which brought together passenger figures and projections for the future growth of passenger numbers and revenues. An economic appraisal then followed. The proposal would have to be completed by December 2006, when it would be submitted to Government for incorporation into their December 2007 Comprehensive Spending Review.

The Northern Ireland Executive's draft budget for 2008/09 was announced on 25 October 2007 by the then Minister for Finance and Personnel, Peter Robinson. The Minister confirmed that £182 million had been allocated for investment in Translink services. As such, the draft budget included provision for the following: the purchase of 20 new trains to replace existing rolling stock and provide additional capacity; the purchase of around 200 new buses; the completion of Londonderry rail line track life extension work north of Ballymena; the commencement of a major track relay project between Coleraine and Londonderry; the completion of significant improvement work on the railway line between Knockmore and Lurgan; and the extension of the Concessionary Fares Scheme to introduce free travel on public transport to all those aged 60 years and over (excluding all-Ireland or cross-border travel). In January 2008, the final budget was approved by the Northern Ireland Assembly. The over-60s free travel scheme would commence on 1 October 2008.

New Train Order

An important date in the procurement of the 20 new Class 4000 trains was 25 March 2009. This date marked the formal signing of contracts drawn up between CAF, the new trains supplier selected by means of a rigorous tendering exercise, the DRD and Translink. The £114 million order was funded by the DRD. It was estimated that the first new train would be delivered in April 2011, with all 20 trains to be delivered within 15 months.

It had been determined that when the 20 new trains entered service, NIR's 13 oldest trains would be retired. At that point, the company would be operating 37 train sets, as opposed to 29. The significant increase would translate into enhanced service frequencies and capacity for rail passengers. Other major and related work to be carried out under the new trains project included the building of a new train maintenance depot at Adelaide, and a platform extension programme to ensure the accommodation of the longer six-car trains during peak periods.

Senior Staff Changes

The Translink Chief Executive, Keith Moffett resigned on Friday, 22 December 2006. As the announcement was made just as the Christmas holidays had commenced, the news only became public through the local media on 27 December. The Chief Operating Officer, Philip O'Neill took up the post of Acting Chief Executive until the recruitment process had been completed.

Catherine Mason was appointed as the new Group Chief Executive, from Monday, 3 March 2008. She had previously been Managing Director with Arriva Midlands, the bus and rail services operator serving the East and West Midlands in England.

In 2010, an important new post was created within NIR – that of in-house solicitor. JP Irvine was appointed on 7 July that year as Head of Governance and Legal, and he was to be based in the NITHC building in Belfast. Since we dealt with a lot of legal matters within the Secretariat, this appointment was bound to bring changes to our department. My first meeting with JP was on 4 August 2010, and we continued to have these regular meetings as a matter of course. Around this time, my job title was changed to Head of Prosecutions.

Trip of a Lifetime

In the autumn of 2008, my wife Lucinda and I decided to travel to Australia to visit relatives in the west and east of the country. Knowing this would likely be a one-off visit, I took the opportunity to schedule into our itinerary a trip along one of the most long-distance train routes in the world.

So, on Saturday, 8 November 2008 we arrived at Sydney Central station to board the early afternoon "Indian Pacific" train for Perth, almost 2,500 miles away, for a trip which would take the guts of four days. We had decided to travel in Gold Class and this was a real treat.

The train was composed of one diesel locomotive and 15 carriages, which had aluminium bodyshells to reflect the heat. Our compartment had a big picture window with a very comfortable seat, and ensuite toilet and shower facilities. This service is not known for its speed, as its journey includes travelling up through the Blue Mountains, and I would hazard a guess that in some areas, we were travelling at about 25 mph! The dining car was something else: silver service, linen tablecloths, luxurious furnishings and five-course meals were the order of the day. While you were at the dining car, according to the time of day, the carriage attendants would either set your compartment bunks up for night time, or by taking these down, get the compartment ready for day-time use.

Each day at selected stops, there was a bus tour from the train, giving us the opportunity to see the sights along the way. The first such tour was at Broken Hill, and we travelled around the local area and then to the museum. The next trip offered was a tour of Adelaide, but Lucinda had arranged to meet her relatives at the station at this point, so we did that instead. As advertised, the train also stopped in what the brochure called the "Middle of Nowhere", which was a station named Cook. Right in the heart of the desert-like Nullarbor Plain, this was basically a railway depot where drivers rested and changed trains. The final bus tour was from Kalgoorlie station, when we were taken to the gold mines at the Super Pit, a vast hole in the earth, where the lorries which scurried around looked like Dinkey toys. Eventually, the train arrived in Perth on the morning of Tuesday, 11 November. It had been a memorable trip indeed!

Early Thoughts of Retirement

In April 2009, I put out some feelers with my boss about the possibility of an early retirement package, as our Human Resources department had asked for applications. I submitted an expression of interest and received a quote back from the company, but it wasn't the right timing, nor was the offer sufficient for me to be able to proceed then. The truth is that I had never really thought of working past age 60, and the thought of working until I was 66 certainly did not sound good. I had always felt a pull towards Scotland, where I had been going for holidays since I was about 15 years old. Lucinda also liked Scotland very much – we had even gone to Inverness for our honeymoon! We didn't have any precise plans at that stage, but the idea of Scotland was somewhere at the back of our minds.

Move to NITHC Premises

As our Secretariat department was still based in Milewater Road in Belfast, this in a sense created a physical barrier between us and the key members of staff we were working with, now that the new Company Secretary and legal senior were in place at the NITHC premises. For this reason, as well as other, non-work related ones, it would have made much more sense for me, Maureen and Karen to work at the NITHC building too.

Discussions between senior staff went on in the background for some time, until it was finally announced, on Thursday, 7 July 2011, that the three of us would be transferred to the NITHC building, possibly sometime that September. After a few delays along the way, we moved over to the NITHC premises at Great Victoria Street on Tuesday, 31 January 2012. However, as Maureen still held the shared work role with the Director of Finance as well as with me, she continued to work in Milewater in the mornings. Otherwise, working in the city centre was a real change for us all, especially in terms of our travel to and from work. The railway station was now 300 yards away, and of course all the shops were just outside the door.

Long Service Event for Staff

On the evening of Thursday, 7 June 2012, a special function was held for staff with more than 35 years' service within the Translink group. The venue for the event was the Railway Gallery at the Transport Museum at Cultra, and just over 70 members of staff and their guests came along for the evening.

Tables were set around the railway exhibits and on the covered turntable at the Museum, and a sumptuous meal was served to all present. Each member of staff was asked to choose a gift from a brochure which had been circulated in advance: I had chosen a lovely Swiss watch. The Chairman, John Trethowan and the Group Managing Director, Catherine Mason presented these gifts to each member of staff, while the Director of Human Resources, Gordon Milligan read out some light-hearted background details on each of us. A copy of this information, along with a photo of the person from the time when they first started at the company were also given as a memento of the occasion. As well as this, official photos were taken at the event, and copies of these were sent to staff as well. This function was really well organised, and it was generally hoped that this would be the start of a new tradition at the company.

The author and his wife, Lucinda at the Translink long service event held at Cultra on Thursday, 7 June 2012. *(Author)*

Early Retirement

In April 2011, I applied again for early retirement. At this point, the company were looking to recruit a new legal assistant, and so my request was put on hold until someone was in place. Further discussions took place eventually with my new boss, JP Irvine, which resulted in a meeting with the Human Resources Director on 15 May 2012. We agreed in principle that I would be offered voluntary redundancy with a possible leaving date of the end of the calendar year. Less than a month later, I received my first detailed letter from Human Resources with an offer based on a departure date of 28 February 2013. Then, at the beginning of August, I was advised by my boss that the company had accepted my request for voluntary redundancy from February 2013, as discussed.

A few days later, I advised Maureen and Karen about my leaving plan and the office restructuring which would in all likelihood follow. They had both known for a few years that I had been looking into early retirement, but on the day I broke the news, they were still surprised and no doubt had their own worries about the future.

By this time, Lucinda and I had some plans in place for our own future, including a move to Scotland, and our house was also up for sale. All of the doors where opening for us in these plans, and for me, as a born-again Christian, a Bible verse came to mind: "The Lord hath done great things for us, whereof we are glad." (Psalm 126: 3). We knew that the Lord's timing was perfect.

By November 2012, interviews were being carried out for a new Company Lawyer (partly to replace me), with a start date in January 2013. With this in mind, certain very difficult decisions had to be taken. Another new role had to be created, and after much discussion, Karen Hutchinson was appointed the new Prosecutions Officer for Translink. Maureen had decided to return to Milewater Road to work full-time for the Director of Finance. Her last day in our office was Friday, 11 January 2013, and it was sad indeed to lose her after eleven years of working together. Maureen had been of immense help to me over the years at work; she was a really dependable colleague and always a great representative of the company. She was also a personal friend, and we have our own memories of many incidents, good and bad, over the years. My own leaving date had now slipped back to Friday, 31 May 2013, but I was happy to help out in the new department in the meantime.

Pre-Retirement Trip

As the date of my retirement came closer, I decided to take a few days' leave and, with the one British Rail staff pass I still had left, I thought I would go on one of the trips that I had undertaken many years before. (As an NIR employee, I was entitled to two first-class BR passes; I had already used the first one.) On Monday, 4 March 2013 I flew to London Gatwick with Flybe, and from there, took the train into central London. At King's Cross station, I boarded the *Highland Chieftain* high-speed train, taking the 12.00 hrs (East Coast) service from London King's Cross to Inverness. I travelled First Class, and enjoyed the in-seat catering service. The *Highland Chieftain* was formed by a Class 254 Inter-City train, which had entered service in 1976. The seating arrangements and space available are far superior to a lot of other trains in service today. The first stop on this 125 mph service was York, and from there, we made limited stops en route to Inverness. Finally, after around 570 miles, we arrived into Inverness at 20.04 hrs (five minutes early – how about that!).

The next morning I set off on one of the most scenic railways journeys in Europe – Inverness to Kyle of Lochalsh. This two-coach diesel train runs at the more sedate speed of around 50 mph, but the scenery is breathtaking, especially when there is snow lying, or the sun is shining – a very nice way to see the Isle of Skye! I returned that day on the 14.37 hrs to Inverness, travelling back home again on Wednesday, 6 March.

New Prosecutions Officer

From Wednesday 1 May 2013, Karen Hutchinson became Prosecutions Officer at Translink. In the weeks before my retirement at the end of the month, I was able to take Karen by car on a detailed tour of the NIR railway routes, as requested by Philip O'Neill, the Chief Operating Officer. To this day, I am glad that the work I initiated at the company has continued, and that Karen has followed me with real enthusiasm for what she is doing and with an eagerness to get the job done. It is great to know that, over two years since I left the company, the work has continued apace under Karen's very capable management, and that the new legal team is working well.

Translink's New Prosecutions Officer, Karen Hutchinson, May 2013. *(Author)*

My Last Day at Work

After clocking up almost 40 years' service, I now faced my very last day at Translink. On Friday, 31 May 2013, I arrived into work early and had my last informal meeting with Philip O'Neill. The office had been well decorated with old photographs, and a few "Trespassers Prosecuted" signs were on display too! Along with my wife, about 60 of my work colleagues turned up for the occasion.

Around 10.30 am, Philip O'Neill gave a speech, followed by my boss, JP Irvine. I was pleased to see Mrs Mason there also. A generous sum of money had been collected by my colleagues and, as indicated on the envelope in which it was presented to me, was to be used to purchase a season ticket for Inverness Caley Thistle Football Club (I followed these instructions!). I also received a great surprise – and in fact it was a "rail" treat! – when I was presented with a name board from a Castle Class train: *Bangor Castle*. I received other gifts from various colleagues, and my wife Lucinda loved her bouquet of flowers.

The day I left the office for the last time, I knew I would miss my friends and colleagues, and of course this has been the case. However, with two or three trips back to Northern Ireland each year so far, I have able to see most of them again. I also keep in regular contact with Karen, who is a personal friend, and we still have a laugh from time to time as we recall many memories from the past.

Unsurprisingly, since our move, I have kept up with my enthusiasm for the railways. Although the Dr Beeching report of the mid-1960s brought about a major withdrawal of railways on the mainland, including in the north-east of Scotland where we now live, fortunately, there are a few railway preservation societies in existence, including the Keith & Dufftown Railway, of which I am a member. Lucinda and I also enjoy walking along old railway routes in our area (now footpaths), and exploring stations and infrastructure in the locality. We venture back of course to the

Presentation of
Bangor Castle train
name board to
Edwin, by Philip
O'Neill and J P Irvine,
Friday, 31 May 2013.
(Author)

real railway (Scotrail) too, and have travelled on many routes, starting from either Keith or Inverurie stations, depending on our itinerary. It continues to be a pleasure not to have to go to work each day!

NIR DURING THE TROUBLES:
1972–1977

As noted in Chapter One, there have been many periods of civil unrest in Northern Ireland since 1920; the most recent of these, known as "the Troubles", started in 1969, and was ongoing throughout my entire career at NIR. Even by the time I retired in 2013, there were still a number of incidents occurring, although thankfully on a much smaller scale. The detailed records I kept at the time, some of which I will be reproducing in this book and its Appendices, bear testimony to the fact that, even in incredibly difficult and challenging circumstances, the railways very often succeeded in keeping going. The trains may not have run on certain sections of track at times, and there may have been delays for many passengers, but thankfully travel services were maintained by the provision of substitutionary buses from the two main bus companies, as well as on occasion from private coach operators. This in itself was a remarkable achievement in such difficult times.

Literally thousands of terrorism-related incidents took place over the span of my 40-year career at NIR – far too many incidents to record here. The most intensive period of terrorist activity however, on the railways and indeed elsewhere, was between 1972 and 1977, and in Appendix A, I have recorded each individual railway-related incident over this six-year phase. Some incidents of course were of a more serious nature than others, and unfortunately led to fatalities and injuries among passengers and staff, as well as extensive damage to NIR and CIÉ trains, and the very infrastructure of the railways. I have covered these major incidents in more depth in this chapter as best I can. Incidents about which I have provided more detail in this chapter have been marked as such in the corresponding entry in Appendix A. In Appendix B, I have recorded only a selection of terrorist incidents from the period 1978 to 2013, some of which, again, I discuss in more detail in the next chapter.

Where possible, I have included photographic records of the incidents being referred to. Due to the security clampdown at major incident scenes, some of the photographs from amateurs and train enthusiasts show the later rather than the immediate aftermath; since official press photographers and journalists were generally permitted on the scene straight away however, the photographs I have included from such sources tend to reflect what things looked like just after incidents had happened.

The Early 1970s: Terrorism on the Railways Intensifies

As stated previously, I joined NIR in 1973, but there were of course a number of incidents in the preceding years. I have detailed some of the most significant of these here.

Security swoop on train from Dublin on 6 May 1971. *(News Letter)*

On 6 May 1971, security forces made a surprise swoop on the evening Enterprise train from Dublin to Belfast at Meigh level crossing in South Armagh. Once the train was stopped at the level crossing, security forces used ladders to board it; during this time, a soldier on the ground was struck by a bottle thrown from the train. As the train continued on its journey to Belfast, nearly 120 troops and police carried out a systematic search of passengers, their luggage and every nook and corner inside the compartments, while a radio-linked helicopter flew low overhead. Once in Belfast, the train was shunted into a siding, where a thorough search was made below the carriages by troops using metal detectors, but again, nothing was found. The police party was from the Special Patrol Group based in Musgrave Street in Belfast, and the troops were from the 4th Field Squadron Royal Engineers.

This was the first reported "snap-check" by the security forces, in a drive to stop any possible smuggling by train of arms and ammunition. In a statement to the press, an RUC Inspector explained that this would serve as a warning to terrorists, that surprise swoops by the security forces would be made on the railways as well as on the roads.

The next day, Friday, 7 May 1971, the IRA tried to derail a train on the Londonderry line by blowing out a section of rail. Fortunately the driver of the train saw the broken rail and managed to stop in time. Riots, explosions and the number of fatal shootings around Northern Ireland intensified from Friday, 14 May. Fire bombs and incendiary devices were also being used on a limited basis around this time.

A track walker was carrying out a routine morning inspection of the track at 8.20 am on 21 June 1971, when he noticed explosives under the lines at Silverwood bridge, near the Goodyear factory at Lurgan. (At that time, it was standard procedure for each section of the railway to be walked by track walkers on a daily basis from Monday to Friday.) In this instance the walker immediately raised the alarm, and all trains were stopped until an Army bomb disposal team arrived on the scene. They managed to make safe four separate 2 lb gelignite bombs, despite the fact that these were wired together. This was a serious incident, in that the bombs had failed to

Terrorism intensifies on the railways: *Belfast Telegraph,* 21 June 1971.

Six trains pass over mines on track to Dublin

BOMBS FOUND ON BUSY RAIL LINE

explode only because the timing device was defective, and also because no warning about the devices being on the line had been given. Lurgan police station had been attacked by terrorists a few hours earlier. Another frightening consideration was that before the explosives were found, six trains had already passed over the live devices, including the 08.00 hrs Enterprise service from Belfast to Dublin. The Enterprise was carrying hundreds of passengers, including a party of schoolchildren.

On Tuesday, 22 June, a police car was lured to a trap by the IRA close to Carnalea station. The car was hit five times by gunfire, and police returned fire. The perpetrators, suspected to be from the IRA, escaped through the railway subway and into an awaiting vehicle in the station car park.

Less than six weeks later, on Thursday, 5 August, more than 60 train passengers were evacuated from the 20.42 hrs Bangor to Belfast service at Craigavad, when a suspicious parcel was found on board by a passenger. Dozens of people from nearby houses were also evacuated while the police carried out a search. The hoax package was made up of sticks, tied together with insulating tape and with a rough "fuse" attached. Trains on the line were delayed for one hour.

Introduction of Internment

Internment – imprisonment without trial – was introduced in Northern Ireland on Monday, 9 August 1971, when approximately 300 people were detained. The days which followed saw heightened violence throughout Northern Ireland, with 35 Troubles-related deaths and over 100 bomb explosions.

As a direct result of the introduction of internment and the heightened threat of terrorist attack, one immediate precautionary measure taken by NIR was to ensure that most of the Bangor line Multi-Engine Diesel (MED) rolling stock was stabled in Bangor overnight. Each evening, from around 21.00 hrs, the following pattern would now be the norm: six cars at Platform One; six cars in middle road; three cars at Platform Two; and eight cars at Platform Three. These precautions continued for some time. The photograph shows an MED set running over to Platform Two, which was the only platform free at this time. The photograph was taken in late August 1971.

Stabling of rolling stock in Bangor, August 1971.
(Author)

Around this time too, bus services were badly affected, and Belfast City Corporation buses ceased operating completely after the evening rush hour. Ulsterbus services were curtailed throughout the country: for example, from 8.00 pm each evening, Bangor to Belfast buses only ran between Bangor and Holywood.

The civil unrest showed no signs of abating as autumn approached. On the evening of Wednesday, 8 September 1971, two bombs were found near a CIÉ freight train at the Grosvenor Road freight yard in Belfast.

Although bombs were being found on the railways or in railway premises with increasing frequency around this time, one of the first instances of bombs actually exploding onsite was at Kilmore near Lurgan on Tuesday, 2 November 1971, when two 10 lb gelignite bombs exploded on the track at 01.00 hrs. This was another "no warning" bomb incident. Very fortunately, there were no injuries or fatalities, but tracks were damaged – although the precise location of the damage was not traced for several hours. One track had a section blown out and the other track was badly buckled. Permanent way gangs (gangs of about six men, tasked with maintaining the railway on a daily basis) were able to repair both tracks, and only a few early morning trains had to be either cancelled or delayed.

Interior of Belfast Queen's Quay Station, 27 November 1971. *(Victor Patterson)*

Unfortunately it wasn't too long before there was another terrorist incident on the network. On Saturday, 27 November at 09.00 hrs, a male walked into Belfast Queen's Quay station with a smoking bomb and gave a five-minute warning to staff that they should get out. But the terrorists had miscalculated, and the 15 lb bomb exploded within three minutes, injuring six passengers and railway staff. Considerable damage was also caused to the station's refreshment room, shop and ticket barrier area. Glass and debris littered the station. Four other explosions were reported in Belfast during the same day, but the one at the train station was the most serious.

On Thursday, 2 December 1971, train services were delayed again by an elaborate hoax device, which was left on the up line at Lurgan. Again, the track walker came across the shoe box on his patrol duties and, following a check by the Army, it was discovered that the taped-up box contained stones and soil. There was to be no let-up in the pre-Christmas period either, and on the afternoon of Monday, 20 December, a small explosion damaged the station building at Whiteabbey on the up side.

January 1972 and Bloody Sunday

In terms of the ongoing civil unrest in Northern Ireland, matters took a serious turn for the worse on Sunday, 30 January 1972. A Civil Rights march was taking place in the Bogside area of Londonderry city, when the British Parachute Regiment became involved. As a tragic result, 13 marchers were shot dead, 14 others were injured and 50 people were arrested. This day became known in history as "Bloody Sunday". There is incidentally no record of any terrorist-related incidents on the railways on this date.

The next two major incidents, which took take place in February 1972, were not directly related to NIR, but I am including them because of the involvement of British Rail and for local interest, as typical examples of the nature of terrorist plots at the time.

On Wednesday, 16 February, 700 passengers, including 300 soldiers, travelled on the British Rail night sailing from Heysham to Belfast, completely oblivious to that fact that a terrorist bomb had been hidden on board the ship in the course of the journey. The 40 lb bomb was only discovered in a suitcase by a member of the crew half an hour before the ship was due to dock in Belfast after the eight-hour voyage. The crew member lifted the suitcase and thought it was rather heavy for its size. The case was then declared to be suspicious, and left to one side for the remainder of the journey. As soon as the ship docked in Belfast, all of the passengers, including the soldiers, were evacuated from the *Duke of Argyle*, before Army bomb disposal experts moved in to defuse the bomb.

The terrorists obviously thought that they had secured some good publicity for themselves from of the incident of 16 February, since, just a few weeks later, on 29 February, they decided to put another shipload of passengers through a similar ordeal. The *Duke of Argyle* had left Belfast on the evening sailing to Heysham, with over 300 passengers on board, when a bomb alert was received by the security forces. The ship was travelling down Belfast Lough when the alert came through, resulting in the vessel returning to Belfast port at once. All of the passengers were evacuated and, after a thorough search during which no suspicious devices were found, three hours later the ship set sail again.

Several years later, local sea transport would be targeted again, when on the evening of Saturday, 20 July 1974, a bomb exploded on the *Ulster Queen* in Belfast Harbour. There was damage to the First Class lounge of the Liverpool-bound ship, but, very fortunately, no injuries or fatalities were reported.

On the afternoon of Friday 3 March 1972, services on the Portadown line were suspended for four hours, as a mark of respect for the funeral of a train driver, who had been shot dead in his Lurgan home by two gunmen. Sergeant Henry Dickson was also a member of the security forces.

Destruction at Great Victoria Street station, 22 March 1972. (*News Letter*)

March 1972: Destruction at Great Victoria Street Station

Terror struck in the centre of Belfast on the afternoon of Wednesday, 22 March 1972, when a bomb containing 150 lb of gelignite planted in a van exploded in a car park at the rear of the Europa Hotel and Great Victoria Street station.

A total of 71 people sustained injuries in the blast, fortunately mostly of a minor nature, with one person being detained in hospital overnight. The high toll of injuries was the result of there not being enough time to clear people away from the area. A youth of about 20 years old had parked the hijacked van in the car park and shouted, "You have 30 minutes to get out!" before running off towards the Grosvenor Road. However, barely ten minutes had elapsed when the large bomb exploded, leaving a crater in the concrete surface of the car park which was five feet wide and three feet deep.

In the car park, 70 cars were destroyed by the blast, all of the glass panels in the railway station roof were blown out, and two trains were badly damaged, including BUT railcar No 133. Damage was also caused to the bus departure stands in the adjacent bus station, and every single window at the back of the Europa Hotel was shattered.

Gelignite Found on Ayrshire Railway

Barely a fortnight later, on Tuesday, 4 April 1972, Northern Ireland's problems threatened to affect those living further afield too. Thirteen sticks of gelignite were found by a signalman on the Ayr to Stranraer railway line at Killochan in South Ayrshire. An Army bomb disposal team were brought in and managed to safely remove the explosives, which had in all likelihood been dumped by a frightened terrorist from Ulster.

Barrel Bombs stop Cross-Border Trains

All cross-border trains were halted on Saturday, 24 June 1972, following the discovery of deadly barrel bombs on the South Armagh section of the railway at 02.30 hrs. The drama had started when the driver of a Dundalk to Adelaide Yard freight train observed two beer kegs blocking the line, two miles north of the Border. The crew got out, threw the barrels down the embankment and proceeded on their way as usual. As nothing untoward was reported, the line remained open. Sometime later, some of the crew on a freight train, again travelling from Adelaide Yard to Dundalk, observed another keg on the line near the same location. The driver got out, put the barrel on board the train and headed to Dundalk, where he took it to the Stationmaster's office and left it on his table.

However, someone in the office heard a noise coming from the barrel, and realised that it was a bomb. The Garda were called, as well as an Irish Army bomb disposal team. They confirmed that if the barrel had been hit by a train, it would have detonated. The railway between Dundalk and Newry was subsequently closed, while the British Army made safe the other two barrel bombs north of the Border. Cross-border services resumed by mid-afternoon the same day.

It should be noted that beer kegs were routinely carried on freight trains in open wagons. Depending on the state of the track or the way the train was being driven, such kegs could sometimes bounce about and end up on or at the side of the track. No doubt the crew on both freight trains that day spent some time after the event, contemplating just how close an escape they had had!

July 1972 and Bloody Friday

Another very black day in Northern Ireland's history was "Bloody Friday", on 21 July 1972. The deadly tally for the day was 11 people killed and 130 injured. There were no less than 39 explosions throughout the day across Northern Ireland, with a further three bombs being defused by the Army. In Belfast alone, 22 bombs exploded, with public transport services being targeted at the city's main train stations at York Road and Great Victoria Street, and at several bus depots, including Great Victoria Street and Smithfield.

The most serious incident was at Oxford Street bus station, where a bomb left in a stolen Volkswagen estate car detonated, killing seven people and leaving 40 others injured. At the scene, body parts were found over 30 yards away from the blast, which had also destroyed the station. Four of those killed at Oxford Street were Ulsterbus employees. Upwards of 80 buses were damaged in the attacks at the bus depots. The railway network did not fair too well either in that day's country-wide onslaught. A summary of the eight railway incidents is given in Appendix A.

The first railway incident on Bloody Friday was in the early hours of the morning, when the 23.55 hrs overnight freight train from Londonderry to Dublin was attacked by terrorists at Boilie level crossing, between Lurgan and Portadown. The locomotive and first six wagons passed over the crossing safely, but then a 50 lb bomb detonated under the seventh wagon. The following ten wagons were derailed and blown off the track, and over 200 yards of track was destroyed. A six-foot deep crater marked the spot of the explosion. Miraculously, the train crew were uninjured. The Army commented at the scene that the bomb had been detonated from some distance away. Later on that day, train services resumed, using single-line working between Lurgan and Portadown.

Meanwhile, mid-afternoon that day, a youth and a female walked into Belfast York Road station and left a suitcase there. No warning of a bomb was given, but fortunately a passenger noticed the unattended suitcase and raised the alarm. A member of staff opened the suitcase, which was found to contain explosives, and the station was evacuated. The bomb exploded shortly afterwards, leaving a crater in the concourse of the station.

Attacks continued around Northern Ireland overnight into Saturday 22 July, with the further incidents at NIR locations which are summarised in Appendix A. Lurgan station came under attack yet again, when a huge 50 lb bomb devastated the entire station.

Derailed freight train at Boilie level crossing, following an explosion on 21 July 1972. (*Victor Patterson*).

Hijacked Train at Lurgan

After the death and destruction of Bloody Friday, the rest of the summer of 1972 was an extremely tense time across the country. On 9 August, for example, the 23.55 hrs freight service from Londonderry to Dublin was stopped at Lurgan at 04.00 hrs, when a gang of ten youths altered the signals at Bells Row level crossing. The CIÉ crew were ordered off the train and the gang proceeded to hurl petrol bombs at the wagons, which were covered with canvas tarpaulins. The resulting fire damaged the locomotive as well as the wagons themselves, before firemen from Lurgan managed to extinguish the flames.

My Dad's Bus

I have to record this next item for my dad's sake. As I explained in an earlier chapter, my father, who had a 47-year career in the Northern Ireland transport industry, was an Ulsterbus driver for many years. On Monday, 16 October 1972, during his last run that day from Belfast Oxford Street to Bangor, his bus was hijacked by armed men in East Belfast. This was a terrifying experience for him and indeed our entire family, as communication methods in 1972 were not the best. There were of course no mobile phones then, and so we didn't hear what had happened for a number of hours, in fact until my father had eventually turned up in Bangor.

The bus, which was due to arrive in Bangor at 23.30 hrs, was hijacked at 22.35 hrs. The terrorists took the vehicle, but Dad held on to the Company's money, taking it with him as they made their getaway, so that he could pay it into the office later. The passengers dispersed and soon my father found himself in a side street of the Albertbridge Road. Luckily, an unknown man came to his aid and drove him to Bangor bus depot; they arrived there at around 2.00 am. We never found out the stranger's name or anything more about him. As an RAF man during the Second World War, my dad had been in danger before, but he never talked very much to us about the bus hijack – or indeed the war. I think the incident stayed more with my mother, who constantly worried about him when he was on late shifts in Belfast at such a difficult time during the Troubles.

The kind of danger my father experienced was something many transport workers in Northern Ireland at the time risked being exposed to in the normal course of their duties – a fact which most were very much aware of, and understandably unhappy about. On Thursday, 9 November 1972, for example, the majority of CIÉ cross-border freight services ground to a halt, as up to 60 train crew staff were demanding danger money for manning services into Northern Ireland. The resulting loss of freight into Northern Ireland during this period equated to about 2,000 tons per day. Although the Labour Court in the Republic had issued a recommendation about increased payments, the train crews had rejected the offer. The dispute carried on and was not settled until Tuesday, 21 November that year, when newspaper reports stated that the staff had "now accepted what they describe as an adequate offer".

Fatality

In Northern Ireland during this time, vehicle checkpoints on roads were very common; these were aimed at preventing terrorists from moving around freely. When such checkpoints were close to the railway, a member of the security forces would often be deployed somewhere on the line nearby to keep watch for his colleagues – however, this could be very dangerous because of the proximity of the trains, and in some instances, injury or even death resulted.

One such incident took place on the morning of Sunday, 12 November 1972, when a soldier from the 1st Battalion Argyle and Sutherland Highlanders was protecting his patrol from the railway line near Cloghogue Chapel. Tragically he was struck by a passing train and died shortly afterwards.

February 1973 and a Train Raid

On Tuesday, 20 February 1973, eight armed men held up the 08.00 hrs Enterprise service from Belfast to Dublin at Dundalk station. The hijackers, some of whom spoke with Northern accents, were believed to be members of an illegal organisation.

Earlier that morning, the Enterprise had pulled out of Belfast on time at 08.00 hrs. It was later confirmed that three of the eight robbers had bought tickets in Belfast and travelled on the train to Dundalk. These three men were armed, and wore suits and overcoats. Meanwhile, at around the same time that morning, other members of the gang had hijacked two cars at gunpoint in Dundalk. The drivers had been tied up and left in a deserted house outside the town, but they were later able to break free.

Two armed members of the gang then mingled with passengers at Dundalk station and, as the Enterprise pulled in, they burst into the Stationmaster's office and ordered the staff out. Meanwhile on the platform, other armed men told waiting passengers to stand against the station wall, or they would be shot. Customs men and railway staff tried to stop the attackers from entering the guard's van, but they were overwhelmed by the number of armed men. Next, eight leather mailbags were thrown out of the train onto the track; other mailbags were left behind: it seemed that the gang knew exactly which bags they wanted. The raiders then picked up the mailbags from the tracks and ran out of the station to a nearby housing estate, where two of their companions were waiting in the hijacked cars.

It was initially reported that the raiders might have got away with up to £50,000, but later this was corrected by the authorities, who advised that all they had managed to seize was C$2,000 and a number of legal documents and deeds. Within two weeks of the robbery, two men from Northern Ireland were extradited to the Republic for questioning.

Another Day of Torment on the Railways

On Friday, 18 May 1973, two main Belfast railway stations were badly damaged by explosions in separate incidents occurring within three minutes of each other. Ten-minute telephone warnings were given to a local newspaper.

The first explosion blasted Queen's Quay station, as a 15 lb bomb went off in the gents' toilets. Windows in a stationary train were smashed. The second blast took place just three minutes later, this time at Great Victoria Street station, when a 50 lb bomb exploded; it had also been planted in the gents' toilets. Train services were thrown into chaos for a period of time, while clear-up efforts were being carried out. Several commuters were treated for shock.

Further chaos was planned for later that evening, however. Another duffle bag bomb had been left in the gents' toilets at Lisburn station. However this time someone had spotted it and alerted the security services, and the bomb was later defused by the Army. While the situation was ongoing, a Portadown to Belfast train had to be evacuated in Lisburn station.

August 1973: A Hijacked Freight Train in South Armagh

On Thursday, 16 August 1973, an early morning north-bound freight train travelling from Dublin was stopped by signals, one mile south of Meigh level crossing in South Armagh. Earlier, four armed and masked men had entered the signal box, ordering the signalman to put the signals to danger, which of course would stop the train. The signalman initially had disappeared and it was feared by his colleagues that he had been kidnapped, but he turned up later, having raised the alarm with his superiors, who had called the security forces.

Next, the four armed men had climbed into the cab of the locomotive and stuck guns into the ribs of the driver and the guard, who were simply told to, "Get the hell out of it!" The two CIÉ staff ran to Meigh village to raise the alarm. Meanwhile the train lay in the mist and fog, and this gave the armed gang time to place explosives on board. Before they left the ten-wagon train, they stole mail from one of the wagons.

Later, after the fog cleared, an Army helicopter swooped overhead with searchlights.

Hijacked Freight Train in South Armagh, Thursday, 16 August 1973. (*Belfast Telegraph*)

Through an examination of the scene with binoculars, they were able to ascertain that there were two milk churns in the cab of the locomotive: these appeared to be wired together, ready for detonation by remote or by radio control. Photographs of a similar locomotive cab were made available to the Army bomb disposal team for the purposes of assessment. An Army spokesman said that they were being very cautious, as the terrorists had a habit of leaving booby traps for the security forces.

Army marksmen then tried to defuse the bombs by firing at the fuses connecting the two milk churns. Unfortunately the ninth shot set off the two large bombs, the explosion starting a fierce fire in the locomotive. Observers more than 600 yards away later recounted that they felt their clothes being plucked at by the blasts.

Even after the explosion, the Army did not approach for some time, for fear of booby traps. Fire engines from Newry stood by on the road about 300 yards from the train, but their crews were not able to move in either.

During the 19-hour closure of the railway between Dundalk and Portadown, passengers were transferred by bus between both stations. While train services suffered subsequent delays, on that day at least, everyone managed to get safely to their destinations.

Further Attacks on the Railways

As the summer drew to a close, train passengers suffered cancellations and delays once more, as terrorists made a concerted attempt over a two-day period to disrupt services on all lines leading out of Belfast. On Thursday, 30 August 1973, a small blast bomb was set off on the down line at Erskine's Bridge at Whitehouse on the Larne line, causing slight damage. Shortly afterwards, there was a small explosion on the Bangor line at Rockport, near Holywood, leading to the cancellation of 12 trains. Anonymous telephone calls had given ten-minute warnings of these bombs.

The next day, coming up to the evening rush hour, suspect packages were found on the track at Tates Avenue bridge near Adelaide in Belfast. Two children had spotted a "thing" near the line, and thought it was a joke. They picked up the item, which turned out to be an alarm clock – the timing device – and the detonator exploded in their faces, causing minor injuries. After the blast the boys realised what the device was, and lifted the explosives away from the line. A rail worker whose attention had been alerted by the bang, took the bomb from the boys before alerting the security forces. The Army sealed off the area, and then discovered a second device buried beneath the track. Fortunately, they were able to defuse this safely. In a statement at the time, a spokesman from the Army said that the boys had been extremely lucky that only the detonator had gone off, and warned children about the dangers of playing on the railways and tampering with suspicious objects. The line was closed for five hours and remained closed through the evening rush hour due to the incident.

Earlier on the same day, 31 August, at 11.35 hrs, masked men had ordered the signalman out of his box at Dunmurry. Subsequently a bomb exploded, destroying the signal box.

Terrorist Attacks in London

By autumn 1973, the terrorists were not confining their activities to Northern Ireland. On Saturday, 8 September, terror came to the railways in London too, when five people were injured by a small explosion in London Victoria station. This was followed by further chaos on Monday, 10 September, when a series of small bombs exploded in London Euston and King's Cross stations, injuring six people.

Friday, 12 October 1973: Another Black Day for Ulster's Railways

If there were any patterns emerging from terrorist activity on Northern Ireland's transport services, it was that part of their strategy was to attack railways on Fridays. The most likely reason for this was that, since people would be trying to get away for the weekend, such attacks would cause more havoc and maximise "publicity" for the terrorists' efforts. This was certainly the case on Friday, 12 October 1973. The timeline of the events which unfolded that day was as follows:

12.50 hrs: A bomb warning was given over the phone about the 12.10 hrs Belfast to Portadown train, which had just left Lurgan, en route to Portadown. On arrival at Portadown, passengers were quickly ushered well clear of the station, which was then sealed off by the security forces. Nothing was found, but this incident closed the line for approximately 60 minutes.

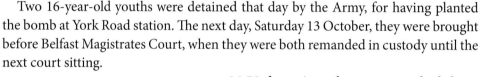

14.22 hrs: Two youths were seen carrying a red suitcase into the toilets at Belfast York Road station. A few minutes later, they left again, but without the suitcase. Summoned to the scene, an Army bomb disposal team blew open a toilet door, however this set off the 20 lb bomb, which demolished the toilet block and caused considerable damage to the booking office. Train services were delayed for approximately 90 minutes.

I remember that day clearly myself, in fact, since I was working in an office only a couple of hundred yards away at the time: my colleagues and I were nearly blown off our seats and to the floor due to the force of this blast. Although we were working in a city in which at the time such incidents were commonplace, we were still shocked and surprised when the explosion happened. Once we had checked ourselves over and ensured that our colleagues in the adjacent offices were alright, our thoughts turned to the possible victims – those who had been unlucky enough to be caught up in the explosion: did they get a warning or did the bomb just go off?; were any members of the security forces caught up in it also? – and so on. After taking a while to gather ourselves, and a cup of tea all round, then we just got on with our work, knowing that we would find out what had happened before very long on the local news.

Two 16-year-old youths were detained that day by the Army, for having planted the bomb at York Road station. The next day, Saturday 13 October, they were brought before Belfast Magistrates Court, when they were both remanded in custody until the next court sitting.

MED trailer No 506, blown up at Marino station on Friday, 12 October 1973 (photo taken at Queen's Quay). *(Author)*

14.50 hrs: A male passenger had been noticed boarding the 12.20 hrs service from Belfast to Bangor at Queen's Quay: passengers had observed that he was carrying a suitcase. However, this man left the train at Holywood, with no suitcase, and strolled along the platform and away from the station. The train was drawing away from Holywood station, when the alarm was raised; at the next stop, Marino, the train was evacuated. With an Army bomb disposal team already on the scene, a 30 lb bomb exploded on the train, wrecking MED intermediate coach No 506, and badly damaging power car No 15. The coach remained out of service for extensive repairs for almost two years. Train services on the line were cancelled for over four hours.

15.08 hrs: Belfast Great Victoria Street station was operating normally, with railway porters going about their duties, taxi drivers standing beside their cabs, and passengers waiting in a queue in the Ulsterbus depot. The train service had arrived in from Portadown at just a few minutes after 15.00 hrs. Suddenly a 100 lb suitcase bomb went off in an empty train at Platform Four. No warning had been given. It was only after the explosion that it was recalled that a male had jumped off the Portadown train at Lisburn, and it was assumed that he had left the suitcase on the train. Apparently the same man had asked a woman in front of the station for directions out of Lisburn.

Train blasted at
Great Victoria Street
station, Friday,
12 October 1973
(*Author's collection*)

Seven people in the area were treated for shock, but, incredibly, no one had been injured. MED power car No 12 was completely wrecked, and there was damage to two other trains and the station. Minor damage was also caused to the Ulsterbus booking office and the Europa Hotel. Train services were disrupted for approximately 60 minutes.

Freight Train Blown Up in South Armagh

Little more than ten days later, another terror attack on a train crew took place, this time very close to the Border. On Tuesday, 23 October at 03.00 hrs, a masked man went to the signal box at Meigh and ordered the signalman to make sure the signals were set to stop the next freight train; he was then told to leave the area.

As the 02.30 hrs freight service from Dundalk approached Meigh level crossing and stopped, it was boarded by a gang of about six masked gunmen, who ordered the crew off the locomotive. Explosives were then placed on board, and before the gang left the train, they set alight all the newspapers and mail bound for addresses in Northern Ireland. They also set fire to one of the wagons on the train and, finally, to the signal box.

For the remainder of that day, no security forces personnel approached the train or the surrounding area, in case booby trap devices had been left by the terrorists. Instead a helicopter circled overhead, keeping a lookout for possible ambushes.

They did not have too long to wait. At approximately 12.30 hrs that day, two booby trap bombs exploded in the immediate area of the hijacked train. Rocks, stones and debris were thrown up over a wide area, just missing reporters and cameramen who had been waiting to see what would happen to the train. The bombs of course were intended for the security forces, who had wisely remained back from the scene. Not long afterwards, at 14.00 hrs, the locomotive of the train was completely wrecked, when a bomb went off inside it.

CIÉ Locomotive destroyed by explosion at Meigh level crossing, Tuesday, 23 October 1973 (*Victor Patterson*).

Train services resumed at 15.00 hrs the next day, following a clearance operation by the Army and the recovery of the damaged train by CIÉ. Despite their best efforts, the terrorists could not keep the trains out of action for very long.

Meigh was the scene of another incident in the late evening of Thursday, 1 November 1973. A gang of four armed men drove a green tipper lorry on to the level crossing. Again, the signalman was ordered out of the box, while the gunmen placed a beer keg at the front wheels of the lorry; there were further kegs in the back of the lorry. The next day, the Army arrived in the vicinity of the crossing, but did not approach the lorry because of the potential danger from snipers and hidden land mines. An Army helicopter circled overhead, however thick fog prevented any attempt to examine the kegs and, as darkness fell, the Army withdrew until Saturday, 3 November. Train services between Portadown and Dundalk were cancelled for approximately 40 hours during this incident. The Army were finally able to clear the area of suspect devices and on this occasion, none contained explosives.

Erskine's Bridge Whitehouse Demolished

A small bridge at Greencastle, between Belfast York Road and Whiteabbey, was destroyed by an explosion on the night of Monday, 12 November 1973. The river

Railway personnel at the scene after a bomb caused major structural damage to Erskine's bridge at Whitehouse on the Belfast–Londonderry line, Monday, 12 November 1973. (*Victor Patterson*)

bridge, known as Erskine's bridge, was completely wrecked by the 500 lb bomb, and train services did not resume for 43 hours, until a temporary culvert bridge was put in place. During the closure, buses replaced trains between Belfast and Whiteabbey, and single-line working was introduced over the up line from 17.00 hrs on Wednesday, 14 November. Double-line working was restored at 16.50 hrs the following day. The estimated cost of replacing the bridge was £130,000.

The aftermath of explosions and fire at Great Victoria Street station on Saturday, 2 February 1974. *(News Letter)*

Great Victoria Street Station Destroyed in Attack

Belfast's newly renovated Great Victoria Street railway station was gutted by a raging fire, which swept through it after two bombs exploded there on the afternoon of Saturday, 2 February 1974. The booking office, the cafeteria, liquor bar and telephone kiosk were all destroyed, and the station roof caved in.

A fireman fighting the blaze and two ambulance men were hurt in one of the blasts, but not seriously. Four fire appliances tackled the flames but couldn't get in too close because of the danger of further unexploded bombs.

The first alert had come when a passenger noticed a suspicious object in the station cafeteria and people were evacuated. Eight minutes later, the Samaritans received an anonymous phone call: the caller warned that four bombs had been planted in the GNR station and that they would explode in ten minutes. It was actually 40 minutes later that the first bomb exploded, followed by the second blast 15 minutes after that: this is when the injuries occurred, since the device had been hidden. The station, the Europa Hotel and traffic in Great Victoria Street all resumed their normal activities at around 18.00 hrs.

First Incendiary Attack

A new phenomenon to appear on the terrorism scene in the Northern Ireland of the mid-1970s was the use of "incendiaries". These were devices which contained relatively small quantities of explosives, but which, once detonated, were capable of starting ferocious fires within seconds. The first incendiary attack on NIR took place on Sunday, 3 March 1974 at Belfast York Road sidings. At 21.00 hrs that night, several incendiaries exploded at the scene. Three MPD (Multi-Purpose Diesel) power cars were damaged in the attack, while trailer No 543 was completely destroyed.

Incendiary devices would prove a lethal tool in the terrorists' campaign of violence.

MPD trailer No 543 destroyed in an incendiary attack on Sunday, 3 March 1974 at York Road sidings. *(Author)*

While not strictly related to the railways, a key example of the havoc these new weapons could create was the concerted incendiary attack on shops and businesses in Bangor's town centre on Saturday, 30 March 1974. The following stores were razed to the ground by fire: Woolworths, Wellworths, the Co-op, Stewart Miller's and Hazletts. Shops with fire damage were: Smyth & McClure, Charles Neill, Telefusion, Textile Centre, as well as a chemist's and a wool shop. The estimated cost of damage was £5 million (in today's money, the equivalent of approximately £54 million).

March 1974: Another Black Friday

In the first of a series of incidents on Friday, 15 March 1974, terrorists displayed yet again a total disregard for the travelling public and their welfare. Once more, the signalman at Meigh level crossing was ordered at gunpoint to put the signals against two approaching passenger trains which were due at approximately 15.30 hrs. Subsequently, both the up 14.30 hrs Enterprise Belfast–Dublin and the down 14.30 hrs Enterprise Dublin–Belfast were stopped and hijacked by the armed terrorist gangs at the crossing. Over 300 passengers were ordered off the trains, and sent walking in the direction of the main road. With the two trains lying within 400 yards of each other, the terrorists then set about loading explosive devices onto each. It was reported later that up to nine bombs had been placed on the trains.

Officials of the Ulster Boxing Council, who were passengers on the south-bound train, would later recall how everyone had to get out onto the track in torrential rain and biting winds. Members of the group helped elderly passengers off the train and ensured that an eight-month-old baby was taken to safety. It was almost two hours before buses rolled up to collect the passengers, and by that time everyone was blue with cold. It took the south-bound passengers almost six hours to reach Dublin. During the closure, nine buses from Ulsterbus, Sureline and CIÉ were used to convey passengers between Portadown and Dundalk.

Army explosives experts had to carry out a prolonged and careful search of the area before they could be satisfied that no bombs had been planted in the vicinity of the trains. It was then decided not to attempt to go onto the trains until the next day. On Saturday, 16 March, each device was checked by the Army – and each device in turn was declared as a hoax. Finally, the trains were recovered from the area and the line was reopened at 16.45 hrs that day.

Meanwhile, also on Friday, 15 March, two small bombs had exploded on the down line at Erskine's bridge at Greencastle on the Larne line. At 18.05 hrs single-line working over the up line was introduced between Belfast York Road and Bleach Green Junction until the end of the day. Bomb scares were also reported at Finaghy and on the Bangor line that day, at 16.45 hrs and 19.15 hrs respectively, resulting in the closure of both lines for a period of time.

Closure of Meigh Level Crossing

The 15 March 1974 attack at the Meigh level crossing was, as we have seen, just one in a long series of incidents at this very vulnerable spot in South Armagh. It was clear at this point that something had to be done to stop the continuous terrorist activity centred around the crossing. In early April 1974, using the Emergency Provisions Act, the British government took measures to close the public road crossing, which the Army blocked using large concrete slabs. The level crossing gates were removed and the signals disconnected. This meant a diversion of several miles for road users, which continued for many years – but at least there were no longer any signalmen in the direct frontline on this stretch of the railway.

Large Bomb at Ballymena

There was to be no let-up for the railways that spring however. Less than a week later, on Thursday, 21 March, an emergency phone call was made from an anonymous source at 21.20 hrs to say that a bomb had been left in the railway station at Ballymena. Police discovered a device in a dustbin in the station, with an alarm clock timer attached to it. Train services were suspended, and the Army carried out two controlled explosions in the early hours of Friday, 22 March, causing only slight damage to the station. A massive 200 lb bomb had been successfully defused. The railway line remained closed until lunchtime that day; it was also closed north of Ballymena due to another bomb incident at Dunloy, where a 75 lb bomb was also defused by the Army.

At a later date, a Randalstown man was identified as a suspect in relation to the Ballymena incident. Forensic tests had disclosed a number of fingerprints on the adhesive tape attached to the alarm clock, and these were matched to the Randalstown man, leading to his eventual arrest in Stranraer in February 1977. On Friday, 13 January 1978, the Judge at the Belfast City Commission court convicted the man in question of making up the timing device used for the bomb, sentencing him to seven years in jail.

May 1974 and the Ulster Workers' Council Strike

A new local Assembly had begun operating at Stormont at the beginning of 1974. This however had been set up under an initiative agreed only by some – not all – of the parties at Sunningdale in England. The political fallout was about to take over. A new grouping of Protestant workers, who called themselves the "Ulster Workers' Council" decided to organise a strike focused on Northern Ireland's heavy industries, including the power stations.

The strike was initially to be for two days, commencing on Tuesday, 14 May 1974. Some trains were cancelled, as crews were unable to get to their depots. The electricity supply was off from time to time. The self-styled Ulster Defence Association (UDA), formed by thousands of men dressed in paramilitary clothing, took control of many Protestant areas, placing roadblocks on the streets to protect their neighbourhoods. Incidents of civil unrest occurred every day. During this period, I didn't get to work from 20–23 May, due to various terrorist incidents, including these UDA roadblocks.

By the second week of the strike, the instability of the situation was rapidly escalating. On Wednesday, 22 May, a 70-year-old man was killed by a train at Glarryford level crossing, when the warning lights did not operate due to power failures: this was as a direct result of the strike. On the same day, a special train for workers, running at 08.00 hrs from Coleraine to Londonderry, was prevented from leaving Coleraine by a human chain of UDA supporters on the crossing. Hijackings, road blocks and widespread intimidation continued. People walking to work in certain areas were ordered to turn back by club-wielding youths. Also on 22 May, the UWC placed a ban on the movement of petrol and oil supplies within Northern Ireland, as a means of intensifying the strike action. Many petrol stations were without fuel, and those which still had supplies had to operate the pumps by hand within time limits "allowed" by the UDA. The ban on fuel inevitably affected the railway services, which operated on diesel-powered engines. Citybus was only running on three routes: Falls, Whiterock and Glen Road. No Ulsterbus services had been operating into or out of Belfast. Petrol suppliers to hospitals and other essential services were told that all deliveries would have to be "vetted" before being allowed on to the road. On Monday, 27 May the UWC called for a complete shutdown of essential services. Normality of some kind would only be finally restored again on Wednesday, 29 May, when the new Assembly was suspended, and Prime Minister Brian Faulkner resigned. It had been a very frightening time for all of Northern Ireland's population, and most people were very glad when the deadlock ended.

Hijacked Train at Kilnasaggart Bridge

With Meigh level crossing now closed, the terrorists had to change their tactics – and the bridge at Kilnasaggart in South Armagh, just 200 yards from the Border with the Republic of Ireland, would become a new focus for their activity over the next few years.

On Saturday, 3 August 1974, the 03.30 hrs freight train from Dublin to Adelaide Yard in Belfast, carrying newspapers and mail, had just crossed the Border at 04.40 hrs, when the driver spotted a flashing red light ahead. He put on the brakes and, as the train came to a halt at Kilnasaggart Bridge, six masked gunmen appeared and jumped on to the locomotive, ordering the train crew off the train. The driver and the guard then saw the gang loading some packages into the engine compartments. The guard was told to clear off, but the gang took the driver with them in their getaway car, eventually releasing him once they were across the Border, north of Dundalk in the Republic.

Meanwhile, an anonymous caller had advised the security forces over the phone that there were bombs on a train heading for Portadown. When the freight train did not arrive in Portadown on schedule, an Army helicopter from Bessbrook was dispatched to look for it. Once it was sighted, the Army searched the area around the train first, before they boarded the locomotive. Following some skilled work by the Army Technical Officer, 400 lb of explosives were made safe and removed for inspection.

During the 28-hour closure of the line, four buses were used to convey passengers from Portadown to Dundalk. However, unbelievably, these buses were also delayed, due to another terrorist incident on the main Newry–Dundalk road. A hijacked CIÉ bus was blocking the main road at Killeen: it had lying there from the previous Tuesday, awaiting further action by the security forces, who needed to be extremely cautious in dealing with it, again because of potential booby traps.

A similar incident followed on Wednesday, 21 August, when the same train was stopped in the same fashion. This time, a milk churn was placed on the locomotive. Army bomb experts were later able to defuse a 200 lb bomb, and the line was eventually reopened, after a 29-hour closure.

In the late evening of Tuesday, 8 October 1974, for once however the terrorists did not get their way. A CIÉ light locomotive, travelling from Adelaide to Dundalk, was passing through the Meigh area when the driver noticed a red light in the distance. He spotted terrorists at the side of the track ahead, but this time he decided to make a run for it. The locomotive duly arrived safely in Dundalk. Obviously frustrated, the terrorists decided to plant their bomb on the track instead, and the 50 lb device exploded later on the up line, causing some damage to the track. Single-line working was introduced the next morning and normal working resumed at 2.45 pm. Three cheers for the train driver!

A New Low: Terrorists Aim "Bomb Train" at Town

The 03.30 hrs freight service from Dublin to Adelaide was again targeted by terrorists on Friday, 8 November that year. The train was hijacked by an armed gang at Mountpleasant on the Irish side of the Border, and the train crew were ordered off at gunpoint. It would seem that explosives were packed into the locomotive and it was then sent on its way into Northern Ireland without the train crew. This was a new dimension in ruthlessness – and cowardice – on the part of the terrorists!

A phone call advised staff at Portadown station that the train was heading towards them and that it was laden with explosives. With only a few minutes to spare, they managed to clear the station of any passengers, while engineers went onto the track and took out a rail on the Dublin side of the station, in order to stop the train. It is estimated that the train could have been travelling at up to 80 mph as it approached Portadown. As it came around the sharp curve, it suddenly jumped the rails and ploughed into the parapet of the bridge leading to Obins Street.

Army bomb disposal teams set to work at once, checking the train for booby trap devices and explosives, while families in nearby houses were evacuated and the roads around Portadown were blocked by the security forces. The first train out of Portadown in the Belfast direction left at 08.48 hrs, but then the Army sealed off the area again, to make sure that no explosives were on the train: in due course, this was confirmed to be the case. The line for Belfast traffic was reopened at 10.30 hrs, and the line for Dublin-bound trains resumed services on Saturday, 9 November at 15.00 hrs.

Hijacked freight train crashes at Portadown station, Friday, 8 November 1974. *(Author's collection)*

There were five other terrorist-related incidents on Friday, 8 November, as detailed in Appendix A.

81-hour Line Closure

On Thursday, 21 November 1974, a report came in at 23.00 hrs, indicating that a bomb had been left in the Meigh area of South Armagh. Accordingly no train services were allowed to run the next morning, as the Army were inspecting the scene. A milk churn was found on the embankment and, as was the usual procedure, a complete clearance operation of a large area had to be carried out by the Army before they would approach the suspect device.

The following day, Saturday, 23 November, an International rugby match was due to be played at Lansdowne Road in Dublin. The Army had not yet given clearance of the line in the Meigh area, and so NIR tried to arrange for the transfer of over 600 rugby fans by bus to Dublin for the match against New Zealand. Unfortunately this was not to be, as sufficient buses could not be found, and fans had to somehow try to make their own arrangements. During the closure period in fact, there were no substitute buses for most of the scheduled trains.

Finally, on Sunday 24 November at approximately 17.00 hrs, the Army blew up the 100 lb milk churn bomb. However the line could not be reopened as it had to first be walked by permanent way staff. It was eventually reopened at 07.30 hrs on Monday, 25 November, with no damage reported.

More Chaos for Rugby Fans

Encouraged no doubt by the media attention the disruption of rugby fans had attracted, it seemed that the terrorists were determined to arrange a repeat performance of the mayhem they had caused. So they struck again on Friday, 17 January 1975, parking a car on Smith's accommodation crossing at Faughal Upper in South Armagh. Since however there was an IRA ceasefire in effect until 00.01 hrs that Friday, the terrorists duly waited until the deadline had passed, leaving the car on the level crossing just a few minutes later, at three minutes past midnight, when they also issued a warning to the authorities.

The next day, Saturday 18 January, over 600 rugby fans had booked to travel, on two special trains from Belfast to Dublin, to see Ireland play England at Lansdowne Road, and again, due to the closure of the line, their plans were ruined. Once more, insufficient buses were available and refunds were given to passengers, who were left to make their own arrangements.

The Army dealt with the car at the crossing on the Saturday at approximately 14.00 hrs, detonating two bombs in the vehicle in controlled explosions. One of the bombs was 100 lb, and the other 50 lb. The force of the blast lifted the car and threw it down the track by 30 yards. A short section of track was damaged, as well as telephone cables. The up line was reopened on Sunday, 19 January at 10.00 hrs, and the down line followed suit at 11.00 hrs. This incident closed the line for 62 hours.

Fatality on Belfast Central Railway

On the afternoon of Monday, 28 April 1975, a man working for a contractor involved in the construction of the Belfast Central Railway was shot dead by masked gunmen on the track at the Donegall Road near the City Hospital. One of his companions was also wounded in the attack. Two men were charged with the murder in July 1975 and appeared at Belfast Magistrates Court.

Enterprise Delayed by Ambush Warning

On Monday, 4 August 1975, a telephone warning was received at the Civic Guard Headquarters in Dublin Castle, advising that the 17.30 hrs Enterprise Belfast–Dublin service would be ambushed and blown up. The train was extensively searched before it left Belfast, and throughout the journey was preceded by DH locomotive No 3 with security forces on board. By 23.30 hrs, the Enterprise, which would have generally been carrying about 100 passengers on this service, had only just reached Poyntzpass. A helicopter kept watch overhead as it crossed the Border. The service finally arrived in Dublin just after 01.00 hrs on Tuesday, 5 August – over five-and-a-half hours late.

Extensive Damage to Lurgan Station

During most of the weekend of 8–10 August 1975, there was widespread rioting in Lurgan. In the early hours of the Friday morning, the crossing keeper's hut at Lake Street level crossing was petrol-bombed, and all of the internal fittings were destroyed.

On Sunday 10 August at 02.25 hrs, two bombs exploded at Lurgan railway station, causing extensive damage to the buildings and the new footbridge. One bomb had been left on the up platform and the other bomb on the down platform. Telephone, electricity and water supplies at the station were all severed as a result of the explosions. Responsibility for the bombing was later claimed by the Provisional IRA.

The station had been due to be officially reopened on Monday, 18 August, having been refurbished after suffering widespread damage due to terrorist action in November 1973. In a statement from NIR, Managing Director, Hugh Waring said he was astonished to think that the railway should be made to suffer for the alleged actions of unrelated parties. After all, he continued, the railway was a public service

Two brown NIR vans, used for carrying mail, were destroyed by fire in Belfast York Road yard on Saturday, 6 September 1975. NIR van No 680 was destroyed, and NIR van No 684 was badly damaged. Following an inspection of the vehicles, it was determined that an incendiary attack was most likely to have caused the fires. *(Author)*

providing facilities for people of every class, colour and creed: it was tragic that it should suffer the kind of destruction that had occurred in Lurgan. Mr Waring concluded by saying that the station would be rebuilt as soon as possible. Workmen began salvage operations as soon as clearance was given by the security forces, and trains were kept running.

The Provisionals' statement claimed that the station had been blasted in retaliation for the continued harassment of local people by the Army, and the actions of the RUC in dealing with riots at the Wakehurst and Shankill estates in the town in previous week.

Incendiary Attack September 1975: A Renewed Campaign of Terror

Monday, 22 September was another of those dark days in Northern Ireland when many people across the country were affected by terrorist incidents. A total of 18 bombs exploded around the country, six of these in Belfast, and two more were successfully defused by the Army. The railways of course were targeted too that day.

Londonderry station was extensively damaged, when a duffle bag bomb exploded at around 04.30 hrs in the gents' toilets at the front of the station. Later that afternoon, the 17.15 hrs freight service from Dundalk to Lisburn was stopped just south of the Border by armed and masked men, and the crew were ordered to take the 18-wagon train to Kilnasaggart Bridge, just into Northern Ireland. Bombs were placed on the locomotive and, shortly afterwards, at 18.30 hrs, once the crew had been ordered off the train, two explosions ripped through the cab of the locomotive, causing extensive damage. Several rails on the track below were buckled, and sleepers were broken.

The Army were cautious about approaching the train and did a sweep of the surrounding area first, looking for booby trap bombs. On the morning of Thursday, 25 September, the damaged train was finally hauled back to Dundalk. During the line closure, a bus substitute service operated between Portadown and Dundalk to ensure that travel was still possible. The line was not fully reopened until midday that day. This had been a 52-hour closure.

However, very shortly after the reopening, a telephone warning was received, claiming that there was now a bomb on the line between Portadown and Newry. This meant a further three hours' closure while a search was carried out.

Yet Another Attack at Kilnasaggart

Just a few weeks later, on Wednesday, 15 October, the 07.00 hrs freight service from Dundalk to Adelaide was stopped at Kilnasaggart Bridge by four armed men. The train crew were ordered off the train and milk churns were placed on the locomotive. This was the eighth train to be hijacked by armed men in South Armagh within three years! The Army commenced their clearance operations and carried out two controlled explosions. The locomotive was slightly damaged in the blast - but the two massive 225 lb bombs had been successfully defused.

A BBC television camera crew came under fire near the scene that day. The cameramen were getting out of their car to film the hijacked train, when three shots hit ground close to them. Fortunately however none of the BBC team were injured. A couple of days later, a PIRA spokesperson said the organisation could no longer guarantee the safety of journalists visiting South Armagh.

During the clearance operation, buses were brought in to replace trains between Portadown and Dundalk, and all freight services were cancelled. The line finally reopened at 22.10 hrs on Saturday, 18 October: at 87 hours, yet another long closure.

Freight Train Derailed at Goraghwood Deviation

After the terrifying incident in November 1974, when terrorists had sent an unmanned 'train bomb' from Mountpleasant to Portadown, a major security review had been ongoing, with a view to preventing the same thing happening again. The proposed solution, which would involve the putting in place of two "preventative measures", would be unique to NIR, and was probably unique on a main line railway anywhere in the UK. The deterrents would take the form of deviations off the main tracks, which could be used to quite literally sideline – and stop – trains which had been hijacked.

The main deterrent would be installed on the down main line to Belfast at Goraghwood, 12 miles north of the Border. The site housed an old station, which was once used as a railway Customs post, as well as the now disused Great Northern Railway Quarry, which at one time supplied ballast for the GNR. The large quarry area had more than enough space for the laying of a deviation of the Down main line, which would provide a detour from the original route, leading through part of the quarry site and then returning to the main line. A 15 mph speed restriction was placed on the deviation.

If for some reason a hijacked train was not stopped at Goraghwood, then the second deterrent would come into play: a set of trap points on the main down line from Dublin, just north of Poyntzpass. These points could be operated by the signalman at Poyntzpass, when a scheduled train approached and the main line was set. If the train was deemed to have been hijacked or in any way suspicious, then the trap points would remain open, resulting in the train being ditched into an adjacent field (fortunately, the terrorists never stooped so low as to keep passengers aboard a hijacked train without a driver).

The main deterrent proved its worth for the first time on Thursday, 20 November 1975, and was effective in stopping a hijacked train from running on to Portadown. The 17.15 hrs freight service from Dundalk to Lisburn had been hijacked that day by five armed men at Kilnasaggart Bridge. The train crew had been ordered off and managed to escape. At 18.10 hrs, a telephone message from the IRA was received at

Hijacked freight train derailed at Goraghwood, Thursday, 20 November 1975. *(Victor Patterson)*

the Maze Prison, claiming that a bomb was on board the train. After the hijacking, terrorists had set the train in motion without the crew, and it was spotted moving north from the bridge at 18.43 hrs by an Army helicopter. As had been hoped, the locomotive and most of its 20 wagons derailed at the Goraghwood deviation; both the down and up lines were badly damaged as a result. It was reported at the time, although not confirmed, that two of the terrorists had been on board but had managed to jump off just before the train crashed.

In the meantime, the 17.30 hrs Enterprise service from Belfast was stabled in Portadown, and the 17.30 hrs Enterprise from Dublin was stabled in Dundalk. Passengers were transferred by bus. The up line reopened at 16.30 hrs on Friday, 21 November, with single-line working in operation, and the then Secretary of State, Merlyn Rees visited the scene on the same day. The down line and deviation remained closed until the following Thursday.

Christmas 1975: A Close Shave for Enterprise at Kilnasaggart

On Monday, 29 December, a major train crash was narrowly averted, when the 17.30 hrs Enterprise service from Belfast to Dublin ground to a halt, only 250 yards from a hijacked freight train with a bomb on board. A short time earlier that day, the 17.15 hrs freight service from Dundalk to Lisburn had been stopped at Kilnasaggart Bridge by at least six armed men. Ordering the train crew to leave the train, they placed a bomb on board.

The Enterprise, carrying approximately 200 passengers, was waved down by the crew of the freight train, who were on the tracks. Just as the Enterprise screeched to a halt, the bomb on the freight train went off, wrecking the freight locomotive. The Enterprise was returned to Poyntzpass, where the passengers were detrained, and buses took them onwards to Dundalk.

In a public statement, Hugh Waring of NIR praised the CIÉ freight train crew for their prompt action, as well as the Enterprise driver for his quick response by stopping the train. Secretary of State, Merlyn Rees and the PIRA soon became involved in a war of words over the incident. Commenting from Stormont Castle, Mr Rees remarked that a crash had been only narrowly averted, and that passengers had been put at serious risk; he concluded that the incident illustrated the reckless criminality of those PIRA who were responsible. The Provisionals retorted that a 30-minute telephone warning had been given to the railway authorities in Portadown about the hijacking at Kilnasaggart, and there had been no question of civilian casualties on the passenger express. An Army spokesman later endorsed Mr Rees' statement, saying that the wreckage from the bombed locomotive had been scattered across the south-bound track and could have derailed the Enterprise, had it not stopped in time.

The Army did not begin their clearance procedures until Tuesday, 30 December; in the meantime an Army helicopter hovered permanently over the scene. Checks were made for landmines and booby trap devices, but nothing further was found. A bus substitute service between Portadown and Dundalk kept the service running during the lengthy closure. The line was not re-opened until Friday, 2 January 1976: at 88 hours, this was surely one of the longest closures yet.

Enterprise Derailed by Explosion

A little over a month later, however, there was yet another incident, and this time, unlike the last, it seemed that it was the terrorists' aim to deliberately derail the Belfast–Dublin Enterprise service. It was however a blessing that a temporary speed restriction was in place at the scene of the incident due, to planned track repairs. Whether the terrorists took this into account is another matter, but it is to be hoped that they did, as the train would have usually been travelling at 50 mph at this point.

On Friday, 6 February 1976, the 17.30 hrs Belfast–Dublin Enterprise service was approaching Scarva (eight miles south of Portadown). The train was formed by a CIÉ train set of one locomotive and six coaches. It had slowed down to 20 mph, in accordance with the temporary speed restriction on the track. Half a mile north of Scarva, at 18.10 hrs, a 5 lb bomb exploded in front of the train, at milepost 80.25. (Every quarter of a mile on the railway, there is a milepost which is used by railway staff to identify where they are, and to mark infrastructure and speed restrictions.) The locomotive derailed but remained upright due to its weight; the four following carriages, however, fell over onto their sides in the railway cutting. The train skidded along the track for about 100 yards before coming to a halt. Two hundred passengers were on board, and four passengers were injured, including a six-year-old girl. Had the train been travelling at its normal speed, then it could have smashed into the side of a bridge, just 10 yards in front of the locomotive. The track below the train was completely ripped up for several hundred yards.

Once the extent of the injuries became clear – i.e., that no-one was seriously hurt – everyone quietened down from an initial state of panic. Passengers were literally left in the dark, as suitcases fell from overhead luggage racks. Male passengers led the rescue operation, lifting women and children out of the train, before forming a human chain to help them up the embankment to the Tandragee–Gilford road. The alarm was raised by people living near the scene; they then opened their doors to the distressed passengers and brought out their best china for cups of tea all around. Back near the train, the 19-strong Ladybird singing group from Newtownabbey led community singing to keep up peoples' spirits. Those passengers who had not been picked up by relatives were taken on a fleet of buses to Scarva, where a cup of tea was awaiting them in a church hall.

Enterprise derailed at Scarva following explosion, Friday, 6 February 1976. *(Charles Friel)*

The majority of passengers eventually continued their journey to Dublin by train from Poyntzpass: the 17.30 hrs Enterprise from Dublin to Belfast had been stopped at Poyntzpass and returned to Dublin with the passengers of the derailed train. Others went back by bus to Portadown and then by train to Belfast. By this time the train driver had also made his way to Scarva station, to warn any approaching train of the danger and to inform the signalman at Poyntzpass.

The Chairman of NIR, Myles Humphreys, who was also Lord Mayor of Belfast at the time, visited the scene and described it as "pretty gruesome". He went on to say that he was very glad however that it was not a major disaster in terms of lives and that thankfully the train had not been going fast. He remarked too that up until this incident, terrorists had left passenger trains alone, but that that day's despicable action presented a very worrying picture for the future. If this was a new tactic in the terrorists' campaign, it would have to be looked into very seriously – however for the time being, the company fully intended to keep the rail service between Belfast and Dublin operating.

On Saturday, 7 February the scene was cleared by the Army, after which recovery of the train and track relaying could be attended to. The first train to run through the area again was the 17.30 hrs Enterprise from Dublin to Belfast on Tuesday, 9 February; services returned to normal the following day from 17.20 hrs.

Weekend of Terrorist Incidents

In late February 1976, a new spate of terrorist attacks on the railways was launched over a single weekend. Once more, things kicked off on the last day of the week, and from Friday, 27 February to Sunday, 29 February, 18 incidents took place, as listed in Appendix A. What was a bit strange was that the incidents did not start until 20.25 hrs. As a rule, the terrorists' aim would have been to disrupt the maximum number of people, and so this was a late start for a weekend campaign late, given that the rush hour would have ended several hours previously.

Three of the incidents over that weekend were of a more serious nature, and I have detailed them here. On Saturday 28 February, the 19.00 hrs service from Lisburn to Belfast was met by a reception party of sorts at Derriaghy – they hijacked the train, and ordered the train crew and passengers off. Suspicious objects were placed on board the two-car 80 Class set formed by Nos 736 and 84. The Army were eventually able to clear the objects, which were declared as hoaxes. The line was closed for 95 minutes.

On the Saturday night, the 21.45 hrs service from Bangor to Belfast Queen's Quay was hijacked at Sydenham station by "passengers" who had joined the train at Holywood. The train crew and remaining passengers were ordered off the train. Two fires were started in MED trailer No 509, causing damage to seats and the floor. Thankfully neither of these fires took hold. Further minor damage was caused by the Army, who shot at suspect devices that had also been left on the train. The train, with only the driver and conductor on board, eventually arrived into Queen's Quay at 23.50 hrs.

On the night of Sunday, 29 February the third incident which could have caused major damage, took place at Belfast York Road's signal box. At 00.30 hrs, the signal box was attacked and a fire started. The south end of the signal box was badly charred: the flooring was damaged, there was smoke damage to the entire interior, 20 panes of glass were broken, and chairs and tables were destroyed, along with other smaller items.

March 1976: London Trains Targeted

A small PIRA cell was blamed for a terrorist attack on British Rail in the spring of 1976, which could easily have caused a massacre. On Thursday, 4 March, a 10 lb bomb exploded on an empty train at 08.45 hrs at Borough Market Junction, just as it was moving from London's Cannon Street station to a maintenance depot. The bomb ripped off part of the roof of the carriage in which it had been planted, and destroyed all the seats in the fourth carriage. Eight passengers in a nearby train were slightly injured as the windows of their train were shattered. There were widespread fears that this was the start of a new campaign of terror on the mainland by the PIRA.

Only minutes earlier, almost 1,200 passengers had got off the same train: the 07.49 hrs service from Sevenoaks to London Cannon Street. It was surmised that the bomb could have been placed on board at any time during the 46-minute journey. Police said that they wanted to interview everyone who had been on the bombed train. Cannon Street station did not reopen until 16.00 hrs the same day.

Just over ten days after this incident, a London tube train was attacked. On Monday, 15 March passengers on the 16.34 hrs service from Barking noticed smoke pouring from the bomber's holdall. He hurled the holdall from one end of the compartment to the other, and ran from the train, before the bomb exploded, ripping off the roof and one side of the train. The tube driver and a Post Office engineer ran after the bomber, and managed to corner him in a goods yard at West Ham underground station. It was then that the bomber, bleeding from wounds caused in the premature explosion, opened fire on his pursuers, killing the 34-year-old tube driver and hitting the engineer in the chest. The bomber then turned the gun on himself – but he survived, and was taken to hospital along with the nine passengers who were injured.

Another attack followed, only 28 hours later. On Tuesday, 16 March at 21.00 hrs, a bomb exploded on a train at Wood Green underground station on the Piccadilly line. Luckily, this time the train had been emptied shortly before the small blast and only one man was injured.

A Very Close Call

In our NIR office at York Road – like many other work places in Belfast in the mid-1970s – you would often hear bombs going off in the distance somewhere, or emergency sirens as vehicles shrieked past our windows. On occasion, however, you got a chilling reminder of just how close you had been to a bomb without knowing it.

One of those occasions for us was on Wednesday, 24 March 1976, when, at around 16.45 hrs, a 150 lb van bomb exploded outside York Road police station, which was approximately 400 yards from our offices. We hadn't received any warnings of course, and our building shook, with dust flying everywhere and a few things falling off the walls and desks. After regaining a bit of composure and giving yourself a shake, the next thing to do was to find out where the bomb was and what had happened – and then you just got on with your work again. (By the way, there was minimal damage to the police station.)

Armed Robbery

People get into the habit of doing certain things in a certain way at certain times, as we know, and of course at the height of the Troubles, there were others out there who were just watching and waiting for an opportunity to seize upon. Wages were generally still paid in cash and of course at the same time on the same day each week. One such incident was on Thursday, 25 March 1976, when a gang of armed men (probably terrorists) came into Belfast Queen's Quay station at 15.15 hrs, and stole £2,500 worth of wages from the staff in the station.

May 1976: Murder on the 17.40 hrs to Portadown

Disaster struck on Friday, 21 May 1976, when a 21-year-old female passenger, Miss Roberta Bartholomew from Richhill, was killed and ten other passengers were injured, including the conductor of the train. A 10 lb bomb had exploded without warning on the 17.40 hrs service from Bangor to Portadown, as the train was in the vicinity of Broomhedge accommodation crossing, about 1.5 miles on the Moira side of Knockmore Junction.

A fleet of ambulances and fire appliances raced to the scene, and the ten injured were treated on the spot. Five were taken to hospital, one of whom was in a very serious condition. The remaining passengers were taken to nearby farmhouses and given tea, before being taken to their destinations by taxi.

Then Secretary of State, Merlyn Rees issued a statement, condemning the bombing and asking members of the public who had any information to give it to the police. In a further twist, a man claiming to speak for the outlawed Ulster Volunteer Force said that they had been standing by and had warned the Provisionals that if they did not stop the slaughter, they would retaliate; actions in the past had shown that they would have no mercy. The statement concluded by stating that no further warnings would be given.

The train was formed by a five-car 80 Class set: Nos 81, 761, 732, 738 and 88. Car No 81 was extensively damaged, with other damage caused to Nos 761 and 732. The train was cleared by the Army and then moved back to the Belfast Service Depot at 00.30 hrs on Saturday, 22 May.

Earlier on that day, before the explosion, a conductor on the train in question had noticed a suspicious rucksack, just as the train was leaving Botanic station. He had thrown it out onto the railway embankment and informed NIR Control. At 18.20 hrs, as the police were clearing the built-up area in the vicinity of the embankment, the bomb exploded, injuring one police officer. The train was allowed to proceed on its journey towards Portadown.

Police later advised that a Lisburn newspaper had received an anonymous telephone call at 18.15 hrs that day, warning that a bomb was due to explode in ten minutes at "the new station" in Belfast. A further telephone call at 18.20 hrs, from a different man, warned that there was a bomb in the "Albertbridge station" – presumably meaning Belfast Central. Although it seemed clear that the intended target was the new Belfast Central station, the phone calls from the terrorists were somewhat misleading. This was later reported in the press as a possible PIRA blunder.

In the aftermath of the event, police, trying to jog passengers' memories, placed large posters at railway stations along the route. These bore the headline, "Were You Travelling On This Train?", and asked people to come forward with information. More than 2,000 smaller posters were also circulated by the police, warning passengers that they should, "be observant and be suspicious of unattended objects".

On Thursday, 10 June 1976, at a special court in Lisburn, a Belfast youth was charged with the murder of Miss Roberta Bartholomew, who had died on the train. The 17-year-old youth from East Belfast was remanded in custody to Belfast Magistrates Court until 14 June. A report from Lisburn court on 24 November 1976 stated that the teenager now faced two additional charges, namely of causing an explosion on the train and of being a member of the PIRA. He was further remanded in custody.

The trial of the 18-year-old commenced on Tuesday, 25 January 1977 at the Belfast City Commission. During the trial, the teenager admitted planting two bombs on the train, but in evidence to the court, he confirmed that another man was involved and that he had promised a warning would be given. The teenager believed that the intention was to damage Central Station in Belfast, but not to kill or injure anyone. The Judge was satisfied that the teenager was not a criminal or a vicious type, and said he would rather have had before him those who stayed safe and secure in the background and used others: they were the ones who were legally and morally responsible for the death and injury caused. The teenager was ordered to be detained at the pleasure of the Secretary of State for the murder of the young woman passenger. He escaped a mandatory life sentence for murder because he was only 17 at the time of the offence.

Class 80 motor coach No 81, which was extensively damaged in the explosion, returned to service on Friday, 2 June 1978.

British Army
helicopter flying
above the Enterprise
train, June 1976.
*(Courtesy Alain Le
Garsmeur)*

Helicopter Escort for the Enterprise

A story appeared in a local magazine in June 1976, showing some dramatic photographs of what it was like to be a passenger on some of the Enterprise passenger trains that ran on the Belfast to Dublin line, especially when travelling through South Armagh. The reporter, Philip Jacobson and photographer, Alain le Garsmeur travelled on the 08.00 hrs Enterprise service and, as the train went south of Portadown, they became aware of a clattering noise which was nothing to do with the locomotive. Instead, a camouflaged army helicopter dipped into view, then took up its post a few hundred feet above the carriages, swooping from side to side, sometimes close to the ground. The escort remained in place for 30 miles, shadowing the train through the fields of South Armagh, also known as "Bandit Country", where for the past four years the PIRA had obliged the authorities to adopt security measures not normally associated with inter-city rail travel.

The magazine report concluded by remarking that the cross-border train services, and above all the Enterprise expresses, were among the most visible tokens of Northern Ireland's determination to preserve a framework of normal life even as the Troubles raged on. As such, these services had become temptingly soft targets for the terrorists, and needed to be accordingly protected.

Special Train Redirected

On Saturday, 7 August 1976, an unattended suitcase was discovered on the rack of carriage No 763 at Botanic station, which was part of the 12.30 hrs service from Portadown to Bangor. The three-car 80 Class (Nos 89, 763 and 737) had stopped at Botanic, when it was noticed that the suitcase had no owner. The train and station were evacuated, to give the Army the opportunity to carry out a controlled explosion; they also fired shots at the case in the hope of destroying the detonator. Considerable damage was done to carriage No 763, including seven broken windows, and damaged interior panels, luggage racks and seats. As it transpired, there was nothing in the suitcase. The line was only cleared at 17.24 hrs, and in the meantime, Dublin-bound services ran to and from Lisburn station.

As a result of this incident, a special train, that had been due to run from Belfast Central to Lisburn with 575 members of the Belfast Junior Orange Lodges, was redirected to Sydenham on the Bangor line. There, all the passengers were transferred to buses for the journey to Lisburn. For the return journey back to Botanic station, an eight-car MED train was supplied.

Nightmare Attack on Bangor-bound Train

On Friday, 8 October 1976, a passenger boarding the 20.40 hrs service from Lisburn to Bangor handed an unattended bag he had found to the porter on the platform at Belfast Central. The porter left the bag on the platform for a short time, intending to take it up to the station's lost property office later. The train proceeded towards Bangor. Not long after, just after 21.30 hrs, the bag exploded on Platform 4, causing damage to the roof covering

Bomb damage to the platform roof at Belfast Central, Friday, 8 October 1976. *(Author)*

Platforms 3 and 4. The Inspector's office was badly damaged, several glass panels were blown out in the passenger ramp, and there was lighting damage also. The bomb was reported to contain 10 lb of explosives, and this was the first instance of terrorist-related damage to Belfast Central station itself.

As the same train travelled on towards Bangor, a female passenger noticed another unattended bag on the train at Holywood. As she felt inside the bag, she unwittingly separated the detonator from the explosives. This action no doubt saved lives! No warning had been given in relation to either of the bombs that the terrorists had left on this train. Fortunately though, NIR Control had passed information about the Belfast bomb to the crew on the Bangor-bound train. The conductor decided that he was not taking any chances, and promptly stopped the train at Seapark, between Holywood and Marino. The passengers were de-trained and taken by bus to Bangor, while local residents were moved from their homes and nearby roads were closed. Army bomb experts safely dismantled the 40 lb bomb, and the empty train eventually arrived in Bangor at 00.27 hrs the next morning.

A Suspect Briefcase on Train: My Own Involvement in Evacuation Efforts

As a result of previous attacks on trains, unattended objects were treated with great suspicion. This was the case on Wednesday, 10 November 1976, when a briefcase was found by the conductor on a luggage rack at Sydenham station on the 08.15 hrs service from Lisburn to Bangor. No one claimed the item, so the train was evacuated and the passengers sent off towards the Holywood Road for a bus. The Sydenham Bypass was also closed during the incident, which caused serious tailbacks.

On the same day, I was travelling on the 08.30 hrs service from Bangor to Central, when we were stopped by a signal approximately 400 yards from Sydenham, where the service normally stopped. We could not return to Holywood, as there was another train sitting in the station, bound for Belfast. I assisted the train crew in assembling all of the passengers of the train; we then managed to make a hole in the fence at the side of the track, to enable them to walk up to the Holywood Road for a bus to Belfast.

The Army carried out a controlled explosion on the briefcase on the Lisburn to Bangor train; as a result, minor damage was caused to MED coach No 29. The line was reopened after three hours, from 08.50 hrs. Just after the controlled explosion had taken place, a passenger had rung NIR to say that he had left his briefcase on the train earlier that day!

Justice is Eventually Served

On Sunday, 14 November 1976, police received a phone call from an anonymous source, claiming that three bombs had been planted on the railway at Ballycarry, Magheramorne and Glynn stations. Trains were delayed on the Larne line for three hours, while an Army bomb expert dealt with the suspicious objects. These turned out to be oil cans with batteries and wires attached – hoax devices.

At Belfast Crown Court on 2 May 1979, two Larne men admitted planting hoax bombs on the railway that day. They were both given 18-month suspended prison sentences; they were also fined £150 each, when they pleaded guilty to receiving instruction in the use of guns.

A Report of Landmines on Track

As 1976 drew to a close, the terrorists came up with another new twist in their campaign against the railways. All they had to do was to phone up and say that landmines had been laid on the track! This is what happened on Tuesday, 30 November 1976, when a call came through at 18.40 hrs, stating that landmines had been laid between Dunmurry and Lisburn. Services ground to a halt and passengers were cleared from the stranded trains.

No substitute buses were available for local services until the line reopened some days later. However, Enterprise services to Dublin were replaced by buses running between Belfast Central and Lisburn. The Bangor line operated normally, and a service was provided from Belfast Central to Botanic, by running trains wrong line order (i.e., in the wrong direction to normal working) over the down line.

The Army cleared the line after two days of searches. To be doubly sure that everything was safe, however, a new procedure was carried out with the help of volunteer rail workers. This involved a locomotive being sent from Belfast Central to Lisburn and back, to ensure that the weight of a locomotive would not set off any explosives on the track! The line was finally fully reopened on Thursday, 2 December – 45 hours after the alert had first been received. Acts of bravery such as this – being willing to run over a section of the line during a security alert – were frequent at the time, since many rail staff were determined to keep the trains running by whatever means they could. No pressure was put on these staff, who volunteered to put themselves in the frontline. Unfortunately, their courage had to go unacknowledged, since if names had been made known, there was the very real danger that the terrorists would retaliate in some way.

December 1976: Nine Terrorism Incidents in One Day

Things were running normally on the railways on Monday, 13 December – until early afternoon, when disruption affected almost all of the routes on the network. The nine incidents which caused mayhem on this one day, and those which followed, are recorded in Appendix A. Below, I am setting out the events of the day in a different format, which highlights how the Belfast–Dublin line was affected during the subsequent three-day period, as follows:

13.49 hrs: A suspect lorry spotted under the bridge at Cloghogue, Newry – cleared four hours later.

14.37 hrs: A hijacked bus is left on Bells Row level crossing, Lurgan – bomb defused and the crossing cleared one hour later.

14.45 hrs: Bomb scare at Belfast Central – cleared 45 minutes later.

14.49 hrs: Suspect car seen under Ayallogue bridge at the Border – 200 lb bomb defused – line cleared 26 hours later, on Tuesday, 14 December.

15.30 hrs: Reports of landmines on Belfast–Lisburn track – cleared 2.5 hours later, by running inspection trains.

21.45 hrs: Suspect objects found beside track at Silverwood, Lurgan – two bombs defused – finally cleared at 13.06 hrs on Wednesday, 15 December.

You will see how local trains were disrupted for two days, and cross-border services for three days. On the Derry line, during the bomb scare at Lisahally, a bus substitution was put in place between Londonderry and the old station at Culmore. As a matter of record, 28 roads across Northern Ireland were closed the same day, mainly by hijacked vehicles and milk churns. The PIRA were determined to stretch the security forces to the limit. From the standpoint of today, it is hard to imagine the bewilderment and terror caused by this unremitting spate of emergencies, deliberately orchestrated to happen all within the same 24-hour period.

May 1977: Ulster Workers' Strike Disruption

The Ulster Workers' Council had called for another strike throughout Northern Ireland, which was due to start at 00.01 hrs on Tuesday, 3 May 1977. However, even before the strike began, explosions damaged both the up and down lines at Sydenham.

On the day of the strike itself, NIR staff had already been advised to report to their nearest manned station, in order to assist in any way they could, and then to travel to work as soon as practical. So I reported to Bangor station and signal box for 09.00 hrs. Once basic repairs of the damaged track at Sydenham had been completed, along with a handful of passengers, I boarded the first train out of Bangor, at 12.05 hrs. We only got as far as the new Crawfordsburn crossover before we had to stop: both

Police check the line after removing a barricade at Crawfordsburn, Tuesday, 3 May 1977. (*Author's collection*)

lines had been blocked by a barricade constructed of rails, sleepers and barbed wire – material which had not picked up previously by staff after engineering work. Our train returned to Bangor.

Police were informed and they went out to clear the barricade, along with a ballast train which had left the Central Service Depot with engineering staff. Again, with a handful of other passengers, I came out on the next train, which left Bangor at 14.35 hrs, and this time we managed to get to Belfast Central. I didn't stay at work long, returning to Bangor on the 17.15 hrs service. A suspicious parcel at Hilden delayed trains for an hour in the afternoon.

Evening train services were expected to be severely restricted due to the threat of trouble. The last services to run that day were as follows: 18.10 hrs, Belfast–Portadown; 19.25 hrs, Belfast–Bangor; 18.55 hrs, Bangor–Belfast; 18.10 hrs, Belfast–Larne Harbour; 18.50, Larne Harbour–Belfast. This pattern continued for an extended period during the strike.

On Day Two of the strike, services on the Bangor line were suspended, due to a bomb scare at Victoria Park. I was on the first train out of Bangor at 10.05 hrs, but we only got to Bangor West due to another bomb scare at Carnalea. We left Bangor West at 11.15 hrs, and eventually managed to get to Belfast Central.

On Day Seven of the strike – Monday, 9 May – a new railway timetable was brought in, and, as had been previously planned for some time, the new station at Bridge End opened, following the closure of Ballymacarrett the previous day. Services on the Bangor line were suspended once again, this time due to a bomb scare at Victoria Park, but I was on the first train out of Bangor at 09.45 hrs.

Day Nine of the strike saw the situation take a serious downturn. No buses were running in Northern Ireland due to a Citybus driver having been shot dead the previous night. A bomb exploded at Bangor bus depot at 17.20 hrs, causing slight damage, while an explosion on the down line at Victoria Park closed the railway in the evening.

On the following day, Thursday, 12 May, once more, there were no buses running. Due to the damage at Victoria Park the previous night, single-line working was in operation over the up line between Rockport and Bridge End.

As the eleventh and final day of the strike, 13 May, dawned, a bomb scare on the Bangor line meant no trains could depart before 07.30 hrs. Services on the Bangor line were further disrupted, when the company received a warning to the effect that Bangor train drivers were now under threat from the strikers. After a period of time, it was agreed that, as a security measure, police or army staff would travel on Bangor line services for the rest of the day.

This second loyalist strike was an attempt to rerun the previous "successful" one which, as mentioned earlier, began in May 1974 and had the backing of the Democratic Unionist Party and the Ulster Defence Association. Like the first strike, the aim was to show the Government how much power could be exerted on the streets by key elements of the Protestant workforce, and the extent to which they could potentially influence against the political and security situation in Northern Ireland. However, without the same support as in 1974, this second workers' strike fizzled out on Friday 13 May without any great consequence.

More Incendiary Attacks

As 1977 year drew to a close, there was no let-up in incidents with incendiaries on the railways. On Wednesday, 21 October, as the 21.55 hrs Lisburn to Bangor service was due to leave Lisburn station, an incendiary device exploded in a carriage, causing minor damage and, fortunately, no injuries. When the train was checked by security forces, a further three incendiaries were found concealed in seats. Another device was then found on the station platform. It was later reported that four girls had been acting suspiciously in the vicinity of the train, and it was assumed that they had planted the bombs.

A matter of weeks later, on Friday, 4 November, a member of staff at Bangor station found an incendiary under a seat in a train which had just arrived in from Lisburn – the 21.55 hrs service to Bangor. A controlled explosion was carried out by the Army and only minor damage was caused to the train. Although this was the same train involved in the Lisburn incident the previous month, the security forces were satisfied that this was a new device planted that day, and not one which had remained undiscovered from the last time.

Although it seemed at times that the railways were being constantly targeted in this way, NIR was, relatively speaking, far less prone to such attacks than shops and other commercial businesses around Northern Ireland. In the late 1970s, both Bangor and Newtownards town centres, for example, suffered further episodes of multiple attacks on a number of premises on the same day and at the same time. As with the railways however, those who found themselves targeted in this way were determined to recover from the damage and resume business as usual as quickly as possible: in this sense, they would not let the terrorists win.

NIR DURING THE TROUBLES:
1978–2013

While the early 1970s are often regarded as some of the most intense years of the Troubles, there were many periods in the subsequent years which were equally violent and deadly for the general population, and as we know, there would be no real let-up in the three to four decades which followed. This chapter "telescopes" the events which took place in a 35-year period, not because there were fewer of them or they were of any less significance than those of the early years – quite the opposite was the case at times of course – but simply for the purely practical reason that the records I kept while at NIR are not nearly as comprehensive for this period, since the recording procedures within my job had changed. In this chapter therefore I have highlighted the more important and serious terrorist incidents of these years; in Appendix B I have also provided a list of all of the incidents I was able to record at the time.

May 1978: More Concerted Attacks on NIR

Tuesday, 2 May 1978 saw the beginning of a series of attacks on NIR over the next four days. By that first evening, three bridges had been badly damaged by explosions – one at the Border, and two on the Londonderry line. The Provisionals claimed responsibility for each of these attacks.

The first incident was at Kilnasaggart bridge near the Border, when the stone arch bridge was extensively damaged in an explosion. It was clear that the bridge would have to be rebuilt, but in the meantime, temporary measures were put in place so that the line could be reopened by 07.00 hrs on Friday, 5 May 1978. Another bomb scare that morning would close the line again for one hour.

Also on this Tuesday evening, two bridges were damaged in the Limavady area: a large hole was blown in the Roe River bridge, and the Burnfoot River bridge was also damaged. Again, repairs were made as soon as possible, and both bridges reopened at 14.30 hrs on Friday, 5 May.

Then, on Wednesday 3 May, the Londonderry line service was further disrupted by bomb scares at Dunloy and Kellswater, only to reopen at 12.15 hrs that afternoon. The next day, Thursday, an early morning attack by terrorists in Londonderry Waterside station left the station devastated. Three armed men had entered the station and left four bombs, which subsequently exploded. One demolished the booking office; the second one demolished the toilets; the third one completely destroyed 80 Class driving trailer No 737; the fourth bomb went off inside 80 Class motor coach No 87, damaging the engine. A 70 Class driving trailer was also damaged in the explosions. It was clearly a well-planned attack, as the trains in question were being kept in the station, due to the bombing incidents in the Limavady area a couple of days beforehand.

Only a matter of weeks later, Kilnasaggart bridge was damaged once again, by a further explosion on Friday, 26 May 1978. Temporary repairs had only just been completed after the previous incident, when the Army uncovered two further bombs in the vicinity. These were successfully defused on Sunday, 28 May, and the line was reopened the next day at 16.30 hrs.

Fire at Seahill Station

On the evening of Sunday, 8 January 1978, approximately 140 yards of the down platform at Seahill was destroyed by fire, in a suspected terrorist incident. Train services were disrupted for three hours, as fire crews dampened down the wooden platform which was constructed of old wooden sleepers. Only one coach length of the platform was available to stop trains at safely following the fire, as the remainder of the platform had been destroyed. One fireman was taken to hospital after being overcome by fumes. It was estimated that the damage to the station would cost more than £30,000 to repair.

A Black Day for NIR: First Terrorism-Related Fatality on the Enterprise Service

On Thursday, 12 October 1978, the 08.00 hrs service from Dublin to Belfast Central had almost reached its destination when, just over half a mile short of Belfast, between Botanic station and the Ormeau Road bridge, four bombs exploded on board. As a result, a Dublin woman in her 50s on a shopping excursion to Belfast was killed outright, and eight other passengers were injured. An RUC statement issued just after the incident accused the bombers of perpetrating a "reckless, indiscriminate" act of terrorism against ordinary people.

Dublin woman dies as bombs explode on Enterprise train, Thursday, 12 October 1978. *(Pacemaker Press)*

Bomb-damaged Enterprise returning to Dublin – photo taken on the approach to Belfast Central, Sunday, 22 October 1978. Badly damaged coaches Nos 1512, 1534 and 1553, can be seen here. No 1913 was undamaged; a further coach, No 1146, sustained some damage and was covered in a tarpaulin, since it had been reported that the frame of the coach contained asbestos. *(Author)*

More than 100 passengers had been on the CIÉ train as it approached Belfast. The first bomb went off in the toilet compartment at the rear of the restaurant coach, where the woman who was to be fatally injured was sitting. The adjoining second-class coach was where many of those to be injured were sitting. Damage to the coaches was severe. Restaurant staff were later praised for their efforts in helping the injured. Strange as it seems, most of the other passengers in the other coaches were unaware that the disturbance they heard had been caused by a bomb. As soon as he could, the driver brought the train to a stop near the Ormeau Road bridge. Passengers weren't evacuated immediately, but, following a second explosion and then a third, passengers disembarked hastily and ran down the track, some scrambling up the steep embankments on either side of the line. Dense smoke billowed from the train as the fire took hold, and at times the train was virtually invisible. Firemen broke through nearby derelict houses and walls beside the track in order to reach the train as quickly as possible.

The bombs had exploded at 10.29 hrs; it was reported that an anonymous female phone caller had rung the Samaritans in Portadown at 10.07 hrs, claiming that ten bombs had been placed on the train. The information was passed on to the police, and then to NIR. One of the theories looked into at the time was that the target for the bombs had been Belfast Central station, as the train was due in at 10.20 hrs. However the train had been running approximately ten minutes late, due to engineering works on the line south of Portadown.

Later on, on the evening of the day of the attack, a caller purporting to represent the Irish Freedom Fighters – believed at the time to be a cover name for the Provisionals in Armagh – had called Downtown Radio to claim responsibility for the attack. A further report from the 1st Battalion PIRA in North Armagh admitted having carried out the train bombing, but blamed the railway authorities for causing the death and injuries. In the statement they claimed that all possible measures had been taken to prevent injury or loss of life, and that a full half-hour warning had been given to the Samaritans. They further stated that, had NIR used the adequate signalling system which was in use throughout all railways, then the operation would have successfully destroyed the train without loss of life; that, since the death and injuries were a result of the delay, responsibility for these must rest with both the RUC and NIR. Finally, they extended their sympathy to those injured and to the family of the dead woman. Roy Beattie, NIR's Chief Executive, dismissed the PIRA statement out of hand, as did the RUC, who commented that it was a mercy that more deaths had not been caused.

After the tragedy, high-level meetings were held between the railway companies, the RUC and the Gardai, to discuss security on the railways, including the possibility of placing radios in the cabs of cross-border trains. NIR decided in favour of this measure, but CIÉ staff based in Dundalk were resistant to the idea: apparently they felt that agreeing to such a system might result in intimidation from those who might perceive this as being overly complicit with security forces in the North.

The CIÉ train that day was formed by locomotive No AR 030, with the following hauling coaches: 1913, standard brake; 1553, standard; 1534, standard; 1512, standard; 2417, restaurant car; 1146, full First; 3174, steam van. The damaged train was taken to the Central Service Depot later on that day and would remained there until Sunday, 22 October 1978, when it was returned to Dublin.

There were other, separate incidents on 12 October 1978. At 11.45 hrs that morning, three youths held up the signalman at Dunmurry, leaving a bomb which subsequently went off and started a fire, destroying the signal box. A warning had been given by a caller, claiming to represent the PIRA. During that day too, other bomb scares on the railway were dealt with: between Belfast and Bangor, between Belfast and Larne, and at Central Junction in Belfast.

The day after the fatal attack, Friday, 13 October, the terrorists did not let up. At 12.57 hrs, I received a phone call from NIR Control, passing on a report from CIÉ Control, to say that they had received an anonymous call stating that bombs were on the Belfast to Dublin trains. At that point, the 11.00 hrs Enterprise Belfast to Dublin was at Drogheda, and the 11.00 hrs Enterprise Dublin to Belfast was at Portadown. Both trains were duly evacuated and checked by the security forces, who declared them safe at 14.30 hrs. There were also two bomb scares on the Bangor line during the day.

More Trouble at Kilnasaggart

The 06.20 hrs freight service from Dundalk to Belfast Adelaide was hijacked by an armed gang at Kilnasaggart Bridge on Monday, 20 November 1978. The train crew were ordered to take the train a further two miles up the line to Newtown Bridge, where six more masked men were waiting. Several boxes and cylinders were loaded onto various parts of the train, which was carrying 2,000 barrels of Guinness and Harp. When the crew were released, they went to raise the alarm.

Passengers on subsequent services were transferred between Portadown and Dundalk by bus. Once the security forces were on the scene, an Army helicopter circled constantly overhead, as it was feared that the area had been booby-trapped.

During the clearance operation, the Army defused two 150 lb milk churn bombs found in the cab of the locomotive, No AR 021. The line was closed for six days, eventually reopening on Saturday, 25 November 1978.

Train Strikes Bomb on Track

On Tuesday, 28 November 1978, the 15.55 hrs service from Belfast to Bangor train, carrying schoolchildren and others, struck something on the line at Sydenham. The train driver reported the incident; the object had also been spotted by some boys on their way home from school. The Army were immediately called in, and the object was confirmed as a bomb, which, fortunately, they were able to defuse following two controlled explosions. The device had been knocked off the track and the train wheels had severed the wires. No warning had been given relating to the device. The Bangor line was closed, along with the adjoining Sydenham Bypass, which resulted in traffic chaos in East Belfast. The route was cleared at 18.46 hrs, and the first train out was the 18.50 hrs service Belfast Central to Bangor.

April 1979: Freight Train Damaged by Explosion

On Saturday 21 April 1979, an armed man flagged down a Dundalk to Adelaide freight service at Newtown bridge. The man then produced a gun, and ordered the train crew to take the train to Killeen bridge, about 200 yards ahead. Once there, six armed and masked men carried two milk churns into the driver's cab of the locomotive. The train crew were ordered off and within minutes, a massive explosion ripped through the locomotive and started a fire. The locomotive was destroyed and two wagons were damaged.

80 Class coach No 748, destroyed by explosion and fire, Friday, 25 May 1979. *(Author)*

The train had been sitting directly below the bridge which carried the main road between Belfast and Dublin: this also had to be closed. The railway reopened for single-line working on Monday, 23 April; the road bridge and road were also cleared around the same time.

Killeen bridge was the focus for a further terrorist incident on Monday, 21 May 1979. Three hijacked lorries were driven on to the bridge and a beer keg was placed on the track. By the end of the night, all obstacles had been safely removed by the Army.

Trains Extensively Damaged by Explosions

On the eve of the North West 200 motorcycle event in Portrush, Friday, 25 May 1979, the 20.10 hrs service from Belfast Central to Londonderry, which was carrying supporters for the races, was blown up by terrorists between Crumlin and Antrim stations. An observant woman passenger saved the lives of her fellow passengers, when she noticed a suspicious parcel under a seat and called the conductor. He immediately let the driver know, and he stopped the three-coach 80 Class train 1.5 miles on the Antrim side of Crumlin.

As the passengers were ushered off the train and began to walk along the track to safety, the driver detached the motor coach from the two carriages, in order to try to salvage it. Meanwhile the conductor ran up the track to Antrim station for assistance. Police vehicles ferried the passengers to Antrim.

Shortly afterwards, the package exploded, starting a fierce fire. Minutes later, a second bomb exploded. The fire brigade attended and three hours later, the area was declared safe. There had been no

70 Class coach No 722, destroyed by explosion and fire, Friday, 25 May 1979. *(Author)*

warning from the terrorists for this incident. Driving trailer No 748 was completely destroyed and intermediate trailer No 767 sustained slight damage.

Meanwhile, at Belfast York Road station on Friday, 25 May 1979, two bombs exploded on the 20.15 hrs service from Larne Harbour to Belfast. The train had arrived and was empty when the explosions occurred. There were no injuries, fortunately; once more, no warning had been given by the terrorists. The train was formed by 70 Class Nos 78, 722 and 701. The passenger compartment of No 78 was destroyed, intermediate trailer No 722 was destroyed and the driving trailer received slight damage.

A Controller's Nightmare

When the telephone rings at 02.05 hrs, you usually think, why on earth would someone be calling at this time? But, as a duty NIR Controller, I had come to expect such calls. And so when on Thursday 5, July 1979 I picked up the phone at this unearthly hour to someone from Force Control, Police Headquarters, I knew that something serious was up. The caller went on to say that they had received a bomb warning for Ballymena to Cullybackey, and asked if we had any trains running. I had to think quickly – at that time of the morning, most of the network was closed. However, after wakening up a little, the first thing that came to my mind was the 01.25 hrs freight service from Lisburn to Londonderry! I immediately phoned the signalman at Ballymena and told him to stop the freight when it arrived with him. I didn't get line clearance again until 05.20 hrs and had to be into work again for 09.00 hrs, so I was pretty tired, as you can imagine!

Goraghwood Deviation Proves Its Use

On 23 July 1979, the 06.45 hrs freight train from Dundalk to Adelaide was hijacked on the Irish side of the Border by masked and armed men. The crew were ordered off and the train was sent on its way, unmanned. Terrorists were by now of course aware of the deviation at Goraghwood, so they probably knew that the train would not make it around the sharp curve on the deviation of the main line. The locomotive derailed as expected, and all the wagons followed suit, derailing across both main

Derailed freight train at Goraghwood, Monday, 23 July 1979. (*News Letter*)

lines. The locomotive – No AR 004 – burst into flames, and firemen were called to deal with the blaze. The up line reopened at 15.30 hrs that day, and the down line followed at 17.50 hrs. Most of the wreckage was put into part of the old GNR quarry, adjacent to the down line, for recovery at another time.

This type of activity was attracting publicity for the terrorists, so again, on Tuesday, 11 September 1979, they did exactly the same thing. The 06.45 hrs freight Dundalk to Adelaide was hijacked, this time at Cloghogue bridge south of Newry, and the train sent on with no crew. On this occasion the two "B" Class locomotives remained on the track, but the 15 wagons carrying Guinness and Harp were all derailed, ripping up the track. After the Army had checked the area for explosives, the up line was reopened at 14.30 hrs that afternoon, with single-line working in operation for several more days.

September 1979: Train Blown Up at Balmoral

Two bombs exploded on the 22.05 hrs service from Lisburn to Bangor on Wednesday, 19 September 1979. A phone call had been made, with the caller claiming that five bombs had been left on board this train. Minutes after passengers had been evacuated, the first bomb exploded, starting a fierce blaze. Three fire engines rushed to the scene, but could not get as close as needed, due to the threat of more bombs.

A second explosion went off shortly afterwards, and the entire area around the station was cleared: this was only yards away from nurses' and doctors' accommodation at the Musgrave Park Hospital. The line was closed for up to two hours, and passengers on other services had to be delayed or diverted. The train was formed by a three-car 80 Class, Nos 741, 770 and 68. Driving Trailer No 741 and Intermediate Trailer No 770 were completely destroyed. No 68 had smoke damage.

80 Class set blown up at Balmoral, Wednesday, 19 September 1979, seen later at the Central Service Depot. (*Author*)

Railways caught up in Bombing Spree

Another wave of terrorist activity was unleashed across Northern Ireland on Monday, 26 November 1979. A total of 25 devices were left at 15 locations throughout Northern Ireland, including four devices on the railways. Fifteen people were injured, one of them seriously.

At Belfast Central station, soldiers from the Royal Engineers removed two bombs from the 16.10 hrs service from Bangor to Portadown. The two sports bags containing the devices were placed on the platform, and the station was evacuated at 16.57 hrs. One of the bombs went off at 17.03 hrs on Platforms 3 and 4. The other device was defused by the Army.

On the same afternoon, two bombs exploded at Adelaide station on the 16.15 hrs service from Lisburn to Belfast Central. The train was stopped and searched at Adelaide after the passengers had been taken off. Half an hour later the two bombs exploded, starting fires which destroyed carriages Nos 769 and 733. The train was formed by a three-car 80 Class, No 99 *Sir Myles Humphreys*, No 769 and No 733. The Bangor line was then closed by a bomb scare at 17.00 hrs, and passengers had to try to make their own way to Bridge End in order to catch a train when the line did reopen. The first train from Bridge End left at 19.00 hrs that evening.

January 1980: Three Die in Train Blast

On Thursday, 17 January 1980, as the 16.55 hrs service from Ballymena to Belfast Central was travelling through Dunmurry near the M1 bridge, bombs exploded on board the train, killing three passengers and injuring five others, two of these with very serious burns. No warning had been given about the devices. After so many recent incidents on trains where passengers had narrowly escaped death, there was a sense in which this had been bound to happen sooner or later. This did not make the event any less shocking, of course.

As the fireball bomb ripped through the two carriages of the train, panic-stricken passengers, many with their clothes ablaze, leapt from the train. The three people who died were so badly burned that their sex could not be established when firemen and forensic experts later examined their charred remains in order to try to identify them. Police said that the deaths and injuries had been caused by burns from blazing petrol, rather than by the force of the explosion: this led them to conclude that the bombs had been incendiary devices, each containing just a small amount of explosives, attached to a can of petrol. The train involved in the incident was a two-car 80 Class, Nos 93 and 734, and both coaches were destroyed. The three passengers killed were in No 93.

The stricken train did not stop automatically – it was stopped near the M1 bridge by the conductor pulling the emergency handle. A train heading from Belfast to Portadown drew up beside the driver's cab and asked what was going on. The other driver was able to reverse his train back to Finaghy, where he summoned help.

Police were soon appealing for the assistance of two teenagers, who had been standing on Dunmurry platform, waiting for a train coming from Belfast to Lisburn. They had witnessed the explosion as the train passed by, and had gone to tell the

The wreckage of the 80 Class set engulfed by fire after a bomb at Dunmurry that left three dead and two seriously injured, Thursday, 17 January 1980. *(Pacemaker Press)*

signalman at Dunmurry, before they left to catch a bus.

At the scene, NIR's Chief Executive, Roy Beattie stood contemplating the wreckage, horrified. He commented that words simply could not describe what had happened; that he was just disgusted that human beings – so-called human beings – could have done such a thing. His voice shook with emotion as he concluded that there could have been absolutely no justification for it. Secretary of State, Humphrey Atkins joined with other politicians and churchmen in condemning the train bombing too. After a meeting with the DUP and Euro MP, the Reverend Ian Paisley at the House of Commons, Prime Minister, Margaret Thatcher said she was very alarmed by the development, and promised a full inquiry.

The day after the incident, Friday, 18 January, a news agency report suggested that two of the three people killed in the blast might have been PIRA men, but this claim was regarded with scepticism. The report went on to say that the two PIRA men would have been on active service when the explosion occurred. A police spokesman however emphasised that the victims had not as yet been identified, as their bodies had been burned beyond recognition.

However, on Saturday, 19 January, a statement from the PIRA admitted that one of those killed in the train blast had indeed been a PIRA man – Kevin Delaney, a 26-year-old accountant from Belfast, and one of their members. The statement went on to assert that the bombs were meant to have exploded in Belfast Central station, and concluded with the PIRA offering their deepest and heartfelt sympathy for the victims, and their apologies for the premature explosion on the train.

The police in Northern Ireland later issued a statement too, confirming that two of the dead, regular passengers on the train, were from Finaghy and only hundreds of yards from their home station when they died. They were 17-year-old student, Mark Stuart Cochrane and 36-year-old father of three, Aboyonni (Max) Olorunda. The minister at the funeral of Mark Cochrane stated that the PIRA's statement of apology was sickening and hypocritical, and suggested that in future they should keep their explanations and sympathies to themselves.

As if the train bombing at Dunmurry was not bad enough for one evening, two other bombs exploded on the Larne line on the same fateful day. Thankfully, both bombs were spotted in time and removed from the trains. No warnings had been received for these devices either. A passenger found one on the 17.35 hrs service from Belfast York Road to Carrickfergus. It was carried to the platform, where it exploded, causing slight damage but no injuries. The second device was found on the 17.35 hrs service from

Carrickfergus to Belfast York Road. Again, the device was lifted onto the platform, this time at Greenisland, where it exploded. Fortunately there were no injuries.

A Personal Brush with Danger: NIR Staff in Shooting Incident

On Thursday, 16 October 1980, myself and two other colleagues from NIR were due to be interviewed by BBC News at Belfast Central station. The interview, which had been set for 3.00 pm that afternoon, was to be in relation to some trouble at the station the previous day, apparently caused by 100 football supporters, who had started to agitate the residents of the adjacent Markets estate. Police had had to intervene to try to calm the situation and remove the football supporters from the scene.

At 3.00 pm on Platform Three, the BBC were just coming down the ramp towards us and the interview was about to start – when suddenly, a single gunman opened fire on us from the side of a house in the Markets estate. We all dropped to the ground; I rolled off the platform and on to the track. Five shots were fired, a couple of them hitting and smashing the glass panels in the Platform Two ramp. I crept along the track to the signal box, and managed to phone the police from there. Once they arrived, we were all taken to Musgrave Street police station to give statements. Since the BBC had been present at the incident, it was duly reported on the news that night. For some time afterwards, I couldn't help wondering why the gunman had attacked us that day; how had he known that the BBC were going to be there; and what was the point of his attack?

H-Block Protestors

On Friday, 31 October 1980, about 100 people, protesting about the treatment of prisoners in the H-Blocks at The Maze Prison near Lisburn, came into Belfast Central station. They arrived at around 13.00 hrs and walked around with placards. Although they were very vocal about the H-Block protests, there was no trouble, and they left the station at 14.00 hrs. However, it was an intimidating experience for NIR staff, including me and of course also for passengers, who had to make their way through the crowd of protestors to be able to get to the trains.

In the spring of following year, the first hunger striker in this most recent campaign died. The funeral of Bobby Sands took place on Thursday, 7 May 1981. He had passed away on Tuesday, 5 May, after 66 days without food. Over 300 supporters travelled on the 08.00 hrs Enterprise service from Dublin to Belfast Central to attend the funeral. They were escorted to West Belfast by police using 14 RUC Land Rovers.

March 1982: Another Day of Disruption on the Railways

The up line, the down line and the single line of the Antrim branch were all put out of action by three separate explosions at Knockmore, in the late evening of Monday, 8 March 1982. Rails were severed in each explosion and train services were suspended for a number of hours. Fortunately, all three lines were able to reopen at lunchtime on the following day.

The explosions sent pieces of rail and ballast flying into the air, and some of these parts came through the roof of the Grove Activity Centre, some 100 yards away. The premises were packed at the time with pensioners and teenagers, and there was panic when the metal crashed onto the floor of the badminton courts, narrowly missing one of the players. Several windows in the centre were smashed and vehicles in the car park were also damaged. The Housing Executive had to attend several homes in the area in order to repair broken windows.

Tuesday, 9 March would be a day of widespread disruption throughout Northern Ireland. A suspicious object, which turned out to be a bomb, was found at the closed level crossing at Meigh, near the Border. Fortunately the Army were able to defuse it safely. There were further bomb scares on the Bangor and Larne railway lines at different periods during the day.

Bomb Explodes on Enterprise: August 1985

On Thursday, 29 August 1985, the 11.00 hrs Enterprise service from Dublin to Belfast Central arrived in Belfast at Platform Two at approximately 13.35 hrs, just a few minutes behind schedule. An anonymous caller had just claimed that bombs had been placed on the train. Security forces arrived and were in the process of checking the train, when a bomb went off in the guard's van: the device had been concealed in the frame of a bicycle there. Five police officers and three members of NIR staff were injured. Being a first-aider, I was able to assist the injured at the scene. One of the police officers was later reported to be in a critical condition.

Train services were suspended at Belfast Central right through the evening rush hour, as searches continued for further devices. Bangor line services continued to operate to and from Bridge End, with a bus service to Belfast Central. Portadown and Dublin services ran as far as Lisburn, with bus services taking up the rest of the service to Belfast.

Easter 1986: Emergency Powers Act

On the night of Sunday, 30 March 1986, senior railway operations staff were asked to attend RUC headquarters for an urgent meeting regarding train services the next day. An Apprentice Boys parade was due to take place in Portadown on Easter Monday, and an organised party of 800 Apprentice Boys had been booked to travel by special train from Belfast Central to Portadown. It was estimated that another 1,000 supporters would be making the trip under their own steam. In the preceding weeks, there had been a lot of anxiety on the part of both the public and the authorities at the prospect of trouble at the Easter Monday event.

At this eleventh-hour meeting, police advised NIR representatives that the Secretary of State for Northern Ireland had decided to ban the Apprentice Boys parade the following day, and that, under the terms of the Emergency Powers Act, the RUC would be acting to prevent participants travelling to Portadown. The NIR representatives were advised that the special train, along with any other scheduled services between 09.00 hrs and 13.00 hrs would therefore not now be allowed to operate. Ulsterbus and other bus companies had been advised similarly regarding their services.

And so the next day, Easter Monday, the special train was cancelled and, due to serious public unrest in Portadown throughout the day, services from Belfast to

Portadown were stopped short at Lisburn, right through to the early evening. There was also a demonstration at Belfast Central that morning, when 1,000 Apprentice Boys arrived at around 10.30 hrs, taking up position in the station car park and on East Bridge Street. The station was effectively under siege for approximately one hour. It was only presence of substantial numbers of police which prevented the demonstrators from gaining access to the station buildings.

Security Review of the Railways

In November 1987, I was tasked with carrying out a complete security review of all NIR stations and essential elements of our infrastructure, in conjunction with a member of the RUC Security Branch. Over a period of three days, commencing on Wednesday, 11 November, we travelled all over the network – from Bangor to the Border, and from Belfast to Larne and Londonderry. During our journey through "bandit country" in South Armagh, we were chaperoned from the air by helicopter as we went from location to location.

Such security reviews were essential, as there was a continuing catalogue of terrorism-related incidents happening on the railways in the late 1980s. On Friday, 9 September 1988, for example, two males dressed as postmen boarded the 06.05 hrs Coleraine to Belfast Central service at Lambeg. When the train arrived at Finaghy at 07.40 hrs, these men suddenly got up and shot a passenger twice in the head, before running off and climbing into a getaway car. The car would be recovered by police later at Riverdale Park East at the Andersonstown end of Finaghy Road North. Staff and passengers immediately went to the aid of the injured man, and the train ran non-stop to Belfast City Hospital station, where the victim was taken by stretcher to the Accident and Emergency department. Sadly however, he died a short time later. He was later named as Mr Colin Abernethy – apparently a leading member of the Ulster Clubs, a loyalist grouping.

In another incident, during the early hours of Friday, 1 May 1992, terrorists drove a vehicle up the railway track from the Dublin direction, to a position on the line

A soldier is killed in a massive explosion near Cloghogue Chapel, Newry, Friday, 1 May 1992. *(Author)*

adjacent to an Army road checkpoint, near to Cloghogue Chapel. There they detonated a 1000 lb bomb, which killed one soldier, demolished the checkpoint facility and completely destroyed both up and down lines, leaving a large crater. I was tasked with inspecting the damage the following Tuesday, after the line had been cleared by the Army. It was only then that repairs could commence, and from Wednesday, 6 May, the line was reopened with a temporary speed restriction.

Ceasefires Called, and Ended

On Wednesday, 31 August 1994, the PIRA announced a ceasefire from 24.00 hrs. Some months later, loyalist groupings followed suit, declaring a ceasefire from 24.00 hrs on Thursday, 13 October 1994. So many in Northern Ireland hoped and prayed that the cessation of violence would last as long as possible.

By the summer of 1995 however, although things had been relatively quiet on the terrorism front for NIR as a result of the ceasefires, tensions were mounting in an alarming way over a controversial loyal order parade in the Garvaghy Road area of Portadown, planned for the first week in July. On Friday, 3 July unruly youths rioted around Lake Street in Lurgan and in West Belfast. On 6 July, trouble erupted again at Lurgan, and at 23.30 hrs the railway track near Lake Street was set on fire. Sporadic trouble continued on and off until 13 July, with various bomb scares at Newry and the Border areas.

The 1994 PIRA ceasefire ended in a most dramatic and shocking way in the early evening of Friday, 9 February 1996, when 100 people were injured in an explosion in the financial sector of London at 19.00 hrs. Another bomb exploded on a bus in London on Monday, 19 February, leaving one passenger dead and nine injured. Local repercussions were felt too of course with the ending of the ceasefire. On Friday 9 February at 19.35 hrs, a bomb scare was called through for the railway line at the Red Bridge in Newry. This was not cleared until 17.30 hrs on Sunday, 11 February, with nothing having been found.

As the summer of 1996 approached, the threat of widespread violence in Northern Ireland raised its head once more, due to the difficult situation that had arisen at Drumcree on the outskirts of Portadown. From Monday, 8 July, the railway line was blocked a couple of times, due to protests at Lurgan. This pattern of disruption continued, along with numerous bomb scares, until Saturday, 13 July, which led to the cancellation of two special trains that day from Lurgan to Bangor. The organised parties of loyal order marchers were transported by Ulsterbus instead.

1997: Train Hijacked at Lurgan

The following year, as the "Twelfth Fortnight" loomed again, tensions began to brew once more, over the issue of the proposed Orange Order parades in Portadown. Widespread trouble was reported around Northern Ireland, and would continue for a number of days.

On Sunday, 6 July 1997, a lunchtime train from Belfast to Portadown was hijacked at Lurgan. In an apparently well-planned attack, a couple of passengers had joined the train at Lisburn, and they pulled the emergency handles just as the train was running over Bells Row level crossing on the outskirts of Lurgan. When the train stopped, passengers were told to leave at gunpoint, and they had no choice but to walk along the track towards the level crossing at Lake Street. Meanwhile, three armed men, who had been waiting for the train at the side of the track, were joined within minutes by ten other masked men who had come from the republican Kilwilkie estate. The group then started smashing every single window in the train, and threw petrol bombs inside, starting fires in each of the carriages. Level crossing barriers and a signal relay room were also damaged. The gunmen shouted to the train driver, "You have moved us off the Garvaghy Road, but you won't move us off this road!" – referring to the road at the level crossing. The masked men then all ran back into the housing estate.

Train hijacked at Lurgan, Sunday, 6 July 1997. *(News Letter)*

Rumours of a proposed attack had been circulating in Lurgan from the previous Friday; such rumours were allegedly reported in an article in the Sunday World newspaper on the day in question. At NIR, there was disappointment and frustration that we lost a train because no one had listened to the word on the ground: it was a loss which could have been prevented.

The train which was attacked was formed by two train sets composed of two × three cars: 80 Class, Nos 82, 772, 737, 751, 778 and 93. All four of the trailers were completely destroyed by fire, and the passenger compartments of the two motor coaches were also destroyed. It wasn't until almost two years later, the summer of 1999, that the refurbished six-car set was introduced back into service. Once approval had been given for the repair of the coaches, they were sent to Glasgow, where the two power cars were rebuilt, and the coaches were refurbished and made compatible with 80 Class rolling stock. The total cost of the repairs came to £1.5 million.

1998: Portadown Again

The year after the Lurgan attack, 1998, a different approach was taken by the security forces when the time for the contentious loyal order parade on the Garvaghy Road in Portadown came around again, on Sunday, 5 July. The result was, predictably enough, the easing of tensions in one section of the community, and the ramping up of resentment in the other. As regards train services, a decision was taken to close certain routes after 18.00 hrs that day, and this proved effective in averting any attacks, but was not ideal for any prospective passengers.

The Good Friday Agreement – and the Omagh Bombing

Throughout 1997, talks had been taking place between the British and Irish Governments with the intermediary of a United States senator, in the hopes of brokering a peace deal with the Provisionals. On Good Friday – 10 April 1998 – the Belfast Agreement was finally signed. The Provisionals declared their ceasefire, and a power-sharing, devolved government was to be formed, which would include representatives of parties allied with the main paramilitary groups. Loyalist paramilitary groups declared their ceasefires shortly after. Following the Agreement, the phenomenon of direct terrorist attacks on public transport largely ceased.

However, a few short months after the signing of the Belfast Agreement came one of the worst atrocities in over 30 years of violence. Although this did not directly affect the railways or public transport networks in general, I cannot for the purposes of record let this dastardly deed of terrorism go unmentioned. On Saturday, 15 August 1998 at 15.08 hrs, an explosion from a massive bomb in a booby-trapped car, parked in the main shopping part of Omagh, killed 29 people and injured around 220 others. The "Real IRA", supposedly a breakaway Republican group, were thought to be responsible for the atrocity.

A Relative Peace

Although as I have said, the incidence of terrorist attacks and bomb scares on the railways decreased dramatically after the Belfast Agreement was in place, and across Northern Ireland in general things were very much better, there were still sporadic incidents affecting NIR in the years which followed. In July 2004, for example, the traditional Royal Black Preceptory special train from Lurgan to Bangor, which ran once a year on the 13 July, was attacked by an unruly mob as it passed the Kilwilkie estate. The attack seemingly was well planned, judging by the number of objects thrown at the train by the assembled crowd. The GM locomotive with nine Gatwick carriages was attacked with petrol bombs and paint bombs, as well as being heavily stoned. Several passengers reported injuries from flying glass.

The train reached Bangor in a sorry state, with its exterior showing the scars of the attack. The police advised NIR that the train would not be returning to Lurgan in the evening, and that buses should be provided in its stead. Sadly, the train option for this particular traditional outing is still not available to the organisers to this day, due to the security situation in Lurgan.

The July "marching season" continued to be a time of the year when civil unrest could flare up very quickly in Northern Ireland. On Monday, 12 July 2010 trouble was reported in Lurgan and by the afternoon, it had spread to the railways. As the 16.10 hrs Enterprise service from Belfast Central to Dublin was making its way between Bells Row and Lake Street level crossings in Lurgan, an unruly mob managed to stop the train. They attempted to gain access into the driver's compartment, and also tried to set the train on fire. Thankfully local community representatives were on hand to try to quell the trouble, and they saved the day. With some of these representatives on board, the train was eventually allowed to move on, and proceeded on its journey to Portadown without further incident.

In more general terms too, there have still been incidents in recent years with the power to shock the community and potentially destabilise the Peace Process. In 2009, two such events occurred within a couple of days of each other, threatening to shake the fragile peace. On Saturday, 7 March that year, two British soldiers were gunned down and killed at an Army barracks at Antrim, while the following Monday, a police officer was shot dead as he responded to a call in a residential area of Craigavon.

And Finally . . .

Before I close this chapter, I should share a couple of the more humorous incidents that come to mind when I look back on those difficult years, when we at NIR struggled to keep the railways running through some of the country's worst times.

One of these lighter moments happened during a bomb scare at Belfast Central. A team from the Army had assembled in the inner station car park before going out on the track towards Botanic, where a suspect device had been spotted on the line near the Blackstaff river bridge. I was in the Railway Control office with other colleagues, and we could observe the Army on our CCTV systems. Trains of course had been stopped between Belfast Central and Botanic, so the service was badly disrupted.

After a lengthy period of time, I noticed that the Army had still not moved. Deciding to investigate, I went down to the car park and asked the officer in charge if there was a problem, and if he had any indication of how long they would be. He responded by saying that they had been waiting for authorisation to proceed onto the railway, once the electric current had been turned off! I quickly advised the officer that NIR had no electric railways, as all motive power was diesel. The Army then finally proceeded out onto the track to look at the suspect device – which turned out in any case to be a hoax.

Another incident involved the NIR Works & Buildings Manager on one occasion when he was in South Armagh to carry out his routine bridge inspections. He had begun at Kilnasaggart bridge, and from there would be heading north through "bandit country". The inspections were quite detailed and he spent quite some time at each bridge. I remember him telling me how after a while, he began to feel really annoyed, as no one from the security forces had approached him as yet, and he could very well have been a terrorist sizing up the bridges for his own purposes. However, just as he was travelling up a narrow road towards the next bridge, he was suddenly confronted by two British soldiers, who stepped out from some bushes and aimed their rifles at him. He stopped the car at once and they began to question him as to why he had been at each bridge for such long periods of time: they had his itinerary and all the timings for each bridge carefully noted down. They had obviously been watching him the whole time! He quickly explain who he was of course and was only released once he had been thoroughly checked out…

These two chapters on the Troubles can only give an idea of what it was like for railway staff and passengers during this dark period in Northern Ireland's history. The reality of working through these difficult times was often all the more frightening for members of NIR staff, like myself, who were asked to carry out our day's work in spite of the inevitability that some of us would be caught up in terrorist incidents and exposed to danger. I had my fair share of such situations, and a number of near misses, but I feel privileged to have stood alongside my many brave and determined colleagues.

SPECIAL TRAIN MOVEMENTS AND ROLLING STOCK

Since I spent my schooldays in Bangor, my initial knowledge of the different types of rolling stock used by NIR was limited, and in the mid-1960s, I was witnessing the last days of steam due to the closing down of Belfast Central Railway. After this, for many years, the only type of train to be seen on the Bangor line was the Multi-Engine Diesel (MED) train.

However, as I got older and travelled about a bit more locally, I discovered the many different kinds of rolling stock in use at Belfast's two other train stations, York Road and Great Victoria Street. There they had 70 Class stock, Multi-Purpose Diesel units, parcels vans, Hunslet locomotives and coaches, BUT coaches, AEC coaches, CIÉ locomotives, and Park Royal and Cravens coaches. The Bangor line was certainly just a branch line – as opposed to a main line – in many respects, not least in terms of the limited range of rolling stock in use there.

70 Class Diesel Train

First used by NIR in 1966, these trains were built by the Ulster Transport Authority, and were sometimes referred to as the "River Class". Eight motor standard class coaches were built, along with intermediate and driving trailers. The motor units were all numbered and named after rivers, as follows: 71 *River Bush*; 72 *River Foyle*; 73 *River Roe*; 74 *River Lagan*; 75 *River Maine*; 76 *River Inver*; 77 *River Braid*; 78 *River Bann*. Each of these motor units had an English Electric four-cylinder turbo charged engine, developing 550 hp and weighing in at 62 tons. The engine took up half the capacity of the coach; the remainder housed 53 seats.

Londonderry–Belfast six-car 70 Class railcar between Bleach Green Junction and Whiteabbey, 1966. *(Author's collection)*

The first photograph I acquired of a 70 Class railcar, taken in 1966, was of a six-car set near Whiteabbey, which was travelling from Londonderry to Belfast.

The Hunslet Locomotive

Three Hunslet English Electric locomotives were introduced by NIR in 1970, and these were intended for use on the Belfast to Dublin Enterprise service. They were built by British Rail Engineering Limited at Doncaster, acting as sub-contractors for the Hunslet Engine Company. The three locomotives were fitted for push-and-pull working, and were to be used as either one locomotive and driving trailer, or one locomotive at either end of the train. They were dual-braked and had power output for electric train heating.

The locomotives were numbered and named as follows: 101 *Eagle*; 102 *Falcon*; 103 *Merlin*. These names were taken from the famous Great Northern Railway steam locomotives of 1932. The maximum locomotive speed was 80 mph, and they weighed in at 68 tons, with a Bo-Bo wheel arrangement. The engine was English Electric 1350 hp turbo blown.

Hunslet DL 101 *Eagle* being prepared for the new cross-border service, commencing on 1 July 1970. *(Author)*

In 1970 also, a fleet of eight coaches was acquired for the new cross-border train, comprising four standards (Nos 821–824), two brake driving trailers (Nos 811–812), one First Class (No 801) and one grill/bar car (No 547). These were built by British Rail Engineering using a standard BR Mark IIB bodyshell, and weighed 32 tons each. In 1972, a further five coaches were introduced into the fleet: four standards (Nos 825–828) and a First Class driving trailer (No 813). Some of these coaches were supplied complete, and others were supplied as shells and finished in the NIR workshops at Belfast York Road.

Multi-Engine Diesel Trains (MED)

As I have said, in my teenage years, the only rolling stock we had on the Bangor line was the MED stock. These were built in Duncrue Street Works, Belfast, from 1952 by the Ulster Transport Authority, and they served well for over 25 years.

Three-car MED (led by No 27) at Bangor West, 17 August 1971 – notice the station building on the up platform. *(Author)*

The official date for withdrawal of these units was 17 July 1978, and the last printed entry in the Diesel Roster was dated 3 July 1978. The set was only due to run 60.5 miles per day. The last remaining powered set comprised Nos 32, 509 and 21, and in fact after the official end date, this set ran for another 1,027.5 miles.

The last special working of this MED set was on 2 September 1978, for an outing related to a Senior Citizens' Free Day Out. The set managed a few more runs in the roster before its last day of operation, on Thursday, 28 December 1978, when it ran three services: the 06.55 hrs Belfast–Bangor;

MED No 18 in middle road, and another set at Platform One at Bangor station, 17 August 1971. *(Author)*

the 07.35 hrs Bangor–Lisburn; and the 08.35 hrs Lisburn–Belfast.

The set was withdrawn early in the New Year, due to a fire in the engines of power car No 21 at the Central Service Depot on 2 January 1979. Even though the set had not been run since 28 December, due to the very cold weather the engines had been left idling for the interim days, so that they could be started again without too much difficulty when required. As a result, the engines and exhaust systems would have been extremely hot and this, along with the abundance of oily and highly flammable substances around, meant that the chances of a fire breaking out were high.

Disposal of the coaches proved difficult, due to a number of them having been lined with blue asbestos, a very dangerous substance – as such, they could not be cut up or burned. Several possible schemes were proposed, including sinking the coaches in the North Channel. However, it was only after the necessary permission was granted (as is required for the dumping of blue asbestos), that they could be disposed of in a quarry near Crumlin.

A siding was installed on the down side at Crumlin, and the coaches were initially taken by rail and then onwards to the quarry by low loader lorry. They were then dropped into the water-filled quarry, where they eventually sank into the deep water. It is sad to record that not one of these coaches was preserved for posterity in the Transport Museum, after 26 years of service.

The history of the use of MED units on Northern Ireland's railways is an interesting one. It was only towards the end of 1948 that a British vehicle manufacturer produced a horizontal, diesel-engined bus, and UTA technical staff carried out research into the possibility of incorporating this flat engine as the propelling unit in existing types of railway rolling stock.

This resulted in an experimental train, consisting of three coaches, being trialed on the Bangor line in August 1951. The train, which was effectively the first MED train in Ireland, employed four AEC flat diesel engines, two each on the leading and rear coaches, with a non-powered intermediate coach. It quickly proved to have considerably lower running costs, when compared with steam traction.

Further developments to this first model were then explored by the British manufacturers and the UTA, which resulted in the perfecting of control gears capable of synchronising and modulating the power output of eight Leyland flat diesel engines. The total output – 1,000 bhp – would be capable of propelling a train of six to eight coaches, having a gross weight of 185 to 225 tons, over average rail track formation at a speed of up to 73 mph. This would be the first instance of using of multi-powered units to such an extent in rail traction in Ireland.

By April 1952, the first six-car MED train had been built at the UTA workshops at Duncrue Street in Belfast, using existing coaching stock, with four powered coaches and two non-powered intermediate coaches. An additional new feature on this train was the provision of wide, power-operated sliding doors which were under the control of the guard. The total seating capacity would accommodate 48 First Class passengers and 356 Standard Class passengers. Following the successful running of the first sets, it was decided to proceed with the modification of existing stock and the construction of 26 new vehicles. Of the new vehicles, 18 would be of lightweight steel construction and the remaining eight would constitute lightweight bodies built on standard underframes, which the UTA had in stock. The design and fabrication of the integral vehicles and the lightweight bodies were carried out by Metal Sections Ltd of Oldbury in Birmingham, and the final assembly was completed in the UTA workshops in Duncrue Street.

New Rolling Stock and a Delayed Order

As mentioned in Chapter One, in February 1972, the purchase of new rolling stock for NIR was announced by the government: ten new trains would be ordered, at a cost of £1.5m. The details of the trains are given in the 80 Class section below. Following the announcement, it was decided that British Rail would build only the bodyshells and that, in order to provide employment in Northern Ireland, the finishing work would be completed in NIR's own workshops in Belfast York Road.

On Wednesday, 23 January 1974 however, it was reported by NIR that the completion of the contract for the new train sets was being delayed due to a steel crisis in England. Delivery of the 22 new vehicles being built by British Rail at Derby had originally been due to commence in late 1973, but this would now be delayed until 1974.

The urgent need for NIR's new rolling stock was highlighted by a newspaper article of 23 August 1974, in which the reporter commented on how, on a lovely calm summer morning in the city, a huge cloud of black fumes had been seen to descend onto the Sydenham Bypass, as a train was leaving Sydenham station for Belfast. In response to this and other comments from the public, NIR's Managing Director at the time, Mr Hugh Waring said that the company was all too aware of the problems being presented by the old rolling stock. Both engines and the stock were simply worn out, he explained, and so much was obsolete that some trains were running only because the company's engineers had machined up vital parts themselves, as spares were no longer available. Mr Waring went on to reassure railway users that NIR were taking on nine new train sets over the next four months, initially on the Portadown line. When the new Belfast Central Railway opened, these sets would also be running through to Bangor. He concluded his explaining by confirming that NIR could not even cannibalise the redundant stock, since none of the components was compatible with one another. The company had, for example, a legacy of Leyland-engined MED coaches on the Bangor line, AEC engine stock on the Portadown line, and a few BUT vehicles from the old Northern Counties – but none of these could be used together and all the spares were different.

The First 80 Class Test Run

The first 80 Class motor coach from the 1972 order – No 89 – arrived into Belfast York Road from BR in Derby on Saturday, 21 September 1974. This particular unit arrived complete, but future units were to be finished in Belfast, as previously mentioned. Transport for these would be organised by Pickford's Heavy Haulage, and the motor coaches, weighing 62 tons each, would be taken from the British Rail Engineering York works and transported to Belfast via the Heysham to Belfast ferry.

The numbers designated for the first motor coaches ran from 81 to 89. When a second batch of sets was ordered, as detailed later in this chapter, the numbers reverted to 67 to 69, and from 90 to 99. The driver's and engine compartment in this model took up almost half of the coach, with the remainder housing 45 passenger seats. The engine was an English Electric four-cylinder turbo charged, developing 560 hp. Also supplied were Intermediate trailers (with a capacity of 87 seats) and driving trailers (with 81 seats), built at British Rail's Derby Litchurch Lane plant. Only a couple of the motor coaches would be named at later dates. The last motor coach in this contract left York in the middle of January 1975.

As the photograph below left shows, on 27 September 1974, No 89 was taken for its first test run to Greenisland and back. We see it here being prepared outside the diesel shed at Belfast York Road, after which it would have attached to its two new trailers. The exterior colours for the fleet were Moroccan maroon and Caribbean blue. The set formations would be four × three-car sets and five × two-car sets.

By Thursday, 12 December 1974, the status of the new 80 Class motor coach fleet was as follows: No 84: just arrived that day; No 83: in the NIR workshop, being finished off; Nos 89, 81 and 82: already in service.

Motor Coach No 88

On Friday, 24 January 1975, the shell of diesel electric motor coach No 88 arrived at Belfast York Road. This was the last motor coach to arrive for this order. The previous day, the fifth set to go into service, comprising Nos 84 and 736, had been sent from Belfast York Road to Great Victoria Street. The very last 80 class vehicle of this order

Below: 80 Class Motor Coach No 89 being prepared at Belfast York Road for its first test run to Greenisland, Friday, 27 September 1974. *(Author)*

Below right: Shell of Motor Coach No 88 arrives at Belfast York Road on Friday, 24 January 1975. *(Author)*

to arrive in Belfast York Road was driving trailer No 739, which was delivered on Tuesday, 4 March 1975.

Special Trains: 1973–1976

On the evening of Thursday, 1 November 1973, a local football derby was to be played as the Gold Cup final at the Oval (Glentoran's ground) in East Belfast. The Gold Cup final was between Bangor and Ards, and ended up not such a good event for Bangor, as they were beaten 4–1. A special train for 500 Bangor supporters ran from Bangor to Ballymacarrett, departing at 18.45 hrs. The return train left Ballymacarrett at 21.45 hrs; the return fare was 25 pence.

For the occasion of the official opening of the new station at Larne on Wednesday, 3 July 1974, a special train left Belfast at 12.20 hrs for Larne Town. The train was composed of Hunslet No 102 *Falcon*, and three of the new 80 Class coaches.

In the early to mid-1970s, Loyal Order special trains were a good source of annual income for the railway, and many specials ran over the years. On one such occasion, for example, two six-car MED special trains ran from Bangor to Holywood for 12 July 1975. These services left Bangor at 11.15 and 11.25 hrs, returning from Holywood at 17.15 and 17.25 hrs.

Hunslet No 102 being prepared at Belfast York Road for a special, 3 July 1974.
(Author)

First 80 Class on Bangor Line

On Monday, 12 January 1976, a very *special* special train ran from Belfast Great Victoria Street to Bangor. An empty 80 Class inspection train, formed by Nos 82 and 739 (driving trailer leading to Bangor), this would be the first train to run from the Great Northern and on to the County Down line since 1965. The train left Great Victoria Street at 10.30 hrs, departed Belfast Queen's Quay at 11.15 hrs and was gauged in all three platforms in Bangor. It began the return journey from Bangor to Great Victoria Street at 12.00 hrs that day.

Following on from this, on Tuesday, 13 January 1976 a special train, formed by Nos 88 and 738, left Botanic station at lunchtime, with the NIR Board and senior officials as its passengers. The train stopped at Belfast Central station, allowing the party to view progress there, and then continued to the Lagan bridge. The train ran on to Bangor, arriving at Platform 2.

The passengers on board the special were welcomed by the then North Down Mayor, Councillor Jack Preston and officials of the Bangor Tourist Development Association.

First new train allocated to the Bangor line, Tuesday, 13 January 1976 *(Author's collection)*

At a reception afterwards, recently appointed NIR Chief Executive, Roy Beattie said that the new train in which they had travelled would be put into service on the Bangor line the next day. This would be the first new rolling stock to run on the Bangor line for 25 years.

True to the Chief Executive's word, the new train entered passenger service on Wednesday, 14 January 1976. Initially it was running on off-peak services and then very soon it was deployed for rush hour services. Some initial comments from passengers were that they were amazed at the comfort it provided, in comparison to the old train types, which were still in operation at that point. Some however disliked the higher step down from the train onto the platform, and some were not sure about having to open the door by a handle again.

First Special Train from Bangor to Dublin

Following the opening of the Belfast Central Railway, rail excursions between Bangor and Dublin became a reality for passengers again. On Thursday, 6 May 1976, the first special train ran on this line in over eleven years. A five-car 80 Class train, it was chartered by the Bangor Tourist Development Association, along with the Chamber of Trade. An impressive 323 out of 339 seats were booked on the special that day. The return fare was £2.95, and refreshments and drinks from a minibar were served in one of the guard's vans.

The five-car 80 Class set was made up of coaches Nos 82, 739, 735, 764 and 83. My mother (Mary Ellen) and I were among the passengers that day, and I recorded the schedule and actual timings as follows:

	Scheduled	Actual		Scheduled	Actual
Bangor dep.	08.40	08.43	Dublin dep.	17.55	17.59
Dublin arr.	11.40	11.22	Bangor arr.	21.10	21.00

Travelling on the train too were the Mayor of North Down Council, a number of councillors and members of both the Bangor Tourist Development Association and the Chamber of Trade. Following our arrival in Dublin, there was a great flurry of press photographers and local journalists to greet the hundreds of passengers. Receptions for the many dignitaries who had made the journey were held at the Gresham Hotel and later at the Mansion House of Dublin.

Although the day was a great success, some commentators brought up the fact that no Enterprise-type train would be able to undertake the same run, due to the fear that bridges on the Bangor line were too small. (As enthusiasts will know, each type of train differs in its actual height and width, and will not necessarily fit through each bridge or platform on a specific line. This was the case in relation to the Enterprise-type train – it wouldn't fit on the Bangor line without certain basic infrastructure changes being carried out.) NIR commented that it would have to be sure that proper clearances were available at all of the bridges on the Bangor line, but that this could not be undertaken until Enterprise locomotives were available for the necessary checks. In fact, CIÉ had originally also planned to run an excursion from Dublin directly to Bangor on the forthcoming Bank Holiday Monday, 7 June, but due to this issue of the lack of clearance on bridges, passengers had to change trains at Belfast Central for the run to Bangor station.

A second special train from Bangor to Dublin ran just a month or so after the first, on Thursday, 10 June 1976, but for some reason or other, this time the occasion was a disappointing flop. The same scheduled timings as before applied, but only a two-car 80 Class train was allocated, as such a small number of passengers were travelling – only 26 in total (including myself).

In September 1976, the main obstacle blocking the line to Bangor for Enterprise locomotive-hauled trains was removed. This obstacle was the remains of the steel footbridge at the disused Kinnegar station. See Chapter Eight for further details.

May 1976: Steam Train Special into Bangor

On Saturday, 22 May 1976, the Railway Preservation Society of Ireland organised a special steam train to travel from Whitehead to Bangor. There was great excitement among enthusiasts, as it had been almost eleven years since a steam train had been seen at Bangor station (the last one had left on Wednesday, 28 July 1965).

The steam special left Whitehead at 07.45 hrs that day, travelled to Belfast York Road and then onwards to Antrim, before running down the branch line to Lisburn. From there, it went on to the Belfast Central Railway and then stopped at Cultra, before arriving in Bangor at 11.35 hrs.

The 13.10 hrs RPSI Steam train, Bangor to Whitehead, Saturday, 22 May 1976. (*Author*)

The train was hauled by locomotive No 4, which was built in 1947 and had been used extensively on the Bangor line in the early 1950s. Seven carriages were in the formation, including a restaurant car. The shunting of the carriages was carried out by a four-car MED set, formed by Nos 35, 19, 502 and 22.

As the train left Bangor again at 13.10 hrs on its homeward journey to Whitehead, many local people assembled to say farewell. For some of the crowd who lined the Brunswick Road bridge, as well as the path running alongside the railway, this would be their first glimpse of a real, live steam engine.

More Specials in 1976: Apprentice Boys, Bangor Market and an Historic Steam Tour

On Thursday, 12 August 1976, for the first time in 12 years, a Portadown contingent of Apprentice Boys travelled to Londonderry by train for the annual parade there. The train was formed by a Hunslet locomotive hauling ten BUT carriages. The train traversed the Lisburn to Antrim branch line.

The 10.45 hrs Londonderry–Belfast service (four-car 70 Class) crosses the 09.00 hrs Bangor–Londonderry special steam train at Dunloy, 25 September 1976. *(Author)*

August 1976 was also a very busy time on the Bangor line for special trains. During that month alone, an average of six special trains ran every Wednesday between Belfast Central and Bangor, in order to accommodate the numbers of passengers wishing to travel to the seaside and to the weekly market in the town.

On Friday, 24 September 1976, steam locomotive No 4 and six carriages ran from Whitehead to Bangor in preparation for a special run the next day. The train arrived in Bangor at 20.15 hrs on the Friday evening. The following day at 09.00 hrs, the steam train left Bangor for Londonderry, with 250 passengers – including me. We did not have a good start, however, as the train encountered very bad wheel slip, and took 15 minutes to get beyond Bangor West station!

The train stopped at Dunloy station, which was to be an historic occasion as the station was to be closed from 18 October 1976. Another historic stop on the run was at Limavady Junction station, which was also due to be shut down on the same day in October.

We then ran on towards Londonderry and passed the crossing loop at Lisahally. The Belfast end connection had already been removed, but the Londonderry end turnout was still in position. In fact, on the following day, Sunday, 26 September 1976, the loop would be used to cross the 09.30 hrs service Belfast to Londonderry with the 08.00 hrs ballast train from Coleraine (a three-car MPD set).

Onwards then we went to Londonderry, where the frontage of the station had

had been badly damaged by a bomb just a few months previously. For the return journey to Belfast York Road, the steam train left Londonderry at 15.35 hrs. Bangor line passengers were transferred to Belfast Central by a special bus; thankfully, the 18.45 hrs service train to Bangor was delayed by ten minutes to allow our party of enthusiasts to purchase tickets and board the train. It had been a memorable day for us all!

Refurbishment of the 70 Class Trains

During 1977, an extensive internal modernisation project was carried out on the 70 Class diesel sets at Belfast York Road workshops. The work involved the complete renewal of all seats, floors, partitions and panelling. Several of the side-corridor type coaches were converted to open saloons, and modern windows were fitted.

Once the refurbishments were completed, the fleet would consist of eight power cars, seven driving trailers and eight intermediate trailers. The original four driving trailers in the fleet would have additional coaches – Nos 701, 702 and 703 – which were formerly First Class brake coaches.

Four-Car 80 Class Set

For a period of time in the late 1970s, a four-car 80 Class set, motor coach No 89 and three trailers, was formed and used for busier services, basically to provide more passenger seating: a three-car set had 213 seats, while the four-car set could offer 300 seats. One of the runs this train was allocated was the 17.15 hrs express service from Belfast Central to Bangor, which regularly had a need for this kind of passenger capacity. On one occasion, during rush hour on 25 November 1977, I recorded the running times as follows: departed Belfast Central, 17.15 hrs; Craigavad pass, 17.27 hrs; arrive Bangor West, 17.34 hrs; arrive Bangor, 17.39 hrs. As can be seen, even on the express run the set did not particularly fare well, slowing timings down by four minutes, as recorded. On stopping services however, the times were even worse, due to the slow start-up time of the train. The problem of course was that an extra 33 tons had been added to the train's total weight, without any more power being provided. It was not surprising therefore that the four-car set in this formation did not last long.

1978: Completion and Delivery of Additional 80 Class Order

In 1975, following successful completion of similar vehicles by BREL in 1974, NIR had placed an additional order for new 80 Class stock. This order included 13 power cars, nine intermediate trailers and 12 driving trailers. The power cars were to be built at Derby Litchurch Lane, while the trailers would be assembled at Wolverton works, using bodyshells and bogies constructed in Derby. The expected completion date for delivery was spring 1978.

On 7 December 1977, at an official ceremony in Derby to mark the handing over by British Rail Engineering of the first power car in the additional order, NIR Chairman Sir Myles Humphreys was presented with a key for the new power car. The order was duly completed and delivered over the following months, until finally, on Thursday, 7 September 1978, it was NIR's turn to play hosts to BREL representatives, who travelled to Belfast Central station to present the last power car in the Phase II order of rolling stock. In the tradition of British Rail, this power car, No 99, was named *Sir Myles Humphreys*, after the NIR Chairman. The new car and its nameplate were unveiled at a ceremony in the station.

Refurbished Enterprise Set

On Monday, 3 July 1978, NIR launched into service its newly refurbished Enterprise train set. The train was formed by Hunslet No 101 *Eagle* and six Mk II carriages. The set had been brought round from Belfast York Road to the Central Service Depot on Saturday, 1 July. On launch day, Chairman Sir Myles Humphreys stated that it was a proud day for the company, in being able to offer new facilities for a route which had seen a 35 per cent increase in passengers over the previous 12 months; it was also clearly a great development for travellers too. The reconfigured Enterprise train firstly did a special run, leaving Belfast Central at 08.50 hrs and returning at 11.15 hrs from Dublin, before taking up its regular duties and running that day's 14.30 hrs Enterprise Belfast to Dublin service.

It was not all plain sailing for the Enterprise immediately thereafter, however. On

Refurbished Enterprise set at Belfast York Road, Saturday, 1 July 1978. *(Author)*

Thursday, 6 July 1978, the newly painted Hunslet failed in service while operating the 11.00 hrs Enterprise from Dublin to Belfast Central. The following day, when Hunslet No 101 was heading the 14.30 hrs Belfast Central to Dublin service, it failed at Dundalk, with over 300 passengers on board. The truth was that the Hunslet locomotives operating this service were now eight years old, and they had not been without mechanical problems over the years and in fact throughout their lifespan.

Special Trains 1977: the Irish Cup Final and the "Jamborora Express"

The 1977 Irish Cup Final was held at the Oval football ground in East Belfast on Saturday 23 April, where Coleraine would face Linfield. Most of the Linfield supporters who travelled by train arrived at Ballymacarrett on the 13.30 hrs Portadown to Bangor service.

Meanwhile 500 Coleraine supporters travelled on a 12.50 hrs special train from

Coleraine to Ballymacarrett, which was formed by a six-car MPD set, Nos 54, 536, 45, 541, 51 and 64. This was the first time an MPD set had been seen on the Bangor line – at this stage, these trains were operating mainly on the Larne and Londonderry lines. The MPD set ran empty to Bangor station, and left Bangor at 14.55 hrs, also empty, returning to the Central Service Depot for

The 12.50 hrs special Coleraine to Ballymacarrett MPD set, as well as the 14.05 hrs service Bangor to Lisburn at up platform, 23 April 1977. (Author)

fuelling and cleaning. Even though Coleraine won the final 4–1 on the day, the special return service to Coleraine from Ballymacarrett had seven windows smashed, with four seat cushions being thrown out of the train.

In June 1977, a series of special trains ran from Londonderry to Cultra station – a station which had not been used since 1957. The first schools special, a six-car 80 Class, ran on Friday, 17 June 1977; the second, a three-car 70 Class, on Tuesday, 21 June; the third and final schools special ran on Wednesday, 22 June and was formed by a six-car 80 Class.

In late July 1977, the 50th anniversary of the founding of the Catholic Boy Scouts movement was held at an International Jamboree in the Waterford area. For the return journey of the Northern Ireland contingent on Friday 5 August, a special train, the "Jamborora Express", left Cahir, near Tipperary, at 10.25 hrs and, with 750 Scouts on board, ran on to Belfast Central, arriving at 16.25 hrs (35 minutes late). The train

Looks like CIÉ have taken over at Belfast Central on Friday, 5 August 1977, the day the NI contingent returned from the Scouts' International Jamboree in Waterford! Here, at Platform One, we can see the special train which ran back to Dublin empty; at Platform Two, the seven Mk II coaches for the 17.30 hrs Enterprise to Dublin; and at Platform Three, locomotive No 012 running around the train. (Author)

was formed by "A" Class locomotive No 052, hauling ten Park Royal carriages. The 340 Scouts for the Londonderry line were transferred on to a special five-car 80 Class set, which left Central at 16.37 hrs from Platform Two (17 minutes late).

Special Trains 1978: a Peace Train, a CIÉ Civil Engineering Train and Others

On Saturday, 18 February 1978, peace movement supporters were urged to catch the "Peace Special" train for a major protest outside Provisional Sinn Féin's headquarters in Dublin. The nine-car 80 Class train ran from Londonderry to Dublin and was hired by the Peace People as part of a protest at recent murders in the Province. The demonstration, at 14.00 hrs in Kevin Street in Dublin, was timed to coincide with other rallies in Oslo and parts of Norway. Over the next 12 years or so, further peace trains would run at various intervals. On 12 October 1989, for example, a couple of large special trains connected to peace demonstrations (a GM locomotive and 11 coaches, and a nine-car 80 class) left Belfast for Dublin at 08.10 hrs and 08.30 hrs respectively.

Wednesday, 22 February saw the arrival at Belfast Central of an AR CIÉ locomotive No 012. The civil engineering train, with five wagons of continuous welded rails for the Bangor line, and a sixth wagon carrying unloading equipment, had left Dundalk at 10.15 hrs, and from Belfast Central had travelled onwards to Bangor to stable for the night in the middle road.

This was the first time since 1965 that a train from south of the Border had run on the Bangor line. The wagons carried 18 lengths × 300 feet welded rails that had been prepared in the CIÉ rail plant at Portlaoise. The locomotive ran around its train the following morning, and left Bangor at 09.30 hrs to discharge the rails between Holywood and Kinnegar during a period of single-line working.

The civil engineering train from Portlaoise to Bangor passes through Belfast Central on Wednesday, 22 February 1978. *(Author)*

Up until 1965, many special trains had run from the "Great Northern" to the "County Down" via the old Belfast Central Railway. With the new link now in operation, some of the special traffic returned, including two special trains for the Royal Black Preceptories from Lurgan, which were the first specials to run on this route again, on Thursday, 13 July 1978. One train was formed by a nine-car 80 Class, and the second was formed by a six-car 80 Class. Again, on Tuesday, 18 July that year, Poyntzpass and Scarva Sunday Schools combined forces to run a special train from Poyntzpass to Bangor; this was formed by an eight-car 80 Class train.

1978 was also the first year for the Belfast contingent of Apprentice Boys to travel by train from Belfast Central to Londonderry, which they did on Saturday, 12 August. The train was formed by a five-car 70 Class set hauling six BUT carriages. This would be the last year of operation for the BUT carriages.

Special Trains 1978–1979: Firsts for the 80 Class in Bray, Wexford and Claremorris

On Saturday, 17 June 1978, the North West of Ireland Railway Society organised a special train from Londonderry to Bray. The "Foyle Enterprise" was a six-car 80 Class train, formed by Nos 67, 771, 740, 732, 763 and 94. I travelled on the train from Lisburn to Bray. The train left Londonderry at 07.05 hrs and arrived in Bray at 12.05 hrs. The vast majority of passengers detrained at Dublin Connolly and a small number, including myself, went on to Bray. Clearance for the train between Dublin and Bray at the time was achieved by simply completing the necessary paperwork – unlike in 2015, when clearance would only be permitted following the running of a train with only clearance engineers on board first.

Foyle Enterprise in Bray, first 80 Class to Bray, Saturday, 17 June 1978. *(Author)*

First 80 Class to Wexford

On Saturday, 5 August 1978, a special train was chartered by the Irish National Foresters to run from Belfast Central to Wexford. I travelled on this service myself as a railway enthusiast and off-duty employee, as the train would be running on a part of the Irish Rail network it hadn't been on before. The five-car 80 Class set, formed by Nos 96, 764, 749, 746 and 95, was so full that I had to sit in the guard's van the whole way with the catering crew. This was the first time for an 80 Class set to visit Wexford and here again, the run was gauged as a paper exercise.

When the train left Belfast Central at 07.35 hrs, all was fine, however No 96 started overheating at Skerries. Thankfully, Inspector Val Ryan joined at Dublin and allowed the train to continue with No 96 cutting in and out. Between Dublin and Bray, the Inspector cut the No 96 engine out to give it a rest, restarting it on the journey up Bray bank and through the tunnels, which worked well. (The engine in the train's other coach, No 95, was working normally and therefore able to keep the train running, albeit at a slower speed.) The service finally arrived in Wexford 55 minutes late, at 13.15 hrs. There

The first 80 Class in Wexford, Saturday, 5 August 1978. *(Author)*

was a plan to run on to Rosslare Harbour for refuelling but this was not required. The train was stabled in Wexford yard, and the engineers had a look at it before its return journey, on Sunday, 6 August departing at 17.50 hrs. Fortunately, there was no further trouble on the way back.

First 80 Class to Claremorris

Another historic first run for an 80 Class set was on Sunday, 8 April 1979, when a chartered five-car 80 Class set ran from Belfast Central to Claremorris, a return trip of 498 miles. I travelled on this train (in the rear cab), which was full of pilgrims heading to the Knock shrine. On this occasion a paper exercise for gauging purposes was not sufficient, and one of CIÉ's requirements was that all centre steps had to be removed from the train, and the centre doors locked. On the journey from Dublin to Claremorris, engineering staff either allowed the train through each station at slow speed, or stipulated that the train was to be stopped for physical measuring, between other step boards and platforms. The train was due to leave Belfast Central at 07.40 hrs, but left six minutes late, arriving in Claremorris 20 minutes late, mainly due to these gauging procedures.

As a result of these checks however, the line was cleared for future operations of this type, as it had been established that there were no obvious engineering difficulties, and that the removal of centre steps would not be required.

The photograph shows part of the line-up for return specials from Claremorris, as follows: Extreme left: 2 × GM locomotives and 10 coaches for Limerick; Left: 2 × GM locomotives and 11 coaches for Limerick; Right: five-car 80 Class for Belfast Central; Extreme right: 2 × GM locomotives and 14 coaches for Dundalk. Also, not visible in photograph would have been at the rear, one GM locomotive and 14 coaches for Dublin Heuston.

The return NIR journey departed Claremorris at 17.48 hrs (23 minutes late), due to the large number of passengers and specials at the station. Our train, which arrived in Belfast Central at 23.29 hrs (six minutes late), was formed by Nos 67, 765, 731, 763 and 92.

Claremorris special trains, including one from Belfast, Sunday, 8 April 1979. (Author)

Cross-Border Football Specials

Wednesday, 20 September 1978 was the date of a much-anticipated football match between the Republic of Ireland and Northern Ireland at Lansdowne Road in Dublin. Two special trains were provided for travelling fans: a six-car 80 Class and a three-car 80 Class. Both sets ran through to Lansdowne Road, and the three-car set was stabled in Dun Laoghaire until the return journey. On the way back to Belfast, there was a bomb scare at Scarva, which blocked both specials for over an hour. Frustration grew among the supporters and as a result train windows were broken, seats thrown out, seats slashed and interior side panels kicked in. Incidentally, the result of the game was a nil-all draw.

Belfast and County Down Railway Museum Trust Special Trains

In December 1978 I was responsible for commissioning a special train from Bangor to Dublin under the auspices of the Belfast and County Down Railway Museum Trust, for which I was the fundraising officer. One of this organisation's aims was to encourage railway preservation by, for instance, trying to bring a preserved railway back to the Ballynahinch area of County Down, and other such initiatives.

We chartered a five-car 80 Class train from NIR, and 295 passengers out of a possible maximum of 339 travelled on Saturday, 2 December. The special rate fares being offered were £3.50 for an adult return, and £2.50 for a child return. The Trust also had catering facilities set up in one of the guard's vans. My mother and two other ladies made eight loaves of sandwiches to sell on the trip. The train left Bangor at 08.00 hrs, and arrived Dublin at 11.02 hrs – 6 minutes late, which was partly due to the special train not stopping at Bangor West to pick up passengers there, and us having to subsequently wait for these people to arrive via the scheduled service. The return service left Dublin at 17.45 hrs and arrived in Bangor at 20.45 hrs. The train was formed by Nos 92, 772, 743, 750 and 81. A tidy profit of £146 was made for the Trust.

Further trips from Bangor to Dublin on behalf of the Trust took place the following year. These included a special on Saturday, 12 May 1979, which was formed by a three-car 80 Class, with 185 seats filled out of a potential total of 213. A trip on Saturday, 1 December 1979 was also successful, with 205 passengers out of a possible total of 213, as was an excursion on Saturday, 15 December 1979, when with 210 passengers travelled and there were only three seats to spare. On this occasion, however, there were ten passengers missing on the homeward journey, who had most likely used the cheap ticket for a single trip. Incidentally, a passenger on both these December trips was my girlfriend Lucinda, who of course was to become my railway enthusiast wife!

Football Specials

A total of 500 Cliftonville football supporters travelled from Belfast Central to Bangor on Saturday, 7 April 1979 to see their team play against Bangor. The train was initially to have been a Hunslet and five coaches, but as these had been signed off as needing repairs, it was formed instead by a five-car 70 Class set. Thankfully no damage was caused to the train, despite such a large number travelling. The RUC were out in force and used nine land rovers to escort supporters to and from North Belfast, and to and from Bangor's football ground.

Just four weeks later, on Saturday 5 May, the biggest football special to have ever operated before on NIR ran from Belfast Central to Bangor. A huge crowd of 685 Cliftonville supporters travelled on the midday special, returning from Bangor at

17.15 hrs. Twelve windows were broken along the way. The train was formed by Hunslet No 102 hauling eight MPD trailers. A large police contingent was present both at Belfast Central and in Bangor.

Busy Times for Bangor

On Saturday, 19 May 1979, Bangor saw one of its busiest days for many years. Within the space of 15 minutes, 23 railway carriages arrived in the town. A massive 800 members of the Junior Orange organisation had come from Portadown and Lurgan, followed by 700 members of the Portadown Free Presbyterian Sunday School. The trains were made up as follows: a five-car 80 Class hauling three MPD trailers; a four-car 80 Class; a nine-car 80 Class hauling two MPD trailers. A lot of shunting had to take place in order to move the MPD trailers into the correct platforms for the return journeys in the evening. The evening specials were delayed for a short time due to football supporter trouble at Adelaide station.

Special Loyal Order Trains

Northern Ireland's traditional "marching season" always created a demand for special train services. On Thursday, 12 July 1979 for example, a special train running from Bangor to Holywood and back was organised for Bangor District Orangemen. The train was formed by a five-car 80 Class hauling five Enterprise carriages. The following day, the Lurgan and area Royal Black Preceptory came by train to Bangor. The two specials, carrying 1,300 passengers in total, were formed by a nine-car 80 Class set, along with a four-car 80 Class set with five Enterprise coaches.

The next month, on Saturday, 11 August 1979 the Belfast Apprentice Boys special to Londonderry was formed by a four-car 80 Class hauling five MPD trailers. The 07.40 hrs special was full on its outbound journey, and 100 passengers were left behind to catch the next ordinary service train.

Autumn 1979: Visit of Pope John Paul to Ireland

The visit of His Holiness Pope John Paul II to the Republic of Ireland from Friday, 28 September 1979 to Monday, 1 October 1979, was a momentous occasion for many people, and a very large number of special trains was laid on for those wishing to travel to the many venues on the Pope's itinerary during his stay. The detailed Córas Iompair Éireann Supplementary Circular of, which I have kept a copy, records a total of 279 special train movements.

There were a number of other exceptional measures taken to accommodate all the additional train services. For example, Ashtown station, on the line between Dublin Connolly and Clonsilla (for Phoenix Park Dublin) was reopened especially for the occasion – the first time since its closure in 1934. On Friday, 28 September at 11.30 hrs, a temporary signal box was deployed at the Liffey Junction end of the station. This signal box remained in use until Monday, 1 October, when it was taken out of commission again. Ashtown station would be permanently reopened on 12 January 1982.

There was also a good provision of special train movements from Northern Ireland to the various venues. On Friday, 28 September, for example, the 14.30 hrs Enterprise

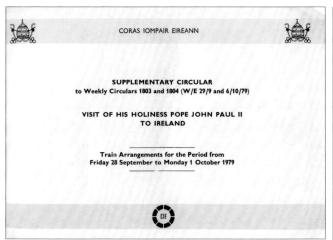

CORAS IOMPAIR EIREANN

SUPPLEMENTARY CIRCULAR
to Weekly Circulars 1803 and 1804 (W/E 29/9 and 6/10/79)

**VISIT OF HIS HOLINESS POPE JOHN PAUL II
TO IRELAND**

**Train Arrangements for the Period from
Friday 28 September to Monday 1 October 1979**

CIÉ

Above: Front cover of the CIÉ Supplementary Circular for the Visit of the Pope to Ireland, September 1979. *(Author's collection)*

Right: Page 2 of NIR Weekly Notice for Saturday, 29 September 1979. *(Author's collection)*

N.I.R.   2
NOTICE NO. 45
SATURDAY, 29th SEPTEMBER (Contd.)

TRAIN CANCELLATIONS

Central/Dublin
The usual Enterprise service has been withdrawn. The full cross border service for ordinary passengers is shown under columns 4, 10, 13 and 16 on pages 2 and 3.

Lisburn/Ballymena
All local trains between Lisburn and Ballymena will be cancelled. Stations between Lisburn and Antrim will be served by certain Londonderry trains (see Train Alterations).

TRAIN ALTERATIONS

08.00, 10.50, 14.40, 17.10 Londonderry/Central ┐ will call at all stations
11.15, 14.10, 15.55, 18.00 Central/Londonderry ┘ between Lisburn/Antrim.

14.30 Bangor/Portadown - will depart 14.45 and run correspondingly later to Central, thence 10 minutes later to Portadown.

18.00 Dublin/Central - passengers for Londonderry line must be advised to change at Lisburn.

22.05 Lisburn/Bangor - will depart 22.14 if 20.35 SP Drogheda/Central is on time. If 20.35 SP Drogheda/Central is running late, 22.05 ex Lisburn may be held at Central until 22.45.

SPECIAL TRAINS

Station		(1) SP	(2) EC	(3) EC	(4) A	(5) SP	(6) SP	(7) SP	(8) LE	(9) EC	(10) A	(11) ED
Depot	dep.	05e45	08.00	08.35		08e25		12e10	14.45	14.50		
Central	arr.	05e50	08.05	08.40		08e30		12.15	14.50	14.55		
"	dep.	06.35			09.00	09.35		12.30			15.00	23.00
Lisburn	dep.	06p46			09p11	09p49	10e08	12p41			15p11	23p12
Moira	pass	06.52			09.17	09.55	10.15	12.47			15.17	23.19
Lurgan	arr.	-			-	-	10e22	12e54			-	-
"	dep.	06p58			09p23	10p01	10.30	13.10			15p23	23p25
Portadown	arr.	07.04			09.29	10.07	10.37	13.17			15.29	23.31
"	dep.	07.05			09.30	10.08	10.38	13.18			15.30	
Poyntzpass	pass	07.17			09.42	10.20	10.50	13.30			15.42	
Meigh	"	07.33			09.58	10.36	11.06	13.46			15.58	
Dundalk	arr.	07.45			10.10	10.48	11.18	13.58			16.10	
"	dep.	07.55			10.15	10.55	11.28	14.03			16.15	
Drogheda	arr.	-			10.41	11.22	11.55	-			-	
"	dep.	08p21			10.42			14p29			16p41	
Dublin	arr.	08.58			11.18			15.05			17.15	
"	dep.	09.05						15.15				
Ashtown	arr.	09.17						-				
Ballinasloe	arr.							18.00				

No. 1 - 9 car DE (80 Class).
No. 2 - DL and 7 coaches.
Nos. 3 and 9 - DL and 5 coaches.
Nos. 4 and 10 - 2 DL and 12 coaches.   A - Enterprise
Nos. 5 and 11 - 6 car DE (80 Class)
No. 6 - 6 car DE (80 Class)
No. 7 - 6 car DE (80 Class)
No. 8 - DL

---

service from Belfast Central to Dublin was formed by two Hunslet locomotives and 12 coaches. A special service was laid on too for an expected increase in passenger numbers in the evening: this train, which left at 17.10 hrs, was formed by a Hunslet and five coaches.

On Saturday, 29 September 1979 special parties related to the Papal visit were listed as follows:

639 passengers: Belfast Central to Ashtown, 06.35 hrs special and return from Connolly

426 passengers: Belfast Central to Drogheda, 09.35 hrs special and return same day

426 passengers: Lurgan to Drogheda, 10.30 hrs special and return same day

426 passengers: Lurgan to Ballinasloe, 13.10 hrs special and return Sunday evening

To give some idea of how these specials were formed and the train alterations that had to be made accordingly, page 2 of the NIR weekly notice for the day in question is reproduced here.

On Sunday, 30 September 1979, the six-car 80 Class special with 426 passengers for Lurgan left Galway at 17.15 hrs and arrived in Lurgan at 22.10 hrs. Some smaller organised parties returned to Belfast from Dublin on Monday, 1 October.

New Rolling Stock: 1980–1983

In December 1980, six new 50-tonne capacity, vacuum-braked, bogie rail-carrying wagons were delivered to NIR. Built by CIÉ at their Inchicore works in Dublin, each wagon had been fitted with two petrol-driven crane units, enabling a total load of 50 rails to be loaded or unloaded by two men within about half an hour. The new wagons were numbered C476 to C481, and replaced NIR's existing 40-tonne bogie timber trucks, which dated from 1911.

In the same month, two new General Motors locomotives for NIR ran from Dublin to Belfast York Road via the Antrim branch. They were allocated NIR numbers 111 and 112. Similar to those which had been purchased by CIÉ and known as the 071 Class, the new locomotives had been built at the General Motors factory at La Grange, Illinois, USA. Their wheel arrangement was Co-Co and, with a weight of 99 tons, they could achieve 90 mph with their 2250 hp engines. They had been shipped from Milwaukee almost a month earlier, on 20 November 1980, bound for Dublin. On Thursday 29 January 1981, a test run was undertaken by GM No 111 with the refurbished Enterprise coaches from Belfast York Road to Antrim, and onwards to Belfast Central and return. All went smoothly on this occasion.

A naming ceremony for the new locomotives was held on the morning of Monday, 2 February 1981 at Belfast Central station, with executives from General Motors and Sir Myles Humphreys and others from NIR in attendance. Locomotive No 111 was named *Great Northern*, and No 112 was named *Northern Counties*. The special train then set off to Dublin, running double-headed to Portadown, with locomotive No 111 leading.

Unfortunately however, the day had not started off very well, with an NIR employee being struck by the new train during shunting movements at the Central Service Depot. The train ran over the employee, and he lost both legs and one arm. Very sadly, he died later in hospital.

A third General Motors locomotive was ordered in the autumn of 1983, and was delivered the following spring. The locomotive, No 113, was named *Belfast & County Down* at a special ceremony in Bangor on Tuesday, 7 August 1984; Sir Myles Humphreys and Mr John Gable from General Motors Corporation, who had travelled from Illinois, unveiled the nameplate. Locomotive No 113 would be used on the Belfast to Dublin route and for other special train movements.

Double-headed special Enterprise at Belfast Central, Monday February 1981. *(Author)*

In the spring of 1982, NIR took delivery of a dining car, which had been purchased from British Rail. The Mk 11F dining car, which was allocated Number 546, was fitted with the same catering equipment as on the BR Advanced Passenger Train, and it had originally been in service between Birmingham and Glasgow. As well as the self-service buffet, which included refrigerated display units, there was a full range of catering equipment, including an electric cooker, grills, deep fat fryer, microwave oven and two fridges. The dining car was also fully air-conditioned: the first vehicle with this feature to be introduced on NIR. It was expected that it would be available for service in June 1983, after being decorated with NIR livery and given new bogies.

Using a portion of a claim settlement paid by the Northern Ireland Office relating to criminal damage to rolling stock, NIR purchased Railbus No R3 from British Rail Engineering Limited. The Leyland Railbus had been built in 1981 by BREL at the Litchurch Lane Works in Derby. Its engine was a Leyland 690, producing 200 hp, capable of a maximum speed of 75 mph. Weighing 19 tons, it had a seating capacity of 56. There were driving cabs at each end; also at each end was an air-operated, folding bus-type door.

The Railbus, which had previously operated in the Bristol area, had to be converted to the NIR gauge, as the plan was to use it on certain off-peak services. On Friday, 30 July 1982, the Railbus was taken on a test run from Belfast York Road to Bangor, via the Antrim branch. This was also used as an opportunity for a gauging run.

The new acquisition was used on a Ministerial visit on 15 September 1983, when Mr Richard Needham and Mr Chris Patten, along with NIR senior staff, travelled from Belfast York Road to the Monkstown area to see a tamping and lining machine in operation. The next stop was at Crumlin, where lignite deposits had been found. A site for possible new sidings was viewed, which could be provided if the mining company undertook bulk transportation of lignite by rail. The visiting party then viewed the jointly owned (NIR and CIÉ) ballast cleaner at Lisburn station, before returning to Belfast Central.

Railbus on an Irish Railway Record Society special, passing Seahill on Sunday, 8 August 1982. *(Author)*

Railbus No R3 had been one of three manufactured as prototypes, and it was used as a demonstrator on many railway systems before being sold to NIR. Another of these three prototype Railbuses was sent for evaluation to the Old Colony & Newport Railroad in the USA, where it operated on a leisure and suburban route on Rhode Island from July 1984.

NIR intended to use Railbus No R3 mainly on the Portrush branch, but it would also be used on weekend services on the Bangor, Ballymena and Larne lines. Unfortunately however, after a number of trial runs, it became clear that the Railbus could not be relied on to work track circuits within the signalling system, due to the fact that it was a single vehicle and quite light. On one occasion, when it had run into the loop at Crumlin, it had simply disappeared off the signal panel. Given these considerations, it was decided that the Railbus would operate mainly on the Portrush branch, as there were no signalling issues there; however, due to the number of students travelling to the University, on many occasions the use of the Railbus was restricted to off-peak times only.

On 22 May, 1985, Hunslet No 103 and two NIR Enterprise carriages ran from Belfast York Road to Dublin, to pick up two new Irish Rail Mk III carriages. The train then ran back to Belfast, with the two IÉ carriages Nos 7130 and 7602 attached to NIR carriage No 813. The train was gauged from Newry to Belfast Central and returned to Dublin later in the day.

More New Rolling Stock: the 450 Class Train Arrives

NIR's first new 450 Class train was available for test runs from 9 September 1985. The sets had been built by BREL at York Works and Derby Litchurch Lane Works. Most of the components were re-cycled from other items of rolling stock. The undercarriage was from old BR Mk 1 coaches, the engine units and wheels were taken from the NIR 70 Class units and refurbished, while the power unit for set No 457 was salvaged from an 80 Class motor coach No 88. The only new parts were the British Rail Mk III bodyshells and the interiors.

Three sets had originally been ordered in the autumn of 1983, but further negotiations had brought another order for six more sets in May 1984. The engine was English Electric producing 550 hp, and the motor coach weighed 62 tons. (The weight of all trains purchased by NIR up until the 1990s was recorded in imperial tons). As the engine took up half of the coach there, were only 38 passenger seats, as well as 13 tip-up seats if required. The intermediate trailer, weighing 30.4 tons, had 78 seats with 15 tip-up seats. The driving trailer had 68 seats with 15 tip-up seats, and weighed 32.4 tons. The exterior colour scheme was light cream and carnation red.

The trains were all to be named after castles, as had been the tradition on the Northern Counties Railway when naming locomotives. The 450 class of train was also

First 450 Class train at Belfast York Road, Nos 451, 791, 781, 9 September 1985. *(Author)*

known soon after as "the Castle Class" set. The numbering sequence was taken from similar trains on British Rail, the motor coach numbers and names allocated were as follows: 451, *Belfast Castle*; 452, *Olderfleet Castle*; 453, *Moiry Castle*; 454, *Carrickfergus Castle*; 455, *Galgorm Castle*; 456, *Gosford Castle*; 457, *Bangor Castle*; 458, *Antrim Castle*; 459, *Killyleagh Castle*.

The official launch for the new trains was held on Monday 28 October

1985 at Belfast York Road station, when two new trains, *Belfast Castle* and *Olderfleet Castle* were introduced. Around 150 guests, including Sir Myles Humphreys, the Deputy Lord Mayor of Belfast and the Chairman and Managing Director of British Rail Engineering Ltd (BREL), watched as the Secretary of State for Northern Ireland, Tom King, drove off in the first new train, the *Belfast Castle*. This was the first train of the £6 million Rolling Stock Development Programme which had been announced by Government in May 1984.

The last Castle Class set, No 459, arrived in Belfast in 1987, and had its official launch at Portadown station on Wednesday, 8 July 1987. *Killyleagh Castle* was duly christened by the Rt Hon The Lord Grey of Naunton in the presence of NIR's Chairman, Sir Myles Humphreys.

More Special Trains

As in previous years, on Wednesday, 13 July 1983, special trains from Lurgan to Bangor ran for the Lurgan and area Royal Black Preceptory. These trains were formed by a nine-car 80 Class set, and an eight-car 80 Class set. Tragedy struck however on the return journey, when a boy fell out of the first special at Crawfordsburn and died. Due to fact that the two trains were carrying 1,200 passengers in all, and that the security forces were waiting for the parade in Lurgan, the delay due to the accident had to be kept to a minimum, to allow the trains to proceed as quickly as possible.

An international scout jamboree took place at the National Forest Park at Portumna, County Galway, from 30 July to 8 August 1985. Up to 10,000 scouts took part in the event. On Tuesday 30 July, a special three-car 80 Class train left Bangor at 06.45 hrs and attached to a further nine-car 80 Class set in Belfast Central. The 12-car set with 822 scouts on board left Belfast at 07.15 hrs and arrived at Ballinasloe at 12.35 hrs. Meanwhile, 100 scouts travelled from the Londonderry line and boarded an Enterprise service, to join one of the many specials from Dublin. The special parties arrived back in Northern Ireland on Friday, 9 August.

On the morning of 9 September 1985, a special train of an unusual kind arrived at Belfast Central: the station's first freight train! The arrival was unscheduled of course, as this was the 07.25 hrs freight service from Dundalk to Belfast Adelaide, made up of AR 015 and nine cement wagons. The points on the down main line at Adelaide, which were there to allow the train into the yard, had failed, and so the train had been sent on to Belfast Central, where it arrived at Platform One. The locomotive ran round the wagons and returned to Adelaide later that morning.

October 1985: A Special Farewell Run for the 70 Class

To mark the end of an era and say farewell to the 70 Class, the Railway Preservation Society of Ireland organised a special run on Saturday, 12 October 1985. The train for the occasion was formed by a three-car 70 Class, motor coach No 75, trailer No 728 and motor coach No 77.

The aim of the special event, non-stop run on the day – to travel from Belfast York Road to Londonderry within 100 minutes – was geared to match the fastest overall timing scheduled for the route in the 1959 Summer Timetable. This schedule

Special farewell to 70 Class: Belfast York Road, Saturday, 12 October 1985. *(Author)*

remained in operation until the end of the summer of 1966. For most of the seven years of this non-stop service, the train was operated by an MPD set, but for the last few weeks of the 1966 Summer Timetable, the then new 70 Class sets had appeared on the run with power cars Nos 71 and 72.

The special 70 Class train left Belfast York Road at exactly 10.44 hrs and arrived in Londonderry at 12.08 hrs – a time of 84 minutes and 8 seconds! The train departed again from the old station in Londonderry at 12.40 hrs and ran back to Belfast Central at a more leisurely pace, stopping at some stations along the way and arriving at a few seconds before 16.19 hrs. It had been a great send-off – although there were however the following week, a few complaints murmured by NIR management about the alleged speed of the train!

On Easter Tuesday, 1 April 1986, a 70 Class was used to operate a special train from Larne Town to Belfast York Road which was commissioned to carry supporters of a loyal order demonstration in Larne. Although trouble had already started at Larne, the supporters were put on the train and sent on their way without police escort. The train had only got as far as Magheramorne Loop, when it was forced to stop because groups fighting on board and wrecking the interior. Police had to come from Larne to intervene and remove many of the youths on board. Unfortunately the coaches sustained quite a bit of damage.

As with the MED coaches, because of problems with asbestos, most of the 70 Class coaches ended up being moved to Crumlin and dumped into the quarry. Two 70 Class coaches which did not have asbestos in their make-up eventually ended up on the Downpatrick & Ardglass preserved railway. Coach Nos 713 and 728 were transported from Adelaide freight yard to Downpatrick in September 1991.

1986: NIR Metropolitan-Vickers Locomotives

Six spare CIÉ Metropolitan-Vickers locomotives arrived in stages onto the scene in NIR. Two of them were noted at Belfast York Road on 2 January 1986; newly painted No 109 was seen at York Road later that year, on 7 May. The NIR designation for the locomotives was 104 Class, and they were to be used on ballast and shunting trains. They had been introduced into CIÉ between 1956 and 1957, and there had been 34 locomotives in the full fleet. They weighed 61.5 tons, and the original engine was a Crossley at 550 hp, to be replaced in the mid-1970s by a General Motors engine of 1100 hp.

Special Trains to Bangor: 1986 and 1987

Monday, 14 July 1986 saw the traditional Lurgan to Bangor specials run for the loyal orders. This year the specials were formed by a GM Locomotive and eleven Enterprise coaches, as well as an eight-car 80 Class but with a strange formation – two three-car sets with two spare driving trailers in the middle of the train.

1987 saw further interesting trains run for the loyal orders. On Monday, 13 July, an eleven-car 80 Class was chartered from Bangor to Holywood and back. On Tuesday, 14 July, two specials ran from Lurgan to Bangor. One was GM locomotive, No 113 hauling nine coaches; the other was a first-time run – a nine-car 450 Castle Class set.

Most of the trains mentioned above were managed locally, as they were too long for some platforms on the network but that did not deter railway operations from running them. I don't recall anyone falling from the long trains at platforms, but due to revised health and safety measures, we in Northern Ireland will probably not see the like of any of these long trains again.

Cable Plough Train

In November and December 1987 the Irish Rail cable plough train made several visits to the Belfast to Bangor line. The train was hauled by GM locomotive No 111 on the first run, and GM locomotive No 112 on the second run.

1988: Enterprise to Dun Laoghaire

From 16 May 1988, a new through service operated from Belfast. The 17.00 hrs service from Belfast Central was extended to Dun Laoghaire, in order to connect with the 20.45 hrs Sealink Ferry to Holyhead. The evening service was scheduled to depart at 19.55 hrs and arrive in Belfast Central at 22.40 hrs, to connect with the 14.45 hrs Stena Sailing. The 08.00 hrs service from Dublin to Belfast started back from Dun Laoghaire to give a connection with the 03.15 hrs Stena Ferry from Holyhead.

These new services provided a convenient service for travellers from Northern Ireland to the Midlands and London with the minimum of changes of train, and the overall journey times were quicker than the Stranraer route.

Autumn 1988: 80 Class Refurbishment

Wednesday, 7 September 1988 saw the first of the fully refurbished InterCity 80 Class railcar sets being officially launched into service on the Londonderry line. Power car No 96 was officially named *Glenshane* at a ceremony in Londonderry station. This three-car set had been completely refitted, with new two plus two seats, and tables with new interior panelling. Driving trailer No 754 had been converted from former Hunslet coach No 811, and had a large van for parcels and mail. The new Inter City livery colours were silver grey and Prussian blue. The same treatment would be applied to six Inter City sets, Nos 94 to 99. Trolley catering services had also been introduced on the line.

Cultra Siding Special Train

The first passenger train use of the new siding at the Transport Museum at Cultra took

First passenger train to use Cultra siding temporary platform, Wednesday, 9 August 1989. *(Author)*

place on 9 August 1989. The 11.05 hrs service from Londonderry stopped on the down main line near Craigavad and reversed into the siding to a temporary one-coach platform built of scaffolding and timber planks. The train was 80 Class No 96 and two trailers, and the temporary platform was on the down side of the train.

More Special Trains

On 10 September 1989, the RPSI organised a special train to run from Belfast Central to Bangor they called "The Bangor Belle". The three wooden-bodied carriages were supposed to be hauled by a DH locomotive for a last run, as the locomotives had been declared surplus. Unfortunately the DH locomotive had broken down earlier, but it would be replaced by a surprise locomotive, Metro-Vic No 104.

April 1990 saw two other special trains of interest run. On Saturday, 7 April the Southern Rail Tours organisation chartered a 12-coach Inter City train, hauled by NIR GM No 111, from Belfast Central to Westport and back. The outward journey was made via Dublin, Mullingar, Athenry and Tuam, whilst the return trip was via Roscommon. Every one of the 586 seats had been booked.

Two weeks later, the Irish Traction Group chartered a train to run from Bray to Londonderry and back to Dublin. The train was hauled from Coleraine to Londonderry and back to Belfast Central by Hunslet No 101 *Eagle*. The tour was referred to as "The Hunslet Farewell". The run from Belfast Central to Dublin was scheduled for the 17.00 hrs Enterprise, but the 12-coach train was hauled as far as Dundalk by two NIR GM locomotives, Nos 111 and 113.

Special trains were still very much the order of the day in 1991. On Friday, 12 July, a special formed by an eleven-car 80 Class, ran from Bangor to Holywood at 11.30 hrs. Saturday, 13 July brought the usual two specials into Bangor from Lurgan: a nine-car 450 Castle Class, followed by GM locomotive No 112 and eleven Enterprise-type coaches. The following year however, the Lurgan specials did not run, due to a bomb incident and its aftermath in the Belfast Central area over two days. The loyal order passengers travelled by alternative bus arrangements instead.

1993: The Transport Museum Moves

Until 1993, the Transport Museum for Northern Ireland had been tucked into a small side street in East Belfast. The old shed had a bit of character, but it was quite difficult to see the large exhibits properly due to the confined space. A much anticipated change of venue for the Museum was to finally happen in 1993, and so I paid my last visit to the Witham Street premises on Thursday, 31 December 1992, knowing that it would be closing its doors for the last time a few days later, on Saturday, 2 January 1993.

I can well recall the various proposals put forward at the time on how best to move the railway rolling stock from Belfast Witham Street to the Museum's new site at Cultra. One idea was that the large items of stock could be transported by road using low loaders, but this plan was soon scrapped because of the weight restrictions on the over bridge which led from the car park area of the new gallery site to the sea facing side of the railway. It was agreed however that, depending on their weight, smaller items could be brought by road. A second suggestion was that the large items of stock should be moved by rail from Adelaide freight yard to Cultra. This proposal was approved.

On Friday, 5 February 1993, heavy hauliers, GCS Johnson started moving the rolling stock from Witham Street to Adelaide. This process began after the evening rush hour, and the first locomotives to move were B&CDR No 30 and LMS NCC No 74 *Dunluce Castle*.

The heaviest lift was locomotive No 800 *Maeve*, which was moved on Monday, 8 February and carried on a low loader with 40 wheels. LP & HC locomotive No 1 was also moved that day.

The first special train run from Adelaide freight yard to the siding at Cultra took place on the morning of Sunday, 14 February. I was there, along with a small team of other volunteers to assist where possible: we had the tricky task of keeping hundreds of onlookers off the track at Holywood. The leading locomotive was GM No 111, and the trailing brake locomotive was Hunslet No 101, with two steam locomotives and a carriage in between.

Locomotive No 800, *Maeve*, being prepared for the move to Cultra, Monday, 8 February 1993. *(Author)*

The second special train running from Adelaide to Cultra that day was shunted at Belfast Central for positioning purposes in the afternoon. The formation at Cultra was Hunslet No 101, No 74 *Dunluce Castle*, No 800 *Maeve* and GM No 111, which was this time being used as the brake due to the weight of the steam locomotives. Meanwhile, our job controlling the crowds wasn't getting any easier, and, due to the number of onlookers at Holywood as well as quite a few trespassers, I arranged for the 14.30 hrs service from Bangor to Belfast to be held at Marino for 15 minutes. The Hunslet was used to shunt each locomotive into the new Museum shed separately.

The following Sunday, 21 February, the special train was not as glamorous, I suppose, and did not attract the same number of onlookers. It was hauled by Hunslet No 101, and the museum stock was the LP & HC locomotive No 1, Royal passenger saloon No 47 and three four-wheeled vans. The GNR Railbus No 2, which had been completely rebuilt and brought back to life, also ran that day as a special passenger service, from Poyntzpass to Cultra. Gleaming with its new blue and cream paintwork, the Railbus was full of passengers who must have felt it a great honour to travel on such a train and for such a distance on the main line. Sadly however, this Railbus only ran the one trip that day, after which is was consigned to the museum – if there was the will, it could still be used today to run specials on the Bangor line on Sundays…

On Thursday, 30 September 1993, the new Transport Museum held a special Railway Gallery Launch opening evening for specially invited guests, among whom were a number of NIR staff, including me. The Railway Gallery opened for public viewing the next day.

A New Track Maintenance Machine and Farewell to the DH Locomotives

At Belfast York Road on Monday, 14 February 1994, delivery was taken of a new machine capable of carrying out the functions of tamping, lining, lifting and levelling of the track. The new 08 series machine replaced the 07 series machine, and had the capacity to tamp switch and crossing work, which would be a new facility for NIR. As soon as the NIR operators and technical staff were trained, the £700,000 machine could be put to work.

In September 1994, it was time for NIR to say farewell to the three diesel hydraulic locomotives which had been part of the company's stock since 1969. During their time in service, the Hunslet-built English Electric units had been used for permanent way trains and shunting. Their maximum speed was supposedly 40 mph, but during my time in NIR, I was told that they generally only managed 23 mph with a 620 hp turbo-charged 12-cylinder engine. They weighed in at 44 tons and the wheel arrangement was a C (a six-wheel set containing three axles).

Goodbye to the Diesel Hydraulic Locomotives at Lisburn, Sunday, 11 September 1994. *(Author)*

On Sunday, 11 September that year, the three DH locomotives, Nos 1, 2 and 3 made their farewell appearance. Locomotives Nos 2 and 3 had previously been stored at Larne Harbour for a period of time, awaiting their fate, but now a two-car 80 Class set No 67 hauled them from Belfast York Road to Antrim, and then on to Lisburn. The locomotives were secured at Platform Two, while the 80 Class went into the Lisburn yard to pick up DH No 1. Finally, the 80 Class and DH No 1 returned to attach to the two other locomotives. The train proceeded to Adelaide freight yard, where the three DH locomotives would be attached to a southbound freight train at a later date. They were to be passed on to the Irish Traction Group – a railway enthusiast group still operating to this day, which is based in Carrick-on-Suir, on the Limerick Junction to Waterford line.

Spring 1995: First Visit to NIR of 201 Class

On Tuesday, 7 March 1995, the 201 Class locomotive, No 201, from Irish Rail, arrived in Belfast Central. The first locomotive of its kind to visit Northern Ireland, No 201 was in Belfast for a gauging run. The previous spring NIR had ordered, from General Motors in the USA, two 201 Class trains at a cost of £3.5 million. The first of the order, No 209, arrived from Dublin on 21 April 1995. The NIR livery at that stage was an overall blue with a large NIR logo on each side of the vehicles. Although the new carriages for the cross-border route were not due to be delivered for some time, the new 201 Class locomotives in the meantime took up the running of Enterprise services, in the summer of 1995.

A Royal Train for a Royal Visit

For the first time in NIR's history, a Royal Train was to be organised for a Royal visit to Northern Ireland in March 1995, which would commemorate the opening of the new Cross-Harbour Link road and rail bridges. Due to the very strict security surrounding such a visit, only certain information was given at specific times to chosen individuals. Given my involvement in security matters within NIR, I had a role in a number of clearance operations with the security forces relating to the Royal visit.

One of the oddest things I remember during these procedures happened on the day in question, when I was standing at Lagan Junction awaiting further information from security forces. All at once, I noticed a group of about six men coming towards me on the new route from Queen's Quay Junction. At first, I thought they were a permanent way squad, as all were kitted out in high-visibility gear. It was only however when they were a few hundred yards away from me that I realised they weren't permanent way men after all, as I could see that they were carrying rifles slung over their shoulders! Only then did I know they were the Army patrol which I was waiting to meet there, so that I could escort them through some of the search areas.

On the day of the visit, Thursday, 9 March, Her Majesty the Queen and His Royal Highness the Duke of Edinburgh travelled, along with other dignitaries, on the Royal Train from the Dargan Viaduct – the new bridge across the River Lagan – to Belfast Central station. While on board the train, in coach No 785, the Queen and Duke of Edinburgh signed Visitors' Books for NIR and Graham/Farrans. The Chairman of NIR, Bill Smyth then presented the Royal guests with Gold Medallion Rail Passes, while DoE Permanent Secretary, Ronnie Spence presented them with leather-bound booklets detailing the entire Cross-Harbour Bridge project. At 11.30 hrs (5

Royal Train approaching Belfast Central, 9 March 1995. *(Author)*

PROGRAMME FOR
ROYAL TRAIN

Conveying
Her Majesty
Queen Elizabeth II
and
His Royal Highness
The Duke Of Edinburgh

From DONEGALL QUAY to BELFAST CENTRAL
on
Thursday , 9th March 1995

The programme for the Royal Train, Thursday, 9 March 1995. *(Author)*

minutes ahead of schedule), the train left the Dargan Bridge and arrived in to Platform One in Belfast Central; the Royal party however detrained on the opposite side, where a special platform had been built for the purpose on top of the beach siding. The flag pole at Belfast Central was also used for the first time at this juncture, after which the special party were introduced to Government Ministers, including the MP for the area, Reverend Martin Smyth, the Chairman of NIR, Bill Smyth, the train crew and other members of NIR staff and their families.

The Royal Train was formed by a four-car Castle Class, Nos 459, 789, 785 and 455. There had been some controversy from certain political parties over the issue of the refurbishment work which had to be carried out to the train, and the associated expenditure. However, it was money spent which would benefit all passengers in the long-term, since after the Royal visit, the train would, from the following day, be put back into use for ordinary services.

New Cross-Border Service from Newry

In mid-May 1995, a new train service from Newry to Dublin began operating, with the aim of allowing Northern commuters to be in Dublin before 09.00 hours. This new Irish Rail service had a departure time from Newry of 07.00 hrs, with the service due to arrive in Dublin Connolly at 08.59 hrs. The corresponding return service would depart Dublin at 17.19 hrs, to arrive in Newry at 19.03 hrs. On the first morning the new service was in operation, the train was seen off at Newry by the Chairman and Vice Chairman of Newry and Mourne Council, along with a senior manager from NIR.

Autumn 1996: New Enterprise Rolling Stock Arrives

In the summer of 1994, NIR had signed a £14 million order with the French rail rolling stock company, De Dietrich for the construction of 14 main-line express coaches for the Belfast to Dublin line. The contract formed part of an £88 million EU-funded Cross-Border high speed rail project. Accordingly Irish Rail had signed a similar contract with the French company.

The coaches were to be produced on the jigs that were used for the construction of Eurostar trains, which could be easily adapted for the NIR/IÉ coaches; manufacture of the Irish order followed on from a production run of Eurostar coaches. The new coaches would be 23 metres long and, although the bodyshells were a similar shape to those of the Eurostars, the interiors would be much more like those of a TGV coach.

Wednesday, 25 September 1996 saw the arrival in Northern Ireland of the first of the new rolling stock for the Enterprise service. The De Dietrich rolling stock was run from Dublin Connolly to Belfast Central and on through to the depot at York

Road, and this journey also served as a gauging run. The train was formed by GM locomotive No 206 and seven of the new carriages. NIR executives and staff were able to view the interior of the new coaches that day too. The train returned to Dublin later in the day.

As a new train came into service, an old model was on its way out. In September 1997, former CIÉ Metropolitan-Vickers locomotive, which had been renumbered NIR No 106, left Fortwilliam sidings in Belfast and travelled by road the whole way to Cahersiveen to form a part of a permanent exhibition, as the last train of its kind to have been operational on this line in Ireland. For display purposes, the locomotive was repainted in its earlier silver colour and given back its original number, C 202.

Ten Years of the Modern Railway Society of Ireland

To mark the tenth anniversary of the Modern Railway Society of Ireland, a special train was chartered for a long-distance run on Saturday, 24 May 1997. The train was formed by GM locomotive, No 111 with six Mk II coaches, and was named "the South-West Enterprise" for the occasion.

The South-West Enterprise train was due to leave Belfast Central at 06.35 hrs that morning, but didn't arrive into Belfast from York Road yard until 06.53 hrs. There was a quick loading of passengers on board – I was one of them – and we were away again at 06.56 hrs. With one stop in Dundalk to allow the up Enterprise through, we arrived in Dublin Connolly at 09.35 hrs (33 minutes late). With no time made up in the interim, it was decided that a couple of station stops should be cancelled, and so, apart from a change of crew at Inchicore, there was a non-stop run to Cork. Our arrival time there was just after 12.25 hrs (precisely 9.5 minutes early). After a short break, the train was on its way to Cobh, then to Tralee and back to Belfast Central, where we finally arrived at 23.52 hrs (2.5 minutes early, to be exact). Working out at a distance of 704.5 miles for the round trip, it had certainly been a long run, and a great day out!

Special Trains, 1998–1999: Various

On Saturday, 13 June 1998, the MRSI had chartered a special train for another long-distance run, this time of 597 miles. The train was formed by GM locomotive, No 113 and nine Mk II coaches, Nos 912, 927, 924, 933, 926, 546, 901, 903 and 915. The "Shannon Crystal Railtour" would celebrate 150 years of railway services – 1848 to 1998 – at Limerick Junction, Tipperary, Thomastown and Bagenalstown.

On the day in question, the train left Belfast Central at 06.22 hrs (2 minutes late), and ran to Dublin Connolly, with a stop at Drogheda to allow the up Enterprise through. Although only 5 minutes late into Dublin Connolly, the train left again for Athenry with a delay of 16 minutes, at 09.46 hrs. Part of the treat for us railway enthusiasts was to run down the freight-only line from Athenry to Ennis. To secure the necessary permission from Irish Rail for our train to run there, we had to agree to a provision of two additional coaches on our train, since the special would be acting as the 13.50 hrs service train from Ennis to Limerick for Irish Rail. I can still remember standing on the platform at Ennis that day, and seeing two ladies coming along to ask the Irish Rail member of staff, "Where is this train going to?" to which he replied, "Belfast". The two ladies looked puzzled: they were only going to Limerick and didn't know that a train could run from Ennis as far as Belfast!

From Limerick, our special train ran through to Carrick-on-Suir, for a stop to allow the enthusiasts to see the three NIR DH locomotives, Nos 1, 2 and 3, as well as to photograph CIÉ locomotive, No B103. The special then headed to Waterford and after that, back to Dublin via Carlow. On our return journey, although we left Dublin 28 minutes late, at 21.08 hrs, we managed to arrive in Belfast at 23.22 hrs, with a delay of seven minutes. Another very enjoyable outing on the railway!

Another chartered train for the MRSI was operated on Saturday, 19 September 1998. On this occasion however, an NIR GM locomotive was not available, as all three of them had failed. The tour name for our train was the "Beet 'n' Boat Route Railtour": "beet" referred to the sugar beet special trains that ran around the south west of Ireland (including on the line from Rosslare to Limerick Junction and on to Mallow, which was part of our route that day too); "boat" referred to the part of our route which ran to Rosslare Harbour, from which ferries to Wales and France can be taken.

Our special train left Belfast Central at 06.24 hrs (4 minutes late), with IÉ GM locomotive, No 071 taking charge of the seven coaches on the tour: Nos 912, 901, 903, 546, 926, 920 and 915. We headed to Dublin Connolly, again with a stop at Drogheda to allow the up Enterprise through. A change of locomotive was made at Dublin, with IÉ GM locomotive, No 072 taking over the run. The special then transferred over onto the Cork main line, ran to Limerick Junction and then onwards to Waterford and Rosslare Europort. From there, the train ran back to Belfast Central, arriving at 23.28 hrs (2 minutes early). Another enjoyable tour, this time with a total distance of 534.5 miles.

New Year 1999 started well for railway buffs, with a different type of Railtour to enjoy, as the MRSI operated a special "Four Loughs Railtour" on Saturday, 2 January. The train was formed by GM locomotive, No 112 and five Mk II coaches.

The journey commenced officially from Yorkgate at 07.04 hrs, running to Belfast Central. The first run of the day left at 07.25 hrs (4 minutes late) for Larne Harbour, and it was back to Belfast again at 09.03 hrs. For the next trip, the special was off to Londonderry via the Antrim branch, arriving at 13.02 hrs (2 minutes late). A bus was organised to take us to Buncrana, on the trail of the closed and lifted Londonderry and Lough Swilly Railway, after which it was back to Londonderry. We then joined the Foyle Valley Railway two-car Railbus, which ran for two miles and then had to stop, as a tree had fallen across the track. Undeterred, we walked the last third of a mile to the end of the line. To end the day, we took the special train which left Londonderry at 16.40 hrs for Belfast Central via the Antrim branch; we arrived just after 19.14 hrs (exactly 5.5 minutes early).

A Big Anniversary for Dundalk Railway

1999 was an important year for Dundalk in railway terms, since it had been 150 years since the opening of the Dublin to Dundalk route, on 15 February 1849. To mark

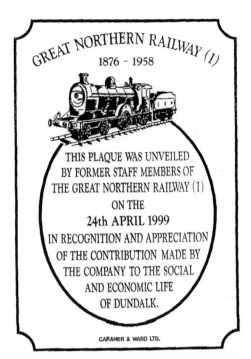

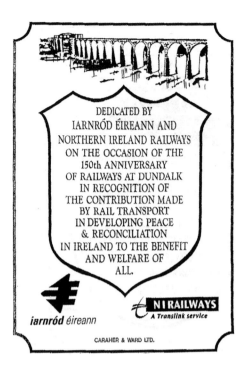

Copies of the plaques unveiled at Dundalk for the 150th Anniversary of Dundalk Railways, 24 April 1999. *(Author's collection)*

the anniversary, special events were to be held at the main station on Saturday, 24 April 1999. RPSI Locomotive No 85 and six Craven carriages ran that morning from Belfast Central to Dundalk, arriving at 12.10 hrs, while RPSI locomotive No 171 and six Craven carriages ran from Dublin, also arriving in Dundalk at 12.10 hrs.

Shortly after this, commemorative plaques were unveiled at the station and at 13.05 hrs, locomotive No 171 and carriages departed to Poyntzpass, while locomotive No 85 and carriages left for Drogheda. The two trains returned to Dundalk by mid-afternoon. In their absence, special events continued at Dundalk station, and invited guests were taken to a Reception at Derryhale. Finally, at 16.30 hrs, the steam trains left Dundalk for the return journeys to Belfast and Dublin.

A Few More Specials

On 26th May 1999, an empty diesel set ventured onto the Bleach Green to Antrim line, which had just opened for 10 mph running exactly a week earlier. It was the first vehicle to run on the line in 18 months, other than an empty set, which had travelled out as far as Kilmakee No 1 level crossing on 28 February 1999 for an emergency plan exercise. The 80 Class set No 81 ran from Great Victoria Street to Antrim and then on to Belfast York Road for 09.24 hrs. However, the line closed again on 30 August that year, awaiting the start of the track relaying process, which would commence on 29 November 1999.

A GM locomotive had run a couple of local train services on the Bangor line for a period of time in 1999, and the last journeys for the GM and seven Mk II coaches would be in June that year. These passenger trains on 11 June were the 08.12 hrs express from Bangor to Belfast Central, and the 17.15 hrs express service from Belfast Central to Bangor.

There was another special run organised by the MRSI on Saturday, 29 December 2001. Featuring a four-car 80 Class (with motor coaches Nos 96 and 89), the tour was named "The David Boyd Memorial Railtour", after a young former member of the Society. The train left Belfast Central at 08.56 hrs and ran to Portadown, then on to Lisburn, down the Antrim branch and to Castlerock, where it arrived at 11.43 hrs (20 minutes late). Due to the delay in arriving, we had lost our path by that stage, and had to sit for 72 minutes before running back to Ballymoney (we didn't make it into Londonderry, as had been originally planned). In Ballymoney, we sat for another 104 minutes before heading to Portrush, and even then, the train had to cover scheduled branch trips. We left Portrush at 15.48 hrs, and ran back to Belfast Central at 17.16 hrs (36 minutes early). The weather was pretty poor that day, with intermittent snow blizzards, and I was convinced that more could have been done by NIR to allow the special to run into Londonderry.

Rolling Stock Disposal and Repairs

On 31 January 2000, approval was given for the disposal of Mk II coaches, Nos 547, 913, 916, 917, 922 and 928. These coaches had been stored in Bangor and at Larne Harbour. Meanwhile, in March 2000, two 80 Class coaches, Nos 780 and 752, were sent to a train repair company in Kilmarnock for major anti-corrosion body work. The total repair bill would come to £300k, and the coaches were not due back in Belfast until August 2000. The revamp was intended to extend the working life of the coaches by three years, by which time, it was hoped, new trains would be in place.

RPSI steam locomotive No 3 arrived at Muckamore by low loader lorry on 18 June 2000. The RPSI had been contracted to haul ballast wagons between Antrim and Bleach Green Junction, and the steam locomotive was used for this purpose until 25 November 2000, when it was removed from the track at Antrim stone dock. NIR could have quoted for the job themselves and made the company a bit of income, but it seems that they weren't willing to release one of their locomotives for this contracted work, and so they just let the RPSI get on with it.

On 6 August 2001, the local GM locomotive set with six Mk II coaches made its last scheduled run, going out as the 05.40 hrs empty from Belfast York Road to Portadown, and returning as the 07.55 hrs passenger service from Portadown to Belfast Great Victoria Street.

Between September and December 2001, eight Mk IIF ex-Gatwick Express carriages arrived at Belfast York Road. Due to be back in service by the end of December 2001, these coaches had been refurbished and re-liveried by Rail Care Ltd of Glasgow. NIR workshops would be reworking the NIR generator vans to render them compatible with the new coaches, so as to provide heat and light. The new coaches would be finally introduced into service in early March 2002, after rigorous technical testing processes were satisfactorily completed. The coaches operated on the Portadown to Belfast line, as well as providing back-up for the Enterprise service.

On 13 November 2001, Hunslet locomotive, No 102, was restarted at York Road depot: the idea was to use it for shunting in Adelaide yard. This would be the first time it had been started since its failure in March 1999. After some further time in service in Adelaide Yard, No 102 was eventually hauled to Whitehead RPSI siding on 28 March 2004, so that it could be preserved for posterity.

A Move for Railbus No 3

On Sunday, 1 October 2000, a well-planned operation took place with the aim of moving Railbus No 3 from the Transport Museum Gallery to Adelaide freight yard, as it was eventually to be rehoused at Downpatrick Railway Museum. For all those involved, including myself, an early start was required, since the down main Bangor line would be blocked until the operation was completed.

It was great to watch the proceedings unfold. GM locomotive No 112 was first on the scene to pull out locomotive No 74 *Dunluce Castle*. In the meantime, a two-car 80 Class set was brought past Cultra platform and was used as a brake for No 74, which was then placed onto it by GM No 112. The GM went back into the Museum Gallery and brought out the GNR Railbus, so that it was parked a few feet away from No 74. It didn't take too long for the NIR engineers to release the brakes of RB3 and off she went, hauled by GM No 112. This train was taken to Adelaide via Bangor; meanwhile the Bangor line was returned to normal working by 10.30 hrs. Eventually, on 31 March 2001, RB3 would be taken by road from Adelaide to the Downpatrick Museum.

Rolling Stock Movements, 2002–2005

On 13 January 2002, a GM locomotive and two Mk IIF ex-Gatwick Express carriages did a clearance run between Belfast and Carrickfergus, and then to Newry. On 17 February 2002, IÉ GM locomotive No 150 and Gatwick carriages, Nos 8911, 8944, 8943, 8946, and 8947, ran a test run from Belfast to Dublin Connolly and back. (Incidentally, written clearance would only be issued by IÉ on 7 February the following year – 53 weeks later – by way of an entry in the IÉ Weekly Circular, No 3023!) A week later, on 24 February 2002, a GM locomotive and two Mk IIF Gatwick carriages did a clearance run via the Antrim Branch, from Belfast to Londonderry and Portrush, and back.

The first passenger run for the Gatwick carriages was on 10 June 2002, when the train formed the 17.14 hrs service Belfast Great Victoria Street to Newry, as well as 18.30 hrs return service. The train was formed by GM No 112 and carriages Nos 8911, 8943, 8944, 8945, 8948, 8947 and 8946.

On Sunday, 16 June 2002, there was a first-time run by 201 Class GM locomotive No 207 on the Bangor line, which was also used as a gauging exercise. The GM was hauling engineering flat wagons, and ran round the wagons in Bangor.

One of only two remaining 70 Class coaches was destroyed by fire in an arson attack at Downpatrick railway station at 03.00 hrs on Boxing Day 2002. No 713 had been originally built in 1924 for the LMS NCC. The station was also damaged in the attack.

Gatwick coaches had their first passenger run to Dublin on 12 February 2003, but the trip was not a success, due to a failure of the Enterprise set. The train, formed by GM 113 and seven Gatwick coaches, ran the 14.10 hrs Enterprise Belfast to Dublin service, departing at 14.47 hrs. The return 16.50 hrs Enterprise Dublin to Belfast, formed by GM 209 and seven Gatwick coaches, did not depart until 17.15 hrs and ended up failing at Newry. Passengers were transferred to a local set for the rest of the journey to Belfast. They should have just let GM 113 operate the Enterprise back to Belfast! Instead, it was returned to Belfast hauling a freight train the following day.

On 30 March 2003, the full set of nine Gatwick coaches was used for the first time on the 08.45 hrs rugby special from Belfast Central to Dublin, returning at 17.40 hrs from Dublin to Belfast. The second generator van was not ready for service by this date, so passengers that day likely had a bit of a chilly journey to and from the match!

Some ten days later, the Gatwick coaches made a gauging run to Bangor, with IÉ GM locomotive No 186 and two additional coaches. This was followed, on 10 April, by GM No 111 and seven coaches. I just happened to be at Belfast Central at the time, and was able to have a run on this 14.22 hrs empty special. We travelled at full speed, clocking up a memorable seven minutes from Belfast Central until passing Seahill. The train returned to Belfast at 15.00 hrs.

A special train ran on 12 April 2003 for the IRRS, travelling from Dublin to Belfast Central, to Antrim via Bleach Green, to Lisburn via the Branch, then to Bangor and finally back to Dublin. The special was operated on different sections of the route between GM No 111 and No 113 with seven coaches.

In preparation for an RPSI special train service on 17 April 2004, a further gauging train ran on the Bangor line on 14 April, formed by GM No 111 and four Cravens.

A week after the RPSI event, the IRRS had planned a day trip with the Gatwick coaches. On Saturday 24 April 2004, however, the carriage set which was due to go to Dublin to pick up the special party, failed in Belfast York Road at 05.30 hrs. So the IRRS party had to travel instead on the 09.35 hrs Enterprise from Dublin to Belfast, and then transfer into a special four-car 80 Class set, with motor coaches Nos 91 and 94. This train left Belfast Central at 11.53 hrs (33.5 minutes late) for Castlerock and then Portrush, leaving again for Belfast Central at 15.43 hrs. The special party returned to Dublin on the Enterprise set instead of the special train.

At the beginning of May 2004, a gauging train was operated for the newly acquired RPSI Mk II coaches. Steam locomotive No 85 and 5 Mk II coaches ran from Whitehead to Bangor. The coaches did a further cross-border gauging run between Belfast and Dublin on 10 May 2005.

The next gauging run to be undertaken was for an Irish Rail 2900 Class CAF four-car set, on 8 May 2004. This train ran from Dundalk to Belfast Central via the Antrim branch. Tests were not fully completed on that occasion, and a second run took place on 26 June 2004. The train would not make its first passenger appearance until 5 June 2005, when an eight-car 2900 Class operated the 15.00 hrs Enterprise Dublin to Belfast, and the 18.15 hrs Enterprise Belfast to Dublin services.

A 201 Class locomotive, IÉ No 218, made its first appearance on the Coleraine line on 3 August 2004, when it ran from Belfast York Road to recover the NIR Welder, which had failed. Fortunately the locomotive had been lying idle in York Road.

Spring 2004: New Rolling Stock and the CAF Trains

The first three-car train from manufacturer CAF arrived in Belfast docks on Monday, 19 April 2004. The ship on which it was transported had travelled direct to Belfast from the Port of Bilbao on the north-west coast of Spain. This would be the first set of a total order of 23. The train was unloaded on Tuesday 20 April, and was taken by road to Belfast York Road depot by Mar-Train Heavy Haulage. The second train set from CAF arrived into Belfast York Road yard on Wednesday, 5 May.

New CAF coaches, Nos 3001 and 3401 on board ship at Belfast Docks, Tuesday, 20 April 2004. *(Author)*

Each coach on the new train sets was powered by its own engine, with an auxiliary power unit for all onboard lighting, heating and air-conditioning systems. The main engine was a MAN six-cylinder with an output of 453 hp. The auxiliary engine was a Cummins six-cylinder with an output of 107 hp. Each coach was just over 23 metres in length, with a weight of approximately 50 tonnes.

Test runs and gauging exercises for the new set No 3001 commenced on 17 May 2004. The first run was at 00.10 hrs, from Belfast York Road to Mossley West and back. Further runs took place and these were soon extended to Magherabeg. Only once the tests were complete, and 2,000 miles of fault-free running had been accumulated, were the new trains approved to begin public service. The second CAF set's first outing was on 7 June 2004, when it ran from Belfast York Road to Lisburn at 00.25 hrs.

In the summer of 2003, a new train driving simulator to aid driver training had been delivered to offices at Adelaide freight yard. The simulator was built by French firm CORYS, and it replicated the new Class 3000 cab layout.

The new train was on show to the public at Belfast Central station on 15 and 16 June 2004. Gauging runs took place as follows: 21 June: Bangor line; 28 June: Newry line; 5 July: Londonderry line; 6 July: Portrush line; 7 July: Antrim branch. New trains had to be tested to their extremes, and on 25 October 2004, the highest speed recorded on a CAF test train, travelling through Templepatrick, was 106 mph.

The first passenger runs with CAF train No 3001 were on 24 November 2004: the 09.25 hrs service Belfast Central to Portadown, and the 10.32 hrs service Portadown to Bangor. The train returned from Bangor as a 12.15 hrs express special to Belfast. A reserve CAF train, No 3002, also ran from Portadown to Bangor at 10.38 hrs, in case something went wrong with No 3001. A special, limited edition First Day Ticket was printed for the occasion and issued to the first 1,000 passengers to have travelled on one of the first scheduled passenger services operated by the new C3K trains. My ticket, number 000165, is shown overleaf.

The first rostered service for a CAF train ran on 25 November 2004 – this was the 06.15 hrs service Belfast Great Victoria Street to Bangor. On 20 December 2004, the first passenger run with a CAF train on the Londonderry line was operated by CAF No 3002, and was the 12.25 hrs Belfast Great Victoria Street to Londonderry service, returning from Londonderry at 15.05 hrs to Belfast Great Victoria Street. The first CAF test train between Belfast and Dublin was run on the night of 15 February 2005.

On Tuesday 21 June 2005, I travelled from my office in Milewater Road Belfast to Bangor and boarded a 14.30 hrs special train from Bangor to Belfast Central, for the launch of the new train service, which had begun operating on Monday, 6 June. On the journey from Bangor, a commentary was given by the NITHC Chairman, Mrs Joan Smyth and footage from the front-facing camera were also shown on a projector within the train. Another special train travelled from Portadown that day, departing at 14.15 hrs and running to Belfast Central, as part of the celebration of the "New Rail Service Central Corridor between Bangor and Portadown". A special Invitation Ticket was printed for the event.

On the platform at Belfast Central, a banner with the words "New Train Service" was ceremonially cut by dignitaries, followed by an afternoon tea served in the concourse of the station. Later on that evening, I also went to a farewell function for the NITHC Chairman, Joan Smyth, who was retiring on 30 June that year.

The last new CAF train set, No 3023 was unloaded at Belfast docks on 18 July 2005. The first passenger CAF train didn't run on the Carrickfergus line however until 12 October 2005, due to the relaying of the track on the Larne line. The first cross-border passenger run for a CAF train was an unscheduled one on 31 December 2005, when set No 3009 ran empty diesel Portadown to Dundalk to then work the 17.40 hrs Dundalk to Belfast (which was the 16.50 hrs Enterprise from Dublin), since the Enterprise set had failed earlier. A replacement five-car 80 Class set had also been sent to Dundalk earlier to take up this running, but it had failed on arrival.

The first CAF to run through to Dublin was set No 3005, which formed the 10.30 hrs Enterprise Belfast to Dublin and the 13.20 hrs Enterprise Dublin to Belfast services on 2 January 2006. The IÉ Enterprise set had failed in Belfast Central. On the same day, CAF No 3001 operated the 18.10 hrs Belfast to Dundalk, and empty back to Portadown.

Gatwick Coaches

Gatwick coaches were dispersed on 23 January 2005: five to the middle road in Bangor, and four to Adelaide freight yard, hauled by a GM 201 class. The heavily loaded morning and evening Newry trips were now operated by a six-car 80 Class in the roster from 24 January 2005, and a six-car CAF in the roster from 28 February 2005. Meanwhile a GM locomotive hauled three Gatwick coaches from Adelaide to Belfast York Road for repair on 12 December 2005.

September 2005: The "Longest Day" Railtour

On Saturday, 24 September 2005, the MRSI ran an 80 Class railtour which they had christened, "The Longest Day". The train was formed by a six-car 80 Class set, with Nos 83, 779, 734, 733, 766 and 89. As part of the agreement to allow this train to run, NIR had asked for the use of the special to cover the scheduled services of 13.58 hrs Coleraine to Londonderry, and the return to Coleraine at 15.05 hrs.

The train left Belfast Central at 05.46 hrs (one minute late), and arrived in Dublin three minutes early, at 07.54 hrs. From Dublin the special travelled to Lisburn, down the Antrim branch to Portrush and then on to Coleraine. The service run to Londonderry and back was then completed and, with a brief stop in Coleraine, the special left for Belfast Central at just after 16.11 hrs (5.5 minutes late) via the main line, arriving just after 17.28 hrs (6.5 minutes late).

A GM Railtour: 2006

The following year's MRSI Railtour took place on Saturday, 13 May 2006 and had been named, "The One-One-One Day Tour" – so called, since the train would be hauled by an NIR GM 111 Class locomotive. Prior to the departure of the tour, NIR GM locomotive No 113 had run light engine from Belfast York Road to Whitehead, to pick up the six RPSI carriages and return with them to Belfast Central. The train was late arriving in Belfast, and departed for Dublin Connolly at just after 06.34 hrs (3.5 minutes late).

However, when Irish Rail heard that locomotive No 113 was to be operating the special train, they removed it in Dublin without prior notice, and stabled it in the yard there. Their concern was that this particular locomotive had not been further afield than Dublin in recent years. In its place, IÉ provided IÉ GM locomotive No 080 for the rest of our run, and we left for Rosslare Europort at 09.27 hrs (7 minutes late). After a short break there, the train set off to Waterford, where the locomotive was changed yet again – this time to IÉ GM No 074. After that, it was onwards to Limerick Junction and to Dublin Connolly, where we arrived at 19.38 hrs (7 minutes early). NIR locomotive No 113 was returned its proper place that evening, leaving Dublin at 19.53 hrs (22 minutes early) and arriving in Belfast at 22.03 hrs (32 minutes early).

2007: Irish Rail Ban Special Trains

Since Irish Rail were embarking on an intensive period of driver training for new rolling stock, they decided to impose a ban on all diesel or locomotive-hauled railway enthusiast special trains on the network. An announcement was made that the ban would be effective from 1 June 2007 until January 2009.

Spurred on by the imminent special train ban and determined to make the most of the time left, the MRSI organised a special tour, "The Mayo Explorer" for Saturday, 19 May 2007. On the day the light GM locomotive No 111 ran from Belfast York Road to Whitehead at 04.30 hrs, to pick up the six RPSI carriages, returning to Belfast Central for a 05.57 hrs departure to Dublin Connolly. Again, once in Dublin, the NIR locomotive was removed to the yard, and, for the trip to Westport, a pair of Irish Rail GM locomotives, Nos 146 and 149, took its place. The locomotives were refuelled at Westport from a mobile road tanker. On the return journey, we got a treat at Claremorris, when we crossed the 08.35 hrs timber freight service to Westport, which came through the station at speed at 16.05 hrs. Back in Dublin, the locomotives were changed again, and the special train arrived back at Belfast Central at 22.41 hrs (4 minutes late).

Rolling Stock Movements, 2006

In 2006, the Gatwick coaches reappeared again, commencing test runs between Belfast and Portadown on 21 August in a formation with GM locomotive No 113 and seven of their number. From 25 September 2006, the Gatwick set was used to operate a passenger service departing Portadown for Belfast Central at 07.45 hrs (avoiding Great Victoria Street). The first run was formed by GM locomotive No 111 and seven coaches. Meanwhile, the previous day, NIR GM locomotive No 112 had returned to Northern Ireland after having worked freight trains on IÉ for several years.

A newly operated Sandite train commenced operations at NIR on 18 September 2006. The train was formed of 80 Class units Nos 89 and 97; equipment had been placed in the train to allow for the application of Sandite to the rails in certain locations, as required.

A Refurbished 80 Class Set

In the autumn of 2008, a four-car 80 Class refurbished set commenced service on the Larne line. The train was fitted with door interlocking. A second four-car 80 Class refurbished set entered service in January 2010; I travelled on this 80 Class set most mornings, as it was on my connection as the 08.20 hrs Belfast Central to Yorkgate (travelling on to Whitehead). Only a limited number of conductors were trained to operate the set with its new interlocking doors, and this often caused problems, since of course when the conductor due to operate the service had not been trained in the system, the set would have to be cancelled altogether.

More Rolling Stock

In late June 2009, a driving trailer for the Gatwick train set arrived at Belfast York Road. The last Gatwick run was the 07.50 hrs service from Portadown to Belfast Central (avoiding Great Victoria Street), on 22 June 2009. That August, a number of Gatwick coaches were moved from Belfast York Road to Adelaide yard. Two of these coaches were brought back to York Road again on 4 October 2009, for testing along with the new driving trailer, in a test journey between Belfast York Road and Fortwilliam depot. The driving trailer was never used in passenger service. The

Gatwick strategic set, as it was known – comprising four Gatwick coaches and a generator van – was moved from Adelaide to Lisburn on 16 April 2010.

2009: New CAF Class 4000 Sets

On 25 March 2009, an official ceremony was held to mark the signing by NIR of a new contract for a further twenty CAF trains. Due for staged delivery between 2011 and 2013, these trains would be similar in many respects to previously ordered CAF Class 3000 sets. For the new order however, there would be a number of variations and improvements in the sets. There would be no auxiliary engine, as the main engine now provided power for all the requirements of each coach. The small toilet compartment was not included, and a number of additional bays would be provided for prams and bicycles. From a distance, the front of the trains would look slightly different around the lower lights, and the area above the driving cabs would be painted black.

The first new CAF set of the second batch, No 4001, arrived in Belfast York Road on Monday, 14 March 2011. The first test outing by a new CAF Class 4000, on 31 March 2011, was run from Belfast York Road to Donegall Quay and then to Fortwilliam depot. From Tuesday, 5 April 2011 a series of test runs were carried out at night time between Belfast York Road and Magherabeg.

Gauging of the Londonderry and Portrush lines was carried out on 31 July 2011. Mileage accumulation trains for the CAF Class 4000 trains were run from 1 August. Three return-journey training trains were scheduled on the Antrim branch from 27 September.

The launch of the new CAF train into passenger service was held on Thursday, 29 September 2011; the set used was CAF No 4002. A number of dignitaries, including officials from the Department of Regional Development, boarded the train at Belfast Central. The train formed the 09.42 hrs service from Belfast Central to Larne Town, returning to Belfast as the 11.00 hrs service from Larne Town, where a number of other guests had boarded. At 12 noon in Belfast Central, speeches were made,

CAF Class 4000 No 4001, arriving at Belfast York Road, Monday, 14 March 2011. *(Author)*

My special ticket, No 0018, for the launch of the new CAF Class 4000 train on Thursday 29 September 2011. *(Author's collection)*

including one from the then Transport Minister, Danny Kennedy, and afterwards a buffet lunch was provided in the station concourse.

A special ticket was produced for the launch day, which certified that its bearer was one of the first 1,000 passengers to have travelled on one of the first scheduled NIR passenger service operated by the new CAF Class 4000 trains. My ticket, No 0018, is shown here.

On 29 March 2012, a CAF Class 4000 gauging run was operated from Belfast to Portrush Platform Three, and travelled back on the Antrim branch to Belfast York Road. That July, the last of the new CAF trains, set No 4020, arrived in Belfast from Spain.

Farewell to the 80 Class

The IRRS ran a final outing for a four-car 80 Class on 14 May 2011. The train ran from Lisburn to Larne Harbour, back to Belfast, and then on to Bangor, Lisburn and finally back to Belfast Central once more. The last scheduled passenger timetable runs for the 80 Class on the Larne line took place on Friday, 23 September 2011. The set was formed by Nos 8094, 8752, 8749, and 8090.

A few days after these final services ran, the MRSI organised a farewell tour to commemorate the end of passenger service for the 80 Class trains. The "Class 80 Finale – The Last Thump!" ran on Sunday, 25 September, with a special train formed by Nos 8090, 8749, 8752, and 8094.

The train left Belfast Central for Dundalk at 09.00 hrs and after a break, departed again at 11.24 hrs (1 minute late) to run non-stop to Coleraine via Belfast Central, arriving at 13.48 hrs (only 2 minutes late). The set was refuelled, but due to a service train in the station having mechanical problems, the special was delayed, only departing Coleraine at 14.38 hrs (13 minutes late), and then running to Belfast Central via the main line. The set then travelled to Larne Harbour, back to Belfast and onwards to Bangor, with a 16.5 minute non-stop run in both directions. The set performed very well, although it was also a good idea to have a travelling NIR fitter on board!

It is hoped to preserve an 80 Class set, but in the winter of 2015 the last remaining units were still carrying out Sandite duties. However, at that point, NIR had started a tendering process to acquire a MPV, which could also carry out Sandite duties. It is hoped that an 80 Class set will eventually end up in preservation at the Downpatrick & County Down Railway, possibly in 2016.

Antrim Branch

On Sunday, 9 October 2011, the Antrim branch was used as a diversionary route for Londonderry trains, due to a replacement crossover being

Farewell to the 80 Class train tour, Bangor, 25 September 2011. *(Author)*

installed at Belfast York Road on the main line. The crossover had been assembled at the old sidings at Ballymacarrett, and then taken by road to York Road. Five return passenger trips were operated over the Antrim branch.

On Sunday, 23 October in the same year, a similar operation took place for the replacement of a crossover at Bleach Green Junction. A number of railway enthusiasts, including myself, took the opportunity of travelling on the Branch that day. I took the 14.53 hrs Lisburn to Antrim service, returning on the 15.50 hrs Antrim to Lisburn.

Rolling Stock Movements

From 1 February 2012, a GM locomotive and hoppers test train operated on the Antrim branch for a couple of days for driver training purposes, in preparation for the Londonderry relay later in the year. On 13 February that year, the GM locomotive and hoppers train ran from Londonderry at night, to establish ballast tips at specific points along the route of the relay.

On Thursday, 19 April 2012, I was able to observe, from a vantage point on the Milewater Road footbridge, the first nine-car CAF Class 3000 to operate. Set Nos 3002, 3023 and 3004 ran up and down Belfast York Road yard several times around 10.45 hrs. The intention was to use the nine car for rugby specials and other such trains. I don't believe this has happened as yet.

February 2012: Farewell to the Castle Class

A special tour to mark the retirement of NIR's Castle Class trains was organised by the MRSI for Saturday, 18 February 2012. The tour train was formed by Nos 8785, 8795 and 8455. At this stage, two other Castle Class sets, Nos 454 and 459, had been stored in the beach siding at Belfast Central. Two other sets, Nos 453 and 457, were to be stored in the middle road at Bangor station, and were taken there on Sunday, 22 January 2012, by a special movement run by another Castle Class, making it the first nine-car set to be seen on the railway in a number of years.

On the day of the farewell tour, the special train left Belfast Central for Dundalk at 09.04 hrs (9 minutes late, due to a conductor having some issues): Irish Rail had

The Farewell to the Castle Class train tour, Saturday, 18 February 2012. (*Author*)

given special permission to allow the train into Dundalk. The MRSI members from the South boarded the special at Dundalk, and the train left at 10.46 hrs (1 minute late), travelling to Adelaide station so that the party could view the new depot from the footbridge. The train then ran non-stop to Antrim in 32.5 minutes. A trip up the Antrim branch was next, calling at Crumlin and Ballinderry stations and onwards to Bangor. The special was delayed in Bangor, due to a passenger on board being unwell, and returned to Belfast Central after the 15.57 hrs service train.

I am happy to be able to report that one of these Castle Class train sets has been preserved. On Thursday, 25 September 2014, set No 458 *Antrim Castle* was shunted in Belfast York Road yard by GM No 113 (appropriately named *Belfast and Co Down*), with assistance from the 80 Class Sandite train. A low loader from Moveright International in England was then used to transfer the coaches to the Downpatrick & County Down Railway in Downpatrick. Driving trailer No 788 was taken to Downpatrick on Saturday, 27 September, and intermediate trailer No 798 and power car No 458 were moved on the following day. Ramping of the coaches onto the track at Downpatrick proved somewhat complicated, due their semi-permanent coupling. However, a coupling bar had been provided by NIR and this helped with the shunting of the low loader, using locomotive No B146. The train was formally handed over to Downpatrick by NIR officials on 22 November 2014.

During my time at NIR, passenger rolling stock was altered on many occasions, so that it was very different from what was in place at the start of NIR. Major progress has been made in passenger comfort and safety through the years. My favourite trains during the time I worked at the company were undoubtedly the 80 Class diesel sets. They were reliable, and the fact that you could build the train up from a two-coach to a twelve-coach was a great asset for railway operators. The bench-type soft cushions were really comfortable and the trains could certainly pick up speed, especially those with just two coaches. The modern trains we have now are fine of course, but for a railway enthusiast, those run locally lack variety and interest, as they are all so similar, apart from the cross-border trains. There is really no type of rolling stock available now locally to run a special train on NIR, and there are effectively no long trains any more, which is disappointing for those of us interested in trains and hoping to see something a bit different!

CHAPTER 8

STATIONS AND INFRASTRUCTURE CHANGES

There have been many great advancements and changes to stations and the railway infrastructure in Northern Ireland since the inception of NIR – a complete turnaround from the last days of the UTA. In this chapter, I will look in detail at some of the changes since 1973; the main changes prior to this I have recorded in Chapter One.

Press Conference

At a press conference on Wednesday, 3 October 1973, an NIR representative gave a review of infrastructure projects currently in hand, as well as forthcoming work soon to be underway. It was anticipated that the new Belfast Central Railway project would be up and running by May 1975, and this would mean that all rail services from Dublin, Portadown, Londonderry and Bangor would be able to use the new station at Belfast Central. Since the beginning of operations at NIR in 1968, approximately 75 miles of new track had been relayed with concrete sleepers and new rails. The relaying programme was set to continue at a rate of approximately ten miles of track per year, until eventually the entire track mileage would be replaced. Stations at Lisburn, Coleraine and Bangor had been modernised and similar work was underway at Londonderry. In conjunction with the road authorities, work had begun for the provision of a new station at Larne Town, while a new station was also being constructed at Portrush. Also planned for rebuilding and renewal was Lurgan station, which had been extensively damaged by a terrorist explosion.

Belfast Central Railway Update

By January 1974, the Chairman of NIR was predicting that the new Belfast Central station and railway would be open by June 1975. One of the major structures on the route would be the new bridge over the River Lagan. The old iron bridge was in the process of being demolished, and already the spans over the road and two spans over the river had been removed. The new bridge would be more imposing, as it would carry double track, whereas the old bridge had been for single track only. During construction, the River Lagan was partially dammed, with the permission and cooperation of the Belfast Harbour Commissioners, who in turn saw to it that the bridge in progress left sufficient clearance for the passage of river traffic and was equipped with suitable navigation lights. During the building process also, road traffic had to be halted at a certain stage, to enable workmen to remove iron spans over the Laganbank Road. Work was also being carried out on East Bridge Street, which was reduced to a single lane.

The original iron bridge had been completed in 1870, and had made history on 4 September 1897, when their Royal Highnesses the Duke and Duchess of York (later to become King George V and Queen Mary) passed over it on a Royal Train, which had been provided by the Northern Counties Committee Railway. This was the first time – and perhaps the only time – an NCC train passed over the County Down tracks.

Reopening of the Lisburn to Antrim Railway

As part of the launch of the planned new train service for the Lisburn to Antrim branch line, special inaugural free travel trains ran on Saturday, 26 January 1974. There were four return services that day, and the train was formed by a four-car MPD train, with Nos 51, 536, 541 and 65.

A free commemorative First Day ticket was also printed: as a limited edition, these were only available to be collected from a number of stations. An authorisation instruction was also issued in conjunction with each special ticket, and a copy of a ticket and authorisation are shown here.

Regular timetabled train services from Lisburn to Antrim began operating from Monday, 28 January 1974, with intermediate stations at Ballinderry, Glenavy and Crumlin. However, numbers travelling in the first week were disappointing, with only nine passengers on average per train. On Thursday, 31 January 1974, the train set was reduced to a double-ended MPD unit, No 65. Lisburn market proved a winner however, with 200 passengers travelling there by train on Tuesday, 5 February that year.

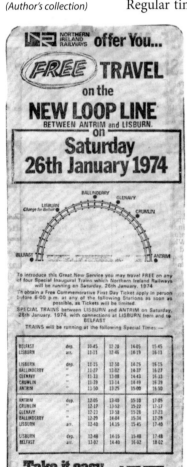

Advertisement for introductory service on the Lisburn to Antrim line, 26 January 1974. (Author's collection)

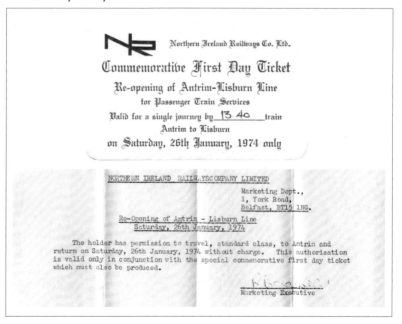

Commemorative First Day Ticket for the re-opening of the Antrim to Lisburn line on 26 January 1974. The accompanying authorisation instruction also shown.
(Author's collection)

The last scheduled passenger service had previously ended on 12 September 1960, and since then the line had been used for scheduled freight services running from the Republic of Ireland to Londonderry, special passenger trains and other empty stock and engineering trains.

Construction Work at Belfast Central: 1974–1975

As 1974 began, work on the new Belfast Central station project continued at East Bridge Street, Belfast. By 16 February, part of

the steel work at the front of the station was now in place and services in the roadway and footpath were being renewed, or redirected. The roadway had been reduced to single lanes to allow the contractors sufficient room to work at the frontage. The work being carried out on the 100-year-old bridge was necessary, as it was not in good condition and was thought that the structure could not stand up to the vibrations from modern trains. Passing motorists would ask what the system of gantries were for, and it was explained that their purpose would be to carry all the telephone, gas and electricity cables which would normally be underground, but now had be above ground while parts of the bridge were being replaced. Although at this time work was on schedule for a proposed opening in the summer of 1975, there were still fears that delays could be caused by an ongoing steel shortage in England.

First special train, the 11.15 hrs Lisburn to Antrim service at Lisburn station, Saturday, 26 January 1974. *(Author)*

Above middle: Quay layout and new track bed, 10 January 1975. *(Author)*
Above: River Lagan Viaduct under construction, 10 January 1975. *(Author)*
Right: Belfast Central Station taking shape, 10 January 1975. *(Author)*

New Stations and Realignments

On Sunday, 23 June 1974, the new curve leading from the Belfast direction to the new Larne Town station was opened at 12.00 hrs. On Wednesday, 3 July a special train ran from Belfast York Road to mark the occasion, and I have covered this in more detail in Chapter Seven.

Also at the beginning of July, a single platform station opened at the down main line at Knockmore, on the outskirts of Lisburn. Although the station would principally be served by trains from the Antrim branch, some Portadown trains would also be calling in the morning and evening peak periods.

Meanwhile, as work progressed on the Belfast Central Railway project, certain other track changes were taking place at Queen's Quay. On Monday, 11 November 1974, Graham contractors were on site and took temporary possession of the down main line from the signal box to Fraser Street bridge. The up line became the down line, and the siding beside the diesel shed became the up main line.

New Belfast Bridges Erected for the BCR

One of the missing bridges on the BCR was at Middlepath Street: the original bridge had been demolished in 1965 as part of a new road layout. New bridge girders were placed into position by Graham's contractors on Saturday, 22 March 1975.

Bridging the gap at Middlepath Street, Belfast, Saturday, 22 March 1975. (Author)

Things didn't all go smoothly in this process, however, for when the contractors arrived on the designated day to carry out the heavy-duty, but nonetheless highly skilled bridge-building operation, they discovered that one of the cranes they were intending to use had been vandalised. It appeared that the previous evening, vandals had run off the crane's engine oil, and cut a fuel pipe. Fortunately, however, the engineers on site were able to make sufficient repairs for the two 70-ton girders, which would span the up and down lines across the bridge, to be hoisted into position.

Meanwhile, work continued apace on other bridges for the BCR. On Sunday, 29 June 1975, Graham contractors spent all day erecting two 75-ton bridge beams into place at Bridge End, Belfast (not to be confused with the location of the railway station at Bridge End).

On Tuesday, 29 July 1975, ballast trains started to run on the new Central line from the Donegall Road end of the line, which was from Central Junction. At the same time, ballast was being laid on the new embankment running from the Fraser Street bridge, near Queen's Quay, towards Middlepath Street.

Bridge Widening at Seahill

The road under Bridge No 29 at Seahill station did not have much clearance for vans and lorries, and when delivering goods to addresses in the area, they often had to

stop and deliver these on foot. To alleviate this problem, the Roads Service decided to widen Bridge No 28 and build a new section of road. The new concrete decking for the bridge was placed into position on Sunday, 10 August 1975.

Knockmore Station and the Third Line

As we have seen above, the Lisburn to Antrim branch line had reopened at the end of January 1974. A new single wooden platform station was built to serve trains at the down main line, and this opened on Monday, 1 July 1974. New concrete platforms were then built for the up direction towards Portadown, and for Antrim Branch trains in both directions via a new third line from Lisburn to Knockmore Junction.

The photograph shows the 14.35 hrs service from Antrim to Lisburn (a three-car 80 Class), calling at Knockmore station main line. This platform was closed the following day, on 31 May 1975. The new concrete platform and new third line can

also be seen here. By this stage, the third line had been laid from Lisburn and was only 300 yards short of Knockmore Junction.

However, plans to open the third line from Lisburn through to Knockmore Junction stalled due to planning restrictions. As more and more objections and proposals accumulated, a Public Inquiry was called for. This would eventually be held in May 1976, as we will see later in this chapter. It took almost three years from when the track was laid along the third line for it to be opened, once the Londonderry line train services commenced on 23 January 1978.

Above left: Bridge beams in place at Bridge End, Belfast, 29 June 1975. *(Author)*

Above: Belfast Central station takes shape, with inner steel roof now in place, 18 July 1975. *(Author)*

Below: Train at main line platform, Knockmore, Friday, 30 May 1975. *(Author)*

Above: First train approaching Ormeau Road bridge, Belfast, Thursday, 4 September 1975. *(Author)*

Above right: First train at the new Botanic station, Thursday, 4 September 1975. *(Author)*

Below left: Frontage of former Belfast York Road station, October 1975. *(Author)*

Below: Frontage of new Belfast York Road station, November 1975. *(Author)*

September 1975: First Special Train on the New Railway

Determined not to miss a first run on a very historic day, I booked the afternoon off on Thursday 4 September 1975, and joined the 14.35 hrs special train from Belfast Great Victoria Street to Belfast Central station. The train was formed by 80 Class set, Nos 88 and 738. The speed over the new line was 3 mph, and we travelled along the up line only, as the down line had not yet been completed. The train could not enter the platforms at Belfast Central, as point and crossing work was still ongoing, so we came to a stop 150 yards short of the platforms, where a special party of officials detrained to inspect the site.

New Station at Belfast York Road

A new station building opened at Belfast York Road on Sunday, 30 November 1975, replacing the former station, which had been badly damaged in previous terrorist attacks. From the photographs, we can compare the frontage of the previous incarnation of the station with the frontage of the new station. The waiting area in the new station was quite small compared to the former, and there would only be

two ticket barriers, one for inwards and one for outwards movement. Behind the ticket barriers and the platforms in the new station, the original area was still in place. The rebuilt station was officially opened by NIR Managing Director, Hugh Waring, at 12 noon on Wednesday, 10 December 1975.

I always found it strange that this station was called "York Road", as it was positioned in York Street, and even the Post Office had it listed as being on York Street. In fact, the frontage of the old station came out on to Whitla Street also. I am sure someone has the answer to that!

Developments for Bangor: 1975

With new signalling being introduced for the BCR, it was an opportune time to replace the banner signals on the line between Holywood and Bangor with two-aspect colour light signals. The down line signals were operational from Sunday, 9 November 1975, followed by the up line signals a week later, on Sunday, 16 November.

Bangor West signals: colour light No U1 and banner-type, Sunday, 16 November 1975. (Author)

The next development, shortly after this, was the connection of the Bangor line to the new Belfast Central Railway. Quite a bit of slewing of the track at Belfast Queen's Quay had to be done to position the track for the connection, and finally, on Wednesday, 3 December 1975, the shed line was connected to the BCR, with the installation of temporary turnout No 16, which led on to the down line of the BCR.

Another historic day for the railway was Tuesday, 9 December 1975, when the first train from Belfast Central ran on the Bangor line. Taking on a load of ballast at the temporary Eliza Street yard, beside the Markets Estate, DH No 3 and six hoppers ran from Belfast Central to Belfast Queen's Quay. This was the first time in over 10 years (since the line's closure in 1965) that a train was able to travel this route. As mentioned before, because I was in the Operations department at NIR, I was fortunate enough to

Belfast Central Railway connected to the Bangor line at Fraser Street bridge, Wednesday, 3 December 1975. The 17.28 hrs service from Belfast Queen's Quay to Bangor (a three-car MED) can be seen in the background. (Author)

know when these special movements were to take place. On this occasion too, I duly took a half-day's leave, and made my way to Belfast Central and Belfast Queen's Quay.

With Mr Hugh Waring and other senior NIR officials travelling in the cab, DH No 3 left Belfast Central at 14.30 hrs to run on the down line from Belfast Central to Fraser Street bridge near Queen's Quay. The train then went on to the shed line, where it propelled on into the yard via No 8 points and then to Platform Three. All had gone smoothly thus far, but

when we were returning to Belfast Central later that day, the first derailment on the BCR took place! Hopper No C337 came off the track at Middlepath Street bridge, and Hopper No C325 was left supporting it until it could be re-railed the next day. This no doubt was a bit embarrassing for NIR, as the wagons could be seen from quite a distance and were in full view of motorists on nearby roads!

The first 80 Class train run on the Bangor line would take place on Monday, 12 January 1976, as detailed in Chapter Seven.

BCR Completion Date Revised Again

As the reader will have realised by now, the date for the opening of the BCR kept being pushed back for various reasons. In December 1975, the completion date was revised again in an official statement from NIR, which cited unexpected and unavoidable engineering problems as reasons for the delay. Vandalism had been a factor too, as valuable signalling equipment had been set on fire and its replacement had also caused unforeseen delays. This time around, wisely, NIR did not give the public a specific completion date; it was simply announced that the new system should be up-and-running by the spring of 1976. Mr Hugh Waring, the then Managing Director, had expected to be there for the opening of the new railway, but he would be retired before the eventual completion date. His successor would be Mr Roy Beattie, a current senior executive.

Since the projected completion date for BCR had been changed so many times, NIR's announcement of the actual opening date was delayed until the last possible moment. Finally, on Friday, 12 March 1976, came an official statement that the first train from Bangor to Belfast Central would arrive at the new station a month later, on Monday, 12 April 1976.

The new Belfast Central station would not be officially opened until Monday, 26 April 1976, by which time rail services from Dublin, Portadown and Londonderry would be able to run into the new station. The new brand name for the suburban services, "Citytrack", and "Inter City", the new name for services north of Ballymena and south of Portadown, would be introduced at the same time.

March 1976: Stations Update

In the spring of 1976, a number of NIR stations were in the news for various reasons.

Lisburn railway station had been presented with a "Heritage Year" award, as part of the European Architectural Heritage Year 1975 awards, for restoration work carried out in the station. Over 1,000 entries had been received from all parts of the United Kingdom. The nineteenth-century station had been given a complete facelift according to an imaginative scheme designed by Ferguson and McIlveen; the work had been carried out by NIR's Works and Buildings Department.

As touched upon in an earlier chapter, in the mid-1970s, the future of the original station at Portrush was very much in question, particularly as a new and smaller modern station had been built just behind the old building. The distinctive old landmark station in mock-Tudor style was put up for sale in March 1976, although it was anticipated that it might not be an easy sell, as it had fallen into a dilapidated state and the facade was listed as an historic building. The overall site area was 18,125 square feet. A possible plus point in selling terms was that there was a well-established licensed premises operating on the site. As well as this, at the time of sale, planning approval had already been secured for a shopping redevelopment scheme.

A third station in the news in March 1976 was Belfast Queen's Quay, which comprised a large station building and grounds. With the forthcoming completion of the Belfast Central Railway project, the station and area where being offered "To Let", and a planning application had already been lodged for change of use to a warehouse. The overall site being offered was approximately one acre, including a concourse area of 11,000 square feet and office space of 18,000 square feet.

Craigavad station and signal box, 26 March 1976. (*Author*)

Another station in transition at the time was Craigavad on the Bangor line. The photograph shows the old station building and signal box there in March 1976. The crossover at the Bangor end of the station was still in existence, but a new crossover had been installed at Rockport, between Craigavad and Seahill. In the image, you will also notice that the up line had just been relaid with new rail and concrete sleepers, which was all part of the ongoing renewal project. By December 1977, the relay had extended to Bangor station. Craigavad station's platforms were still being used for Girl Guide groups visiting the Girl Guides' Lorne Headquarters, just a few hundred yards away. In June 1976, the station building, which had been built in 1863, was put up for sale, with offers in the region of £3,000 being sought.

The Opening of the Belfast Central Railway

The detail of the long-awaited plans for the opening of the BCR was finally revealed to the public on Friday, 2 April 1976. This time it was for real! A public advertisement, shown here, gave the information so many people had been waiting for.

On Saturday, 10 April 1976, trains from Belfast Queen's Quay would travel through the train wash road and along the new No 1 head shunt towards Ballymacarrett station, before emerging back onto the down line towards Bangor. A special train service was in operation on this day. The first photograph overleaf shows the permanent way squad reconnecting the up line near Ballymacarrett to the up line for Belfast Central. The picture was taken from the 11.05 hrs Belfast to Bangor service.

Below: Belfast Central Railway Opening Information, 2 April 1976. (*Author's collection*)

Above: Reconnecting the up line to the Central line, 10 April 1976. *(Author)*

Top right: Belfast Queen's Quay's last day, with two three-car MED sets, 10 April 1976. *(Author)*

Commemorative Last Day Ticket, Queen's Quay Station, 10 April 1976. *(Author's collection)*

NORTHERN IRELAND RAILWAYS COMPANY LTD.

Commemorative Last Day Ticket

Closure of Queen's Quay Station for Passenger Train Services

Valid for a return journey from Queen's Quay Station

on Saturday, 10th April, 1976, Only

A reasonable number of railway enthusiasts, including myself, travelled on the 21.00 hrs service from Bangor to Belfast Queen's Quay and returned on the 21.45 hrs service, which would be the last train out of Queen's Quay. A special commemorative ticket was on sale, to mark the closure of Queen's Quay station: valid for one return journey only on the Bangor line, on Saturday 10 April exclusively, it was priced at £1.00.

As detailed in the public information notice, no passenger trains would run on Sunday, 11 April 1976, so that vital realignment work could be carried out on the track around the Queen's Quay/Fraser Street bridge area.

Monday, 12 April 1976 was the big day, marking the opening of the new Belfast Central station, but the occasion was kept pretty low-key. Only Bangor line services were to use the station for the first two weeks. I travelled up that day on the very first train out of Bangor, which was the 06.50 hrs service; there were only a handful of railway enthusiasts on board. The train was formed by a three-car MED set, Nos 29, 504 and 26. The ongoing timetable simply continued, and I travelled back to Bangor West on the 07.48 hrs service, returning to Belfast Central on the 08.20 hrs service from Bangor West. (A railway enthusiast does those sorts of things – going to the new Belfast station twice in such short succession was always going to better than going just once!) I then travelled to the City Hall on the new Citylink Citybus circular service, which was running mostly at a ten-minute frequency throughout the day, with a flat fare of five pence. My next decision was how to get to my office on York Road, and so I decided on a black taxi, which was cheaper than the alternative, Citybus.

General reaction from the travelling public to the new BCR set-up was mostly favourable, and people welcomed in particular the improved facilities and level of comfort provided at Belfast's new station.

Facilities included a buffet bar, serving restaurant meals, and an all-purpose shop. Due to open in May 1976 would also be a public bar and lounge bar, together with a travel agency and bank. In the midst of all the changes, NIR staff had not been overlooked, and had been provided with brand new uniforms which were modelled on British Rail's continental designs.

Some passengers did make the point that the old Queen's Quay station had been more conveniently sited in terms of access to their work. NIR responded by saying that they were conscious of the need for another station on the Bangor side of Belfast Central. In this respect, planning permission had already been obtained for the building of a new station, to be situated between Fraser Street and Bridge End at the bottom of the Sydenham Bypass. This would facilitate commuters working in the Newtownards Road area at such places as the Sirocco Works.

One of the strange aspects of the new station was a concrete panelled fence which had been built adjacent to Platform Four. On the opposite side of the fence was the newly constructed Markets housing estate; this six-foot high fence was cheap, nasty and far too low. It wasn't too long before trains sitting at Platform Four were the target of stones, and verbal abuse, from some of the locals. Following complaints from passengers and in view of the cost of repairs, it was realised that a higher fence would be required, and contractors were brought in to raise its height to 33 feet.

Saturday, 24 April 1976 was the last day of train services at Belfast Great Victoria Street station. A special train service had been in operation as trains had to travel, single-line working, from Great Victoria Street to Balmoral along the third line and in behind Adelaide station, then over to the down line as far as Dunmurry. As services travelled through Adelaide freight yard, Adelaide station was closed for the day.

True to form, the terrorists continued their ongoing campaign of violence, even Great Victoria Street's last day of operations. At 13.15 hrs, two unattended suitcases were discovered in the station, and services were suspended for 75 minutes. From the evening of Thursday 22 April, cross-border services were also disrupted, and did not return to normal until the afternoon of Monday, 26 April.

Below left: Last day of operations at Great Victoria Street. The 11.30 hrs Enterprise service from Belfast went as far as Portadown only, due to a bomb incident at the Border, 24 April 1976. *(Author)*

Below: Last day of operations at Great Victoria Street – shown here, the signal gantry and fuel point, 24 April 1976. *(Author)*

Above: Last day of operations at Great Victoria Street – note the diesel shed in the background, and fuel point in the foreground, 24 April 1976. *(Author)*

Top right: Last day of operations at Great Victoria Street: near Donegall Road bridge, permanent way squads prepare to connect Central railway with the main lines. DH Nos 2 and 3 with ballast wagons on up main line, 24 April 1976. *(Author)*

On Sunday, 25 April 1976, train services were suspended to allow for the realignment of track at Central Junction at the Donegall Road in Belfast, as well as other necessary works. From 16.00 hrs for one hour, there was in fact a bomb scare at Tate's Avenue bridge, close to the realignment works, which would have closed the line if services had been operating that day. Enterprise services were due to operate from Portadown to Dublin, with a bus connection from Belfast, but due to an incident on the railway at the Border, train services only ran from Dundalk to Dublin.

Not all passengers from the Portadown line greeted the new service on Monday, 26 April 1976 favourably, since the new Botanic and Belfast Central stations were not as convenient for their workplaces or for shopping purposes. Quite a large proportion of passengers chose Botanic station as their first preference.

On the first day of operation, the first through train to Dublin was the 16.10 hrs Enterprise service, due to the line closure at the Border, as mentioned previously. The line was only re-opened at 15.20 hrs, following a 96-hour closure. Services were further disrupted on Tuesday, 27 April, due to a two-hour bomb scare at Kilnasaggart bridge at the Border.

The official opening ceremony for the new Belfast Central Railway took place at Central Station on opening day, Monday 26 April 1976, at 11.15 hrs. Two VIPs almost missed the historic occasion, because their train was disrupted by a terrorist incident at the Border. The Mayor of Dublin, Mr Patrick Dunne, and CIÉ Chairman, Mr St John Devlin had travelled on the 08.00 hrs Enterprise service from Dublin, but ended up having to travel on a substitutionary bus between Dundalk and Portadown, due to the terrorist incident. The Chairman of NIR, Myles Humphreys, who was also the Lord Mayor of Belfast at the time, unveiled the plaque shortly after the two VIPs arrived.

On Wednesday, 5 January 1977, the side entrance to Belfast Central station opened. This included an escalator and stairs from the car park to the concourse. In early October that year, another feature was added to the station with the opening of a new NIR Travel and Information Centre.

Stations Demolished and Rebuilt

The summer of 1976 saw two of Belfast's larger stations come tumbling down, as bulldozers moved in to demolish Belfast York Road station and Great Victoria Street station. A smaller station had been opened at Belfast York Road in December 1975, and the future use of Great Victoria Street was as yet unguessed at. Thankfully, the large site was retained by the Northern Ireland Transport Holding Company, with the only immediate plan being that part of the site would be developed as car parking facilities. This was to prove most opportune, given that the land was ultimately to be used for a new railway station.

Also in the summer of 1976, on 8 July, NIR Chairman, Sir Myles Humphreys and the Mayor of Craigavon, Mr Creith officially opened new station buildings at Lurgan. The station had been previously destroyed by terrorists in July 1972, and completely rebuilt again by August 1975. However, two days before the official opening ceremony took place in 1975, the station was once more decimated by further explosions. Patience had prevailed however, and it was a proud day when, finally, in 1976, the new station could be made available to the public.

Footbridges

Enterprise-type rolling stock had been prevented from running on the Bangor line due to a number of minor engineering problems, but also because of the obstacle posed by the old steel footbridge at Kinnegar station, near Holywood. This hindrance was dealt with in September 1976, during an overnight possession, when the centre span was removed, followed by the steps.

Now that the Bangor line was at last accessible, a Hunslet locomotive ran light from Belfast Central to Bangor for gauging purposes, on Sunday, 3 October 1976. This was followed by the first Hunslet-hauled passenger train (Hunslet No 103 with five carriages), which formed the 10.15 hrs service train from Belfast Central to Bangor, on Wednesday, 6 October 1976.

While the footbridge at Kinnegar was dispensed with in September 1976, a new one would be commissioned for Sydenham in the same month. On 23 September, an advertisement appeared in the press, seeking tenders for the construction of three span pre-cast, pre-stressed concrete beams, to be placed across the Bangor–Belfast railway and the Sydenham Bypass. Tender documents were to be completed by Thursday, 14 October 1976.

Old footbridge at Kinnegar station, 7 September 1976. *(Author)*

Station Closures

The autumn of 1976 saw a raft of station closures across the network, as part of a cost-cutting strategy. A total of seven stations on the Londonderry line were closed on Sunday, 18 October. The fact was that few people were regularly using these stations, and therefore it was no longer viable to stop trains at them. The benefit to regular travellers would be that the journey time from Belfast to Londonderry was to be cut from 2 hours 15 minutes to 2 hours flat. The stations closed were as follows: Drumsough (also known as Cookstown Junction); Cullybackey; Dunloy; Downhill; Magilligan; Bellarena and Limavady Junction.

The following year, on 8 May 1977, further station closures were made: Bleach Green; Trooperslane; Barn; Eden and Kilroot. Ballymacarrett station on the Bangor line also closed on Sunday, 8 May that year, but a new replacement station for East Belfast, Bridge End, was opened the following day near Middlepath Street.

Bangor Line Relaying

The track relay was pressing towards Bangor and to facilitate the work, which was being carried out during off-peak day-times, an additional crossover was installed between the 11.25 and 11.50 mileposts, between Crawfordsburn and Carnalea, and almost directly below Colonel Crawford's footbridge (as mentioned in an earlier chapter, mileposts are located on the railway embankment every quarter of a mile to assist rail staff in identifying infrastructure and fixed points on the line). Installed on Sunday, 24 April 1977, this crossover would allow the following sections of the route to be used for single-line working as required: Bangor to Crawfordsburn; Crawfordsburn to Rockport; Rockport to Belfast Central crossover, No 111.

Summer 1977: Opening of the Lisburn Third Line

Eleven months after the Public Inquiry which followed the outcry by local residents, who were opposed to the creation of the rail link between Lisburn and Knockmore, the Department of the Environment gave NIR the go-ahead to proceed in mid-May 1977. The decision in NIR's favour was subject to two conditions, relating to the carrying out of certain works at the rear of several properties, and the undertaking of landscaping work. NIR were delighted with the result, and planned to introduce the through service from Londonderry to Belfast Central via the Antrim branch by July 1977.

The last full day of operation for Knockmore Junction signal box was 27 May 1977. The final remaining portion of the third line from Lisburn to be laid was only several

Last day of operations for Knockmore Junction signal box, Friday, 27 May 1977. *(Author)*

hundred yards long, and would run directly onto the Antrim branch. The signal box at Knockmore Junction was right in line of this proposed new track, and therefore had to be removed. This would also allow for the construction of a new road bridge, to be built directly above the location of the signal box. The signal box was demolished on Saturday, 28 May and the third line was completed the following day, and ready for through services between Lisburn and Antrim on Monday, 30 May 1977.

Re-routing of Londonderry Trains

Even though the third line had been completed at Lisburn in May 1977, it took another eight months for the big change to take place on the Londonderry line, with the re-routing of the trains into Belfast Central. On Sunday, 22 January 1978, the last passenger trains into and out of Belfast York Road ran on the Londonderry line. The final train out was the 19.00 hrs service from Belfast to Londonderry; it was formed by a six-car 70 Class, Nos 701, 722, 76, 712, 726 and 73. The last train in to Belfast York Road was the 18.25 hrs service from Londonderry, formed by a six-car 70 Class, Nos 71, 727, 702, 78, 725 and 711. A number of railway enthusiasts, including myself, travelled from Belfast to Antrim and back in again on these last trains.

The following day, 23 January, services were diverted at Antrim, ran along the branch line to Lisburn and then onwards to Belfast Central. The advertisement for the new line emphasised the perceived benefits for passengers using the new route, with its connections at Lisburn and Belfast. However, there was still an underlying feeling amongst regular train users that the old route should be restored. The extra journey time was a disappointment for some, and one passenger quipped that it now took just 90 minutes by car from Belfast to Londonderry, whereas, according to the timetables at the time, by train the same journey would now take anything from 123 to 130 minutes. Others had hopes that the Public Inquiry into transport strategies on the network would restore the link to the Belfast York Road direction and then over to Belfast Central, via new cross town bridges.

The first day of operations did not run well at all, with terrorists reminding everyone that they could still cause disruption, no matter how well events were planned. Train services were withdrawn between Lisburn and Dunloy due to bomb scares, and passengers were transferred from train to bus and then to train again along the journey. The first through train out was the 14.05 hrs Belfast to Londonderry service. The first through train in was the 13.20 hrs service from Portrush to Belfast. Even then, the disruption did not end, due to trains being in the wrong place at the wrong times, and also to crossing points on the single line being changed to accommodate the late running services.

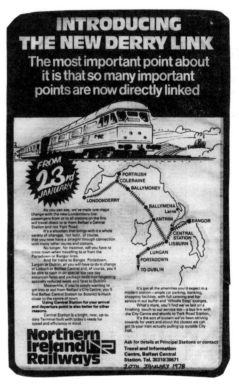

The New Derry Link – what sort of locomotive did they use in the advert, one was tempted to ask! (It looked nothing like any NIR train I had ever seen!) Friday, 20 January 1978. *(Author's collection)*

Tuesday, 24 January, the second day of operations on the new route, saw further disruption because of a bomb scare at Derriaghy. The 06.35 hrs service from Ballymena to Belfast Central was stopped at Lisburn, and passengers were transferred to buses. The line was cleared after one hour. There was still no joy for northern direction passengers however, as another bomb scare between Moira and Derriaghy at 16.05 hrs stopped all rush hour trains for an hour and 30 minutes.

Thankfully on Day Three, all services on the Londonderry line ran as per schedule – the first time for the new service.

On Tuesday, 24 January 1978, Ulsterbus announced that, from the following month, they would be introducing a new express bus service from Ballymena to Belfast, due to a lot of requests for such a service from people working in the York Road area of Belfast, who now had to find their way through the city from Belfast Central. The additional buses would be scheduled for 07.50 hrs from Ballymena, and 17.20 hrs from Belfast's Oxford Street bus station. An NIR official declined to comment on the new bus service.

On Monday, 30 January 1978, to mark the official re-routing of the Londonderry line into Belfast Central, the then Secretary of State, Roy Mason took the controls of a train on the Londonderry line and, with the assistance of the train driver, drove it into Platform 2 at Belfast Central.

1978: Track Relays and More Footbridges

NIR was charging ahead with a number of track relay schemes in 1978, since so much of the network needed attention in this regard. Planned for the year were 30 miles

Old and new footbridges at Sydenham station, Friday, 10 March 1978. *(Author)*

of relaying, with ten miles of replacement on the down line between Greenisland and Whitehead, and onwards to Magheramorne Loop. One-mile sections at Glarryford and at Dunloy would also be tackled, as well as a final half-mile on the up Bangor line. The biggest job would be the relaying of 17.5 miles between Poyntzpass and the Border, where continuous welded rail was to be installed, to permit eventual operation at 90 mph.

The original railway footbridge at Sydenham was fine if you just wanted to cross the tracks, but if you wanted to cross the Sydenham Bypass, then it was a matter of run and hope for the best! However, the Department of the Environment proposed to resolve this issue, by agreeing to erect a new footbridge which would stretch right across the railway tracks and the Sydenham Bypass. By May 1977, the 45-metre long, £60,000 footbridge, with three stairways, was well underway, but would not be completed until the winter of 1977.

Steam crane No 3084, working at Bangor West, Sunday, 2 April 1978. *(Author)*

Both footbridges were in use until Saturday, 11 March 1978; the following day, the old footbridge was dismantled, using NIR steam crane No 3084. This was probably a first-time visit to the Bangor line for the crane, which was hauled by locomotive DH No 2, brought over from the Larne line. Single-line working over the down line was in operation most of the day, to allow the works to proceed.

A few weeks after the Sydenham operation, the 36-ton NIR steam crane No 3084 had another outing on the Bangor line. This time, hauled by DH No 1, the crane was used to lift concrete beams to form the roof of the new station building on the up platform at Bangor West.

Cultra Station and Crawfordsburn Viaduct

The disused station at Cultra was officially reopened for business on Monday, 3 July 1978. Given its close proximity to the Ulster Folk and Transport Museum, several special trains had already called at the station in the intervening years since its closure on 11 November 1957, as detailed in Chapter Seven. Now trains would only be calling at the new station to coincide with the opening hours of the Museum, but NIR had stipulated that, if there was sufficient demand from residents to have it open at other times, then due consideration would be given. One interesting detail about the newly laid platforms was that the edging stones had been brought from the old disused station at Goraghwood near Newry.

Also on the Bangor line, a major piece of engineering work was carried out at Crawfordsburn Viaduct over a period of four Sundays during November and December 1978. The line was therefore closed between Helen's Bay and Bangor on 19 and 26 November, and on 3 and 10 December. A substitutionary bus service ran on these dates.

New concrete decks being installed at Crawfordsburn Viaduct on Sunday, 10 December 1978.

Previously the track had just been set on the steel work of the viaduct, and water was seeping through into the stonework of the structure, causing faults. A new deck was now laid, constructed of forty concrete units, weighing 14 tons each. These units were loaded on to four flat wagons at Bangor station, which was the depot for the engineering trains, and propelled out to the viaduct by a Hunslet locomotive. On site near Helen's Bay, a crane from contractors Farrans was used to lift the concrete blocks from the wagons and place them onto the viaduct. New rails were laid on new wooden sleepers, and for the first time the track on the viaduct was ballasted.

Again, on the Bangor line, in early 1979, the old semaphore and banner signals in the Bangor area were decommissioned during a night possession from Saturday 17 to Sunday 18 February. New colour light signals were commissioned. The Victorian home gantry on the approach to Bangor station was to be donated to the Belfast & County Down Railway Trust for their proposed site at Ballynahinch Junction; the gantry was dismantled by a work party (which included myself) from the Railway Trust on Sunday, 25 February.

New Stations: Londonderry, Ballymena and Lurgan

A new station opened in Londonderry on Sunday, 24 February 1980. The new structure, which was situated 250 yards further towards Craigavon bridge than the previous station, was built on a former car park at Duke Street. The old station building, which had been damaged by bombs several years previously, was closed and the track mostly retained for freight traffic.

The first train out of the new station was the 17.40 hrs service to Belfast Central, which had several hundred passengers on board. The last train to leave the old station on the same day was the 11.30 hrs service to Belfast. The plan was to demolish the old station and platforms, with the exception of the clock tower, which was a listed building. It was proposed that the cleared space would be used for new sidings for freight, as well as to house a car park.

On Thursday, 19 February 1981, a new railway station at Ballymena was officially opened, at a cost of £250,000. NIR Director, Mr Rollo McClure officiated at the opening ceremony. Also in attendance were the station manager, Sam McCrea as well as George Close, the NIR Works and Buildings superintendent, who had overseen the work on the new building. It was revealed that plans had been drawn up for an integrated station for rail and bus, but unfortunately Ulsterbus withdrew its support for the project, and what was built was something of a hybrid, interlacing old and new.

Once again, the station buildings at Lurgan were extensively damaged by terrorist bombs, this time on Christmas Eve 1978. Work recommenced and the newly reconstructed station buildings opened on Monday, 31 August 1981, this time without too much ceremony.

March 1984: Civil Engineering Works at Ormeau Road Bridge

A special train timetable was introduced in March 1984 to allow civil engineering works at the Ormeau Road bridge in Belfast. The track at this location was liable to flooding, as it was below sea level and new pumps had to be installed. The up line was removed from the Blackstaff River at Belfast Central to mid-way between the Ormeau Road bridge near Botanic. The up line was then slewed on to the down line, adjacent the Ulster Television building, with a turnout provided on the Botanic side.

Re-Opened Stations and New Train Service

A new train service for Newry was launched and commenced on Monday, 14 May

1984, which was also the start date for a new NIR timetable. The newly constructed station at Newry (formerly Bessbrook, or Newry main line) was to be served mainly by Enterprise services on the Dublin line. The Newry and Mourne District Council had agreed to provide 50 per cent of the capital cost of the project, meaning that they would be contributing approximately £53,000.

To mark the occasion, a special train that day, departing Belfast Central at 11.05 hrs and calling at Portadown, Scarva, Poyntzpass and finally arriving in Newry at 12.10 hrs. From there, a coach took guests to the Glen Eagle Country Club for a luncheon. The special train left Newry again at 15.00 hrs, to return to Belfast Central.

Newly re-opened stations at Poyntzpass and Scarva also provided a new local service towards Belfast. The local service from Newry to Belfast (Monday to Saturday only) was a bit

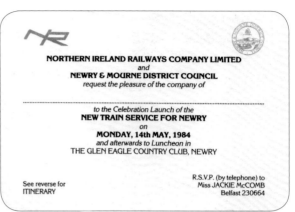

NORTHERN IRELAND RAILWAYS COMPANY LIMITED
and
NEWRY & MOURNE DISTRICT COUNCIL
request the pleasure of the company of

to the Celebration Launch of the
NEW TRAIN SERVICE FOR NEWRY
on
MONDAY, 14th MAY, 1984
and afterwards to Luncheon in
THE GLEN EAGLE COUNTRY CLUB, NEWRY

See reverse for
ITINERARY

R.S.V.P. (by telephone) to
Miss JACKIE McCOMB
Belfast 230664

Celebration launch of New Train Service for Newry on Monday, 14 May 1984. *(Author's collection)*

sparse, with the only commuter train being the 07.10 hrs Newry to Bangor (which left at 07.32 hrs on Saturdays). This was followed by a 08.01 hrs from Poyntzpass to Bangor (Monday to Friday only). The return services were the 16.35 hrs from Bangor to Newry (16.00 hrs Bangor–Poyntzpass on Saturdays), and the 17.40 hrs Bangor to Dundalk (Monday to Friday only).

To allow these new services to operate, Meigh signalbox had to be upgraded, so that it could be opened for part of the day. New signalling for the Poyntzpass–Dundalk section had been planned for the 1984/85 budget period, with a new crossover to be provided north of the Craigmore viaduct.

1985–1986: More Station Infrastructure Works

The new access tower from the car park to the side of Belfast Central station was under construction during May 1985. This allowed for the creation of a new entrance hall at car park level, with a new stairwell and escalator.

Bangor station was also undergoing a makeover in May 1985. A fresh frontage and interior had been completed in August 1985, at a cost of £100,000. The transformation was wholeheartedly welcomed by the travelling public, as it obliterated the station's formerly drab, grey exterior and dull, grubby interior. The Buffer Inn had also been refurbished, and an area of the station had been converted into shop units.

In late January 1986, work had commenced to create a new railway cutting at the Ulster Folk and Transport Museum at Cultra. A trailing siding was being installed with a turnout off the down main line, leading in to the Transport Museum Gallery. The siding was laid in January 1987, along with the installation of the turntable, which came from Athenry.

On a far less positive note, most of the station building on the up island platform at Greenisland was burned to the ground on the evening of Tuesday, 6 May 1986, the result of a malicious fire.

New and Refurbished Stations: City Hospital and Ballymoney

On Monday, 6 October 1986, a new station opened at Belfast City Hospital. The station would have no staff and was designed to help discourage vandalism, with two steel cladded shelters and a few steel seats. Not so good for passengers and not so good for revenue protection, in terms of attracting new customers!

Back in 1984, when a new hospital tower block had been built, the Eastern Health and Social Services Board had approached NIR to investigate the viability of building a station adjacent to the City Hospital complex. A survey had been carried out and the subsequent report identified that the addition of a station at this location could generate around half a million journeys per annum. By the end of 1985, the decision to build the station had been taken. The cost of the new station project was £225,000.

The formal reopening of Ballymoney railway station on Monday, 30 April 1990 was presided over by NIR Director, Mr W de F Smyth. Extensive restoration work had been carried out at the station at a cost of £200,000, which included a new glazed screen enclosing the passenger concourse, restored canopies and a footbridge. At the same time, a new signalling system was installed by Westinghouse between Coleraine and Ballymoney, at a cost of £350,000. To mark the opening too, an 80 Class motor coach was also named on the day by the Mayor of Ballymoney, Councillor JA Gaston. Coach No 97 was named "Glenshesk".

Replacement of Bridges at Holywood and Portadown

In 1987, a programme to replace two railway bridges at Holywood had been drawn up, which meant the closure of the line between Holywood and Bangor, and services being replaced by buses. The first bridge to be replaced was Bridge No 10, the pedestrian under-bridge on the Bangor side of the station. The second to be replaced was Bridge No 11, which crossed the road and led to the Esplanade and the Army's REME facility. Over the years, there had been a number of incidents involving lorries colliding with this particular bridge.

The replacement work was programmed for the weekend of 12–13 September 1987. All went according to plan at Bridge No 11, but unfortunately replacement units did not fit properly at Bridge No 10. Train services were due to resume first thing on Monday, 14 September, but the line had to remain closed until later in the day, with bus services being provided between Bangor and Holywood. During the work, passengers and pedestrians could not access the walking route under Bridge No 10, and so a temporary footbridge was erected across the tracks, mid-way along the platforms at Holywood.

In September 1990, the Bann River Bridge, No 242, which carries the railway over the River Bann at Portadown, was replaced. A report following a detailed survey of the bridge superstructure had been submitted in June 1989, and this indicated serious deterioration of its condition, to a degree that immediate replacement of the complete superstructure was required. The demolition of the existing superstructure and the construction of its subsequent replacement, involving over 300 tonnes of new steelwork, was completed within the planned full possession period of two weeks, during the weekends of 7 and 14 September 1990.

Late 1980s: Belfast Cross-Harbour Railway Project

The major contract for the construction of road and rail bridges for the Belfast Cross-Harbour Railway project was won by the Graham/Farrans joint venture, who were up against highly competitive European tenders from Holland, Germany and France. The overall cost, including acquiring land, would be somewhere in the region of £87 million, and the EC was paying 75 per cent of the £31 million construction costs. A special casting factory was built at Wolff Road in the Belfast Harbour Estate for the manufacture of the concrete box units, which would link together to make the carriageway or the railway. The factory would be able to make three such boxes each day, each four metres in length. Each box unit weighed in at 90 tonnes and, when lifted into position, they would be literally "glued" together in segments. The technique of joining the pre-cast concrete boxes, known as "match cast glued segmental construction" was at the forefront of technology, and this was the first time it had ever been tried in Ireland. The only major hiccup reported was the collapse of one span of a flyover at York Road.

The first sign of any work starting on this major project was on 13 August 1990, when a 110-foot high pile driver arrived at Belfast York Road yard. This was to be used for placing piles for the new railway between York Road and Belfast Central stations. By May 1991, work to clear the route from York Road towards the city was well underway. The new railway would be more than 1.5 kilometres long, and the elevated section of road would be 900 metres long. The new Cross-Harbour Rail Link spanning the River Lagan was to be known as the Dargan Bridge, named after the entrepreneur William Dargan (1799–1867), one of Ireland's most famous engineers.

By March 1992, the new alignment for Lagan Junction was starting to take shape; the area where Queen's Quay station once stood was a mound of earth; coffer dams were being constructed in the River Lagan, and platforms were under construction at the new Yorkgate railway station.

Yorkgate station under construction, 25 May 1992. *(Author)*

As part of the transformation at the York Road end of the project, Belfast York Road passenger station was to close after the last train service on Friday, 16 October 1992. It was a historic moment for a station which had originally opened on 11 April 1848. A good number of railway enthusiasts, including myself, were present, and quite a few of us travelled out on the last trains to Carrickfergus, and back again to York Road. The last train out was the 22.00 hrs service Belfast York Road to Larne Harbour, formed by Castle Class set, No 454. The last train in was the 21.50 hrs service from Larne Harbour to Belfast York Road, formed by Castle Class set, No 457.

Yorkgate Station

On Saturday, 17 October 1992, the new station on the Cross-Harbour railway at Yorkgate opened for passenger services. The station had been named after the large shopping centre which was just a few hundred yards away from it. At the early stages of design in fact, some consideration had been given to the option of having a covered, high-level walkway built between the station and the shopping centre. The station would serve as a temporary terminus for the Larne line trains until September 1994, when the opening of the complete link would relegate Yorkgate back to through-station status. The first passenger train to use the new station, a week before services officially began, had been an 80 Class special train, "The Gate Opener", which was operated by the MRSI. This train was formed by Nos 98, 779 and 97.

By November 1992, the first concrete box units forming the railway viaduct were in place at Middlepath Street and Queen's Quay, and most of this section was in place by December 1992. Meanwhile, the elevated road and rail highway was cutting a swathe through the city, at more than 50 metres a week. Three of the concrete sections were being slotted together per day.

New railway viaduct at Middlepath Street, Belfast, 3 December 1992. *(Author)*

By December 1992, the platform canopies and platforms at the closed Belfast York Road station had all been all swept away, in preparation for building the new train sheds which would replace the facility at the Central Service Depot (formerly Queen's Quay).

The concrete piers were now in position in the River Lagan, and on 8 June 1993, the first concrete supporting unit to form the railway was in place in the river. By late November 1993, the new steel bridge section crossing Bridge End road was positioned on the new railway route, just north of Lagan Junction. Around this time too, the steel work was being erected for the new train shed at Belfast York Road depot.

By April 1994, the railway route was complete and ballasted, ready for the track laying, which commenced the following month. The crossing loop at Donegall Quay was in place in May, and the track at that stage was only 100 yards short of Lagan Junction. On 12 August 1994, the point and crossing work at Lagan Junction had been completed, and the track across the River Lagan bridge was being relayed at the same time.

The first empty diesel train, formed by a three-car Castle Class set, traversed the route on Wednesday, 21 September 1994.

The Opening of the Cross-Harbour Railway

On Saturday 26 and Sunday 27 November 1994, special charity trains ran for the public from Belfast Yorkgate to Belfast Central. The Rail-Link bus service which ran between the two stations also ceased operation at the end of services on the same Saturday.

The new link would provide passengers in Northern Ireland with a unified rail network for the first time ever. The final cost of the Rail Link was £29 million, of which 75 per cent was provided by the European Regional Development Fund. A double-track section had been installed at Donegall Quay, which meant that trains could cross at this point along the single-line section. This location was also earmarked for a new high-level station, which was still on the list of proposals at this stage.

On Monday, 28 November 1994, the Cross-Harbour link between Belfast Yorkgate and Belfast Central became operational. Along with some other railway enthusiasts, I was on the first train out of Central station, which was at 06.35 hrs. I went as far as Greenisland, to return on the first train in, which was the 06.20 hrs service from Larne Harbour to Belfast Central. The morning rush hour went well on the first day of the new system.

Also on Monday, 28 November came good news in the form of an announcement from the Government that the line between Bleach Green Junction and Antrim would be relayed, and that Londonderry and Portrush trains would be directed through to Belfast Central along the new line. This would probably mean that the line between Lisburn and Antrim would have to close.

Station Developments

On 1 December 1993, the newly refurbished station at Whitehead was officially opened by Mr Ian Doherty, the new Chairman of the Northern Ireland Transport Holding Company. The restoration of the station had been a joint venture by NIR and the Holding Company, and had also received 68 per cent funding from the European Development Fund. The total cost of the project was around £360,000. The architects were able to sympathetically combine the original Edwardian character of the buildings with the requirements of a modern railway station. Facilities included a ticket office, enclosed waiting room and toilet amenities.

Meanwhile at Seahill station, the wooden platform surfaces had deteriorated badly, and a number of malicious fires over a period of time had wreaked more of their own damage. A decision was taken to rebuild the platforms, again in wood, and the job was not an easy one due to the station's elevated site. This work was carried out between November 1994 and February 1995. Half of each platform was initially removed on both sides, to allow new sections to be built, and when this was complete, the other half platforms were rebuilt. During the work, a temporary footbridge, constructed of scaffolding equipment and planks, was put in place mid-way along the platforms and access was gained through a piece of wasteland on the Seahill Road.

The old Queen's Quay depot area was handed over to the Department of the Environment on 1 January 1995. The area would soon be completely changed, as the M3 motorway was to run through the site, to link up with the Sydenham Bypass.

1995: Reopening Of Belfast Great Victoria Street

By March 1995, work was well underway on the Great Victoria Street rail project, the new railway formation at Blythefield curve was in position, along with a new bridge in place. Six houses had to be demolished to allow the curve to be built, and accordingly, six new houses had to be built at the corner of Belfast City Hospital station. Construction of the new station was also taking place, and the bus yard behind the Europa Buscentre had been partially sectioned off to allow work to continue. The site for the platforms and track had been completely cleared. During the weekend of 31 March, City Junction was installed; the line between Botanic and Adelaide was closed to allow the work to proceed.

Commemorative First Day Ticket for Great Victoria Street station for the opening on Saturday, 30 September 1995. *(Author's collection)*

On Thursday, 14 September 1995, I travelled on a special train at 15.20 hrs from Belfast Central to Great Victoria Street: this was my first run in to the new site. A few weeks later, on Thursday 28 September, special trains ran from Belfast Central to Great Victoria Street, for an NIR staff and families open night. My family and I went on the 18.02 hrs train to see the new line and station, and took the 1840 hrs special train back out. During the next few weeks, there were plenty of meetings in NIR and many journeys in and out of the new site on special trains.

Saturday, 30 September 1995 saw the opening of the new station and track

STATIONS AND INFRASTRUCTURE CHANGES

layout, with a new train service in operation from that day. The first train out was the 06.30 hrs service to Larne Harbour. There were of course a good number of railway enthusiasts in attendance that day.

NIR marked the occasion with the issue of special commemorative tickets for the first 1,000 passengers using the station on its first day. I was on duty for part of the day and went in again that evening, to ensure that security arrangements were in place for the end of the night. The celebratory events that weekend were really memorable, but for most of Northern Ireland's railway enthusiasts, the icing on the cake would be on Sunday, 1 October, when former Great Northern steam locomotive, *Merlin* would haul the first steam train out of the new station, with more than 300 enthusiasts on board!

Monday, 2 October 1995 was the first full day of rush hour services, and everything ran well, apart from one train failure at 08.20 hrs. The station was officially opened by the then Secretary of State, Sir Patrick Mayhew at a special ceremony on Tuesday, 7 November 1995.

More Stations: Crawfordsburn and Carrickfergus

The last day of operations at the wooden platform station at Crawfordsburn was Sunday, 31 August 1997. I made sure to go to the station that day, and bought a ticket from the conductor for Crawfordsburn to Bangor, but sadly the print on the ticket faded away very quickly!

Work on a complete refurbishment of the buildings at Carrickfergus station had commenced in the spring of 1995. Phase One of the project involved the strengthening of the roof beams and of sections of the walls. Once this was completed, Phase Two would see the refurbishment of the whole station, with particular attention being given to the rotting timberwork throughout the structure. Careful consideration would also to be given to the fact that the station was a DoE historically-listed Building. The work was being carried out by Henry Brothers of Magherafelt, at a total cost of about £850,000.

The refurbished station at Carrickfergus was opened fully to the public from the last week in August 2001. The new facilities included more spacious waiting areas, public toilets, a shop and a refreshment room. A large park-and-ride car park was also provided. The official opening ceremony took place on 30 November 2001, when a commemorative plaque was unveiled by the then Minister for Regional Development, Mr Peter Robinson.

1998: The Belfast–Lisburn Relay

The track relay between Central Junction and Lisburn finally commenced on 2 March 1998, having been delayed by almost a year for various reasons. Both the up and down lines were to be relayed on the 8.5 mile route, the work was to be done in three phases.

The first phase, involving the stretch of the line between the north end of Lisburn station and Central Junction in Belfast, was carried out by an external contractor, Mowlem (Railways), working under a series of short single-line possessions. Each single-line phase was about 1.2 miles in length and took approximately four weeks to complete. This allowed train services to continue to operate in each direction at four trains per hour. Mowlem also carried out the second phase of the work, between City Junction in Belfast and the north end of Belfast Central station. The third phase of the relay took in the main line platforms at Lisburn, to tie into the continuously welded rail on either side of the station. This task was carried out by the NIR in-house relay squad, working under a number of weekend possessions between February and July 1999.

Although one aim of the project was to provide for a maximum speed of 90 mph throughout, there were a few curves in the route, where the combination of a sharp radius and the maximum allowable cant, or super-elevation of the outer rail, made it necessary to maintain a local speed restriction of less than 90 mph. The line between Lisburn and Belfast was returned to double-line service on 15 December 1998.

The following year, further such work was carried out. On 23 May 1999, the line between Belfast Central and Central Junction was closed to traffic for track relay and other work, including the installation of continuously welded rail, the replacement of the track drainage system and the building of a new pumping station at the Ormeau Road bridge. The closure would also facilitate the construction of a concrete deck, which was to be built above the airspace of the track between Botanic station and Shaftesbury Square tunnel. Botanic and City Hospital stations were closed during the relay. A special bus service operated between Belfast Central and Great Victoria Street stations to facilitate passengers during the closure.

During this line closure too, services from Londonderry, Lisburn, Portadown, and Enterprise services on the Dublin line terminated at Belfast Great Victoria Street station. To facilitate the running of Enterprise services, the platforms at Great Victoria Street were finally lengthened, just prior to the closure of the line. The line reopened on 30 August 1999.

Bangor Station Reconstruction

In the autumn of 1998, Lord Dubs, the Minister of the Environment for Northern Ireland, announced that a new integrated bus and rail passenger station would be built in Bangor, at a cost of £4.2 million.

To make way for a new combined station to be built on the site, the demolition of Bangor bus and rail stations commenced on Monday, 7 June 1999. The old bus engineering sheds and bus wash were also demolished, to be rebuilt further back up the yard. Existing bus operations were to be temporarily moved to the Abbey Street car park, to allow the work to proceed. The projected date for the opening of the new station was November 2000.

Living in Bangor myself and of course taking a great interest in the railway, I closely observed the progress of the new station. I noted a number of developments during the demolition and construction process, as follows:

After the demolition of the old station, a mains water pipe was dug up by a JCB in the middle of the site. This water main had not been on the drawings, and so the contractor had no idea of its existence. As a result, the site was flooded for a couple of weeks, the project delayed.

Bangor railway station, just days before demolition, June 1999. *(Author)*

The wave profiles of the roof were impressive. The gap between the platforms was however supposed to be joined by another part of the roof, sweeping from one platform to the other, which would have enclosed the whole area. Unfortunately funding issues removed this feature from the project.

Concerning the down side, or the sea side, of Platform Three, there weren't sufficient funds to provide large glass panels, to keep the effects of the weather from passengers. Instead it was proposed that these panels would be open mesh, for security purposes only. Luckily however, Mr Hesketh stepped in, and somehow ensured that a number of glass panels would be provided to protect the passengers from the elements.

The new building was planned so as to integrate seamlessly into the existing urban context, yet to make a modern and confident statement at the same time. The result was a striking building, featuring the dramatic use of glass and steel in its construction, along with a pleasing nautical theme, which provided impressive and comfortable public transport facilities. The curved "wave" profile of the undulating roof canopy covers quickly became famous, and, along with other design features, was a clever way to pick up and reflect elements of the station's seaside location. An escalator, a lift and a staircase would be provided to take rail passengers from the concourse level to another waiting area and to the platforms.

The new integrated bus and rail station at Bangor opened in stages. Rail passengers were the first to benefit, when the station partially opened for train services on 22 January 2001. Bus passengers had to wait a few more months, until 5 March, before they could make use of the new station. The official opening was held on 5 April 2001.

1998: Bleach Green to Antrim Relay

It was announced in the autumn of 1998 that the direct railway line between Belfast and Antrim, which had been closed since January of that year, was to be reopened. The long-awaited announcement was made by Lord Dubs, Minister for the Environment in Northern Ireland.

After a lengthy delay, the main contractor for the track relay between Bleach Green Junction and Antrim was announced as Farrans from Dunmurry, who had been up against significant international competition. The £14 million undertaking commenced on 29 November 1999, and with a projected 51-week time frame, was due to be completed by late 2000. The project would include the building of new stations at Mossley West and Templepatrick, the relaying of 15 miles of track, and new signalling. Before the main track relaying contract began, two smaller contracts with a total value of £1 million had been awarded, for the carrying out of minor repairs on 28 small bridges along the route, as well as to the listed structure, the Bleach Green Viaduct near Whiteabbey.

Ballast locomotive for Bleach Green–Antrim relay, arriving at Muckamore, Sunday, 18 June 2000. *(Author)*

The contract for supplying ballast to the track was won by the Railway Preservation Society of Ireland, who supplied steam locomotive No 3. The locomotive was taken by road from Whitehead to Muckamore on 18 June 2000, and placed on the track, where it would haul ballast wagons between Antrim and Bleach Green Junction. The locomotive was removed from the track at Antrim stone dock on 25 November that year.

The first test train for the contractor, Farrans ran through the Bleach Green Junction to Antrim section on 26 November 2000. The train was formed by Castle Class set, No 458 and ran a few times, with the best time being a departure from Antrim at 12.14 hrs, to pass Whiteabbey at 12.31 hrs. The following day, the line was handed over to NIR by the contractor, to allow training trains to commence.

The first passenger train over the Bleach Green Junction to Antrim route was on 16 December 2000 for the Irish Railway Record Society. Formed by NIR GM locomotive, No 112 and six Mk II carriages, this train ran from Belfast Central to Ballymena. It was also the first service to stop at the new, as yet uncompleted station at Mossley West.

Following a derailment at Antrim which temporarily closed the Antrim branch to Lisburn, passenger trains operated over the new line from 16 March 2001. The first train on the line was the 09.27 hrs Belfast Central to Antrim, which was formed by a Castle Class set. The next was an 80 Class set.

For gauging purposes, and for also the first time, a spare De Dietrich train set (GM Locomotive, No 220 and 8 coaches) ran from Belfast Central to Ballymena via Bleach Green on Wednesday, 25 April 2001. The train returned to Belfast Central via the Antrim branch. On the same day, an RPSI train, formed by Locomotive No 171 and six coaches, ran from Belfast Central to Antrim via Bleach Green, back to Belfast via the Antrim branch and then on to Bangor.

On 17 May 2001, and once more for gauging purposes and also for the first time, an Irish Rail Class 201 locomotive and eight Mk III coaches ran from Belfast York Road to Antrim via Bleach Green. The train was in Belfast on a charter trip from Dublin. Finally, after a long wait, on Sunday, 10 June 2001, passenger services commenced between Belfast Central and Londonderry via the new Bleach Green to Antrim line.

The official launch ceremony for the new line was held on Saturday, 9 June 2001, beside the new Mossley West station. Guests included the then Minister for Regional Development, Gregory Campbell. However, although the station at Mossley West was ready for use, it wasn't opened for passenger traffic until 15 October that year, due to planning restrictions. A limited passenger service was retained on the Lisburn to Antrim branch following the opening of the Bleach Green line, but these services were eventually withdrawn on 30 June 2003. The day after the official launch, on Sunday, 10 June 2001, a railway Family Fun Day for staff and families had been organised to mark the opening of the new line. Special trains ran to and from Antrim, and I travelled with my family on the 14.25 hrs six-car 80 Class special to Antrim, and then the 15.41 hrs special back to Belfast. A steam train was also used for some of the special trains. Light refreshments and entertainment were provided at the Waterfront Hall in Belfast, with souvenirs also being distributed.

Tickets for the reopening of the Antrim to Bleach Green line, Sunday, 10 June 2001. *(Author's collection)*

Summer 2000: Portrush Branch Track Replacement

If you travelled on the Portrush branch in 1999 and in early 2000, you will know that the track needed a lot of attention at this juncture. I remember travelling there on an 80 Class set on one occasion when the buckeyes were coming up and down so much that the coaches could have detached!

Looking out of the train window on the line in September 1999, you would have seen piles of old rail from the Belfast to Lisburn relay stacked at the side of the track on the branch at the Shell Hill bridge, awaiting for urgently needed work there to proceed. I have chosen the sub-title of this item carefully, as some people were calling the work to be done on the Portrush branch a "track relay", while others called it "track replacement" – however the official term being used within the company was "heavy maintenance". The possible use of three different terms to describe the same job was down to the materials being used on this occasion. A track relay usually entails brand new materials, however the Portrush branch line was to be replaced with old materials originally from the Belfast to Lisburn relay – which is why it was officially called a heavy maintenance project.

The Portrush branch closed for the work on 19 June 2000. First, the old track was completely removed. Then the "new" rails were used under the crop and weld procedure. Basically the old rails were fine, apart from a foot or so at each end, where the rails had dipped. Then the rails were welded together, forming a six-mile, continuously welded rail section. The line reopened on 11 September 2000, in time for the start of the university term. It was a job well done, in a timely fashion and within a small budget.

Coleraine Station and Other Infrastructure Work: 2000–2001

In the spring of 2000, approval was given for a £1.9 million project to build an integrated bus and rail facility at Coleraine Station. The original features of the Lanyon designed railway station, including the platforms, would be preserved and integrated with new modern facilities, including a cafe, waiting area and modern offices for staff. Work commenced in the summer of 2000.

The new station opened to both bus and rail passengers on Monday, 26 March 2001. The official opening was not held however until 21 September 2001, as work on restoring the Lanyon building had not been fully completed. The Minister for Regional Development at the time, Gregory Campbell officially opened the new £4 million integrated transport centre.

Otherwise that summer, there was a five-day closure of the line between Lagan Junction and Sydenham from Monday, 14 August, while the steel bridge over the Connswater river at Victoria Park was being replaced. The bridge had been in a poor state of repair, and a temporary speed restriction of 20 mph had been in place for some time. A replacement bus service between Sydenham and Belfast Central was supplied for passengers while the work was being done.

In the autumn of 2000, two landslides over a three-month period blocked the Bangor line. On Friday, 29 September, the up line was blocked by a landslide at St Columbanus bridge, while on Friday, 8 December, another landslide blocked the up line, 200 yards on the Cultra side of Seahill station. The line was closed for several days for clearance, with most of the repair work being carried out during nighttime possessions of the track.

Belfast Central Refurbishment

On 28 August 2000, major refurbishment work at Belfast Central station began, under a 71-week contract costing £4.2 million. The work would include the removal of the two passenger ramps from the concourse on to the two island platforms: these were to be replaced by two walkways, known as air bridges, which would lead from the ticket barrier area towards the platforms. From the air bridges, a staircase, lift or escalator could be used to reach the platform level, where there would also be a new heated waiting area. Although not part of the original plan, in the event a further air bridge was provided, linking the first two, and offering passengers a route between the platforms without having to re-enter the main part of the building. A glazed exterior would overlook the rails, providing a good viewing gallery.

Additional space was made available in the concourse area of the station, allowing the provision of more seats in the open-plan area. This plan flowed through to the open food court, shop and toilets. The station's catering facilities would provide more choice, with three outlets available – Little Chef, Upper Crust and Taste. The onsite newsagent's shop would also offer the usual newspapers, magazines and snacks.

A new extension was to be created at the side of the station, which would be known as the side atrium, and would greatly improve the access between the car park and bus stop at ground level, and the station concourse level. A new lift and escalator would be provided as well as a staircase. Work would also be carried out to extend the ticket office and frontage of the station. The number of spaces available in the car park would increase to over 200, with dedicated spaces for passengers travelling First Plus on the Enterprise service.

Although the vast majority of the refurbishment work had been completed by November 2002, the official reopening of the station was scheduled for the 25 March 2003. The guest of honour on the big day was the Departmental Minister, Angela Smith. To welcome in the new station on its first day of operation of course, train services were disrupted for a time, courtesy of a bomb scare at Lurgan.

Bangor Line Relay

As mentioned in an earlier chapter, 75 per cent of the money for the project to overhaul the Bangor line was coming from European funding, and NIR was waiting for the DRD to provide the remainder as agreed. As part of the preparatory work and to give more height for road users, the railway bridge at Station Road, Craigavad had to be replaced. This work was carried out over the weekend of 29 June 2001, and during this period, a temporary road had been laid through the Royal Belfast Golf Club, exiting towards Seahill. Then, on Saturday, 7 July, the Bangor line was also closed for the weekend in preparation for the relay.

Work was to be carried out in four stages. The first two stages would take place between Bangor and Craigavad and entail single-line working. The remaining two stages would be between Craigavad and Bridge End, and require single-line working. On Monday, 15 October 2001, a new timetable came into effect to allow for single-line working in several stages as work progressed.

On the day itself, however, the single-line working did not commence, neither did the relay – but the new timetable did! Additional buses were part of the timetable provisions too, and operated only in the morning and evening peak periods, calling at Bangor West, Cultra, Marino and Holywood, to set down only. Single-line working between Craigavad and Bangor finally commenced on Thursday, 18 October. On this first evening, my 17.27 hrs train from Yorkgate was 22 minutes late. On getting in to Central, I missed the only train, at 17.40 hrs, and so I travelled on the 18.00 hrs special bus, arriving at Seahill at 18.40 hrs (a journey which would normally have taken 18 minutes by train).

Work continued through the night during this period, and on 22 October, between 02.10 hrs and 03.10 hrs, there was as much noise as during the daytime, with lorries driving up and down the track and, when reversing, making sharp beeping sounds. Local residents were complaining a lot about the reverse beeping noise!

On 9 December 2001, the up line was laid through Seahill. The line was closed on Saturday and Sundays, and a replacement bus service was provided. The fields around the up side at Crawfordsburn were transformed into a civil engineering yard, with a large pile of hundreds of tons of ballast, rails and sleepers. Another ballast dump was created on the down side of Seahill, half a mile on the Bangor side. A couple of residents close to the sites had to move out to bed and breakfasts on several occasions, due to the noise in the area during the night!

The relay train from the USA, supplied by Harsco New Track Construction Company, was brought in for the project: this would be the first time this vehicle was to be used in the UK. The machine was used to lay new track; its motive power was a caterpillar, and its speed was in the region of 1 mph. One of the problems with the relay train was trying to keep it constantly fed with concrete sleepers. A GM locomotive with six hoppers was in continuous use, dropping ballast along the new track.

In the early hours of Sunday, 24 February 2002, two engineering trains operated by the contractors collided, adjacent to the Belfast City Airport. A special Unimog train was operating on the same line as the 07/5 tamping and lining machine. Tragically, the driver, who was from Mowlem's contractors, was killed in the collision.

From Good Friday, 29 March 2002 to Sunday, 7 April inclusive, there were no

Relay train laying down line between Seahill and Helen's Bay, Saturday, 9 February 2002. (Author)

trains on the Bangor line, so that relay work could proceed. Buses ran in place of trains. Double-line working was restored on the Bangor line some weeks later, on Monday, 20 May, but the relay had not been fully completed. Additional peak hour train services were able to operate on the line, until a new timetable commenced on Monday, 1 July 2002.

By the end of the contract, the status of the relay work was as follows: Bangor station yard: dug out and completely relayed, including point and crossing work; Bangor to Seapark (Holywood): dug out and completely relayed, including two new crossovers at Craigavad and a new turnout at Cultra museum; Holywood: curves re-railed and new ballast; Holywood station to Kinnegar old station: dug out and completely relayed; Kinnegar to Middlepath Street bridge: re-railed and new ballast; Middlepath Street bridge to Lagan Junction: no work done; bi-directional signalling: not completed between Bangor and Bridge End.

As advised by NIR in a *Neighbourhood News* sheet, essential finishing work on the Bangor line had yet to be carried out. The work still required involved the final alignment of the track, the replacement of damaged sleepers and a tidy-up of the site. While this was all being done, the Bangor line closed on Saturdays and Sundays for four weekends in September 2003. All rail services were replaced by substitutionary buses, with earlier start times from Bangor.

First-Time Use for Steel Sleepers

Discussions regarding the possible use of steel sleepers went on for some time at NIR. These had been successfully used by Railtrack in GB, but had not been used in Ireland before. In March 2003, however, a batch was finally purchased, to be used in Portadown. Platform One and Two roads there were relayed using the steel sleepers; Platform Three road was not relayed.

The first use of steel sleepers on the main line in Northern Ireland was in April 2004, at Bangor West. The new track had only been laid for just over two years however, when it had to be taken up to allow the up line to be lowered, in preparation for the new CAF trains, which were due to arrive in a few months' time. Over half a mile of new steel sleepers were laid during the Easter closure, from Saturday, 10 April to Tuesday, 13 April inclusive. During the closure, ballast was brought to the site using Irish Rail's 201 Class locomotive No 217.

2005: Infrastructure Work and the Larne Line Relay

On 11 March 2005, the cast iron footbridge at Ballymoney was removed and taken to storage and a temporary footbridge constructed of scaffolding items took its place. In the same month, Knockmore station platform (up line) closed; the last train to call there was the 18.45 hrs Bangor to Portadown service. The platform remained in place for some years, until it was removed on 18 May 2012.

On Saturday, 26 March 2005 (Easter Saturday), the £25.2 million relay of the Larne line commenced. The work was to be done between Bleach Green Junction and Whitehead, where the track would be replaced, with new drainage and ballast. New signalling equipment would also be installed.

Phase One of the project ran from 26 March 2005. The down line would remain intact for the operation of three trains only, each way, Monday to Friday in the rush hour, until June 2005. Trains from Larne Harbour to Belfast in the morning were at 06.45 hrs, 07.25 hrs and 08.05 hrs. Evening services back to Larne Harbour were at 15.56, 16.37 and 17.15 hrs. These trains were generally formed by two six-car 80 Class sets and one five-car 80 Class set. No trains ran on Saturdays or Sundays, and a bus substitution operated. The last trains ran on 3 June, and no further trains would be scheduled until October 2005.

Phase Two of the project operated from 4 June 2005, when no rail services operated on the Larne line. A special bus substitution timetable was in operation until October 2005.

Phase Three of the project operated from 3 October 2005, when a limited train service resumed between Carrickfergus and Belfast. It was planned that all rail services would resume in December 2005.

Track relay in progress at Jordanstown, Wednesday, 16 June 2005. *(Author)*

Once more, the RPSI steam locomotive No 3 came to the rescue, as the contracted ballast locomotive for the relay. The locomotive was transported by road from Whitehead to Greenisland on 4 August 2005.

By September 2005, the contractor had advanced enough to allow gauging trains on to the newly laid track. The first train into the Bleach Green Junction to Carrickfergus section was CAF No 3018 at 20.45 hrs on Thursday, 22 September, followed later by Castle Class No 455. On 2 October 2005, after the tests were completed, the contractor was able to hand this section of track back to NIR. This allowed, from 3 October, three trains to run from Carrickfergus to Belfast Central in the morning rush hour, and three trains back to Carrickfergus in the busiest evening period.

With a new timetable in operation, the Larne line reopened between Belfast Central and Carrickfergus on Monday, 10 October 2005 (after seven months). The portion of line between Carrickfergus and Whitehead and to Larne remained closed, and buses continued to operate there.

The first train between Carrickfergus and Larne Harbour ran on 5 December 2005, and was a GM locomotive and six ballast hoppers, discharging between Whitehead and Larne Harbour. The following day, gauging trains ran between Carrickfergus and Whitehead. The first train in was Castle Class 455 at 09.30 hrs, followed later by an 80 Class. A CAF train only got as far as Downshire, as the RPSI locomotive No 3 and hoppers had run through the points at Kilroot.

On 17 December 2005, the line between Carrickfergus and Whitehead was handed back to NIR by the contractor; however the Whitehead pedestrian crossing was not commissioned until early February 2006. On 22 December 2005, a gauging run by a CAF train No 3023 operated between Belfast York Road and Larne Harbour.

Although the line between Whitehead and Larne Harbour had not been included in the relay project, track renewal was carried out at five specific sections with a total length of three miles. These sections were as follows: Whitehead to Slaughterford (1150 metres); Camerons (700 metres); Magheramorne to Glynn (1150 metres); Howdens (1535 metres); and Larne Station (300 metres). This work was costed at £2.1 million and was carried out in nine weeks.

On Monday, 13 February 2006, train services resumed between Belfast Central and Larne Harbour, following the completion of the relay between Bleach Green Junction and Whitehead, and with the partial relay from Whitehead and Larne Harbour. A new timetable, which was due to commence on 16 January, had to be aborted due to a dispute between train drivers and NIR management.

Fortwilliam Train Care Depot

In late 2003, a new £11.4 million train care depot site was under construction, but the project had to be delayed for a time, due to the discovery of an electricity power cable running through the site. At the end of August 2004 however, contractors moved onsite to construct the building. The new facility was designed to accommodate the cleaning of the 23 new trains, and would be capable of stabling and allowing the cleaning of up to ten of the new three-car sets at a time. The support beams were 170 metres long, 30 metres wide and 10 metres high, and the cladding was aluminium. The first train to enter into the new sidings and cleaning area, on 2 July 2005, was a GM 201 class and six NIR ballast hoppers. The first CAF train ran into the depot on 15 August 2005.

The new facility opened for business on 24 October 2005, on time and on budget. The Depot was officially opened on 6 December that year. To mark the occasion, a special train arrived from Belfast York Road depot, with a number of dignitaries on board.

Disability Enhancement Programme

In April 2007, work began on a package to upgrade rail stations and halts across NIR. The project, known as the DDA (Disability Discrimination Act) Station Enhancement Programme, would be implemented in two phases. The work included the installation of new shelters, lighting, seating, signage, as well as re-surfacing.

Phase One of the project was carried out between Bangor and Newry. Phase Two of the work commenced in January 2008, and covered the Larne and Londonderry lines. The main contractor in the £17 million project was Cleary Contracting, along with their sub-contractors.

North of Ballymena Relay and Finaghy Bridge Works

Scheduled work on relaying in the Ballymena area commenced in the summer of 2008. The Phase One work involving the digging out of wet beds on the track, and this required the imposition of a temporary speed restriction of 20 mph. Phase Two of the project began in the winter of 2008, and entailed the converting of existing jointed track into continuously welded rail throughout the section of track between Broughdone (north of Cullybackey) and Coleraine. Because of this work, combining relaying and re-railing of various kinds, the line between Ballymena and Coleraine was closed from 30 March 2009. A substitutionary bus service was provided during the line closure. The line re-opened on 29 June 2009.

Meanwhile, between June and September 2008, Finaghy Road North bridge underwent major engineering work. Following a serious incident on the mainland, when a motor vehicle careered off a road bridge onto the railway, causing a major train crash, road over rail bridges all over the UK had to be subject to certain protective measures, depending on the circumstances of each bridge. During this work, a temporary footbridge for passengers was erected across both platforms, approximately half-way along the platforms.

Newry Station

In the autumn of 2005 an appraisal was being advanced by NIR relating to a new railway station at Newry. The aims of the project would be multiple, including: the erection of a new station building on the up side of the track (the side near Newry city); the creation of a new link road into the site; the upgrading and lengthening of the platforms; the provision of a new internal footbridge, with additional lifts and the creation a new park-and-ride facility for 300 cars on the up side, with a space for a connecting bus to the centre of Newry. The car park on the down side would still be available for occasional use. Work on the new £12.6 million project began in February 2008. The main contractors were local firms, Felix O'Hare & Co for the buildings and park-and-ride, and Fox Building Engineering for the access road.

The new station was operational from 7 September 2009. It was officially opened on the morning of Wednesday, 25 November 2009 by the then Regional Development Minister, Conor Murphy.

Antrim and Portrush Branch

On 6 May 2010, Bridge No 3 at Lissue on the Antrim branch was removed to facilitate works at the Lissue level crossing on the Lisburn to Portadown main line. There was repair work to be done to the bridge itself too, since Bridge No 3 had been damaged by a lorry the previous December. The bridge was repaired on site, and both it and the track were put back in place on 5 September 2010.

In the spring of 2011, a £1.3 million engineering project to upgrade the Portrush branch was carried out, necessitating a line closure from 12 March to 28 March. The re-railing project would give passengers a more comfortable journey and would allow the maintenance of the 70 mph speed limit on the route.

Infrastructure Work

Work on a £9 million programme to extend railway station platforms on the Larne, Bangor and Portadown lines commenced in November 2010. The project involved extending 37 platforms at 20 stations and halts. This was required to allow six-car trains to stop at designated stations. Additional lighting, and extra shelters and seating would also be provided, with the possibility of some signal alterations being carried out as well. In earlier initiatives of this kind, Holywood platform had been extended for six-car CAF operations from 22 December 2006, and Cullybackey from 24 January 2007.

2011–2012: New Adelaide Depot

Construction of the new £27.8 million Train Care Maintenance Facility at Adelaide commenced in May 2011. The new depot would include: an engineering depot; staff accommodation facilities; a refuelling facility; train wash; train stabling facilities; and a material storage area.

The first train movement into the new yard (at the north end) was a six-car CAF Class 4000, in the early hours of the morning of 7 June 2012. New signalling was commissioned on 2 July 2012, and trains were running within the depot from 9 October.

The official opening of the Adelaide depot was on 12 December 2012. Dignitaries and others were taken there from Belfast Central on board an RPSI steam special (Locomotive No 186). In preparation for the occasion, the steam train had operated a gauging run to the depot on 8 December.

Ballymoney Footbridge

In the spring of 2012, a £1.3 million investment project was announced, which would benefit rail users, pedestrians and cyclists in the Ballymoney area. The result of a successful collaboration between the DRD, Translink, Ballymoney Borough Council and national charity Sustrans, the project would see the construction of a new, fully accessible, traffic-free bridge at the station and an additional 35 park-and-ride spaces for the increasing number of people travelling by rail. The new footbridge opened at Ballymoney station on 1 November 2012, with an official opening ceremony on 7 November.

Bridge End Reconstruction and New Stations for Antrim and Portadown

On 9 January 2012, work began on the reconstruction and extension to the platforms at Bridge End station. First of all, new platforms were constructed at the Belfast Central end of the station and were in operation from 14 February 2012, with a temporary footbridge in place. Work then began on the removal of the old wooden platforms on the Bangor end, to allow for their reconstruction. A new, long, high-level walkway was then to be installed, to allow access to the down platform without the need for a footbridge. The old sidings area at Ballymacarrett was used as a work and storage yard during this time. The official launch of the new station took place on Wednesday, 28 March 2012, when it was renamed Titanic Quarter.

In the spring of 2011, Translink unveiled development plans for Antrim bus and rail stations, which would involve the construction of an integrated, modern and sustainable passenger facility to serve the local area. The construction of the new £2.2 million combined bus and rail station commenced on 16 January 2012. Glasgiven was to be the contractor. The initial work was to put in place a new traffic management system and a park-and-ride facility.

The actual renovation and extension to the station commenced in the summer of 2012. This was to be Northern Ireland's first sustainable, low-carbon bus and rail station. It would to be a mix of old and new elements and influences: the original station's Grade "B" architecture and facade would be restored, incorporating it with environmentally sound technologies and major eco-refurbishments. Other features would include: park-and-ride for 180 cars; an enclosed accessible passenger waiting area; electronic passenger information facilities; an integrated ticket and information office; a canopy construction to cover most of the platform area; covered bicycle parking; and a passenger lift for access to both platforms. The station was officially opened by the Minister for Regional Development, Danny Kennedy in the summer of 2013.

The construction of a new station at Portadown began in February 2012, at a projected cost of £3.6 million. The new station would see a redesign and modernisation of current passenger facilities, new lift access from Obins Street, new lifts and a new footbridge to give improved access between all platforms, new automatic doors, and enhancements to the station's external appearance. The completed station was opened for passengers on 19 April 2013 and would be officially opened in the summer of 2013, once more by Danny Kennedy.

Londonderry Relay
Work on the Coleraine to Londonderry rail line was to be carried out in three phases, due to the necessary funding not being available to complete the project within a short timescale. The new scheduling of work was detailed in the summer of 2011, as follows:

Phase One: Track closure from July 2012 to the end of March 2013, for the full relay of the line between Coleraine and Castlerock, and from Eglinton to Londonderry. In addition, new continuously welded rail to be laid between Castlerock and Eglinton.

Phase Two: Re-signalling of the line between Coleraine and Londonderry, with a new passing loop. This work to be completed in 2015, to enable the provision of an hourly service.

Phase Three: Completion of the fully relay of the track between Castlerock and Eglinton in 2021.

Phase One of the project duly commenced in July 2012 with the line between Coleraine and Londonderry closed for a track relay at 01.00 hrs on Sunday, 29 July.

The programme would consist of a full track relay between Coleraine and Castlerock, re-railing from Umbra level crossing to Eglinton, and a full track relay from Eglinton through to Londonderry.

Prior to the closure, civil engineering rolling stock was moved into place. On Sunday, 22 July 2012, GM locomotive No 111 ran from Belfast York Road to Londonderry and stabled. The next train was GM locomotive No 113 and three ballast hoppers, which also ran from Belfast York Road to Londonderry and stabled. Tamping and lining machine No 07/5 ran from Ballymena, and stabled in the cutting at Downhill.

Point and crossing work also needed to be replaced at the Londonderry end of Coleraine station, and to facilitate that work, the Portrush branch was closed from Saturday, 15 September until 23 September 2012.

On Sunday 6 January 2013, a new timetable was implemented for the whole NIR network. The most interesting development was the introduction of an hourly service between Belfast and Portrush. The line between Coleraine and Londonderry was handed back to NIR at 06.00 hrs on Monday, 4 March 2013. Test trains commenced with a six-car CAF and a GM locomotive.

Scheduled services from Londonderry to Belfast recommenced on Sunday, 24 March 2013 with two-hourly intervals. The hourly pattern from Portrush to Belfast was continued. Prior to the reopening, a special train for dignitaries ran on Friday, 22 March; special free trains for the public ran between Coleraine and Londonderry the following day.

The former Ulster Transport Authority's lack of investment in the railway infrastructure system in Northern Ireland meant that by 1967, the railway system was in a sorry state. In the 40 years since however, the Holding Company Board and management of NIR have brought the infrastructure up to a standard which is superior to those of many other railway companies in the British Isles. Within the NIR network, all the region's main towns and cities have new and modern stations, while even unattended stations have been brought up to a level which would match or better their mainland counterparts.

However, the same diligence has not been applied to the upgrading of track speeds over the same period. While track has been renewed, the maximum speeds achievable on most of the network have not moved beyond the 70 mph which was the norm when NIR was first formed. The company itself has not generally been responsible for this failure, but rather, the powers-that-be: those who dictate what the budget for projects will be, and who prioritise and weigh up the associated benefits. Therefore, while all of the trains now operating on NIR are capable of running at 90 mph, only small sections of the track are able to support such speeds. This of course begs the question: what is the point of buying trains that normally run at 90 mph for a track which restricts them to 70 mph? Unless upgrades are approved in the near future, there is the distinct possibility that the track and current maximum speed limits will remain in situ for another 40 years.

ANTI-SOCIAL BEHAVIOUR, THE
RAILWAY PATROL AND PROSECUTIONS

My first experience of being on a train that was attacked by stone throwers was at Victoria Park on Saturday, 23 January 1971. A large window was smashed on the 17.20 hrs Belfast Queen's Quay to Bangor, and as a temporary measure, staff on the train put four seat cushions up against the window to stop passengers sitting at it or getting too close to it. As I was only 15 years old at the time, I didn't realise the extent to which this type of vandalism could be dangerous and potentially leave passengers with a nasty injury. I suppose though that if I could have got out of the train, I would have thrown a large stone back at the hoods!

Early Court Cases

Some of the first reported NIR prosecution cases to go through the courts were recorded in the *Bangor Spectator*, which gave very good accounts of the incidents. In May 1971, for instance, three Belfast boy scouts admitted throwing stones at trains from the Crawfordsburn scout camp. Three windows were broken on two trains, at a cost of £12. All three youths were given a Conditional Discharge for 12 months. Also in May 1971, this time at Bangor Court, a passenger was fined £5 and ordered to pay costs of £5.25, after travelling from Belfast to Bangor with an out-of-date season ticket – which may seem harsh, but such tickets can be very costly and if a number of passengers did this, the loss of revenue to the company would be substantial! In a more serious incident later that year, at a court case in Bangor on 3 December, a Belfast man was given a three-month prison sentence suspended for 12 months, for having stolen 20 brass railway plates from the disused signal box at Holywood. The signal box was due for demolition before the following Easter.

On 4 January 1973, two Belfast boys appeared at the Juvenile Court in Bangor, charged with ticket offences. They travelled from Belfast to Bangor but their tickets were only valid between Belfast and Seahill. When challenged, they refused to pay the difference and gave false identity details. Both were fined £2.00 each and ordered to pay £8.70 costs each.

More Stone Throwing and Associated Dangers

In 1972, police reported that the incidence of stone throwing at trains in the Lurgan area was higher than it ever had been. Trains were being stoned frequently as they passed the Kilwilkie estate, and the number of attacks had increased since the Troubles had begun. In a particularly bad example, five trains had sustained broken windows in the same day. As well as a gesture of defiance to/of the authorities, such stone throwing was also thought to be a way of attracting the security forces into the area, so that they could then be attacked by local youths in the estates. It was reported at the time that Lurgan was one of the three black spots for stone throwing on the NIR network: the other two were at Ballymacarrett on the Bangor line, and the Donegall Road bridge in Belfast.

Of course it wasn't just youths or political activists who engaged in stone throwing. As I noted in my journal at the time, a police report of 2 July 1972 warned children, and their parents, that they were dicing with death if they took part in a new game, which apparently had become the latest craze at the time: playing "chicken" with trains. (I was surprised when I found this article in my scrapbook, as I thought that the playing "chicken" craze came in later in the 1970s). The game involved children picking up ballast from the track and waiting to see how close a train could get before throwing the ballast and stones at it. After the police report, a warning was issued by NIR that anyone caught doing this could be prosecuted. The same report also revealed that motorists were being targeted in this way in the Belfast area, and that windscreens were being damaged as cars passed under bridges on motorways.

It was rare that stone throwers could actually be caught in the act, but the police were able to do so in Lisburn in October 1972. As a result, four boys attended Lisburn Juvenile Court on 5 February 1973, and were convicted of throwing stones at passing trains at Ballinderry Road bridge. The Magistrate gave them a good telling-off, commenting that because of their actions, someone on one of the trains could have been seriously injured or possibly lost the sight of an eye. Each boy was ordered to pay £9.72 in compensation to NIR, and put on probation for two years.

On Thursday, 15 March 1973, I had another personal experience of being on a train that was targeted by stones. As the 15.30 hrs service from Belfast to Lisburn came through Tate's Avenue bridge, near Adelaide, a window just behind me was smashed. Glass flew everywhere and some shards landed in my hair. The noise of the window breaking was terrible – not a nice experience at all! As a result of this experience and hearing about other such incidents, I wrote to NIR in September 1972 about stone throwing and its effects on passengers. The company wrote back, stating that they were going to be using more Perspex in the train windows, which I was pleased to hear about.

Sometimes, stone throwing was down to sheer vandalism of course. It was well known in NIR, for example, that the south sidings at Portadown were not a great place to stable train sets over the weekend – and this was proved to be the case on Saturday, 9 March 1974, when a crowd of youths stoned an empty MED set from the "Tunnel" area at 17.20 hrs. A total of 17 windows were broken in the set, which had to be taken back to Belfast Great Victoria Street for repairs.

Vandalism Causes Death of BR Driver

A tragic example of what could happen when stone throwing and acts of vandalism go to the extreme, was an incident involving the death of a British Rail train driver in August 1974. Stone throwers had targeted overhead electric insulators and cable supports, causing an insulator to drop into the path of the electric train running from Balloch to Airdrie in Scotland. The driver saw the obstruction at the last minute, but it was too late. He braked and ducked, but the arm and broken insulator (weighing some 40 lb) shattered the cab windscreen and struck him on the head. He was taken to hospital, but died there twelve days later without regaining consciousness.

In a later report from British Rail, it was revealed that during 1973 and 1974, 15 train drivers and 31 guards had been injured as a result of stones being thrown at passing trains. In Northern Ireland stone throwing at trains continued, with daily reports of damage and occasional injury. Thankfully however, train drivers were not usually the target.

Dangerous Conduct on the Railways

Passengers alighting at Bangor West station from the Belfast direction and wishing to go to the Belfast Road area of the town were sometimes tempted to walk to the Bangor end of the down platform and cross the tracks there to the railway path in that direction.

This was a dangerous practice of course, and on Tuesday, 11 March 1975, a 64-year-old female did exactly that. However, as she walked behind the train that she had just travelled on, she stepped straight into the path of the 08.00 hrs service from Bangor to Belfast Queen's Quay, which was approaching Bangor West station. The lady suffered very serious injuries, losing both legs and one arm, and remained in Newtownards Hospital critically ill for some time.

Just a few weeks later, on Monday, 24 March, there were tragic consequences too for two men who were attempting to steal mail on the 13.25 hrs service from Coleraine to Belfast York Road. As he was going about his normal duties, the conductor noticed their suspicious activity near the coach carrying the mailbags. As he approached the men, both of them opened the train door and jumped out at Monkstown. One was killed by the fall, since the train was travelling at speed; the other escaped up the embankment.

Easter Holiday Gang Wars

Easter Monday,
31 March 1975.
(Author's collection)

Cheap day tickets to Portrush, Bangor and Dublin and other locations had been offered by NIR to passengers for travel on Easter Monday, 31 March 1975, and Easter Tuesday, 1 April. The return fare from Belfast to Portrush was £1.65; return from Belfast to Dublin was £2.20. It was hoped that the special offers might help to soften the blow for passengers of the massive fares increase that was to be levied from Easter Sunday.

Unfortunately however the effect of the cheap day returns was to bring a lot of unruly passengers onto the Portrush line, as hundreds of day-trippers travelled there from the Belfast direction. Everyone went on their merry way to Portrush in the morning

without serious incident, but the return journeys were a completely different story.

The 18.05 hrs service from Portrush to Lisburn, the 18.50 hrs service Portrush to Belfast and the 19.30 hrs service from Portrush to Belfast, all carrying hundreds of young travellers, were extensively damaged, as gang wars between rival factions broke out on board these trains. On each occasion, the trouble began shortly after the trains left Portrush for Belfast, and continued unabated until police intervened at Dunloy. Further problems were reported at Ballymena, when police were pelted with broken glass, light fittings and other fittings from the trains. Several youths were apprehended, and some passengers had to be taken to hospital. Police recorded 26 arrests in Portrush during the day, the majority of these for disorderly behaviour.

The 18.05 hrs service was formed by a seven-car MED set Nos 19, 523, 18, 23, 526, 527 and 10. Each one of these coaches suffered damage, with a total of 34 windows shattered, several toilets and wash hand basins smashed, a toilet door missing, and seats slashed and torn off their mountings.

The 18.50 hrs and 19.30 hrs services were formed of ten-car MPD sets. The numbers were not recorded in my records, as so many MPD and 70 Class coaches were damaged. Police boarded the 18.50 hrs service at Cullybackey to quell the trouble.

There were 600 passengers on board the 19.30 hrs Portrush–Belfast service, most of these teenagers. Very soon after the service departed, fighting started amongst groups, and this continued at Coleraine while the train sat in the station across from a Belfast–Londonderry service. As teenagers looked at each other on opposite trains, windows were smashed and shattered. The on-board fighting continued between Coleraine and Ballymoney, with internal fittings being smashed. At Taghey accommodation crossing, the train was stopped to await police, but by the time they arrived, the service had gone on. When the train was stopped at Dunloy however, police were waiting and they quickly boarded. Three arrests were made, and the police remained in place until the train reached Ballymena.

A total of 27 coaches were damaged on the Portrush–Belfast–Londonderry route that day, in addition to the specific damage recorded for the 18.05 hrs service, as mentioned earlier. The coaches damaged were: Nos 36, 41, 44, 45, 57, 60, 61, and 62. Also damaged were: Nos 128, 274, 340, 342, 358, 360, 472 and 586. There was further damage to: Nos 529, 530, 531, 532, 533, 538, 540 and 541, as well as, and finally to Nos 703, 713 and 723.

On that Easter Monday, a total of 232 windows of all shapes and sizes were broken on these trains. As well as this, 30 seats were thrown out of the trains, two seats slashed with knives, and three toilets were smashed. MPD unit No 41 suffered the most damage, with 31 windows smashed (in other words, all of them), and 25 seats were missing.

Thankfully the Easter Tuesday trains were, for the most part, a completely different story. There were no hoards of teenagers, just a variety of passengers with families, and these conducted themselves peacefully. However, on the Bangor line, the day was marred by unruly teenagers who were travelling by train to see the annual Junior Orange Order parade in the town, unlike the parade participants, who had made their way there on special buses. In 10 MED coaches, 22 train windows were broken, along with a number of light fittings.

So, over the period of the two-day Easter holiday that year, 288 train windows had been broken in all, along with other fittings. This left a rolling stock shortage for the remainder of the Easter week, but since traditionally, quite a few people would take the whole week off which eased the burden, meaning fewer rush-hour commuters. The tidy-up effort was a huge one however, and on Wednesday, 2 April, a special train ran from Belfast York Road to Portrush, with crew tasked with stopping where necessary, in order to pick up seat cushions and various other fittings along the way.

The following Easter, to try to avoid a repetition of the massive damage caused, NIR requested that police attend at various stations along the Belfast to Portrush line, in order to keep an eye on passing trains. Some police officers were asked to travel on board certain services. Nonetheless, on Easter Monday, 19 April 1976, a total of 111 windows were broken on Portrush line trains. Two girls and a youth who had been travelling on the 18.25 hrs special train from Portrush to Londonderry, were treated in Altnagelvin hospital in Derry for minor injuries, and were later released. Overall, the police presence had certainly reduced the scale of damage – on the Bangor line trains, only six windows were broken on Easter Tuesday. However it was evident that something else was going to be required in future years to deal with this unruly lot.

Football Hooligans

Teenage day-trippers were not of course the only culprits when it came to vandalism on the railway; clashing football fans also did their fair share of damage. On Wednesday, 29 August 1975, for example, Bangor football club were at home to travelling supporters from Glentoran for a match with a later kick-off. On the return journey, Glentoran fans smashed 15 windows on the 20.45 hrs service from Bangor to Belfast Queen's Quay. The train was a three-car MED set, Nos 32, 505 and 27. No 27 sustained the most damage, with 11 windows broken.

In another such instance, on Saturday, 27 March 1976, Glentoran football supporters travelled to Larne for an afternoon match. On the return journey, 25 Glentoran supporters boarded the 17.05 hrs service from Larne Harbour at Larne Town, which was a special request stop. Police were in attendance at Larne Town station, but did not board the train. Since train windows were being smashed by fans along the way, the signalman at Whitehead called for the police. However, only one police officer turned up and, realising he wasn't able to deal with the situation on his own, he sent the train on to Carrickfergus. A larger police presence was waiting there, and all of the supporters were marched off the train and down to the police station. These fans were returned to the railway station later, to catch the 19.30 hrs service train to Belfast York Road, this time with police travelling with them. In total, 26 windows had been broken and four seats thrown out of the 70 Class set Nos 713, 727 and 78.

On Saturday, 28 August 1976, football fans were embroiled in trouble once more, although this time, they were the targets rather than the perpetrators. Glentoran had been playing an Irish league football match that day against Lurgan's Glenavon. On the return journey from Lurgan, the train the Glentoran supporters were travelling on was targeted at Kilwilkie estate by a crowd of youths throwing bricks, stones and bottles. A nine-year-old boy was badly injured, and four others received minor injuries. The train stopped at Lisburn station, where the injured were dealt with. The boy was transferred to the Royal Victoria Hospital in Belfast with a suspected fractured skull. The train was delayed in Lisburn for almost an hour before continuing its journey to Belfast. Just a few months later, on Wednesday, 1 September, Linfield supporters, who had attended an Ulster Cup match against Glenavon, were also attacked at Kilwilkie estate by stone throwers. No injuries were reported.

In Northern Ireland of course, different football allegiances weren't the only cause of potential conflict. On Saturday, 26 April 1975, a special train containing 400 Orangemen was attacked heavily by stone throwers as it passed the mainly republican Kilwilkie estate. Windows were smashed and one man suffered a fractured jaw.

More Misdemeanours on the Railway

Thirty tons of railway lines were stolen in the middle of May 1975 from Belfast's Stormont Wharf in the harbour estate. It was reported that the stolen rails had been traced by a Mr Hamill, who originally bought the rails for the new Giant's Causeway tram system. The rails were "tracked" down to Ballynahinch and plans were made to collect them and move them to the tramway site in North Antrim.

Another incident in June 1977 was the proof that it is not always young people who flaunt the law. The case in question involved a 52-year-old civil servant from Portadown, who persisted in smoking on a train even when asked to stop doing so; he also refused to give his identity when challenged. The culprit ended up being convicted in court, where he was fined £10 on each charge, and also told to pay costs of £2.

Vandalism Costs NIR £100,000

Given all of this ongoing anti-social activity, it was hardly a surprise when the press reported in October 1976 that broken carriage windows and other forms of damage to trains were costing NIR more than £100,000 per year. NIR Chief Executive, Roy Beattie took the opportunity to highlight that the issue of youngsters throwing stones at trains had become a major problem. Incidents were recurring frequently at Lurgan and Sydenham, as well as in other parts of the network, with passengers sitting in carriages being injured by flying glass from broken windows. Some passengers were so wary that they refused to sit at window seats.

Playing "chicken" on the railways was still a favoured pastime for youngsters in some parts of the country. In 1977, rail chiefs publicly slammed mothers and fathers who allowed their children to play on the railway track. Fencing near the tracks was constantly being vandalised, and the company was holding adults responsible for that. Lisburn was named as one of the main black spots, and within that area were Knockmore, Hilden, Derriaghy and Dunmurry. The local stationmaster commented that if the youngsters didn't realise the peril they were putting themselves in by running across the tracks, their parents seemed to care even less. In one incident at the time, two children had been seen lying between the sleepers at Knockmore, while a train passed by on the other line. They were little more than eight years of age.

NIR representatives had gone out to meet parents in local housing estates to explain the dangers.

On 23 August 1978, an Alliance councillor from Carrickfergus called for the introduction of a railway police force in Northern Ireland to counter vandalism and anti-social behaviour. The call was made as a result of the increasing number of stoning incidents on the Larne line, as well as at Lurgan. The councillor was pressing for a police force similar to the British Transport Police on the mainland.

Continued Vandalism

Meanwhile, damage and destruction on the railways continued unabated. During the night of 22 December 1978, vandals released the brakes of an engineering train in Bangor. The train, which had been stabled in the middle road, ran approximately 100 yards before smashing into the stop blocks and wrecking them.

In the winter of 1979, extensive column inches in the local media were being given over the regular goings-on aboard the 22.10 hrs service from Belfast Central to Portadown, which they were labelling "the late night terror train". It seemed that every Friday night, an uncontrolled mob of around 40 youths would board the train at Botanic station, and, it was reported, from there until Lisburn, there would be no peace in the front carriage. There appeared to be three rival gangs: one from Adelaide, one from Finaghy and a third from Lisburn. As soon as these unruly youths got onto the train, they would start throwing stones at the other groups on board. The atmosphere was frightening for other passengers, the language being used was appalling and there was usually damage caused. The NIR spokesperson at the time was not able to comment on the press reports.

By September 1979, it seemed that putting stones on the line and watching trains running over them was the latest game among the city's children. The problem was reported between Belfast Central and Adelaide, where children were playing in derelict streets and houses, and then running onto the track. Sometimes drivers and conductors had to jump onto the tracks to clear the debris left by such groups, and in a recently reported incident, a seven-year-old boy had shouted abuse at the train crew as he scurried off the track. In a statement to the press, NIR's Chief Executive, Roy Beattie said that the company would prosecute all trespassers. He also highlighted the very real danger of a child being killed by a train, commenting that there was clearly a lack of parental care.

Easter 1980: More Damage and Mayhem

As I would often remark to my colleagues at the time, there just seemed to be something about Easter that brought out the yobs. Maybe there was a full moon! By 1980, the annual ritual of travelling to Portrush, annoying the locals and then damaging the trains on the way home, seemed to be have become the norm among their numbers.

The catalogue of damage caused on Easter Monday, 7 April, 1980 was as follows: 60 train windows broken on the Portrush to Belfast line; 16 train windows broken on the Larne to Belfast line; eight passengers injured, due to fighting on trains on the Larne line.

As well as this, five people were arrested at Belfast Central after a riot involving 200 youths. Ironically, Friendly Street, beside the station, was the target for the vandals who threw stones at passing trains and in the street itself, smashing the windows of both trains and houses. The trouble had started when someone pulled the emergency handle on the delayed Portrush–Belfast train as it approached Central station. Stones were thrown from the Markets estate, and the youths on board then made their way to the area to fight back. Earlier on the same train, it was also alleged that a passenger was stabbed at Portrush, and had got off the train at Ballymoney.

The following year, it was clear that the culture of yobbery still persisted, with 60 train windows broken on the Portrush to Belfast line over Easter 1981.

Tackling the Offenders: I Decide to get Involved

Like all NIR staff, I was intensely aware of the regular instances of vandalism and anti-social behaviour on the railways, and by the early 1980s, these seemed to be increasing all the time. It wasn't just the trains, other passengers or staff that were being targeted either. It was well known at the time, for example, that if you had an expensive car, it was probably not a good idea to use the car park at Belfast Central station. Quite a few cars there were being damaged by stone throwing, and a number of break-ins were happening too. On Wednesday, 18 August 1982, I saw from my office window four youths breaking in to a car in the station car park. So I ran down, picked up two security men along the way, and we caught the thieves in the act. They were duly handed over to the police to deal with. A job worth doing!

Through my work in Operations and as on-call Railway Controller, I knew that, when it came to "ordinary" vandalism and anti-social behaviour, the police had their hands tied, in the sense that they were usually caught up in dealing with terrorists, and so they were only able to assist us when manpower permitted. I had intimated my thoughts about this to my superiors, and as a result, they allowed me a free hand to attempt to resolve some of the issues directly, which included taking on private security personnel contracted by the company to assist me.

On Thursday, 17 November 1983, our first patrol took place, which was really a forerunner of the Railway Security Patrol. Two security men and their Alsatian dog accompanied me, as we travelled to Holywood on the 15.55 hrs service from Belfast to search for trespassers on the tracks, as it was well known that people would try to cross from the up to the down platforms there. All was quiet. We then travelled back to Sydenham, another station where people were known to cross from each of the platforms. There came across 20 people, mostly passengers, who were crossing the tracks behind down trains that had come from Belfast. There was a footbridge just two feet away from where the trespass was taking place! We called the police to verify their names and addresses, and all of the culprits were advised that they would be prosecuted for trespassing. This duly took place at Belfast Magistrates' Court on Tuesday, 10 April 1984, when all 20 trespassers were convicted and ordered to pay £28 each. A very successful first day for the fledgling railway patrol!

The day after this first foray in November 1983, my boss advised me that the Chief Executive, Roy Beattie had been told about my work at Sydenham – apparently, he was

From 1984 onwards, results of prosecutions were published in the staff magazine, *Signal,* in the form of a schedule. Shown here, the first such schedule, from June 1984. *(Author's collection)*

TRESPASSERS WILL BE PROSECUTED

The fight to free the railway, its staff and passengers from the growing problem of trespassers and stone throwers continues; both on the education and publicity front in conjunction with the Police and various safety organisers; and by continuing to prosecute **EVERY PERSON** caught breaking the law. Considerable interest was shown in the article about prosecution in the December 1983 *"Signal"* and the Company is encouraged by this positive response.

All staff are urged to report all instances of trespass immediately they are detected, using the radio if necessary.

In the first few months of this year, 55 people have been prosecuted by the Company and fines totalling nearly £2,000 have been imposed. These are listed below and include two people who were sent to prison (one for a week and one for a month) for refusing to pay the fine.

Date of Offence	Location	Offence	Number Prosecuted	Cost to Offender
16.5.83	Larne/Belfast	Travel Irregularity	3	£50 Each
23.5.83	Balmoral/Finaghy	Trespass	1	£31
24.5.83	Belfast Central	Trespass	1	£34
28.5.83	Downshire	Trespass	3	£33 Each
1.6.83	Portadown	Opened door while train moving	1	£43
29.6.83	Finaghy	Stone throwing at train	2	£35 Each
6.9.83	Barn	Trespass	2	£36 Each
6.9.83	Downshire	Trespass	1	£34
17.9.83	Downshire	Trespass	4	£24 Each
2.10.83	Downshire	Trespass	3	£44 Each
22.10.83	Templepatrick	Trespass	2	£44 Each
26.10.83	Carrickfergus	Trespass	1	£39
31.10.83	Dunmurry	Stone throwing at train	3	£37 Each
12.11.83	Holywood/Sydenham	Trespass	1	£34
17.11.83	Sydenham	Trespass	17	£28 Each
22.11.83	Greenisland/Jordanstown	Trespass	3	£39 Each
9.12.83	Antrim	Trespass	7	£28 Each

pleased with the outcome and had given the go-ahead for me to try other locations as my work permitted. A second patrol was organised for Friday, 9 December 1983, and the same crew travelled with me to Antrim on the 08.25 hrs service from Belfast. Nine trespassers were detected, and the police duly came to verify their identities. Again, all of these people ended up in court.

The Railway Patrol

Following on from these successes, and the author's proposal to formalise the associated procedures, in 1984 senior management at NIR gave the green light for the patrol to be formed, with the formal title, the Railway Patrol. The name was to be printed on both the front and rear of the high-visibility jackets used by members of the Patrol, so that we would be instantly recognisable, as shown in the photograph.

Heading up the Patrol was no mean task, as so often the work meant that we found ourselves in areas of civil disturbance, mostly at night-time and, in certain locations, with the threat of paramilitary attacks hanging over our heads. There were a few occasions on which we had to retreat because of serious situations arising, and where the RUC were not able to offer us support within a certain timeframe. The Patrol had

The author in his high-visibility vest worn by the Railway Patrol. *(Author)*

no formal liaison with the RUC as such, which could ensure that they would attend if we required them, either urgently or as a matter of routine in checking identities, and so on. However, invariable, they did respond as quickly as possible when tasked, and sometimes in large numbers.

Members of our Patrol had no form of physical protection, such as firearms or batons. However I found I was able to perform my duties as necessary, irrespective of this. As a born-again Christian, I was able to call upon a Bible verse, which greatly helped me when doing this dangerous work: "I can do all things through Christ, which strengtheneth me." (Philippians 4: 13 (KJV)).

We soon had official approval to procure a civil engineering Sherpa minibus for evening duties: this would allow us more flexibility and enable us to respond to calls from train crews or station staff when necessary. Travelling on trains was also within our remit if required. The usual routine for me was to pick up the minibus from the Central Service Depot in Belfast on Friday afternoons, take it on patrol with me that evening, and return it to the Depot on Saturday mornings. The evening patrol usually commenced at 18.00 hrs and as before, consisted of myself along with two security personnel and an Alsatian dog, "Prince". Our work usually ended with the last trains in and out of Belfast, with a stop time of around midnight.

The majority of persons apprehended were trespassing or involved in anti-social behaviour, and all ended up either in court or with an official Caution issued by NIR, depending on the circumstances and severity of the offence. During 1984 new legislation was introduced, which increased the maximum penalty for trespassing on the railways from £25 to £50. The maximum penalty for Byelaw offences was expected to be increased in 1985.

The Railway Patrol 1984

Some of the Patrol's successes in its first year were as follows:

Fri 4 May	Bangor West: 9 trespassers apprehended; Helen's Bay: 13 trespassers
Fri 27 July	Lisburn line: 22 trespassers apprehended
Fri 21 September	Dunmurry: two stone throwers caught, following a chase; Holywood: 13 trespassing as a drinking party on the tracks. The two stone throwers were convicted in Lisburn Magistrates' Court on 5 December 1984, fined £117 each.
Wed 10 October	Warning notices placed on cars parked illegally at Belfast Central
Tues 16 October	Derriaghy: 9 trespassers apprehended (during the morning rush hour)
Wed 31 October	First contested cases at Bangor Magistrates' Court for trespassers apprehended on 4 May 1984. I was called upon to give evidence. Seven trespassers convicted and fined £34 each.

There was no shortage of trespassing and other anti-social behaviour on NIR throughout the year, so the Patrol continued its work, expanding its area of operations to include two very difficult flashpoint neighbourhoods at Lurgan and Finaghy.

The Railway Patrol 1985

Some of the excuses given by the folks trespassing or loitering on platforms were interesting, to say the least! These included: "I was waiting in the shelter out of the rain" (it hadn't rained all day); "I saw the train coming, and could have easily jumped out of the road"; "My bike was broken, so I had to walk on the line"; "There was a bogeyman in the subway, so I had to run across the track"; and finally, "Can I not go now, as I need to get home for my dinner?".

Some successful missions carried out in 1985 were as follows:

Tues 26 February	Lurgan, William Street towards Silverwood: 13 trespassers apprehended
Fri 8 March	Sydenham: 15 trespassers apprehended, with RUC assistance
Fri 17 May	Lurgan: 16 trespassers; Lambeg: 3 trespassers; Sydenham: 4 trespassers. As we were observing a serious assault on the up platform at Lurgan, the police arrived quickly. A bottle was thrown at our van as we were leaving the car park at 23.43 hrs – fortunately, it missed us!
Wed 29 May	In court this day, six Marino trespassers contested our case, with their defence solicitor suggesting that the trespass signs should be illuminated! The Magistrate sent all of the defence and prosecution solicitors and defendants to Marino for a site visit. When we all returned to court in the afternoon, all six defendants were convicted: there is no requirement in the legislation for the illumination of trespass signs!
Mon 17 June	Finaghy: 3 trespassers; Lurgan, William Street area: 5 trespassers. We also spent time observing Frazers' occupation crossing on Antrim branch from the bushes and took details of two motorists who left the gates open.
Wed 21 August	Two glue-sniffers convicted at Bangor Magistrates' Court – the police did not have any legislation to cover this offence, but NIR did, through the Byelaws.
Fri 23 August	Belfast–Carrickfergus and Bangor–Lambeg: 16 trespassers. One of those detected at Carrick goaded our dog and, when he was boarding the train, the dog snapped at him and took a chunk out of his trousers. Nothing more was heard from him, until he was prosecuted for trespassing.
Mon 7 October	Whiteabbey to Clipperstown: 12 trespassers (morning)
Fri 18 October	Bleach Green Junction: 2 trespassers; Finaghy: 14 trespassers with an Alsatian dog. We waited 21 mins for police to arrive, and when they did, they had Army backup. All identities taken by the Army and passed to me for prosecution purposes. It was always noted to management that we required more trespass signs at Finaghy, as they are frequently stolen or defaced.
Fri 22 October	Ballymoney: 4 trespassers
Fri 29 November	Balmoral to Central: 9 trespassers

The Railway Patrol 1986

The work with the Patrol continued and intensified throughout 1986. During the 12 months, we were able to apprehend a total of 72 trespassers, as follows: Carrickfergus and Clipperstown: 11; Bridge End: 2; Sydenham: 14; Helen's Bay: 1; Lisburn: 4; Lurgan and Portadown: 18; Antrim: 19; Crumlin: 3.

Here is a selection of entries worth noting:

On Friday, 25 April, while we were patrolling the track around Ballymacarrett to Bridge End, a petrol bomb was thrown at us from over the wall. It missed us, fortunately, but set fire to the embankment.

On 6 June, we were able to apprehend one stone thrower in the act at Victoria Park. On the same day, we ensured that a motorist who had parked his car on the platform at Crumlin station would be prosecuted.

On Friday, 4 July, in conjunction with police, the Patrol supervised the removal of bonfire material by eight NIR Works & Buildings staff from the side of the up line between Sydenham and Victoria Park. The work began at 08.20 hrs, and at 10.00 hrs sharp the NIR staff thought they should stop for their tea break. With some persuasion however, I reminded them where they were and who was likely to be watching the clear-up operation – so the tea break was cut short, in case of agitation from some of the locals. We all withdrew from the area by 12.00 hrs. This initiative proved a successful one in the long run too, as in 1987, we noted that the bonfire material was stacked beside the railway fence on the public footpath, and clear of the railway itself.

On Friday 18 July, the Patrol observed a drinking party on the Six Mile Water bridge, on the Antrim branch line to Lisburn. As there were up to 26 trespassers wandering in the area, we called for assistance from the police. After waiting for over an hour for officers to arrive, at 22.00 hrs, we went to Antrim police station, where I complained to an Inspector about the lack of response.

On Tuesday, 21 October at around 15.30 hrs, this time with assistance from police, we detected six trespassers between Lurgan, William Street and Silverwood bridge. However, after a crowd started to form and throw stones at our Patrol and the police, officers advised us that we should retreat to Portadown. They certainly followed their own advice, and retreated well ahead of us!

On Monday, 17 November 1986, I attended Antrim Magistrates' Court with our solicitor for the prosecution of a number of trespassers. Due to a number of prior adjournments, we ended up with 26 trespassers in court that day. All of our cases were kept to the end of proceedings for that session, as there so many of them. When our turn came, the Magistrate lined all the defendants up in front of the court and quipped, "Did you all come on a special train?" which was met with some laughter from those present. All 26 were convicted for trespassing at Antrim railway station.

A final development of note in 1986 was the introduction by NIR of a new set of Byelaws, which came into effect on Monday, 15 December. These new Byelaws had been in draft form for almost two years, and had eventually been given the go-ahead after the twelfth draft which I had been involved in from the first draft. Additional clauses were included to cover various new offences, and certain perceived loopholes had been addressed. For instance, it was no longer the case that anyone throwing stones or objects at trains or the railway infrastructure could only be dealt with by NIR if they were actually on railway property. Another new clause gave us the right to ban alcohol on train services on certain special days of the year, by the placing of appropriate notices. Some of the new measures had been adopted from British Rail, London Underground and Irish Rail.

Copies of the Byelaws arrived in our office only one working day before the date of their commencement, and had to be sent out by us the same day. The Company had organised a publicity drive in connection with the new Byelaws, and staff who would be involved in their enforcement were asked to attend a training session at the Training School in Portadown from January 1987; I was tasked with delivering this training.

The Railway Patrol 1987

Operations by the Patrol continued apace in 1987, and again, I have highlighted some of the more interesting aspects of the work below.

It had come to our attention around this time that older school children in Lurgan had got into the habit at home-time of walking down the railways tracks from their school in the Silverwood area towards William Street level crossing. On one occasion, we stopped 13 of them for trespassing and were able to obtain their identities with the assistance of the RUC. There is no doubt that an initiative like this acted as a deterrent to a number of other children.

Another ongoing problem at the time was the extent to which motorists were disobeying level crossing warning systems – potentially a very dangerous thing to do, of course. The first related prosecution through NIR was of a motorist who had driven past the red flashing lights at Cromore level crossing on the Portrush branch. He was successfully prosecuted, and ordered to pay £73.

Throughout the year, there were a number of other miscellaneous incidents, which fell within our remit as involving threats to passenger and staff safety in one way or another. On 15 February 1987, for example, a meat cleaver was thrown at a trackman by a person unknown from Finaghy Road North bridge. In the same month, electricity wires at Finaghy station were vandalised, meaning that when passengers touched the metal fencing on the platform, they received an electric shock.

In another development, on Friday, 25 September that year, an NIR Revenue Inspector joined us on our Patrol. Revenue Inspectors were tasked with carrying out random ticket inspections on trains or at stations to ensure that each and every passenger had a valid ticket for their journey. On this occasion, the last service to Bangor was inspected, and it was found that no less than 43 passengers had no tickets; they all paid up after our intervention. From this date, it was decided that Revenue Inspectors would participate in the Patrols on certain occasions. Meanwhile, a trespasser prosecuted at Antrim Magistrates Court on Monday, 16 February attracted the highest fine to date for such an offence: £133. This was surpassed on Tuesday, 1 September in a Ballymena court, where the offender was ordered to pay £182, also for trespassing. Each Magistrate in Northern Ireland has guidelines on how to penalise offenders and, depending on his or her view of a specific case, to impose a higher or lower fine.

The photograph, taken in September 1987, shows my "new" van, which had just been declared surplus from the civil engineers' department, as mentioned earlier in this chapter. Before this, there had been no vehicle available to the Patrol – we had travelled everywhere by train. On the first day we had the van, I took it for a run to Newry station and back, and then left it at the Central Service Depot. You will notice in the photograph that there is a rope coming from underneath the van's bonnet. The

Photographed here, the "improved" Railway Patrol van, Friday, 4 September 1987. *(Author)*

reason for this was that, as I soon learned, the van did not want to start on a number of occasions – the rope was very useful for towing purposes. Sometimes I had to leave the van on the overbridge at Seahill, so that if it didn't start, then I could let it run down the road and start it in second gear. As you can see, we couldn't have done much undercover work done in the van, given the big NIR logo on its side!

The Railway Patrol 1988

Here are some highlights from my records of the Patrol's activities in 1988.

On 11 February, I had the first of a number of encounters with local trespassers at Downshire station. As the Patrol's visits to this station continued over the months, and years, I actually got to know some of the locals by name, as they were persistent in their trespassing. Although they ended up in court a number of times, there were some who still came back to the same place, again and again. One of them held the record at no less than 12 court appearances. It cost him an absolute fortune in fines and costs, as well as the effort of having to attend court each time – but none of this seemed to act as a deterrent!

On Friday 24 June, two passengers got off the last train to Bangor at Marino: one had a slashed wrist, and the other had been head-butted. The patrol was already at Marino station, as I expected trouble there, due to past experiences in previous years. I called an ambulance for the injured passengers, and eventually the train was sent on its way again at 23.50 hrs – 25 minutes late.

In the late afternoon of Tuesday, 5 July, I observed some suspicious activity at Belfast Central car park, involving three cars. We called the Police and they summoned the Army, who had cleared the car by 18.15 hrs. A fully loaded gun had been found in the car, so my suspicions had been justified.

After almost a year of having struggling at times with the old civil engineering crew bus, I got my own, brand new van on Wednesday, 24 August 1988 – an Astra 1600 diesel, with seats in the back and a caged area for the Patrol's Alsatian dog, Prince. With the arrival of the van, my long-standing routine of travelling to and from work by train would come to end, for a number of years at least.

On Saturday, 27 August, the Patrol was in attendance at Ballymena for a loyal order parade. We managed the large numbers of supporters present without too much bother, except for a couple we had to remove from the station and one window being broken. Later on, 10 passengers were removed from the 16.00 hrs service from Ballymena to Belfast by the police.

One female passenger however wasn't as fortunate that day. Rushing for a train due to leave at 17.10 hrs and in a slightly hysterical state, she ran straight at Prince, the Patrol's dog – and he took a snap at her. Thankfully the passenger was not injured, but Prince had taken a right chunk out of her coat! She ended up missing her train, and so we arranged for her to be taken home by a permanent way minibus, which was in the area. In another incident some time later, a prospective passenger was refused entry into the station, and he showed his discontent by kicking and smashing a station door, leaving a security officer injured. The police were called and the culprit was apprehended in the car park.

The Railway Patrol 1989

The work of the Patrol continued in 1989 with a growing number of successes. On Friday, 10 February, for example, we were at Crumlin station with a view to preventing would-be passengers from crossing the track illegally. When we apprehended one man, who was walking his dog, he stated that he had been walking across the track there for years, and simply shoved past us as we attempted to question him further. As he continued on his way across the track, he said that he lived just down the road and was going to phone his solicitor, and invited me to accompany him if I so wished. I obliged, and followed him to his house a few hundred yards from the station. That way I knew I would at least have his address. The police were duly called to obtain his identity, which they actually had some difficulty doing. Eventually however he received his summons to court, and was given a good telling-off there by the Magistrate, which was very effective in helping him change his dog-walking habits! Two other people were also apprehended at Crumlin that day for trespassing.

One part of our routine on evening Patrol work was that we would usually have a break at about 9.00 pm, before the late trains started running, and we would go for fish suppers or such like. We were always sure to get Prince the Alsatian a sausage or something too, and he would show his appreciation by giving me a big lick on the ear!

In the spring of 1989, a new trend came to our attention, which was that at weekends, numbers on the last train to Bangor were picking up dramatically. On Saturday, 18 March we observed the crowd at Bangor station: mainly coming from Botanic, 140 passengers got off at Bangor to make their way to a local nightclub. As the crowd was very noisy and quite a few of them were intoxicated and carrying alcohol, we had to escort about 50 of them out of the station.

It wasn't long before this new trend had become a fresh problem for the Railway Patrol to deal with. At Botanic station on Friday and Saturday nights, dozens of passengers, mainly young people, were turning up for the last trains to Bangor and Portadown, and the majority were either already intoxicated or carrying amounts of alcohol with them to consume on the trains. Clearly something had to be done to protect the ordinary travelling public from such behaviour, so under the NIR Byelaws Nos 18(i) and 18(iii), I organised a ban on alcohol for these trains and at Botanic station. Similarly in accordance with the Byelaws, posters were displayed to the effect that anyone turning up for these trains carrying alcohol would be prevented from boarding; further, if it was deemed that the intending passenger was intoxicated, then they would also be prevented from travelling. As the Patrol had limited powers, the police were asked to assist us at Botanic on a weekly basis.

The ban was effective from Friday, 14 April 1989, which was also the date of the Patrol's first session of Friday night duty at Botanic. We were in attendance there from 21.45 hrs, and police assistance arrived at 22.45 hrs. Anyone presenting themselves for travel was advised that no alcohol could be taken onto the trains, and if they did not appear to be carrying any, they were searched by the police. Any alcohol found was then disposed of – or the passenger could take their alcohol back if they accepted that they could not travel.

On that first night, 110 passengers turned up for the last train to Bangor, which was the most potentially troublesome service, so the Patrol followed the train by van, down to Bangor, so that we could assist on the journey if necessary. Of course we did not always have the train in our sights, but the crew on board were in radio contact with railway control, as were we, so if they made an appeal for assistance along the way, we would have heard it also. At Botanic station, four passengers had been turned away; at Central, three were refused travel. The next night, on our second duty shift, four passengers were refused travel at Botanic.

This Friday and Saturday night pattern continued on and off for a long time, before the troublemakers were finally squeezed out, and a number of them ended up in court. As the Patrol was on the front line, with the RUC in behind us, we often received many threats and insults from would-be passengers. Technical assaults also took place and on one occasion, a guy pushed me in the throat before he was physically ejected from the station by police.

On Saturday 13 May 1989 numbers boarding at Botanic for Bangor had risen to 140 on a regular basis. Police now were turning up in greater numbers to deal with the problems. Two passengers were arrested that night for being obstructive and refusing to hand over their alcohol, and four others were refused travel. When the train finally arrived in Bangor, it was found that four interior panels had been kicked in.

On Saturday, 17 June 1989, the Patrol was on duty at Botanic once again. The line was closed from Bridge End to Lisburn due to a security alert, so the Botanic to Bangor passengers had to be taken by substitutionary bus, which was also covered under the alcohol ban, since it was deemed to be a railway bus. Passengers were searched before boarding, but before one of the buses moved off, we noticed that alcohol had been handed in through the emergency door. After a quick search, two passengers found with alcohol in their possession were removed from the bus, and advised to make their own way to Bangor. Around this time, numbers travelling from Botanic to Bangor started to decrease for a while, as the night club in Bangor had been closed due to a fire in the premises – but when it reopened in late August, the late night revellers were on the increase again.

During 1989 there were a total of 39 patrol visits to Botanic. The Patrol's evening duty commenced at 18.00 hrs and would entail attending certain parts of the railway network, depending on any incidences reported there during the previous weeks. Generally, we would have continued in this vein until the end of patrol duty, just after midnight – but in 1989, due to the ongoing difficulties at Botanic, we would have been in attendance at the station there from about 22.00 hrs for most of our shifts.

Incidentally, on Wednesday, 11 October that year, a different alcohol ban was imposed on passengers travelling on the 08.00 hrs and 09.00 hrs Belfast to Dublin services. The Northern Ireland football team were playing the Republic in Dublin on that day, and trouble on the trains was anticipated. As it turned out, however, only about 60 Northern Ireland supporters travelled on both trains, and the handful of passengers who had alcohol handed it over without protest.

Despite a challenging year, we did sometimes have some lighter moments in the Railway Patrol too. For example, when a small wine shop opened in Helen's Bay that year, the owner decided to place a couple of large empty beer barrels on the station platform close to his shop. He had been advised on several occasions that this was not permitted under the terms of the lease and that he would have to remove them – but he chose to ignore these warnings. So, finally, on Friday 22 September, the Patrol took possession of the two barrels, rolled them along the down platform, and fired them into the undergrowth. The funniest thing was that when we got back into the van and turned on the radio, the song "Roll out the Barrel" was being played!

The Railway Patrol 1990

As well as overseeing the whole NIR network, the Patrol continued to be kept busy throughout 1990 with the weekend situation at Botanic station. My records show that we made a total of 26 visits there during those 12 months.

Level crossing infractions by motorists were another problem on the rise that year. With the aid of CCTV, we were able to catch an increasing number of motorists disobeying level crossing warning systems. This was – and is – a worldwide problem. The most dangerous part of an operating railway is where rail meets road, and for that reason, the best level crossing is a closed one.

On Wednesday, 12 September 1990, two level crossing cases in the Moira area were heard at Lisburn Magistrates' Court, resulting in a fine of £400 for each motorist. The level of the fines was more and more beginning to reflect the seriousness of such incidents. In relation to this, certain changes affecting public transport had been proposed in a new Order, the Transport (Amendment) (NI) Order 1990. The Order came into operation in July 1990 and, among other measures, increased maximum penalties for certain infractions, for example, Railway Byelaws offences went up from £100 to £400, and trespassing on the railway, from £50 to £400. Provision was also made for charging passengers Penalty Fares on both rail and bus services. However, this provision would not be taken up for many years.

Another difficulty that we at NIR had with road users was on roads where railway bridges were lower than the norm, i.e., lower than 16 feet 6 inches. In Northern Ireland alone, there were up to 80 of these low bridges around the network. In the average year, around half a dozen of these would have been struck, mainly by lorries. As mentioned in Chapter Four, monitoring, following up these incidents and taking appropriate action was all part of my prosecutions and enforcement work.

On Friday, 12 January, there was trouble on the last train to Bangor at Marino station, and at 23.15 hrs, I had to deal with a youth who had assaulted another passenger and a security guard. He tried to escape, by running off the down platform, but he tripped and fell onto the line. I fell on top of him and managed to detain him. In the process I injured my left-hand ribs on a rail. Police arrived, identified the youth and took him to hospital. Having been in pain over the weekend, I went to hospital myself the following Monday, and found that I had a fracture of the seventh rib. The youth was later prosecuted for the assaults.

It was Easter Monday, 16 April, and, since we anticipated trouble on the railways, the Patrol was out on duty. As expected, the Bangor line was extremely busy. It seemed that the 14.15 hrs service from Belfast Central to Bangor had a rowdy crowd on board, and we were called to Helen's Bay to deal with the situation. Police were also in attendance, and 30 disorderly passengers for Bangor were removed from the train and sent on their way. Later on, at 16.27 hrs, a relief train from Bangor had only just reached Bangor West when unruly youths on board set about inflicting as much damage as they could. Five windows had been broken, seats were thrown out, and a fire extinguisher had been set off. Three offenders were removed from the train and dealt with.

To some of the readers, this next incident may be funny! It happened on Saturday, 5 May 1990, when the Patrol called in to Adelaide freight yard, to see if all was in order following a break-in the previous night. We were patrolling the yard, along with the Adelaide security man. At one point, when his dog saw Prince, our dog, it made a dash for us – and bit me on the hand and leg … Luckily I had had a recent tetanus injection, so all I could do was wait until the bite marks healed – it was painful, but not unbearably so. Prince, meanwhile, got off scot-free!

Another new problem for the Railway Patrol which arose that year was the phenomenon that on Fridays, large numbers of passengers were flooding Newry station, coming off the 17.00 hrs Enterprise from Belfast, which would arrive at 17.59 hrs. This meant that a lot of cars were arriving at the station car park (down side) and creating a tailback down the road. The road leading from the Camlough Road to the station was owned by Norbrook Laboratories, but NIR had a right of way over it. However, people coming to collect passengers were parking their cars on the right-of-way road, which was sometimes blocking vehicle movements into and out of Norbrook. Despite trying to deal with the problem locally, the difficulties intensified as the owner of Norbrook, Lord Ballyedmond (Edward Haughey) became involved.

The Patrol was asked to intervene, and our first session of duty was on Friday, 2 November. We arrived in good time, at 16.00 hrs. However, things didn't begin well for us, as the line had been closed between Newry and Dundalk that afternoon due to a security alert. The result was that not only was there a problem with cars parking, but we needed to ensure that enough space was left for substitutionary buses to park, with a large turning circle required. We allowed 36 cars and three buses into the car park.

One motorist was refused entry due to no space being available. We left that evening at 18.40 hrs. The next time we were on duty there was Friday, 7 December 1990, and a similar problem occurred again, with the line between Newry and Dundalk being closed due to a bomb scare – this time too, we had to refuse motorists entry.

The ongoing problems with parking at Newry would continue for the next few years, and, in terms of Mr Haughey's involvement, would come to a head in 1992, so I will recount more of that in that year's entry.

The Railway Patrol 1991

Apart from my normal day-time work, my seven-hour weekend evening stints with the Patrol were now also supplemented with our visits to Botanic and Newry. Generally, we did not patrol every weekend, but every third weekend or thereabouts; however when the Botanic problem arose, we worked every Friday and Saturday night for several months. In 1991, we made 23 visits to Botanic, and 11 to Newry. It was intensive work!

In the summer and autumn of 1991, it seemed that someone had taken a grudge against Seahill station, as one or more persons – presumably the same individuals each time – kept setting fire to the wooden platforms there, in the hope of destroying them. There was a series of fires at the station over several months, including those on 9 August, 31 August, 5 September, 17 September and 1 October. After that, no further incidents occurred, so it can only be assumed that the culprits simply got fed up with starting fires, or that maybe they literally got their fingers burnt!

The situation at Newry station continued, as I have said. On Friday, 8 February, during our visit there, Mr Haughey came to introduce himself and discuss the procedures. Because of his standing in the community, I had to forward a report of the conversation to the Deputy Chief Executive the following Monday morning. Our solution that Friday had been to close the road at the bottom of the right-of-way, so that only the allocated number of cars could gain access to the car park: there were generally two security men to man this checkpoint. At times throughout that year, there were up to 58 cars in the station car park, with up to 90 passengers coming off the train. From April 1992, greater numbers of students were travelling to Newry on the 15.00 hrs service from Belfast, which meant that the car park had to be managed for a correspondingly longer period of time.

On Sunday, 15 September, the Patrol were tasked with another, one-off mission at Newry station, since five special trains had been chartered by Down GAA that day, as they were playing in the final in Dublin. As well as being in attendance in case any trouble should arise, another of our tasks was to transfer all of the money collected that morning at Newry ticket office to Belfast Central station, as the cash limits on the Newry safes would otherwise have been exceeded.

The Railway Patrol 1992

The Patrol's last specific stint at Botanic station took place on Saturday, 16 May 1992. Four other visits had been carried out that year, and by that stage the battle had been won. The late-night troublemakers had gone, and passenger numbers had dropped to a reasonable three or four dozen people, with no real problems of disorder being reported on a regular basis. Our persistence had paid off!

During that year, the Patrol did also six stints at Newry. On one of these occasions, Mr Haughey wasn't too pleased at how the cars were able to tailback for a short period of time while we dealt with them. Although the delay had clearly been unavoidable, he attempted to take my photograph, claiming that I wasn't doing my job properly. I warned him that I would take the camera from him, and told him to move away so as I could get on with my duties. He responded by saying he would report me – and of course he did, the following Monday morning. Fortunately my superiors defended me, and the Patrol continued as before.

On Friday, 7 August 1992, we were tasked to Downshire station on the Larne line, which was known for the groups who would congregate to drink there, especially on Friday and Saturday nights. Several repeat trespassers there had been in court on a number of occasions. In any case, the Patrol arrived at the station at 20.37 hrs, and straight away we were able to observe seven trespassers on the track. When the police arrived, up to 20 other trespassers ran off onto the nearby beach; however I was able to advise that they were still trespassing, as the beach was leased to NIR by the Crown Estate. When, along with the police, we pursued these culprits, quite a few identities were taken – however, in order to escape, some of those on the beach just kept walking out into the sea!

During mid-September 1992, reports had been coming in of stone throwing at early morning trains between Victoria Park and Sydenham – possibly, we thought, by boys on their way to school. On Friday, 18 September, I went to the area to observe and sure enough, as previously indicated, two schoolboys started throwing stones at the 08.15 hrs express service from Bangor. I quickly detained them and sought assistance from the police, who arrived a short time later. Problem solved: the boys were dealt with at a later date, and there was no further stone throwing.

Finally 1992 saw the highest number of incidents to date recorded at Belfast Central station car park. A total of 69 cars were damaged: two of these were burnt out, and five stolen. The RUC Markets unit, along with the stolen car squad, would in fact become involved in trying to resolve the problem the following year, such was the level of concern over the situation. Since the problem had first come to our notice in 1988, several hundred cars had been damaged. Some of the vandalism would take place within the enclosed yard itself, and on one occasion in 1993, it was discovered that the regular security dog had been doped with some substance in a piece of meat thrown over the wall. Funding for CCTV for the car park was approved in March 1994, and installed three months later. During the remainder of that year, there were only a handful of incidents in the car park. In 1995, no cars were reported damaged in the first eight months of the year.

The Railway Patrol 1993

This was another busy and productive year for the Patrol. Our work at Newry continued, with nine visits to help control the traffic situation in the vicinity of the station. There were no further interventions from Lord Ballyedmond at this point.

On Easter Monday, 12 April, the Patrol was on duty between 15.00 and 20.30 hrs, mainly on the Bangor line. In the early evening, we were called to Bangor West, where there was trouble on the 17.45 hrs Bangor to Belfast service, with fighting ongoing between a number of youths on board. When we arrived, we witnessed the fighting as reported, but also, among the youths, we could see a little old lady who was standing at one of the train doors, swinging her handbag and laying into some of the young men! The police arrived shortly after, and we assisted them in removing 24 youths from the train. The little old lady calmly resumed her seat in the carriage.

In May 1993, two youths attempted to steal my van at the Circular Road in Lisburn. I had been at Lisburn station due to a bomb scare and, on my way back to the van, I noticed a pair trying to get into it. I gave chase but they managed to run away. They were wearing trainers, while I had steel-toecapped boots!

The July 1993 edition of *Staff Lines*, the NIR staff magazine featured, as well as the most recent Prosecution Schedule (which was by then a regular item), a new column, *Court Briefs*. Staff had expressed an interest in seeing a bit more detail regarding certain court cases and ongoing legal proceedings, and this was the purpose of the new column.

In September, reports had again been received about schoolboys throwing stones at the 08.15 hrs express service from Bangor to Belfast – this time, from a bus stop on the Belfast Road in Bangor. I went to observe the bus queue on Tuesday, 28 September, and saw two schoolboys hurling stones at the train in question. By this stage the school bus was just arriving, so I followed them onto the bus, advised the bus driver of the situation, and asked him to wait until I spoke to the offenders. I duly obtained their identities and reported them to their school – problem resolved!

NIR Court Briefs from July 1993. (*Author's collection*)

July 1993

COURT BRIEFS

On 21 March 1992 a lady motorist attempted to drive through Killagan AHB crossing whilst the warning lights were on. However she was caught when the barrier arm came down on top of her car. Fined £40 and costs of £40.

Trespass at Downshire remains a problem as can be seen from the Prosecution List. Nine prosecutions have been effected since Christmas 1992. A further ten cases are now pending. As each court appearance is costing the defendant approximately £70 this will have an effect of reducing the problem.

Sharp-eyed Botanic barrier staff noticed something wrong with a monthly season ticket when shown by a passenger on 24 July 1992. On examination of the ticket two sections of the ticket had been altered. It cost the defendant £128.80 in fines and costs.

Two stone throwers were apprehended for stone throwing at trains near Sydenham on 18 September 1992. They were both juveniles on their way to school. Although the Juvenile Magistrate gave them a good telling off and ordered them to pay £35 each, it is disappointing to see this lenient approach to a serious problem.

A train driver was injured at Dunmurry on 3 June 1993 as a result of a stone thrown against the windscreen of the train. Four juveniles have been questioned by the Police and one may be charged with throwing the stone.

Seven youths were apprehended at the Bangor end of Central Service Depot on 29 April 1993. Details have been passed to the Company Solicitor for prosecution purposes.

Three of the twelve persons convicted for trespassing at Lurgan on 30 July 1992 have not paid their fines. Consequently they have served a period of one week in prison.

Three persons were apprehended at Greencastle on 11 February 1993 for trespassing and glue sniffing. Court case pending. Under Bye-Law No 19(8) NIR can prosecute for glue sniffing on Railway property. Previous cases have been successful.

E C McMILLAN
TRAIN CONTROL MANAGER

The Railway Patrol 1994

The Patrol's last specific visit to Newry station in relation to the traffic problems was 3 June 1994. Five other visits had taken place up until then in 1994, and by that stage, thankfully, the problem was evaporating. On that final visit, there were only 23 cars in the car park, with just 43 passengers disembarking from the 17.00 hrs service from Belfast. I think we all breathed a collective sigh of relief! A significant number of passengers had transferred to an earlier service.

In early 1994, NIR had been receiving reports that passengers were afraid to use Finaghy station at night because of large, unruly groups assembling there. On Friday, 24 January, up to 20 trespassers were seen in the vicinity of Finaghy station. Having observed this from Finaghy Road North bridge, we sought assistance from the police; within a short space of time, two RUC land rovers, one police car and an Army land rover arrived. Twelve offenders were identified for later prosecution as trespassers.

One of the more notable level crossing incidents of this year involved a guy who jumped over the level crossing barriers at Coleraine and proceeded to run off. The signalman got a good look at him, however, and CCTV also recorded the incident. The next day, just as police were taking a statement from the signalman regarding another incident involving a car, the same man was spotted at the crossing again. He was caught by the police and in due course prosecuted for the offence.

Saturday 14 May was race day for Northern Ireland's North West 200 motorcycle event and the Patrol was in attendance at Dhu Varren. Apart from our usual operational duties, we assisted in the erection of a temporary fence from Dhu Varren bridge to the bus yard, in order to keep trespassers of the track. Five permanent way men arrived to assist us with trespassers. Some people did still manage to make it on to the track, but not as many as in previous years. With all special trains to the event full to capacity, it was a very busy day for the Patrol.

On the evening of Saturday, 2 July, the Patrol were alerted to the fact that youths in a building site at City Hospital station behind the down platform were throwing wooden pallets over onto the platform, presumably for bonfire purposes. When we arrived, we simply began to throw the pallets back into the building site. After a short time, the youths peeked over the wall, and seeing us, they made a quick getaway.

Stone throwing at trains was of course a perennial problem. Having heard reports of stone throwers around the Dark Arch area of Whiteabbey, I went there to investigate at lunchtime on Wednesday, 28 September. I successfully apprehended four stone throwers in the park near the Dark Arch. Due to circumstances which were about to arise out of nowhere, this would be my last solo attempt at catching offenders.

A Sudden End to the Railway Patrol

On Tuesday, 4 October 1994, I was taken aback when my senior manager said he could not sign my overtime sheet for my trespassing and anti-social behaviour work with the Patrol for the three previous months. Even though I had worked out-of-hours, in dangerous situations and achieved many positive results for the company, my claim for 79 hours was being denied, it seemed, as it had recently been agreed at executive level that there was to be a clampdown on overtime. However, no one

Summer 1995

PROSECUTIONS

Date of Offence	Location	Number Prosecuted	Offence Type	Cost to Offender
18.01.94	Old Stone Bridge, Antrim	1	Lorry damaged bridge	£337.50
03.05.94	Umbra L/X	1	Disobeyed Warning System	£100.00
04.05.94	Antrim	1	Passing Forged notes	£0(1)
14.05.94	Finaghy/Dunmurry	2	Trespass	£125.00
18.05.94	Cullybackey L/X	1	Disobeyed Warning system	£85.00
19.05.94	Belfast/Lisburn	2	Travel Irregularity; abusive	£145.00 Total
27.05.94	Lisburn	1	Setting fire to grass bank	£50.00
08.06.94	L'derry/Ballymena	1	Smoking in Non-Smoking area	£130.00
12.06.94	Whitehead/Ballycarry	3	Trespass; Intoxicated	£267.50 Total
17.06.94	Dunmurry	1	Stone Throwing	£60.00
18.06.94	Bleach Green/Whiteabbey	13	Trespass	£790.00 Total
20.06.94	Antrim/Bangor	1	Travel Irregularity	£100.00
23.06.94	Jordanstown	2	Trespass	£60.00
24.06.94	Larne/Whitehead	1	Damage to train	£90.00
03.07.94	Derriaghy/Lambeg	2	Stone Throwing	£125.00 Total
05.07.94	Lisburn	4	Cars obstructing Railway Entrance	£130.00 Total
16.07.94	Templepatrick	10	Trespass	£320.00 Total
21.07.94	Slaght	1	Trespass, glue sniffing	£132.50
02.08.94	Trooperslane L/X	1	Disobeyed Warning System	£130.00
05.08.94	Dhu Varren	1	Travel Irregularity; assault	£0 (2)
05.08.94	Downshire/Whiteabbey	1	Travel Irregularity	£50.00
06.08.94	Antrim	1	Trespass; Intoxicated	£80.00
24.08.94	Larne/Whitehead	1	Travel Irregularity	£55.00
01.09.94	Andersons L/X	1	Obstruction of Crossing	£70.00
06.09.94	Yorkgate	2	Travel Irregularity	£95.00 Total
08.09.94	Lurgan/Portadown	3	Trespass	£100.00 Total
13.09.94	Glarryford L/X	1	Disobeyed Warning System	£105.00
15.09.94	Ballymoney/Antrim	1	Travel Irregularity	£105.00
28.09.94	Whiteabbey	4	Trespass; stone throwing	£120.00 Total
28.09.94	Cullybackey L/X	1	Disobeyed Warning System	£105.00
30.09.94	Lurgan	1	Travel Irregularity	£60.00
07.10.94	Bangor/Botanic	1	Travel Irregularity	£55.00
11.10.94	Trooperslane L/X	1	Disobeyed warning System	£200.00
02.11.94	Crumlin	1	Common Assault	£0 (3)
07.11.94	Lurgan/Lisburn	1	Travel irregularity	£255.00
08.11.94	Whiteabbey	2	Trespass	£100.00 Total
11.11.94	Victoria Park	1	Trespass	£60.00
11.11.94	Carrickfergus/Ballycarry	1	Travel Irregularity	£50.00
11.11.94	Antrim/Belfast	2	Travel Irregularity; Language	£180.00 Total
21.11.94	Lurgan/Lisburn	1	Travel Irregularity	£30.00
23.11.94	Jordanstown/Larne	2	Travel Irregularity	£120.00 Total
24.11.94	Molyneaux's L/X, Crumlin	1	Obstructing the Railway	£305.00
17.12.94	Yorkgate	1	Assault	£0 (4)
20.12.94	Central	2	Travel Irregularity	£90.00 Total
05.01.95	Central	1	Trespass	£60.00

85 **£5597.50**

(1) 2 months imprisonment, 12 months suspended sentence
(2) 11 months imprisonment
(3) 12 months probation
(4) 6 months imprisonment

Summer Staff Lines - 24

The last prosecution schedule to be printed in the NIR staff magazine: Summer 1995 edition. *(Author's collection)*

had thought to inform me of this development, so I was extremely disappointed – a case of really poor people management. No apology was offered by senior management, and not a word of thanks given to me for all the work over the years!

All railway patrols were cancelled right away, including those sessions of evening duty already listed for 7 and 8 October. So my last full shift on duty with the team had been carried out on Friday, 9 September 1994, although I hadn't known it at the time.

The last Prosecution Schedule to be printed in the NIR staff magazine appeared in the Summer 1995 edition, as shown. From then on the only content on such legal issues would be a slimmed-down column on court briefs. With the merging of the bus and rail companies in the formation of Translink, the old staff magazine was replaced by a new combined bus and rail magazine, *Expresslines*. Once the new magazine was "bedded in", the reporting of prosecutions became a regular feature again, albeit in a different format. The first such article appeared in the in Spring 1997 issue, shown opposite.

NIR Byelaws Training

As part of the restructuring of the new merged organisation under Translink, a number of Bus District Managers were now in charge of railway stations as well as the bus depots. Accordingly, on Thursday, 24 October 1996, I gave my first Byelaws training session to eight District Managers at the Europa Buscentre; similar training to another group followed on Thursday, 7 November that year. On Tuesday, 4 February 1997, I delivered such a course to Bus Area Managers also.

Further Developments, 1997–1999

My day-time work in Prosecutions continued apace, in spite of the abrupt stop which had been put to the Railway Patrol.

Rail offenders suffer penalties in court

In a recent edition of Expresslines details of prosecutions in relation to the bus companies were examined. This article details some of the railway incidents which occurred in the first half of 1996 and came to court after a period of time due to various reasons.

There were 87 successful prosecutions which cost the offenders a total of £7,347 - an average of £84.45 each. Of the 87 convictions, 30 were for trespassing on railway property, 23 for various ticket irregularities, five for ignoring the level crossing warning system at Dunmurry level crossing and the other 29 were for offences ranging from damaging a train seat to disorderly behaviour.

The efforts of staff in reporting these offences and attending court is appreciated and a full list of the 87 cases has been sent to each manned railway station for notice boards.

The more interesting cases included:

1 A drinking party at Jordanstown ended when police were called. Twelve youths were convicted for trespassing on railway property and it cost each of them £55.

2 An interim injunction has been awarded to NIR which effectively prevents a person (name withheld) from Bangor from entering any NIR property. This extreme measure was taken after a member of staff was harrassed on various occasions by this person. Recent cases taken by the police in railway-related matters should ensure that this person is prosecuted for alleged criminal offences.

3 Three juveniles interfered with sliding doors on a train as it passed over the Dargan viaduct towards Yorkgate. After a good telling off in court they were also told to pay £46 each.

4 A passenger used threatening language against a conductor on a train near Trooperslane. Courts do not take too kindly to this behaviour - cost £130.

5 A female passenger was confronted by a male passenger who carried out an indecent act. The conductor became aware of the problem and intervened. The girl was brave and acted as a witness. Defendant had to pay £130.

6 An intoxicated passenger who refused to show a conductor his ticket ended up in court and had to pay £130.

7 A resident of Lambeg helped to convict a juvenile for trespassing at Lambeg station. The juvenile 'escaped' before the police arrived but the resident accompanied the police on mobile patrol and found the juvenile in the vicinity. There were allegations, not proven, that the juvenile had vandalised a poster at the station. The effort was worth it when it cost the juvenile £125 at court.

8 Members of staff occasionally report passengers for smoking in a no-smoking coach. One such incident recently cost a smoker £55.

9 Two brothers ended up fighting on a rugby relief train from Dublin and then used foul language against railway staff. They were removed from the train at Portadown and ended up in court paying £63 each.

10 A female motorist who crashed into Cullybackey South level crossing and drove off without reporting the accident was fortunately insured. Police traced the vehicle and apart from paying a £100 fine, the cost of repairs to equipment of £7,045 was recovered.

First prosecution article in new staff magazine, Spring 1997. (Author's collection)

A complete ban on smoking on all NIR trains was introduced from 7 April 1997. The campaign was launched on National No Smoking Day, 12 March that year. An article in the staff magazine about the campaign provided some further detail as follows: "'NI Railways Signals Halt to Smoking on Trains' is the slogan being used to implement the no smoking policy on trains which will be effective from April 1997… NI Railways will liaise with the Ulster Cancer Foundation to reinforce the message that public transport is moving towards a cleaner environment. Station posters and leaflets have been available from 12 March, and on 3 April, public notices will appear in the *Belfast Telegraph*, *Irish News* and *News Letter*."

By the beginning of 1998, the number of students disobeying the level crossing warning system at Jordanstown had started to be a pressing concern. On 6 February 1998, I was asked, along with police and other NIR staff, to observe the problem, and it was clear that something needed to be done. As time went on, a publicity campaign was implemented, aimed at trying to raise student awareness of the dangers of level crossing infractions. Meanwhile the police issued warnings to a number of individuals. After these attempts had run their course, then prosecutions would be undertaken.

In another incident in 1998, a laser pen was shone at a train driver at Lambeg. The juvenile responsible was taken to court, where he was made to pay £70 costs. Meanwhile, five trespassers on the Portrush branch were fined a total of £463. In another case, NIR was granted a Court Injunction against a well-known offender in the Antrim and Ballymena areas. Issued in 1999, the Injunction placed on the subject a ban from all railway property: this was to be served on him in jail, where he was currently in custody.

On Friday, 5 February 1999, an afternoon train from Londonderry to Belfast was travelling in the Greysteel to Ballykelly area, when the driver noticed two trespassers walking on the line in the distance away from him. He sounded the horn, but unfortunately just at the same time, a Chinook Army helicopter was flying in the vicinity of RAF Ballykelly. The two trespassers had not heard the train horn, and the driver was unable to stop in time. Very sadly, both of the trespassers were killed.

On Friday, 5 February 1999 a persistent smoker on the trains was convicted at Newry Magistrates' Court, and ordered to pay £327 in fines and costs. Meanwhile a couple of youths from North Belfast sniffing glue at Whiteabbey, were prosecuted and fined £158 each. In 1999 also, NIR's first recorded streaker took a run up and down the Enterprise train in front of women and children: he was prosecuted and was fined £102. There had been no problem with identification in this case! On Wednesday, 2 June 1999, three "graffiti artists", or, more accurately, people who had caused criminal damage to trains, were convicted at Bangor Magistrates' Court and ordered to pay fines and costs of £4,500 total.

As the time for the North West 200 races approached again in May 1999, it came to light that the organisers were proposing to try to use the occupation crossing at Nobody's Inn, near Portrush for extra facilities for the event. This was seen as a most dangerous move, and, since there had been no consultation with us about the intended use of the crossing, NIR decided to block the proposal through the courts. With the main races due to be held on Saturday, 15 May, not much time was left to deal with this by the time we had heard about it. I was tasked with arranging for barristers and solicitors to be available on Wednesday 12 and Thursday 13 May at the High Court in Belfast. On the Thursday, our case was heard at 14.00 hrs and I gave evidence on behalf of the Company. The Judge awarded NIR an Injunction to prevent the crossing from being used by the race organisers.

Other Issues

As part of a long-running dispute between the shopkeeper at Lisburn railway station and the NITHC, I had to make my way, along with some NIR colleagues, to the station for 05.50 hrs on Monday, 6 September 1999. Our mission was to place a new padlock on the shop's shutters. When the shopkeeper's wife turned up at 06.20 hrs, all we could do was to advise her to take the matter up with their solicitor. The shop remained permanently closed due to outstanding debts, and eventually tea, coffee and snack machines were made available for passengers in the station area.

On Thursday, 2 December 1999, two civil engineering managers asked if I would accompany them to the Dargan bridge in Belfast, to see if a permanent way squad were out oiling the points. We got there at 16.15 hrs and, as the managers had expected, the squad were not on duty! This matter was then to be dealt with through disciplinary procedures.

Bus Prosecutions

Up until the establishment of the new Translink organisation, all of my experience in prosecution work had of course been solely railway orientated. However, now that train and bus operations were under the same roof, so to speak, things would soon evolve. As articles about railway prosecutions continued to appear in the combined staff magazine, *Expresslines*, a number of bus staff began questioning what the

Company was doing for them in that regard. Traditionally passengers offending on buses were dealt with and prosecuted by the police, and so information for staff about results on this front had been sparse.

When I thought back to my father's career at Ulsterbus, I knew that he had had to use his own devices in dealing with unruly passengers, by simply driving them up to the police station door and handing them over. And so, once I had been given the nod by my superior, I started to check out the legislation around what the bus companies could actually prosecute for. To my surprise, there were actually quite a few sections of Public Service Vehicle regulations that covered offences such as fare evasion and anti-social behaviour. The next step was to task the company solicitor to produce a complete list of such enforceable regulations. In the meantime, I decided to keep tabs on any reports of passenger misdemeanours on Ulsterbus and Citybus services.

In parallel to all of this, a preliminary meeting was set up with the Department of the Environment about the possibility of introducing new bus legislation to prosecute offenders. The meeting at River House in Belfast on Thursday, 16 September 1999 would explore the possible introduction of Byelaws for buses along the same lines as those for the railways.

We made good, and rapid internal progress, and on Tuesday, 30 May 2000, the first passenger to be prosecuted for not paying a penalty fare on a Citybus service was convicted at Belfast Magistrates' Court. During the early part of 2001, Bus Inspectors in Integrated Transport Centres at Bangor and Coleraine were instructed on railway law and byelaws. This was important knowledge for them to have since, now that services were integrated, there were parts of stations which were deemed to be under the control of railways and within the remit of railway legislation – and of course bus passengers were using the joint facilities.

February 2003 saw big breakthrough for bus prosecutions, with the publication of the *Bus Prosecutions Guidelines* booklet. This had been formally approved by bus senior management. Overleaf is an article regarding integration at work, which was published in the Easter 2003 issue of the staff magazine. This was referring to the integration of operations of the bus and rail companies for prosecution purposes, as from this point the Company Secretariat department were dealing with both bus and rail prosecutions.

The first successful Ulsterbus prosecution was in March 2003. On 9 December 2002, an intoxicated passenger on the Portrush to Coleraine circular route had pushed the driver, using abusive language while the bus was in operation. In line with PSV regulations, the offender was fined £75 for obstructing the driver, £25 for verbally abusing the driver, and was also ordered to pay £77 in costs.

Between 2004 and 2006, a series of meetings and briefings took place with bus staff all over the country – the purpose of the briefings was to explain to staff what the Company Secretariat department could do to assist them in relation to prosecution of offenders. I was accompanied and assisted at most of these briefings by either Maureen or Karen from our office. The last of this series of briefings took place in the Citybus drivers' canteen in May Street in Belfast.

Prosecutions - integration at work!

Eddie McMillan, Company Secretariat.

Figures released in January for the period July to December 2002 show that successful company prosecutions are continuing at a steady pace. In this period, 61 individuals were prosecuted and the total cost of fines to the offenders was £8,503 for NIR prosecutions.

Among the stiffest fines and charges to offenders were:

- One individual caught carrying a knife and behaving in a disorderly manner at Botanic Station was given a two-month prison sentence.
- Two disorderly offenders at Coleraine/Castlerock who also used foul language and withheld their identity were fined a total of £1,000.
- An individual caught travelling at Antrim, intoxicated and without a ticket and interfering with the comfort of other passengers was fined £213.
- 2 offenders received six months' Conditional Discharge for throwing stones at Carrickfergus.

Prosecution Guidelines for Bus Staff

Eddie McMillan, Company Secretariat, is responsible for handling prosecutions. He outlines how a formal prosecutions procedure is now being introduced for the bus companies. "We are committed to ensuring that travel on our network is a safe experience for passengers and staff and have stepped up our efforts to prosecute offenders. To this end, the company has recently issued guidelines to help us to handle more prosecutions within the bus companies of those minority of passengers who offend against PSV, Transport Order or other regulations with anti-social behaviour on our buses." Eddie continued. "The Secretariat Department staff have worked with colleagues around the bus network over the last year to prepare a guide book on handling prosecutions relating to passenger incidents on board our vehicles."

The booklet, "Prosecution Guidelines for Bus Staff", was published on 17th February. Copies have been distributed to Area Managers, District Managers, Controllers and Bus Inspectors. A separate guidebook for bus drivers is in production and will be issued presently.

The booklet highlights areas where problems may arise and gives reference to the relevant sections of regulations. It includes a schedule of the penalties for offences against the companies, and gives detailed advice on what steps should be taken by staff to help progress a successful prosecution.

"Bus staff will now have the option to deal with unruly and awkward passengers through the courts, as detailed in this document". Eddie McMillan stated, adding, "The Secretariat Department will facilitate this and handle prosecutions arising."

An integrated approach

Eddie highlighted for reader's attention, three recent successful prosecution cases involving co-operation from NIRailways and Ulsterbus staff. These show integration at work within our organisation in novel ways!

- The first case occurred in the Bangor Bus and Rail Centre in November 2001. Two intoxicated young persons were causing a nuisance in the Ulsterbus Stand area and a large number of schoolchildren were present. An Ulsterbus Inspector intervened several times and was followed by the youths into the NIRailways part of the Station where an attempted assault on the Inspector took place. Other Ulsterbus and NIR staff intervened and the Police were called. NIR Bye-Laws were used to prosecute and the Ulsterbus Inspector gave evidence. One youth was ordered to pay £383 in fines and costs and the other was ordered to pay £109."

- A second case also involved an incident in the Bangor Bus and Rail Centre in March 2002. An Ulsterbus passenger used threatening and abusive language against an NIRailways Inspector and then refused to leave the station. Police were called. NIR Bye-Laws were used to prosecute the Ulsterbus passenger and the NIR Inspector gave evidence. The passenger was ordered to pay £182 in fines and costs."

- A third case occurred on an Ulsterbus between Ballymena and Coleraine on North West 200 day in May 2002. The rail line had been closed due to security alerts and rail passengers were using substitution buses for part of the journey. The incident occurred on a bus operated by an Ulsterbus driver with an NIR conductor in charge of passengers. One abusive passenger was warned several times about his behaviour. The bus was stopped at one stage to deal with the passenger and the Police were called. PSV regulations for Ulsterbus were used to prosecute the passenger and the NIR conductor gave evidence. The passenger was ordered to pay £227 in fines and costs." ∎

Article on Prosecutions – Integration at Work, Easter 2003. *(Author's collection)*

Occupation Crossing Muckamore View: An Ongoing Problem

From early 2001, we had been getting reports about the misuse of an occupation crossing situated at Muckamore View, on the Bleach Green Junction to Antrim line. It had been originally known as Crossing No 21, and Crossing No 14; it was also referred to as McCourt's. A telephone had been provided; users of the crossing had to open and close the gates themselves, once they had checked with the signalman that no train was due. Many reports had been coming in of the gates being left open, and the telephone not being used to contact the signalman before people crossed the line.

NIR was in the process of prosecuting a number of members of the public for misuse of the crossing, when unfortunately, due to a signalman's error, a motorist was given incorrect information about an approaching train and a situation arose. Luckily the motorist was not injured, but she was badly shocked. As a result, the crossing was temporarily closed. After this, a member of staff was placed at the crossing with a hut, so this was basically the reinstatement of a crossing keeper. This situation continued for many months. One solution would have been to adopt the national railways' approach to such crossings, which would have consisted of getting the British Transport Police to put a big padlock on the gates. Then, only after a prospective user had signed a declaration to the effect that they would use the crossing properly, would they be given a key for the padlock as and when they wished to use the crossing.

Sadly, however, this approach was not adopted at Muckamore View. To cut a long story short, a new system of warning lights and barriers was installed at the crossing at great expense – but the system was not interlocked with the signalling system. There is another story there. In fact the new crossing was aligned to only one other in the UK, and that was near Pitlochry in Scotland.

The attempt to find a satisfactory solution for this crossing went on for many years, involving yet more expense, including the purchase of a nearby house, as a measure to reduce the number of individuals using the level crossing. This may have changed the way people gained permission in crossing the line, but misuse of the crossing continued. A number of motorists were eventually prosecuted, with the aid of CCTV.

British Transport Police

Every now and then, the idea of having a body of dedicated railway police in Northern Ireland was bandied about by NIR senior executives. In 2001 however, serious consideration was given to a police unit which could actually operate on buses as well as the railways. While the idea would be to align such an operation with the practices of British Transport Police, it was thought that the necessary manpower should be supplied through some alliance with the local Northern Ireland police.

British Transport Police had great expertise in dealing with level crossing misuse, among many other issues. On Tuesday, 15 May 2001, I met with our BTP liaison officer in Birmingham. We travelled to West Wales and Barmouth, to see different types of level crossings and to review the misuse at each one. The next day, I accompanied the police party which was to assemble at Birmingham New Street station to usher the Prime Minister Tony Blair, Gordon Brown and David Blunkett safely off the London train. Further stops on that trip included a visit to the Railtrack offices and the Birmingham power signal box, and a meeting with the BTP Chief Constable. In December 2001, a further flying visit was organised for me, to go to Birmingham to participate in a Conflict Resolution training course with BTP.

Investigations into available legislation used by London Transport buses brought me over to London on Monday 28 January 2002, for a meeting with legal advisors. I also went out on patrol with one of London Transport's bus revenue inspectors between 17.00 and 19.00 hrs issuing Penalty Fare notices on London bus services.

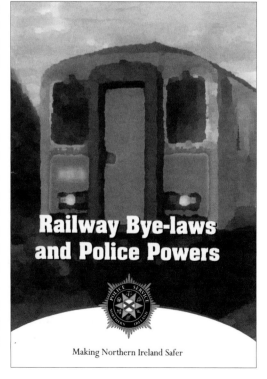

Railway Byelaws and Police Powers booklet. (Author)

My investigations relating to bus legislation continued, and on 14 October 2003, I went for a meeting with an Oxford bus company to see their CCTV operations on the buses and at their workshops. The next day, I attended a Route Crime Conference in London.

Looking at a Liaison Between NIR and Police

Prior to the Travelsafe Conference in March 2004, which I have talked about in Chapter Four, our liaison with the Police Service of Northern Ireland was working well, especially through the efforts of a designated Sergeant, based at Newtownabbey police station. Since police officers in Northern Ireland do not receive any specific training relating to railways, this Sergeant went about producing a very helpful booklet, approved by his senior management: *Railway Byelaws and Police Powers*. This covered railway byelaws, definitions, public order offences, incidents on railways, accessing the track, being on the track, types of rolling stock, and who to contact in NIR.

Prosecutions

In 2004 prosecutions on all types of offences continued, but once again, the most worrying type of infraction was that of motorists and pedestrians disobeying level crossing warning systems. Several dozen people were convicted in this regard at various locations throughout Northern Ireland. A motorist in Lurgan, who failed to observe the warning system at William Street, ended up being prosecuted and paying £3,800 in fines and costs of repairs. Quite a few of the public road level crossings now had CCTV installed, and this proved a great benefit when it came to court.

In 2005, further offenders on buses were being dealt with under the PSV regulations. As an example, a passenger using an altered Freedom of NI ticket between Armagh and Belfast, after being challenged by a bus driver, was convicted and ordered to pay £190.

In 2006, a motorist whose van damaged equipment at Niblock level crossing was convicted and declared liable for £4,800 in fines and costs of repairs. In another incident, an 18-year-old bus passenger, travelling in the Coleraine to Garvagh area, had to pay £228 for interfering with passenger comfort, refusing to produce a ticket, refusing to give identity details and loitering in Coleraine station.

Bus Legislation

Following the preliminary meetings with the DoE which had begun 1999, the message coming across was that it would not be possible to implement byelaws for the bus companies. As this option, which would have been the ideal, had been refused, we had no choice but to explore our second choice of plan – the implementation of some form of additional powers for the bus companies. In 2005, assisted by Maureen, I drew up a new draft Statutory Rule dealing with the prosecution of offenders on bus services and bus stations. It took many months and many drafts before this work became an "official draft". It was presented to the DRD and DoE in 2006, in the hope that this help would move proceedings along within their timeframes. However, even though I did actually see a Statutory Rule in draft form from the government, sadly, I retired before I was able to see the end result of my work (2013).

Penalty Fares

On 11 August 2008, in a bid to deal proactively with the ongoing problem of fare evasion across the bus and rail networks, and avoid the subsequent loss of revenue, a new Penalty Fare scheme was introduced. Passengers caught travelling without a valid ticket for their journey would be issued with a penalty fare of £20, plus the value of their single journey. Those who failed to pay the penalty fare after a period of 21 days could end up being prosecuted in court. Training of staff was undertaken by me, with the assistance of either Maureen or Karen.

More Prosecutions

A driver who crashed into the railway bridge at Old Stone Road, Muckamore in the summer of 2009 was given three penalty points on his licence by the PSNI, while NIR recovered the £3,200 for the damage to the bridge.

In another significant case, in the summer of 2010, a motorist, who failed to observe the warning system at Cullybackey North level crossing and collided with a Belfast-bound train, was fined £250 and three penalty points on his licence, while £39,000 was recovered through his insurance company for damage to the train.

Crossing No 14 Muckamore View, as mentioned above, continued to be a problem spot. On Monday, 1 August 2011, CCTV evidence proved its worth in court again, when two separate cases where heard in front of Antrim Magistrates. The two incidents had happened on separate dates at Crossing No 14 (McCourt's) on the Bleach Green to Antrim line. Both defendants had had narrow escapes, after having ignored the warning system; one of the motorists stated that he had felt his car shake violently as the train missed it by two seconds. Both offenders were convicted and fined £500 each, plus £175 costs.

Shown here: the last prosecutions update report to appear in the NIR staff magazine *Expresslines*, Spring 2012. *(Author's collection)*

Prosecutions Update

During the six-month period, July to December 2011, Translink NIRailways Prosecutions against 69 individual offenders were secured in the courts system by Translink's Secretariat Office.

45 of the prosecutions related to safety offences, including: failure to observe level crossing warning systems, bridge strike and trespassing.
- An individual who failed to observe the warning system at Antrim Level Crossing was charged £594.

- An individual who drove a motorbike with excess alcohol onto the track at Lissue Level Crossing and failed to stop for police was sentenced to 3 months in prison, suspended for 2 years, and was charged £350.

24 of the prosecutions involved ticket, travel and behaviour offences, including: attempted theft, disorderly/indecent behaviour and no valid ticket.
- An individual charged with disorderly & indecent behaviour at Ballymena was sentenced to 4 months in prison, suspended for 18 months.
- An individual charged with disorderly behaviour at Cultra was sentenced to a 120 hours Community service Order.

The total amount recovered, including costs for repairs, came to £10,166.00

I very much enjoyed my work in Prosecutions and with the Railway Patrol during my time at NIR. From my very first year there, I had gained some insight at first hand into the company's procedures and practices in this regard. As time passed by and my involvement increased in this work, my colleagues in the Patrol and I found ourselves in some dangerous circumstances, but the hand of God protected us through the years. For me, it was always very rewarding to be able to assist my work colleagues when they found themselves in difficult situations, and to sit with some of them in court while they got the satisfaction of seeing the offender dealt with and the victim getting some kind of justice.

The senior management of NIR were always very supportive of the work of the Patrol, making available, albeit with delays at times, the necessary finance to provide a vehicle, security staff, the radio telephone equipment and the other items needed to support the patrol. On a couple of occasions in fact, when members of senior management, including the Chairman himself, were approached by friends of offenders, asking them to stop court cases from going ahead, they did not interfere in the legal process, or try to restrict me in my efforts. The running joke in the office in fact was that McMillan would prosecute even his own Granny! The abrupt discontinuation of the Railway Patrol in 1994 was a sad way indeed to end this work.

In terms of the present however, it is great to see that Translink continues to support the work of rail and bus prosecutions, and that this is now in the capable hands of Karen Hutchinson, supported by the solicitors in the legal department.

CHAPTER 10

OPERATIONAL ACCIDENTS AND INCIDENTS

Today's safely running railway systems have evolved over 150 years, and during that time, numerous new procedures and techniques have been devised and implemented, sadly in many cases as a result of accidents. Like all railway companies, NIR and its predecessors have not escaped their fair share of accidents over the years, and although systems can be made safe, human error and unusual circumstances cannot always be planned for. This chapter deals with many of the accidents – both serious and more minor – which happened over the years that I had worked for NIR, including those that I personally attended.

One of the first collisions to happen on the early NIR network occurred on 7 July 1971 at Portadown. One hundred passengers on the evening Enterprise from Dublin to Belfast had a fortunate escape when, at 19.20 hrs that evening, it crashed into the rear of a freight train at West Street bridge in Portadown. The impact drove the freight train 100 yards down the line towards Belfast. Several passengers as well as the guard of the Enterprise sustained minor injuries. On the stationary freight train, two goods wagons and a guard's van were badly damaged, when the train became derailed at a sharp bend in the track. One of its wagons was carrying mail, and 20 mail bags were strewn over the track.

A statement later released by NIR explained that at the time of the incident, only one line on the double track had been in operation, due to the construction of a railway bridge further down the track; a shunting movement was being undertaken by the freight train when the Enterprise arrived and struck it.

Express train collides with freight train at Portadown, 7 July 1971 as reported in the *News Letter*. (Author's collection)

Train Derailments

On the evening of Friday, 10 September 1971, as my diaries of the time confirm, a slow speed derailment occurred as a train entered a platform in Bangor's main station. Although there were 60 passengers on board, thankfully no one was injured, although the train driver was taken to hospital for a check-up. He was later released, with no further treatment needed.

On Tuesday, 13 June 1972, about 150 passengers had a fortunate escape, when the rear coach of an early morning Belfast to Londonderry train derailed between

Dunloy and Ballymoney. No injuries were reported, but 500 yards of the single-line track was ripped up. Services between Dunloy and Ballymoney were suspended, and replacement buses were laid on in the interim. It was later reported that a mechanical fault on the train may have been the cause of the derailment.

Less than a month later, on the evening of Sunday, 9 July 1972, train services between Bangor and Belfast Queen's Quay were disrupted for several hours, following the derailment of an empty train at Belfast. While a crane was being used to lift the carriage back onto the track, trains ran from Bangor to Sydenham, with a replacement bus service to take passengers on to Queen's Quay.

Fatalities and Near Misses

One of the youngest victims on record to be killed by a train during NIR's history was a three-year-old boy, who was struck by a Portadown to Belfast Great Victoria Street train at Finaghy at 17.00 hrs on Tuesday, 27 February 1973. Tragically, the child had wandered onto the track with older children and, by the time the driver realised he was on the tracks, it was too late to stop the train in time.

Later that year, there was another fatal incident on the railway, when a 74-year-old Portadown businessman died in hospital a few hours after falling between a train and the platform at Balmoral station on Thursday, 16 August. At an inquest into the accident on Thursday, 22 November 1973, a witness recalled that the train door was sticking and wouldn't open. However, as the train started to move off again, the door suddenly opened and the man fell out and onto the tracks, in below the train. The train ran over his left leg, and he died later in hospital of his wounds. An open verdict was returned.

Two Men Escape Death

In another incident with a more fortunate outcome, two men escaped death on 14 June 1973, when their car was struck by a freight train at Donnybrewer level crossing, eight miles from Londonderry. The crumpled car was carried 500 yards along the track, and the two men remained trapped inside until the Fire Brigade were able to cut them out of the vehicle. Both were rushed to Altnagelvin Hospital in Londonderry, where one was described as being critically ill, and the other seriously ill. Fortunately, both men survived.

1973: Freight Train Derailments at Boilie

On Friday, 17 August 1973, a CIÉ north-bound freight service became derailed at Boilie near Lurgan. The down line was closed for several hours as the wagons were re-railed and the track was repaired; during this period, single-line working was in operation.

A similar incident involving a CIÉ freight train occurred at exactly the same location on the track at Boilie on Thursday, 22 November. On this occasion single-line working was in operation for most of the day.

A third derailment took place at Boilie the following month, on Wednesday, 5 December. It was clear that there was a problem of some kind with the track at this location, and this time, an investigation was called for. It seemed odd that it took three derailments at one location to commence an inquiry!

A Collision, a Train Failure and Two Derailments

On Friday, 4 January 1974, the 13.20 hrs service from Larne Harbour to Belfast York Road crashed into a lorry at a temporary level crossing at Larne Town, damaging MPD unit No 40. Both the train driver and the lorry driver were taken to hospital, suffering from shock and minor injuries. The temporary level crossing was in place, as a new railway deviation and station were being constructed, for opening in June that year.

Another incident worth noting involved the 08.23 hrs Crumlin to Lisburn branch set, on 8 August 1974. Double-ended MPD coach No 65 failed at Ballinderry at 08.35 hrs, and there was no relief train available for recovery. Efforts to find a replacement bus met with no joy either. Passengers were left stranded, not knowing what to do. Eventually most of them decided to leave, and they walked to the main road, in the hope of spotting a service bus. Hunslet DH No 3 eventually arrived at around 10.00 hrs, and took the failed unit back to Belfast Great Victoria Street for repairs.

On Wednesday, 14 August 1974, the 19.55 hrs freight service Londonderry–Lisburn derailed in Lisahally loop (it didn't get very far!). The set was formed by a three-car 70 Class unit with no wagons, and the two trailers were completely derailed. The train had gone into the loop to cross the 18.00 hrs service from Belfast York Road to Londonderry. After the recovery of the set and a clear-up operation, the line was re-opened at 15.15 hrs on the following day.

October 1974: Runaway Train Crash at Gormanstown

Although this incident did not occur on NIR territory, given its seriousness, I would like to record a few details about it here. On Monday, 21 October 1974, two people died and eleven were injured, in one of the Republic's worst rail crashes for many years. The accident occurred at Gormanstown on the main Belfast to Dublin line. An empty train had stopped between Dublin Connolly and East Wall, when the driver dismounted to inspect suspected mechanical problems. However, while the driver was out of the cab, the train moved off without him. The empty runaway train ran on the down line, until it caught up with another empty train in front of it at Gormanstown, crashing into it and propelling it into the station. This second train struck the platform and rebounded into the side of the 06.50 hrs service from Dundalk to Dublin, which was sitting at the up platform, causing the fatalities and injuries to the passengers on the waiting train.

1974: A Series of Derailments

On Tuesday, 29 October 1974, the 06.10 hrs empty diesel set from Belfast York Road to Whitehead derailed at No 17 points at Whitehead. Train services were disrupted during the morning rush hour, as the carriage was re-railed and returned to York Road for inspection.

The very next day, a Hunslet locomotive operating a spoil train from Magheramorne Quarry sidings to Cloghan Point derailed in the sidings at Magheramorne. This location was the scene of another such incident on Monday, 4 November, when a spoil train running from Magheramorne Quarry sidings to Cloghan Point derailed on the Larne side of Ballycarry bridge at 11.30 hrs. Six loaded hoppers were derailed, with three of them overturning, to be left lying at the edge of Larne Lough. As a result of this accident, approximately 200 yards of track had been ripped up and the single line was closed.

The NIR steam crane was summoned from Lisburn to lift the wagons back on to a temporary track. Unfortunately, as the steam crane was in the process of lifting one of the wagons, it overturned, killing one of its operators and badly injuring two others. At this point, CIÉ was called upon for help, and they dispatched their CIÉ steam crane from Dublin at 18.30 hrs on Tuesday, 5 November. Once the crane arrived at Ballycarry, around lunchtime the following day, the efforts to re-rail the NIR steam crane and the wagons could begin. The apparently long delay in getting the CIÉ crane to the scene was down to the fact that, in both CIÉ and NIR at the time, such steam cranes were not much in use, except for occasional infrastructure work or for the recovery of rolling stock due to accidents (as in this case). The CIÉ crane was based in Inchicore in the west of Dublin, and the first thing to be organised was a train crew to work on it. Next, a suitable locomotive would have had to be sourced to haul the crane on its 125 mile trip north to the scene of the accident. This train would have been restricted in speed due to its weight and structure, so it would have had to "find a path on the railway" to reach the accident scene.

The line was re-opened on Thursday, 7 November at 16.00 hrs; the first service to run through was the 15.35 hrs Belfast to Larne Harbour.

On Tuesday, 12 November, there was yet another derailing incident. This time, the Bangor line was blocked for up to two hours, following the derailment of the 07.15 hrs service from Belfast Queen's Quay to Bangor. The scene of the incident was No 8 points at Queen's Quay, where the rear coach of an MED set came off at Fraser Street bridge, blocking both up and down lines. I travelled on the first service out of Bangor, at 08.35 hrs, and we ran as far as Ballymacarrett station, where the service terminated. Single-line working commenced later, and both lines re-opened at 15.20 hrs that day. That morning I had a very valid reason for getting in to work late, at 10.15 hrs, since I'd had to walk the whole way from Ballymacarrett to our offices at York Road!

A Shunter Injured at Belfast York Road

On the morning of Tuesday, 12 November 1974, a shunter working at Belfast York Road was crushed between two coaches during a shunting movement in the yard. Seriously injured, he was sent to the Royal Victoria Hospital, where he remained unconscious and in intensive care for some time. The job of a shunter can be quite a dangerous one, which requires both skill on his part and that of the train driver he is working with, as well as the careful coordination of their respective skills in each movement. The coupling and uncoupling of rolling stock is carried out in a very confined space, and the shunter has to manhandle the coupling equipment and cables. If a train driver doesn't control his speed properly, the shunter can all too

241

easily end up being crushed between two items of rolling stock – as was sadly the case in this instance.

A Derailment and a Flying Roof Section

Four CIÉ wagons on the night freight from Lisburn to Londonderry were derailed at Knockmore Junction on Wednesday, 20 November 1974. The down main line between Lisburn and Moira, as well as the Antrim branch were closed for most of the following day. Single-line working operated via the up line between Lisburn and Moira until repairs were completed.

As Christmas approached, a special mail train had been organised for the evening of Monday, 16 December 1974 to accommodate last-minute mail. The 70 Class train ran from Belfast York Road to Coleraine; however while it was in transit between Ballymoney and Coleraine, the driver heard a loud noise, and noticed that the large sliding inspection panel on the roof, which covers the engine generator, had blown off in gale force winds. Fortunately, the next day, the roof section was found in a farmer's field and recovered. Even more fortunately, no one had been injured.

1975: Further Derailments

On Tuesday, 11 March 1975, the CIÉ locomotive which had been designated to work the 17.30 hrs Enterprise service from Belfast Great Victoria Street to Dublin, was derailed on a set of points at Great Victoria Street. A relief locomotive was called and the train left one hour behind schedule. The CIÉ locomotive was re-railed at 10.00 hrs the following day.

Less than a month later, on Tuesday, 8 April, four wagons on a CIÉ freight train from Dundalk to Belfast Adelaide were derailed coming out of the Lisburn loop. The incident happened at 13.17 hrs.

Freight train derailed at Lisburn, Tuesday, 8 April 1975. The photograph also shows another freight train passing on the main up line. (*News Letter*).

The main down line was reopened just before the evening rush hour the same day, although there were some cancellations to services. However Platform 3 remained out of use until the line was repaired on the afternoon of Thursday, 10 April.

On Thursday, 10 April, a spoil hopper derailed on the track at Cloghan Point, to be re-railed within 55 minutes. The photograph shows the poor state of the track the spoil trains were running on; it can be seen too that the track had a cant leaning towards the nearside rail.

A few days later, on Monday, 14 April, an empty spoil train running from Cloghan Point to Magheramorne loop derailed between Whitehead and Ballycarry. Two hoppers became derailed, and 700 sleepers were damaged. Between Whitehead and Larne, train services were replaced by buses until late afternoon on Wednesday, 16 April; the first train running through was the 16.08 hrs Larne Town to Belfast York Road, and there was a temporary speed restriction of 5 mph in place.

The next incident recorded was on Friday, 25 April, when a hopper was derailed at Magheramorne loop in the early afternoon. Before the wagon was re-railed, the fast line through the loop was blocked for several hours.

Discharge siding at Cloghan Point, April 1975. *(Author)*

Two Derailments in One Day

Thursday, 8 May 1975 saw two separate derailment incidents. The first happened in the early morning, at 07.15 hrs, at Cloghan Point, and again involved a hopper, this time at the discharge site. The hopper was re-railed at 11.40 hrs. The second derailment took place at Londonderry, when 70 Class trailer No 702 was derailed during a shunting movement in the yard.

More Derailments

In May 1975, re-sleepering work was being carried out on the track at the Maze, and a 15 mph temporary speed restriction was in place. On Tuesday, 13 May, however, the 16.15 hrs service from Belfast Great Victoria Street to Portadown was travelling through the restricted area, when three bogies of the two-car 80 Class became derailed. Single-line working was introduced over the down line between Lurgan and Knockmore Junction, until the up line was re-opened the following day at 16.00 hrs.

On Tuesday, 20 May 1975, an afternoon CIÉ freight train from Adelaide to Dundalk became derailed at Tandragee. A Guinness tanker came off the line, damaging 1¼ miles of track. Single-line working was introduced over the down line between Poyntzpass and Portadown, and remained in place until 15.00 hrs on Thursday, 22 May.

Collision with Train Buffers, and a Fire

On Friday, 5 September 1975, at least twelve passengers were injured when the 08.12 hrs service from Carrickfergus to Belfast York Road ran into the buffers at Platform 3, York Road station. Most of the injured were taken to hospital with fairly minor injuries; it was later reported that no one had been detained.

A few months later, on Thursday, 27 November, as the 17.15 hrs service from Belfast Queen's Quay to Bangor was arriving into Bangor, MED power car No 24, which formed part of the train, sustained extensive underfloor fire damage. The Fire Brigade were summoned to extinguish the fire, and fortunately, there were no casualties.

Autumn/Winter 1975: More Derailments

The 20.55 hrs freight service from Londonderry to Lisburn derailed at Macfin, between Coleraine and Ballymoney, on Thursday, 18 September 1975. Three wagons came off the line, damaging one mile of relayed track, but fortunately only 400 sleepers had to be replaced. A substitute bus service between Coleraine and Ballymoney was laid on for travellers until mid-afternoon on the following day.

In the afternoon of Thursday, 30 October, 80 Class motor coach No 82 derailed in Belfast Great Victoria Street yard, blocking in two train sets for the evening rush hour. Just over a month later, on Tuesday, 2 December, the 07.00 hrs freight service from Dundalk to Adelaide didn't get too far either. Just as the train was leaving Dundalk, nine of its wagons overturned, blocking the down line for most of the day.

New Year's Eve 1975: Train Crash at Wexford

Disaster struck on the railways on 31 December 1975, in the form of a fatal train crash in County Wexford. Five people on the train were killed, including one member of staff, and another 43 were injured, including four members of staff. Again, although the incident did not involve NIR trains or happen on NIR territory, it cannot be passed without mention, given that it was the worst accident in the 30-year history of Ireland's state-run railway company, Córas Iompair Éireann.

The accident occurred when a mechanical digger crane, which was being transported on a 20-ton tractor unit, hit an overhead railway bridge, dislodging the rails and supporting girders. Tragically, before there was time to issue any warnings, shortly afterwards the Rosslare Harbour to Dublin train came hurtling along the line at about 55 mph . All 87 passengers on board were travelling in the rear carriages of the train. The locomotive overturned, pulling the brake van and three carriages down a 14-foot embankment. The fourth carriage came to rest, straddling the bridge, with the fifth carriage telescoped into it.

This is one horrific example of what can happen when a railway bridge is struck by a vehicle. A Public Inquiry into the incident was subsequently ordered by the Irish Department of Transport. Among the conclusions, it was noted that there had been no signs or notices on the bridge, or on the public road approaches to it, to advise road users of the clearance under the bridge. One of the recommendations was that, on all such roads in the Republic, bridges under 15 foot 6 inches should have appropriate signs erected as soon as possible.

Derailments on Belfast Central Railway

There was a series of derailments on the new Belfast Central Railway, even before it was officially open for traffic. The first of these was on 9 December 1975, as detailed in Chapter Eight. A second incident occurred on Wednesday, 14 January 1976, when one hopper on the ballast train from Eliza Street (close to Central Station) derailed near the Ormeau Road bridge on the afternoon run. Luckily, the situation was quickly rectified.

In the early afternoon of Monday, 23 February 1976, a further derailment happened – the third on the BCR before it was officially opened. DH Locomotive No 2 came off the track on the new Lagan River bridge; fortunately, once more, re-railing took place reasonably quickly.

Train Fire at Carnalea

Passengers had a very lucky escape on Thursday, 20 May 1976, when the 20.40 hrs service from Lisburn to Bangor suffered an engine fire at Carnalea. The three-car MED set had stopped at the station, when a passenger noticed flames coming from underneath the second coach. He shouted a warning to the conductor, who promptly evacuated the train. Railway staff tried to tackle the blaze by their own means, but the coach burst into flames and the fire brigade had to be called. The middle coach was almost gutted as a result of the fire, which was thought to have been the result of a mechanical fault. Thankfully, no one on the train was injured. The line was closed for half an hour before the train was moved to Bangor station.

1977: Two Collisions at Central Service Depot

There was a shortage of train sets on the morning of Thursday, 17 February 1977, as well as a number of train cancellations, due to a collision between an Enterprise set and the local Hunslet and coaches set in the Central Service Depot (formerly Queen's Quay). The Hunslet and two coaches were damaged in the incident in the early hours of the morning. The 08.00 hrs Enterprise service to Dublin that day was formed by a three-car 80 Class set, instead of a locomotive hauling seven coaches – there was no first-class compartment, seating space was limited and, with no dining car, there were no hot breakfasts on offer that morning!

Some months later, on Saturday, 7 May, two early morning passenger trains collided at Carrickfergus station. Two passengers and a train driver were injured: luckily, as both trains were travelling slowly, any injuries were minor. The crash happened as one train, approaching from Belfast, entered a section of line which the other, Belfast-bound train was leaving.

More Derailments

On Tuesday, 2 August 1977, the 20.15 hrs freight service from Londonderry to Lisburn derailed at Bellarena. Two wagons came off the line, and approximately one mile of track was damaged. The blame was laid squarely on local rabbits and badgers, which had been tunnelling under and around the track. The embankment was full of holes and this was surely an indication of what could happen when the activities of local wildlife were not kept in check!

DARK DAYS AND BRIGHTER DAYS FOR NORTHERN IRELAND RAILWAYS

Some weeks later, on the morning of Thursday, 22 September 1977, Hunslet No 103 derailed in Portadown yard during shunting movements, with its front two wheels coming off the track. Fortunately, there was no damage done, the locomotive was re-railed and operational again by 15.30 hrs.

September 1977: Family Tragedy at Accommodation Crossing

On Monday, 26 September, the 11.30 hrs service from Belfast York Road to Londonderry collided with a car at an accommodation level crossing at Station Road, Ballykelly. A 25-year-old man, his three-year-old son and a man aged 40 were killed, when the car they were in was cut in two by the force of the collision. Part of the car was carried 400 yards along the track before coming to a stop.

The crossing had been unmanned since 1973, and phones had been provided as a safety measure for anyone using the crossing. However, when checks were carried out at the scene, it seemed that the phones had been ripped out of their boxes, most likely by vandals. The train driver was badly shocked but otherwise uninjured, and there were no reports of injuries to passengers. There was only minor damage to the train, and services resumed later on in the day. The local community were of course devastated by the losses suffered by the families involved.

Further Derailments

On Thursday, 20 October 1977, the 12.45 hrs freight service from Adelaide to Dundalk was travelling over Lake Street level crossing in Lurgan, when one wagon became derailed. The up line was blocked for 90 minutes while the wagon was re-railed and the line checked for damage. In the meantime, single-line working was established on the down line between Portadown and Moira.

Less than two months later, on Friday, 2 December, the 08.30 hrs through service from Bangor to Antrim derailed on all wheels on the approach to Antrim station. It was late in the evening before the set was re-railed, with the help of the NIR 36-ton steam crane which was brought from Lisburn to carry out the heavy work.

The following year, 1978, brought a series of similar incidents. On Thursday, 9 February, one wagon of the 01.25 hrs freight service from Lisburn to Londonderry became derailed near Knockmore Junction. The crew remained unaware of this fact, until the train arrived at Ballinderry. As a result, approximately five miles of track were damaged. After an inspection, three wagons were left on the fast line at Ballinderry until mid-afternoon, when they could be recovered by mechanical engineers. The remainder of the train continued its journey to Londonderry.

On Sunday, 26 November 1978, single-line working was in operation between Bleach Green Junction and Greenisland for planned engineering works. During a shunting movement at Greenisland however, the 09.40 hrs service from Belfast to Whitehead became derailed at No 30 points. The front two wheels of 80 Class motor coach No 91 dropped off, and was re-railed a short time later.

December 1978: Fatal Collision at Lisburn

Unfortunately, there was an incident of a much more serious nature on Wednesday,

20 December 1978, when the 11.00 hrs Enterprise service (CIÉ) Belfast Central to Dublin ran into the rear of the 10.05 hrs service Bangor to Ballymena at Lisburn station's Platform 1. The train driver of the Enterprise, 53-year-old Joseph Reid, was killed in the collision, and thirteen passengers were injured.

Enterprise collision at Lisburn, Wednesday, 20 December 1978. *(Author)*

The Enterprise had struck the stationary 80 Class train at 27 mph, after braking hard. The locomotive cab, No AR 010, was completely crushed, and derailed on six wheels. The 80 Class driving trailer No 742 was badly damaged, although this would not have been immediately evident when you looked at the coach, on which very little could be seen apart from a few buckled marks around the driver's cab. The rear bogie of No 742 was knocked out of place; the track and station canopy were also damaged as a result of the collision.

It was later established that the driver of the Ballymena train had seen the Enterprise coming on the up line behind his train at the last moment, and had immediately climbed into the cab and released the brakes, thus avoiding a more serious collision. The CIÉ Enterprise set was formed of locomotive No AR 010, hauling 3178, 1149, 2420, 1540, 1549, 1539 and 1917. The three-car 80 Class was formed by Nos 69, 768 and 742.

On 29 January 1979, the Department of the Environment for Northern Ireland announced that a Public Inquiry was to be held into the accident. This would commence on 21 February 1979 in Belfast. Driving trailer No 742 returned to service on Friday, 29 February 1980 after extensive repairs.

Winter 1978: Landslides and Heavy Seas

On Friday, 29 December 1978, an early morning inspection of the line revealed that a landslide had blocked the down line between Belfast and Larne at Cloghan Point. During the closure, passengers were transferred between Carrickfergus and Whitehead by bus; the line was reopened on the afternoon of Sunday, 31 December.

Turbulent weather in early 1979 caused further problems on the railways. On Friday, 16 February, heavy seas badly undermined the up line between Whitehead and Kilroot. Parts of the battery sea wall had actually been washed away, and single-line working was brought into operation on the down line until further notice.

As the area was extremely difficult to access by other means, the only way of bringing concrete to the site for repair work was by rail. Two mini-mixers from Handymix Concrete of Dromore were permanently mounted on a flat railway wagon, and had to be hauled out to the site by a DH locomotive from Whitehead. A Thomson A7 pump was then used to place the concrete. The work was ongoing until April 1979.

Fatal Level-Crossing Collision: Summer 1979

On Monday, 9 July 1979, the 17.55 hrs service from Belfast Central to Londonderry ploughed into a car which had stalled on an unmanned level crossing at Artiferral (Tweed's) between Dunloy and Ballymoney. Tragically, when the train struck the car and then completely derailed, a 20-year-old off-duty policeman who was travelling on the train was killed, and twenty other passengers were injured, including the train driver. Seconds earlier, a mother and her three children had managed to jump from the stalled blue Ford Capri. The train, which was travelling at 70 mph and carrying 40 passengers, ripped through the car and carried it another 150 yards down the track.

Fatal collision at Tweed's Crossing, Monday, 9 July 1979. (Author)

Driving trailer No 714, the coach, which had been holding the young policeman and most of the injured, was lying on its side; intermediate trailer No 725 remained upright, but partially down the bank; and motor coach No 71 lay at a precarious angle, if almost upright.

Over 200 yards of track were ripped up in the collision, and to allow work to recover the train to proceed, a temporary track was built alongside. Both the NIR and CIÉ steam cranes were involved in the recovery of the train. The line reopened that Thursday, 12 July.

More Derailments

On Thursday, 15 February 1979, Hunslet locomotive No 103 left Portadown with eleven empty hoppers in tow, in the direction of the Central Service Depot. After the train had passed the Ormeau Road bridge (half a mile from Belfast Central), the sixth hopper became derailed, damaging 330 sleepers. Eventually, just past the Blackstaff River bridge, the hopper dug itself into the down main line by 18 inches. Single-line working was introduced over the up line, but services in the evening rush hour were badly disrupted.

On Wednesday, 15 August 1979, the 14.40 hrs service from Londonderry to Belfast came off the track at the facing points as it entered Castlerock station. The leading bogie of 70 Class No 72 became derailed. The 50 passengers were de-trained, and the Portrush branch set was sent from Coleraine, to enable them to continue their journey to Belfast.

November 1979: A Very Slow Express

On Monday, 19 November, I took the 17.50 hrs express train from Belfast Central to Bangor. Far from being an express service, however, the train didn't arrive in Bangor until 19.08 hrs that evening! The reason for the delay was that we got caught up in the rescue effort of the 17.30 hrs service from Belfast to Bangor, No 89, which had failed at Cultra, and which our set ended up pushing into Bangor. The journey from Cultra to the top of the bank at Craigavad was very slow, as our train was constantly slipping on the rails due to fallen leaves which had formed into a mulch and were sticking to the tracks.

Slow-travelling trains are more prone to slipping in such circumstances, as they cannot obtain sufficient momentum before slipping again – a faster service will just run over the rails and leaf mulch with minimum disruption. Another contributing factor to such slippage on 80 Class trains is that, in a normal three-coach train, only two axles out of a total of 12 axles are powered, which means that the power is not evenly distributed.

In this instance, our solution was for the spare driver and I to walk alongside the rescuing train, putting gravel and small stones on the rails to allow it to get some grip. Once the speed picked up, we were able to board again, while passing through Craigavad station.

Further Derailments: Ballymacarrett and Portadown

In the late 1970s, there were two head shunt tracks running from the Central Service Depot towards Ballymacarrett on the down side. These were essential to allow trains to gain access or to exit from the depot. On Tuesday, 27 November 1979, an empty four-car 80 Class set from the Depot to Belfast Central ran into the buffer stop on head shunt No 1, pushing it towards the nearby electricity pylon, which was only a few feet away. As a result, the leading motor coach No 88 was completely derailed and dug itself into the ground, while the next driving trailer was derailed on one bogie. The driving trailer was recovered within a few hours of the incident; No 88's recovery took longer however, as, with the aid of re-railing equipment, it had to be gently hauled out of the ground and placed back onto the rails. The head shunts are no longer in existence today.

In another incident on Easter Saturday 1980, two coaches of the 14.30 hrs Enterprise service from Dublin to Belfast Central derailed as the CIÉ train approached Portadown station. Fortunately no one was injured in the incident, which happened approximately one mile south of the station. Passengers in the derailed coaches were moved to the front of the train and were able to continue their journey to Belfast. It was thought that the unseasonably hot weather might have buckled one of the rails at the spot in the line where the coaches derailed. Single-line working over the up line between Portadown and Poyntzpass continued until the next day, while work was underway to recover the coaches and repair the track.

June 1980: Runaway Coaches in Bangor

On Saturday, 21 June 1980, several Sunday School "specials" had arrived in Bangor. As usual for such specials, MPD carriages were being hauled behind 80 Class sets, to ensure the provision of more seats on busy Saturdays. On this occasion however, during shunting movements, three MPD coaches were left in the run-round loop at Bangor. When the brakes released, these coaches ran off into Platform 3, crashing into the buffer stops, and demolishing them and the metal fence on the platform. No 49 was leading, and its front bogie was pushed back ten feet. No 64 also sustained some damage. Mechanical engineers had to carry out some repair work, before the carriages could be returned empty to Belfast on Tuesday, 24 June.

NIR Tie Saves the Day!

On Tuesday, 8 July 1980, I was travelling on the 17.15 hrs express service Belfast Central to Bangor, which was formed by a four-car 80 Class set. Just as the train was passing through Kinnegar, the emergency brake came on, due to a very bad low joint on the track. I got out to assist the crew: we discovered that the jumper cable spring clip had broken and the jumper cable had fallen out, causing the train's brakes to come on. As we all stood racking our brains for a few minutes, all at once conductor Tony Campbell simply took off his NIR tie and suggested we use it to tie up the jumper cable! That solved the problem nicely, and so off we went, arriving in Bangor only five minutes late.

August 1980: 13 Killed in Cork Train Crash

A rail tragedy which, although not relating to NIR, cannot go without mention was the horrific train crash which took place on Friday, 1 August 1980 at Buttevant in County Cork. A total of 18 people were killed, of whom 16 were passengers and two were train crew members, and 75 passengers were injured, in what would be the worst train crash in Ireland in a century.

The 10.00 hrs service from Dublin to Cork, with about 230 passengers on board, had been passing through Buttevant station, when the train suddenly left the rails and careered into an embankment, causing the leading coaches to jack-knife across the line. A subsequent Inquiry found that on the down main line, a set of unconnected facing points, which should have been connected to the nearby signalbox, had not been sitting in the correct position to allow the train to pass safely. Due to the layout of the points, the train had entered the siding at 65 mph and derailed.

Autumn/Winter 1981: A Collision, a Derailment and Frozen Points

Thankfully, terrible events such as the one at Buttevant happened relatively rarely. In the aftermath of the tragedy, the usual, more minor run-of-the-mill incidents continued to occur on the NIR network. On Tuesday, 22 September 1981 at Central Service Depot, for example, two 80 Class sets collided during shunting movements. In a sense this was bound to happen at some time, since before the morning and evening rush hours in particular, the depot there was quite tight for space. On this occasion, a train driver was taken to hospital; fortunately there had been no passengers on board.

The rush hour train service was badly disrupted, with the two sets being signed off for inspection.

Again, on Thursday, 29 October 1981, a GM locomotive and seven empty hoppers were returning from Poyntzpass to the Central Service Depot, when the hoppers derailed at the Laganbank Road bridge, near Belfast Central, at 15.00 hrs. The down line was blocked until late evening, and a special bus service between Belfast Central and Bridge End was organised for Bangor line passengers.

Winter brought other problems in 1981, and on Thursday, 10 December, rush hour services came to a standstill when seven trains were reported around the network as unable to operate due to the freezing temperatures. Air brakes on the trains were the problem – as soon as these brakes were applied, they would freeze up. The problem was exacerbated on the following day, when there was a five-inch snowfall. There were no point heaters installed anywhere on the NIR system, meaning that it was up to designated railway staff – known as "the snowmen" – to come along and clear the points manually. The problem continued into the New Year, and on Monday, 11 January 1982, ten sets of points throughout the network were reported as being frozen. On that day, I travelled to work in Belfast on the first train out of Bangor – which was not until 09.40 hrs. Incidentally, the temperature recorded at Aldergrove on 11 January was minus 9°C.

Train driver killed in collision at Hilden, Friday, 25 March 1983. *(Author)*

March 1983: Train Driver Dies in Hilden Crash

Tragedy struck again on Friday, 25 March 1983, with another railway accident which claimed the life of an NIR train driver. As the 17.05 hrs service from Portadown to Bangor was sitting at Hilden station, another train came around the curve behind it, ploughing into the stationary train. The driver of the second train, 59-year-old Herbert Deane, was killed, and six passengers were injured. The injured were taken to the nearby Lagan Valley hospital in Lisburn, but were all released later. An RUC inquiry and an NIR inquiry into the collision were immediately launched. At a later date, it was announced that a Public Inquiry into the circumstances of the accident would also be taking place.

One of the injured passengers later recalled that his train had broken down at Hilden, and that the next thing he could remember was hearing the crash, a loud collision, and being flung up out of his seat along the full length of the carriage. There was a lot of screaming, and he could remember being lifted out of the train. A nurse, who had been travelling along the road in a car and had seen what happened, came to the assistance of passengers. A teenager who had been watching trains at Hilden station recounted seeing the second train ploughing into the other one, and the stationary train being pushed about 75 yards up the track. He also remembered how people were screaming as they were trying to pull the train driver out of the train.

At the Public Inquiry in April 1983, evidence was given indicating that the stationary train at Hilden had broken down with a brake failure. At the same time, it was revealed that there had been an act of vandalism on the track between Finaghy and Dunmurry, which caused the signalman to mistake the whereabouts of the 17.05 hrs train and to allow Mr Deane's train to proceed with caution. When the Lisburn signalman conversed with the Belfast Central signalman about the two track occupations, it was agreed that the 17.05 hrs train was between Dunmurry and Finaghy – whereas it was of course standing stationary at Hilden. Giving evidence, the signalling inspector said that the work of the vandals had led to the fatal error of judgment, and related how, when he had checked the area after the accident, he found that wires had been pulled out of the track, causing a track circuit failure. Further investigations revealed that there could have been other factors too in the accident. When braking tests were carried out by NIR at the maximum cautionary speed of 25 mph, the results indicated that the second train should have stopped 150 yards short of the stationary train. The Inquiry Chairman, Major Holden concluded that the train was doing rather more than the permitted cautionary speed.

In other evidence given at the hearing, the conductor of the 17.05 hrs stationary train said that, after the train driver had tried to repair the fault which led to the breakdown but was unable to, he, the conductor, had begun to make his way back up the track to lay protective detonators, when he had seen the second train coming around the curve. He said he had no idea another train was coming so close behind them. He jumped to the side and could only watch the collision. Afterwards, he looked into the cab of the crashed train but couldn't see anyone.

Class 80 motor coach No 88 was badly damaged; on the stationary train, coach No 712 was completely destroyed and coach No 726 was damaged. It was later noted that No 712 had asbestos lining in the coach interior, and so anyone attending the scene of the accident was formally noted on staff records as having done so, in case of asbestos difficulties in the future (this included me, as I was on the accident investigation team).

January 1984: A Cold Snap

New Year 1984 had a few cold snaps, with big storms up and down the country. On Friday, 13 January, in the worst delay of the day, the 06.20 hrs service from Londonderry to Belfast Central arrived into Belfast three hours and 25 minutes late, delayed by fallen trees and broken level-crossing barrier arms. Passengers at Belfast Central on Monday, 16 January had clearly decided to make the most of the white winter by throwing snowballs across the platforms at each other for a laugh.

In Scotland however, the situation was altogether more serious, when on Saturday, 21 January, the 17.10 hrs Kyle of Lochalsh to Inverness train was reported to have been lost in a snow blizzard near Achnasheen. A rescue locomotive from Inverness also became stuck in the drifts when it got to within just half a mile of the stranded train. The four railway staff in the rescue locomotive decided that they would wait for daybreak before trudging several miles through heavy snow to find the exact location of the trapped train, information which was passed on to the authorities, to enable a helicopter rescue of the passengers. The railway line was blocked for many days before the trains were recovered.

1984–1989: Train Fires, Collisions and Derailments

On the evening of Friday, 23 November 1984, a Londonderry to Belfast Central train was passing through Cullybackey station, when the signalman observed that one of the coaches was on fire. With the departing train in his sights, he immediately phoned the Fire Brigade and told them to attend a train fire in Ballymena station, which was where the service was heading. The signalman thought that this was a better idea than suggesting that the train stop en route, since it would only take a few minutes to get to Ballymena! The 80 Class driving trailer No 747 was badly damaged in the blaze, which was later blamed on an unknown intoxicated passenger who had been smoking and had set down their cigarette on a train cushion. Assisted by the draft from several open windows in the carriage, it was not long before the cushion caught fire and the blaze ignited.

On Friday, 4 April 1986, two train sets collided at the Central Service Depot in Belfast at 06.50 hrs, which resulted in a number of train cancellations in that morning's rush hour. An 80 Class motor coach, No 90 was struck mid-way by Enterprise coach No 915, with both coaches sustaining limited damage.

Once more, I personally witnessed an incident on the railway, this time in early February 1987 when travelling home on the 17.20 hrs stopping service from Belfast Central to Bangor, which was formed by the local Hunslet set with three coaches. When we stopped at Victoria Park, which only held one coach due to the platform's length, a passenger opened a train door at the rear of the train and fell straight down onto the ballast. Any further back, and he could have fallen into the Connswater River – what a thought! Along with the conductor, I got down from the train to help the passenger, who as it turned out, had sustained a broken leg. At the time no announcements were generally made as to the length of a train or the platform at this or other locations with similar dangers. In this instance, the train was too long for the platform at the station in question, but the conductor did not issue the necessary warning to departing passengers – i.e., that they should alight using the front coach only.

There was another derailment incident on Friday, 6 September 1989, when the 08.20 hrs stopping service from Bangor to Belfast Central came off the track just past the Connswater bridge at Victoria Park. The train involved was 80 Class motor coach No 99, with two trailers. The leading bogie was completely off the road. While repair work was underway, a security man sat on board the set for security purposes. The line was reopened on the evening of Saturday, 7 September.

October 1989: Fatality at Seahill

On Tuesday, 31 October 1989 I was travelling home from work in my company van when I overheard a radio telephone message from one of our drivers, reporting that a young boy had been struck by a train on the Bangor side of Seahill. I attended the scene, knowing that you had to be prepared to deal with certain situations as and when they arose.

The conductor of the train travelling towards Bangor was distraught: he had by this time found the six-year-old boy, who was lying on top of a bridge, 700 yards on the Bangor side of Seahill. The child was already dead. He was from the Rockport Community, only half a mile away and it seemed that he had been standing close to the track in some undergrowth, waving at the Bangor-bound train, when the 16.55 hrs service from Bangor to Belfast Central had come up behind him and struck him. The driver had not seen him, and in fact only became aware of what had actually happened – that the boy had been struck by his train – when he was questioned by police at Holywood. To assist the undertakers, an empty set was brought up to the bridge and the boy placed on board and taken back to Seahill station.

When someone is fatally struck by a train, the main focus is naturally usually on the victim's family, which is of course the way it should be. However in such circumstances the train crew can be badly affected by being involved in or witnessing such an incident, and the stress of such a trauma can be a major problem in the period afterwards. Counselling is offered to any member of staff involved in these incidents.

Fatal Collision and a Manslaughter Charge: Slaght, March 1990

The danger of level crossings once more became evident in a terrible accident which happened on Thursday, 1 March 1990. The 20.40 hrs service from Belfast Central to Londonderry collided with a car at Slaght public road level crossing, 1.5 miles south of Ballymena; the car was cut in two and flung down the embankment, killing the driver and front seat passenger – the mother and father of the two children in rear of the car. The children themselves were injured and had to remain in the car with their seat belts on until the emergency services came to release them. Meanwhile, the train derailed and the driving trailer of the 80 Class set No 745 went down the 20-foot embankment on the down side and landed on its side, facing in the opposite direction of travel. One passenger in this coach was killed and 27 other passengers injured, some with serious injuries. The intermediate trailer went onto its side on the top of the embankment, and motor coach No 90 derailed but remained virtually upright. I attended the scene of the accident to assist in whatever way I could. Travelling from the Belfast direction by road was treacherous due to snow on the ground, and I followed a couple of ambulances up the M2 motorway towards the scene.

The level crossing was of the new type which had been introduced on British Rail: an Automatic Open Crossing Locally Monitored (AOCL), which meant it did not have any barriers for motorists to stop at, just warning lights. This had replaced the previous crossing type, which had been an Automatic Half-Barrier crossing, which had half barriers and could be monitored from Ballymena signal box.

Fatal collision at Slaght level crossing, Thursday, 1 March 1990. *(Author)*

On the night of the accident, the train had been travelling normally from Antrim to Ballymena. It had been snowing, and the ground and track were covered with light snow. As the train approached Slaght level crossing, the train driver should have been watching for a white flashing light, which would have indicated to him that the crossing equipment was working and all was in order. In the absence of a white flashing light, the train should have been brought to a halt in advance of the crossing.

The subsequent inquiry, in which I was involved, commenced on Monday, 5 March 1990 and continued for at least ten days. A test train was run on Wednesday, 7 March to assess braking distances around the scene of the accident. It later transpired that the level crossing equipment had failed and timed out at some point during the hour before the train arrived. This meant that the white flashing light could not be displayed. As the train approached the crossing however, the driver did not respond to the fact that there was no light being shown, but simply kept going and collided with the car on the crossing. The motorist would not have seen any warning lights on the crossing and, therefore as far as he was concerned, it was safe to proceed.

The train driver was later charged with manslaughter, to which he pleaded guilty. He was convicted at Ballymena County Court on Tuesday, 12 February 1991, and received a conditional discharge for two years.

Sadly, there were to be more fatal incidents in the years which followed. On 23 July 1992, a local train from Poyntzpass to Portadown struck a car on an occupation level crossing at Aughantaraghan, south of Poyntzpass. The car driver was killed in the accident. At a later date, the crossing was closed along with several others in the area, when a new access road to a number of dwellings was constructed by the Northern Ireland Transport Holding Company.

About six months later, in January 1993, the 20.45 hrs Enterprise service from Dublin to Belfast Central struck a male trespasser on the track at the Botanic end of

City Hospital. By the time the Enterprise stopped, it was through to Botanic station. I was asked to assist with the investigation at the site. The man in question was lying on the track a few yards away from the Botanic tunnel entrance; lighting in the area was very poor. To address this problem, it was decided to bring a GM locomotive from the Central Depot to the scene – its powerful headlights were then used to light up the area, so that investigation could proceed.

Derailments at Bangor

Meanwhile, the problem of derailments continued. On Wednesday, 8 January 1992, for example, the 12.15 hrs service from Belfast Central to Bangor came off the track on the approach to Bangor station. The rear bogie of the third coach of Castle Class No 784, although technically derailed, ran for approximately 100 yards on one rail of the down line and one rail of the up line. The train finally came to a stop adjacent to the signal box. Passengers were detrained using ladders, and then had to walk to the station. It later transpired that the signalman had pulled the points under the last coach as it was approaching the platform.

On Thursday, 5 May 1994, the 17.55 hrs service from Belfast Central to Bangor was scheduled into Platform 1 at Bangor. The train had gone over the point and crossing work but as it ran into the track at the platform, the front bogie derailed due to the track spreading. Fortunately passengers were able to detrain and leave the area safely.

Collision on Antrim Branch

In late October 1994, an 80 Class train operating a local afternoon service struck a tractor on Molyneaux's accommodation crossing, near Crumlin. The first coach of the train derailed, and a number of passengers were injured. The emergency services had great difficulty in locating the train, as there were three crossings with the name Molyneaux. To resolve the problem, police called upon the RAF at Aldergrove to send out a helicopter which would provide an exact location for the derailed train. The line was not reopened until two days later, on Saturday, 26 October. Driving trailer No 739 was taken to the mainland for extensive repairs.

Christmas 1995: Frozen Trains

No trains would run on Christmas Day or Boxing Day, and the first day back to work after the two-day closure was always a difficult day. However the situation on Wednesday, 27 December 1995 was more difficult than usual, due to weather conditions. By 06.15 hrs, it had become clear that only two train sets were available for a service requirement of 25. All of the failed sets had frozen air brakes, and the service was only getting back to some sort of normality by 13.00 hrs that day. The temperature was minus 10°C and the falling snow was lying.

Collisions at Finaghy, Yorkgate and Portrush

From 2 March 1998, the line between Central Junction and Lisburn was being relayed; this work was due to be completed in December 1998. Single-line working sections were in use at various stages, with signalling also being provided to protect these sections.

On Tuesday, 7 April 1998, the first freight train from Dundalk to Belfast Adelaide depot had gone into the single-line section, and had been stopped by a signal at Finaghy. A second freight train from Dundalk to Adelaide was not too far behind, and proceeded to enter the same single-line section. Unfortunately however, the first freight train had not cleared the section, as it was still at the stop signal. The second freight train, GM 071 locomotive, ran into the back of the first train, continuing on into a number of wagons and eventually coming off the track and landing on its side. A couple of Irish Rail staff were injured, and the line between Belfast and Lisburn was closed. Meanwhile, beer kegs from the trains were strewn all over the place. The locals were out in number and, unsurprisingly, quite a few of the kegs mysteriously disappeared from the scene!

In another incident, on Wednesday, 29 April 1998, the 07.00 hrs service from Belfast Central to Larne Harbour struck an empty Enterprise set between Yorkgate and York Road yard. The Larne-bound 80 Class set was formed by Nos 96, 769 and 733. Motor coach No 96 sustained severe damage to the offside and went down the bank onto the motorway sidings. Intermediate trailer No 769 also partially went down the bank, stopping in a precarious position. Driving trailer No 733 remained upright and stayed on the track.

The 07.00 hrs Belfast–Larne Harbour collision near Yorkgate, Tuesday, 29 April 1998. *(Author)*

The Enterprise set, with GM Locomotive No 207, had been due to run from Belfast York Road depot over to Belfast Central station, to form the 08.00 hrs Enterprise service to Dublin. The Larne-bound 80 Class set scraped about ten feet out of the Enterprise's Coach H, while one of its coaches, No 96, hit the Enterprise's locomotive, causing some panel damage, broken cab windows and damage to the fuel tank. The Enterprise set then stopped, straddling the over bridge and the up platform at

Yorkgate station. The line between Belfast Central and Whiteabbey was closed until late in the evening of Wednesday, 29 April, and passengers were transferred by bus between the two stations.

Following an investigation, it was established that the driver of the 07.00 hrs service Belfast to Larne Harbour had gone through a red signal just past Yorkgate station.

On 24 September 1999, there was another collision, when a Portrush to Coleraine branch train had brake problems on an evening service, at Dhu Varren. The train crew were having difficulty in repairing the three-car Castle Class set. The train eventually started rolling backwards and picked up speed, before colliding with the buffer stops at Portrush, causing vestibule damage and two broken windscreens to No 784.

Wheel Slip Problems

On Tuesday, 2 November 1999 I came home on a special six-car 80 Class train which left Belfast Central at 18.55 hrs. The first train out of Belfast since 17.45 hrs, the special had been commissioned because the line to Bangor was completely gridlocked, with four trains blocking the down line, which had been initially obstructed by a failed train at Craigavad, due to excessive slipping on leaves. The recovery train, which had tried to propel the failed train, had stopped too and couldn't proceed; there was also a blocked train at Holywood, and another blocked train at Sydenham.

Running down the up line, our special picked up passengers from all of the blocked trains – soon there were so many passengers, it was like a London underground train in the rush hour! The two guards' vans on the train were also packed out. The special also slipped up the hill between Marino and Seahill, but thankfully didn't get blocked there. As mentioned earlier, this problem of trains slipping on leaves was an issue for many years, and eventually NIR utilised special engineering trains during the night to ease the situation.

November 1990: A Fire on the Enterprise

On Saturday, 4 November 1990, the 12.30 hrs Enterprise service from Belfast to Dublin was formed by a five-car 80 Class diesel unit: the regular Enterprise train was not available due to planned maintenance. When the train was about five miles north of Drogheda, the generator of the rear motor coach suddenly went on fire. The conductor noticed the fire very quickly, and the train was stopped at Galroostown Bridge. The 170 passengers were moved to the front three coaches, and the rear two coaches were uncoupled. Two units from the Drogheda fire brigade were dispatched and were able to bring the fire under control within one hour. The front three coaches continued to Drogheda, where passengers were sent on to Dublin by bus. I thought it strange when NIR received an invoice from the Drogheda fire brigade for the call-out fee!

Summer 2002: Boulder Derails Train at Downhill

There was a frightening incident on the railways on Tuesday, 4 June 2002, as a train driver and eleven passengers were injured when their train struck a large boulder on the track at Downhill, causing the train to derail and career down an embankment and onto the beach. The accident happened as the 12.50 hrs service from Londonderry to Belfast Central was travelling through the old station at Downhill. None of those taken to the Causeway Hospital in Coleraine had serious injuries, although the train driver suffered a broken leg and cracked ribs. A woman passenger sustained head injuries, and five others were treated for angina and chest pains. The train involved was a three-car 80 Class set, Nos 740, 767 and 67.

The boulders had come away from the cliffs (which were known as 'Eagle Rock'), adjacent to the road and railway on the down side of the track: it was reported that a landslide had taken place only minutes before the train appeared. A caller had contacted police about the boulders, which had bounced on to the steep Bishop's Road and then over onto the A2 Coast Road, finally coming to rest on the railway. Police were in the process of passing on the message to the railway, but it was too late for the train to be stopped by the last controlled signal. Emergency calls were sent out by Railway Control via the open channel VHF radio system to alert the driver, but they were not heard or acted upon. As soon as the train driver observed the boulder, he made an emergency brake application but this was too late to have any meaningful effect. It was estimated that the train struck the boulder at 60 mph, causing all three coaches to derail. All the coaches remained upright, although the first two slewed from the normal direction of travel, and the coupling between them parted.

Train derailed by boulder at Downhill, Tuesday, 4 June 2002 as pictured in the *Belfast Telegraph*.

A formal inquiry into the incident was launched by Translink. The DoE Roads Service also carried out investigations, which included questioning local landowners about the state of the cliffs and about what precautionary measures could be taken to prevent rock falls in the area.

The line at the scene had been badly damaged, and a decision was taken to relay the affected track. The line was not reopened until Monday, 24 June 2002.

Viaduct Accidents: Cahir and Malahide

Another incident in CIÉ territory which is worthy of note happened on 7 October 2003 between Limerick Junction and Waterford. A freight train was passing over the Cahir Viaduct on the line, when the bridge deck gave way. The locomotive and a few of the wagons just managed to complete the run over the viaduct – but 13 cement wagons derailed and fell into the river below. The line was closed for a considerable period, only reopening on 24 September 2004, with a new timetable in operation which included a new passenger service.

Some years later, in 2009, another viaduct incident occurred on Irish Rail territory, which had a serious knock-on effect for Enterprise services. The accident happened on Friday, 21 August, when a 20-metre section of the Malahide viaduct collapsed, just as the 18.07 hrs service from Balbriggan to Dublin Pearse (a four-car IÉ CAF) passed over it. Just half an hour or so earlier, the 16.10 hrs Enterprise from Belfast Central to Dublin had passed over the viaduct, and some twenty minutes later, an eight-car IÉ CAF from Dublin Pearse to Dundalk had also just cleared it – meaning that upwards of 1000 passengers had been safely taken across the viaduct just before its collapse. The drivers of the two IÉ trains reported having felt movement of some sort on the track while driving.

The viaduct was a 1966 pre-cast viaduct resting on the 1860 original stone piers. From 1844 to 1860, it had existed there too, as a wooden structure. Round-the-clock engineering work organised by Irish Rail meant that the line was able to reopen well ahead of the New Year 2010 completion date originally anticipated. Before this, on Thursday, 12 November 2009, the viaduct was reopened for test trains. The first down train to cross was the empty 09.15 hrs Enterprise DD (De Dietrich) set from Dublin to Belfast York Road; the first up train was a laden Tara Mines freight to Dublin North Wall. The line opened again for full passenger services on Monday, 16 November 2009.

Yuletide Train Failure

One of those train incidents which passengers at the time talked about for many a day afterwards, happened on Tuesday, 23 December 2003. With two days left until Christmas, most people had plans made for the festive season. I was travelling on the 17.21 hrs Belfast Central to Bangor stopping service, and we had only just travelled out of Central by half a mile, when we were stopped on the River Lagan bridge. It seemed that a train had failed at Marino, and that there were two trains in front of us on the Bangor line. Our train was sitting within controlled signals, ahead of and behind us. So it is hard to believe that we sat in this position for no less than 82 minutes! In their wisdom, Railway Control would not let us return to Central, even though we had a controlled signal and the driver had requested the move. In the meantime, passengers for later Bangor-bound trains were being transferred by bus from Central station. At least they weren't stuck in transit, like me and my fellow passengers!

Summer 2012: Golf Special Drama

In 2012, there was much anticipation around that year's Irish Open Golf championship, which was due to be held at Royal Portrush Golf Club from 28 June to 1 July. Large numbers of supporters were expected to travel to Portrush, and NIR had laid on extra trains to cope with the expected demand. Due to the early start of the tournament, the Antrim branch was also used, allowing trains to head north from the Belfast direction.

On Thursday, 28 June, the 06.45 hrs golf special left Belfast Great Victoria Street for Portrush, to travel via the Antrim branch. The special was formed by a six-car CAF Class 4000 Nos 4006 and 4007. As the train ran north of Knockmore Junction however, the driver of the train got a bit of a shock as he looked at the track ahead, and immediately applied the brakes. A 50-foot section of the embankment had been washed out, leaving the rails hanging in mid-air!

Despite the driver's swift response in bringing the train to a stop, the first coach of the train lay straddled over the washout. After a quick inspection had been done, however, the train was reversed back over the gap and returned to Lisburn. From there, the service, with several hundred passengers on board, was re-routed to Portrush via Bleach Green Junction, and the Antrim branch was closed. After the necessary repairs were carried out, the Antrim branch reopened on Friday, 6 July 2012 – too late however for the final days of the tournament!

When an accident happens on the railway, it usually becomes public knowledge very quickly, sometimes with devastating effects on passengers, staff, the public and on the emergency services. When legal proceedings ensue – thankfully, this happens relatively rarely – many railway staff find themselves unexpectedly in the frame – and even those not directly involved can be affected by seeing their colleagues caught up in legal wrangles seeking to place the blame.

Embankment washout north of Knockmore Junction, Thursday, 28 June 2012. *(Author)*

Although human error is still an incalculable factor in many ways, so much about the railway now is so safe. The one big safety problem which, in my view, we have still not got properly to grips with is the hazard of level crossings, where roads of any sort meet the railway. Unfortunately, a number of motorists are still careless at these junctures and seem to have no awareness that, in trying to save themselves a few seconds by weaving around barriers, they could cause a train derailment with disastrous results. As staff in the railway always say, the best level crossing on a railway is a closed one!

APPENDIX A

Detailed Table of Terrorist Incidents on Northern Ireland Railways, 1972–1977

Date	Day	Location	Details
02.01.72	Sunday	Bells Row, Lurgan	Bomb scare: line closed for 3 hours, 20 minutes
05.01.72	Wednesday	Lisburn–Lurgan	Bomb scare: line closed for 2 hours
11.01.72	Tuesday	Boyne Bridge, Great Victoria Street, Belfast	Car bomb on bridge: services suspended for over 2 hours
19.01.72	Wednesday	Cloghogue, Newry	Malicious fire in permanent way hut: cross-border services delayed
28.01.72	Friday	Helen's Bay	Hoax device: morning rush-hour trains suspended
30.01.72	Sunday	Londonderry	"Bloody Sunday": the day on which 13 civil rights marchers were shot dead by British paratroopers. **NB: See Chapter Five for more details** (no rail-related incidents on this day, however).
31.01.72	Monday	Docker Bridge, Lurgan	Bomb scare: service suspended for 30 minutes
01.02.72	Tuesday	Bells Row, Lurgan	Crossing keeper's hut destroyed by explosion: delays to services
04.02.72	Friday	Killeen, Newry	Lorry blown up near bridge: delays to services
09.02.72	Wednesday	Limavady Junction–Magilligan	Several bomb scares: delays to services
25.02.72	Friday	Belfast, Great Victoria Street	Bomb scare: delays to services
26.02.72	Saturday	Portadown	Track blocked by telegraph poles: delays to services
04.03.72	Saturday	Whitehead Carrickfergus–Barn	Concrete sleepers placed on track: 22.20 hrs Larne to Belfast delayed by 80 minutes Concrete sleepers placed on track
09.03.72	Thursday	Belfast Great Victoria Street	Bomb scare: delays to services for 1 hour
11.03.72	Saturday	Londonderry Londonderry–Bellarena Bells Row, Lurgan	Bomb scare in station Bomb scare: delays to services for 1 hour Parcel strapped to rail: delays to services
13.03.72	Monday	Carrickfergus	Bomb scare for 15 minutes
21.03.72	Tuesday	Londonderry	40 lb bomb exploded in station parcels office: no delays to services
21.03.72	Tuesday	Lake Street, Lurgan	Timber placed on track: delays to services
22.03.72	Wednesday	Belfast Great Victoria Street	A car bomb exploded in the car park behind the Europa hotel–bus and rail station at 14.45 hours: 71 people injured in the blast; rail and bus stations badly damaged, as well as two trains including BUT railcar No 133 **NB: See Chapter Five for more details**
23.03.72	Thursday	Bessbrook Skerries	Bomb scare over 3 hours: delays to services Bomb scare: delays to services
25.03.72	Saturday	Belfast York Road Lurgan	Bomb scare in station for 30 minutes Unattended case found on train: delays to services
27.03.72	Monday	Greenisland	Bomb scare for 20 minutes
05.04.72	Wednesday	Belfast York Road	Bomb scare for 20 minutes
09.04.72	Sunday	Kilmore–Lurgan	Bomb exploded on up line: delays to services
13.04.72	Thursday	Bangor West Adelaide–Balmoral	Bomb scare over 13 hours Bomb scare at White's Bakery for 1.5 hours
18.04.72	Tuesday	Boyne Bridge Belfast Great Victoria Street	Bomb scare for 30 minutes, followed by a further scare later for 20 minutes

19.04.72	Wednesday	Belfast Great Victoria Street Queens Quay York Road	Bomb scares at all three Belfast stations, for 1 hour
28.04.72	Friday	Meigh vicinity	Box found on track – a hoax: delays to cross-border services for 45 minutes
29.04.72	Saturday	Bangor	Bomb exploded at the Feedwell dog biscuit factory: cancellations and delays for 4 hours The 11.20 hrs Belfast–Bangor service had just arrived in Bangor station, passing the factory.
30.04.72	Sunday	Belfast York Road	Bomb scare for 30 minutes
13.05.72	Saturday	Lurgan	10 lb bomb exploded in a suitcase on the platform damaging station buildings 23.55 hrs.
21.05.72	Sunday	Belfast–Whiteabbey	Bomb scare for 1.5 hours.
09.06.72	Friday	Belfast Great Victoria Street	Bomb exploded at Europa Hotel, causing damage to walls and stalls in the station: disruption to services
11.06.72	Sunday	Belfast York Road	Bomb scare for 20 minutes.
12.06.72	Monday	Lisburn	Bomb scare for 45 minutes.
13.06.72	Tuesday	Finaghy	Bomb exploded in Diamond Gardens: delays to services
24.06.72	Saturday	Near Border, also Dundalk	One barrel bomb found on each track: cross-border trains stopped for 6 hrs. **NB: See Chapter Five for more details**
26.06.72	Monday	Kilnasaggart Bridge	Suspect lorry parked at the bridge: cross-border services suspended for 6 hrs.
26.06.72	Monday	Greencastle	Erskine's bridge damaged by a 15 lb bomb at 01.30 hrs
27.06.72	Tuesday	Belfast York Road	Bomb scare for 30 minutes
28.06.72	Wednesday	Londonderry train	Bomb scare on a Derry train: delays to services on the line
04.07.72	Tuesday	Belfast Great Victoria Street	Bomb scare for 20 minutes
11.07.72	Tuesday	Bells Row, Lurgan	Crossing keeper's hut destroyed by explosion: delays to services
14.07.72	Friday	Kilmore	Masked men held up crossing keeper, and damaged interior of hut: delays to services
15.07.72	Saturday	Portadown	20 lb bomb exploded at 20.00 hrs, which destroyed the bar and damaged the station
21.07.72	Friday	Various locations throughout NI	This day was "Bloody Friday". **See Chapter Five for a fuller report**.
		Boilie, near Lurgan	50 lb bomb exploded on up line as a freight train passed over the level crossing: train derailed and single-line working was introduced
		Belfast York Road	Bomb exploded on a platform at 14.23 hrs: extensive damage to station and delays to services
		Finaghy	Lorry exploded on Finaghy Road North bridge: line closed 4 hours
		Belfast Great Victoria Street	Bomb exploded on a lorry parked in Ulsterbus premises near the Boyne bridge at 14.48 hours: two people injured, widespread damage to buildings and 48 buses damaged
		Belfast Oxford Street	A car bomb exploded at the bus station at 14.48 hrs: six people killed and 40 injured, including bus staff
		Near Adelaide	Bomb exploded on Windsor Avenue footbridge: line was already closed due to other incidents
		Lurgan	50 lb bomb exploded: considerable damage caused to the station and platform
		Belfast Great Victoria Street	Further bomb scare: station closed for 3 hours.
22.07.72	Saturday	Whitehouse	Bomb exploded on Erskine's bridge : delays to services
		Kilmore	Crossing keeper's hut destroyed by explosion: delays to services
		Lake Street, Lurgan	Bomb scare at crossing keeper's hut: line closed for 2.5 hours.

24.07.72	Monday	Belfast Great Victoria Street	Bomb scare for 20 minutes
31.07.72	Monday	Belfast Great Victoria Street	Bomb scare for 30 minutes
01.08.72	Tuesday	Lake Street, Lurgan Hilden–Lambeg	Bomb scare for 1.5 hours Bomb scare for 30 minutes
02.08.72	Wednesday	Portadown	Army found explosives and ammunition at the old railway station – delays to services
03.08.72	Thursday	Belfast Great Victoria Street	Bomb scare in nearby premises: Platforms 3 and 4 closed for short time
09.08.72	Wednesday	Lurgan	20.55 hrs Londonderry–Dundalk freight service stopped by armed men at 04.00 hrs and was subsequently damaged by fire. **NB: See Chapter Five for more details**
22.08.72	Tuesday	Whitehouse	Bomb scare in nearby premises for 2 hours
23.08.72	Wednesday	Near Adelaide	Suspect device at Tate's Avenue bridge for 1 hour
24.08.72	Thursday	Antrim	Bomb scare at Shaw's Tyre Depot for 30 minutes
28.08.72	Monday	Belfast Great Victoria Street	Bomb exploded at Europa Hotel: delays to services
13.09.72	Wednesday	Kilnasaggart bridge	Both tracks damaged by explosion: delays to cross-border services
15.09.72	Friday	Greencastle	Bomb scare on overhead road bridge for 2 hours
21.09.72	Thursday	Kilnasaggart bridge	Bomb scare: delays to services
23.09.72	Saturday	Finaghy	Suspicious lorry parked at Finaghy Road North bridge: services suspended for 2.5 hours
06.10.72	Friday	Kilnasaggart bridge	Bomb scare for 50 minutes
10.10.72	Tuesday	Belfast York Road	Bomb scare at North Derby Street for 45 minutes
19.10.72	Thursday	Knockmore	Sleeper placed across track
21.10.72	Saturday	Lisburn	Bomb scare for 1 hour: only freight trains delayed
31.10.72	Tuesday	Lurgan	Bomb scare for 8 hours: cancellations and delays
03.11.72	Friday	Carrickfergus Belfast Great Victoria Street	Bomb scare for 10 minutes Bomb scare: cancellations and delays
08.11.72	Wednesday	Dunmurry	Bomb scare for 45 minutes at Balmoral Furnishings
13.11.72	Monday	Lurgan south of Meigh	Bomb scare for 40 minutes Explosion damaged both tracks at Moore's bridge: cross-border train services were disrupted for 14 hours
16.11.72	Thursday	Greencastle	Bomb exploded on new overhead road bridge: delays of 1.5 hours
17.11.72	Friday	Londonderry	Bomb scare at St Columba's Park for 30 minutes
01.12.72	Friday	Lurgan	Bomb scare at Silverwood bridge for 1.5 hours
07.12.72	Thursday	Lurgan–Portadown	Bomb scare: services delayed for 2 hours
14.12.72	Thursday	Near Adelaide Belfast–Portadown Portadown–Dublin	Bomb hoax at Donegall Road bridge Bomb scare for 2 hours: delays to services Bomb scare for 3 hours: delays to services
20.12.72	Wednesday	Whitehouse Gormanstown (IÉ)	Bomb scare at Erskine's bridge for 2.5 hours Bomb scare for 45 minutes: delays to services
21.12.72	Thursday	Belfast Great Victoria Street	Bomb scare for 30 minutes
28.12.72	Thursday	Portadown	Bomb detonated by Army near Shillington bridge: services delayed by 30 minutes
29.12.72	Friday	Lisburn–Lurgan	Bomb scare for 4 hours: with cancellations and delays
05.01.73	Friday	Dublin Connolly Dunmurry	Bomb scare delayed Enterprise by 1 hour Bomb scare at Moffett's factory for 1 hour

06.01.73	Saturday	Dundalk–Meigh	Explosion on down line: delays to services
07.01.73	Sunday	Belfast York Road	Bomb scare for 2 hours
17.01.73	Wednesday	Dublin–Portadown	Bomb scare for 9 hours, centred around Ayallogue bridge, south Armagh
19.01.73	Friday	Dunmurry	Bomb scare at Moffett's factory for 2 hours
24.01.73	Wednesday	Belfast Great Victoria Street	Bomb scare at Europa hotel for 45 minutes
24.01.73	Wednesday	Dunmurry	Bomb scare at Moffett's factory for 2 hours
28.01.73	Sunday	Belfast York Road	Bomb scare for 2 hours
30.01.73	Tuesday	Dunmurry	Bomb scare at Moffett's factory for 1 hour
01.02.73	Thursday	Dunmurry	Bomb scare at Moffett's factory for 15 minutes, followed later by another scare for 50 minutes
08.02.73	Thursday	Dunmurry	Bomb scare for 1 hour
10.02.73	Saturday	Lurgan	Concrete sleepers, manhole covers and wooden planks placed across track
14.02.73	Wednesday	Dunmurry	Bomb scare at Moffett's factory for 30 minutes
16.02.73	Friday	Belfast Great Victoria Street	Bomb scare for 1 hour
20.02.73	Tuesday	Dundalk	Eight armed men raided 08.00 hours Enterprise service Belfast–Dublin at Dundalk **NB: See Chapter Five for more details**
26.02.73	Monday	Dunadry	Suspicious object on track: delays of 20 minutes
28.02.73	Wednesday	Moira	Bomb scare for 9 hours: cancellations and delays
12.03.73	Monday	Kilmore–Lurgan	Bomb scare for 10.5 hours: cancellations & delays
14.03.73	Wednesday	Poyntzpass area	Explosion heard by signalman, but later cleared as not on railway: delays of 1 hour
22.03.73	Thursday	Belfast Great Victoria Street	Bomb scare for 60 minutes
23.03.73	Friday	Portadown–Dundalk	Bomb scare for 11 hours: delays
29.03.73	Thursday	Balmoral	Explosion in the Balmoral Inn: delayed services
20.04.73	Friday	Bangor	Bomb scare in station: no delays
02.05.73	Wednesday	Legatariff	Sleepers placed on track: freight trains delayed
11.05.73	Friday	Lisburn	Bomb exploded near front of station: delays of up to 1 hour
16.05.73	Wednesday	Lisburn	Bomb scare for 2 hours, with subsequent delays
17.05.73	Thursday	Lisburn	Bomb scare for 2 hours: delays
18.05.73	Friday	Belfast Queen's Quay station	Bomb exploded in gents' toilet area: considerable damage; no cancellations
		Belfast Great Victoria Street station	Bomb exploded in gents' toilet area: considerable damage, delays to services
		Lisburn station	Bomb left in gents' toilet defused by the Army **NB: See Chapter Five for more details**
23.05.73	Wednesday	Lisburn	Bomb found at station – closed for 3 hours
24.05.73	Thursday	M2–Belfast York Road signal box	Bomb scare for 50 minutes
25.05.73	Friday	Belfast Great Victoria Street	Bomb scare for 30 minutes
28.05.73	Monday	Belfast Great Victoria Street	Bomb scare for 20 minutes
02.06.73	Saturday	Portadown	Bomb scare for 2 hours: delays to services
10.06.73	Sunday	Adelaide	Bomb scare for 2 hours: delays to services
15.06.73	Friday	Bessbrook to Cloghogue	Bomb scare for 1.5 hours: cross-border services delayed
21.06.73	Thursday	Belfast Great Victoria Street	A 100 lb car bomb exploded on the Boyne bridge with no damage to the station: delays to services

25.06.73	Monday	Lisburn	Bomb scare for 40 minutes
11.07.73	Wednesday	Belfast Great Victoria Street	Suspect car in front of station: minor delays
		Belfast Great Victoria Street	Bomb scare at Europa hotel for 20 minutes
09.08.73	Tuesday	Camlough	Bomb scare for 20 minutes
11.08.73	Saturday	Belfast York Road	Bomb scare: no delays
16.08.73	Thursday	Meigh	CIÉ freight train stopped and bomb placed on locomotive which exploded: line closed for 19 hours **NB: See Chapter Five for more details**
28.08.73	Tuesday	Ballinderry	19.55 hrs freight train Londonderry–Lisburn struck sleepers on track
29.08.73	Wednesday	Ballinderry	19.55 hrs freight train Londonderry–Lisburn struck sleepers on track
30.08.73	Thursday	Whitehouse	Slight damage to down line: no delays
		Rockport, Seahill	Bomb exploded on track: 12 trains cancelled **NB: See Chapter Five for more details**
31.08.73	Friday	Dunmurry	Signalbox destroyed by bomb: line closed for 5 hours from 11.35 hours
		Adelaide area	Suspect packages on track at Tates Avenue bridge at same time as Dunmurry incident **NB: See Chapter Five for more details**
01.09.73	Saturday	Poyntzpass–Meigh	Bomb scare: slight delay to one service
03.09.73	Monday	Adelaide area	Bomb scare at Lislea Drive for 35 minutes
04.09.73	Tuesday	Adelaide area	Bomb scare at Tates Avenue bridge for 10 minutes.
06.09.73	Thursday	Belfast Great Victoria Street	Bomb scare for 1.5 hours
		Helen's Bay–Seahill	5 lb bomb exploded near St Columbanus Home, causing minor damage: some cancellations
		Holywood–Bangor	Bomb scare for 1.5 hours, following previous incident
07.09.73	Friday	Belfast–Carrick	Bomb scare for 1.5 hours
		Lisburn–Lurgan	Bomb scare for 2 hours
11.09.73	Tuesday	Ballymacarrett	Bomb scare at Frazer Street bridge for 1 hour
15.09.73	Saturday	Dublin Connolly	Bomb scare: Enterprise held up for 15 minutes
19.09.73	Wednesday	Belfast Great Victoria Street	Bomb scare for 50 minutes
29.09.73	Saturday	Tillysburn	2 lb gelignite bomb exploded on track: 10 trains cancelled over 3-hr period
		Bangor	Bomb scare for 30 minutes
		Belfast–Carrick	Bomb scare for 1.5 hours
		Belfast–Lisburn	Bomb scare for 1.5 hours
02.10.73	Tuesday	Newry	Bomb scare for 4 hours: delays
05.10.73	Friday	Carrickfergus	Bomb scare for 3 hours – service ran Belfast–Greenisland during closure
		Belfast York Road	Bomb scare for 30 minutes
		Lisburn–Knockmore	Bomb scare for 1.5 hours
		Finaghy	Bomb scare for 2 hours
06.10.73	Saturday	Portadown–Scarva	Bomb scare for 7 hours: disruption to cross-border services
12.10.73	Friday	Marino	30 lb bomb exploded on a train: one trailer completely wrecked; MED coach No 15 out of service for almost 2 yrs; cancellations and delays for 4.5 hours
		Belfast York Road	20 lb bomb exploded in gents' toilet area causing considerable damage; Two teenagers detained in relation to the incident: delays of up to 1.5 hr
		Lurgan–Portadown	Bomb scare on a train for 1.5 hours
		Belfast Great Victoria Street	100 lb bomb exploded on empty train on Platform 4: MED coach No 12 completely wrecked, other damage to other coaches and station; delays and cancellations for up to 1 hour **NB: See Chapter Five for more details**

13.10.73	Saturday	Portadown area	Obstruction on track: delays to services
18.10.73	Thursday	Finaghy	Bomb scare for 1.5 hours
22.10.73	Monday	Lisburn–Lurgan	Bomb scare for 10.5 hours, from 22.00 hours and overnight into 23.10.73: major disruption
23.10.73	Tuesday and Wednesday	Meigh	02.30 hrs CIÉ freight train stopped and bomb placed on locomotive which exploded, land mines placed in adjacent fields: damaged the down line; mail van also set on fire; crossing keeper's hut destroyed; major disruption to cross-border services for 36 hours. **NB: See Chapter Five for more details**
24.10.73	Wednesday	Whitehouse	Bomb scare for 45 minutes
25.10.73	Thursday	Whitehouse	Bomb exploded on down line at 17.00 hrs: line closed for 2 hours, followed by single-line working continuing until 10.00 hours on 26 October
		Lurgan	Bomb scare for 1.5 hours
26.10.73	Friday	Portadown–Dundalk	Bomb scare for 14 hours, overnight into 27 October. An Adelaide–Dundalk freight train on 26 October was held at Poyntzpass until the next day.
27.10.73	Saturday	Barn station	Suspicious parcel on track: delays to services
31.10.73	Wednesday and Thursday	Poyntzpass	Bomb scare for 6 hours
01.11.73	Thursday, Friday and Saturday	Meigh	Hijacked lorry parked on level crossing: line closed for 40 hours; major disruption to services until Saturday, 3 November **NB: See Chapter Five for more details**
02.11.73	Friday	Belfast–Portadown	Bomb scare for 2.5 hours
03.11.73	Saturday	Sydenham	Suspicious parcel found on train: delays and cancellations
03.11.73	Saturday	Bangor	Bomb scare for 30 minutes
03.11.73	Saturday	Belfast York Road sidings	Two separate incidents: 1) 10 lb bomb defused by the Army in the cab of a power car; 2) 3 lb bomb defused by the Army in a trailer coach. Station closed for 2.5 hours, resulting in delays to services
09.11.73	Friday	On a Derry train	All trains on the Londonderry line stopped and searched: delays to services for 1 hour
10.11.73	Saturday	Belfast York Road area	Bomb scare at Crusaders football ground: delayed services for 1 hour
	Saturday and Sunday	Kilmore	Bomb exploded on Balfour's bridge: line closed for 10 hours and overnight into 11 November
12.11.73	Monday to Wednesday	Whitehouse	500 lb bomb demolished Erskine's bridge: Belfast–Whiteabbey closed for 43 hours, followed by single-line working over the down line **NB: See Chapter Five for more details**
13.11.73	Tuesday	Belfast Great Victoria Street	Bomb scare for 20 minutes
15.11.73	Thursday	Belfast Great Victoria Street	Bomb scare at Europa Hotel for 30 minutes
16.11.73	Friday	Helen's Bay	Bomb scare at two railway bridges leading into village for 2 hours: four trains cancelled
	Friday to Sunday	Meigh	Lorry parked on level crossing, with two beer kegs placed beside it. A CIÉ freight train from Adelaide–Dundalk had no warning of the obstruction and the train struck the side of the lorry, and continued on its way. The line was closed for 44 hours, from Friday evening to Sunday 18 November.
19.11.73	Monday	Belfast York Road	Bomb scare for 30 minutes
23.11.73	Friday	Newry	Bomb scare for 6 hours: delays to services
		Belfast York Road	Bomb scare for 15 minutes
		Glenlough, near Dunloy	Bomb exploded at 00.01 hrs: damage to 15 feet of track; line closed overnight, for 10.5 hours

27.11.73	Tuesday	Lurgan	Bomb scare at Silverwood bridge for 6 hours
		Larne line	Bomb scare for 15 minutes
		Ballymena–Ballymoney	Suspicious box on line: closed for 13 hours overnight, into 28 November
		Meigh	Minibus parked on level crossing near Border: line closed for 21 hours, which included the next entry at Newry (closure overnight, into 28 November).
		Newry	Hijacked bus parked below the Egyptian Arch
28.11.73	Wednesday	Derry line	Bomb scare for 1.5 hours
02.12.73	Sunday	Finaghy	Bomb found at station: line closed for 11.5 hours overnight, into 3 December
03.12.73	Monday	Templepatrick	Suspicious box on track: line closed for 45 minutes
		Belfast York Road	Bomb scare for 35 minutes
05.12.73	Wednesday	Lambeg	Bomb scare for 15 minutes
06.12.73	Thursday	Belfast–Lisburn	Bomb scare for 15 hours overnight, into 7 December
11.12.73	Tuesday	Belfast Great Victoria Street	Bomb scare for 30 minutes
13.12.73	Thursday	Belfast–Lisburn	Bomb scare for 13 hours overnight, into 14 December
15.12.73	Saturday	Bangor line	Bomb scare for 30 minutes
		south of Dundalk	Bomb scare for 6 hours
18.12.73	Tuesday	Cloghogue Ayallouge	One car parked under each bridge south of Newry. Line closed for 13.5 hours and overnight, into 19 December
		Great Northern line	Bomb scare for 3 hours
20.12.73	Thursday	Belfast–Lisburn	Bomb scare for 2 hours
		Belfast Great Victoria Street	Bomb scare for 25 minutes
24.12.73	Monday	Dunloy–Ballymoney	Suspicious box on track: closed for 30 minutes
		Ballymoney–Coleraine	Suspicious box on track: closed for 30 minutes
		Magilligan	Suspicious box on track: closed for 1 hour
29.12.73	Saturday	Lisburn–Portadown Belfast Great Victoria Street Finaghy–Dunmurry Belfast–Dublin	All four incidents were bomb scares late afternoon/evening: line closed for 7 hours
03.01.74	Thursday	Greencastle	5 lb bomb exploded between up and down lines at Erskine's bridge at 20.05 hrs: line closed for 2 hours
	Thursday	Hilden	Hijacked van parked under Bridge No 286; 40 lb bomb exploded in the van at 15.20 hrs: line closed for 2 hours.
04.01.74	Friday	Belfast–Lisburn	Bomb scare for 2.5 hours
		Portadown–Dublin	Bomb scare for 18.5 hours, and overnight into 5 January
10.01.74	Thursday	Finaghy	Two beer keg bombs exploded on the line under Finaghy Road North bridge at 20.50 hrs and 21.30 hours: minor damage. Line closed for 1.5 hrs
11.01.74	Friday	Belfast Great Victoria Street	Bomb scare for 30 minutes
13.01.74	Sunday	Belfast–Portadown	Bomb scare for 10 hours and overnight, into 14 January
14.01.74	Monday	Belfast Great Victoria Street	Suitcase found at permanent way in the yard. Army carried out a controlled explosion and station reopened after 30 minutes.
15.01.74	Tuesday	Portadown–Dundalk	Bomb scare for 3 hours at Knock bridge and overnight, into 16 December
		Portadown	Bomb exploded under Thomas Street bridge at 00.20 hrs: line closed for 7.5 hours
		Bessbrook–Meigh	Bomb scare for 30 minutes
19.01.74	Saturday	Whitehouse	Car bomb exploded under Bridge No 7 at 18.55 hours: line closed for 1.5 hours

22.01.74	Tuesday	Belfast–Lisburn	Bomb scare for 2 hours
		Meigh	Bomb scare for 11 hours and overnight, into 23 January. Driver of CIÉ Light Engine from Adelaide to Dundalk saw that the level crossing gates were closed across the railway, and reversed back to a safe location.
02.02.74	Saturday	Belfast Great Victoria Street	Two bombs exploded in the station at 15.45 hrs: station gutted by fire; service suspended for 2.5 hours. **NB: See Chapter Five for more details**
13.02.74	Wednesday	Greencastle	Suspicious box on track at 08.25 hrs: closed for 1.5 hours
20.02.74	Wednesday	Belfast York Road	Bomb scare for 15 minutes
21.02.74	Thursday	Antrim–Londonderry	Bomb scare for 30 minutes
22.02.74	Friday	Dunmurry	Bomb exploded at Moffett's factory at 22.25 hrs: line closed for 30 minutes
03.03.74	Sunday	Belfast York Road sidings	Incendiary devices exploded in empty carriages in the sidings at 21.00 hours: Trailer No 543 destroyed **NB: See Chapter Five for more details**
07.03.74	Thursday	Sydenham	Duffle bag found on 07.30 hrs Bangor–Belfast service: delays of 30 minutes.
15.03.74	Friday	Belfast–Larne	Reports of four bombs along the line. At 16.00 hrs, two bombs exploded on down line at Erskine's bridge, Greencastle: single-line working introduced, but delays and cancellations unavoidable
		Belfast–Bangor	Reports of ten bombs along the line: line closed for 12.5 hours and overnight, into 16 March, with many delays and cancellations
		Finaghy	Two oil drums found on track – a hoax: line closed for 4.5 hours.
		Meigh	The 14.30 hrs up and down Enterprise services were stopped and hijacked by armed men; passengers removed; reports of nine bombs placed on the trains; all hoaxes: line closed for 25.5 hrs and overnight into 16 March **NB: See Chapter Five for more details**
17.03.74	Sunday	Belfast–Lisburn	Three separate bomb hoaxes at Dunmurry, Derriaghy and Adelaide: line closed for over 4 hours
19.03.74	Tuesday	Bells Row Lurgan	Four armed men told the crossing keeper that there were bombs on the line: line closed for 3 hours
21.03.74	Thursday	Ballymena	Bomb call made at 21.20 hrs; following two controlled explosions in the early hours of 22 March, a 200 lb bomb was defused: slight damage to station; line closed for 14 hours
		Dunloy	Signalman abducted at 21.20 hrs by armed men, who left a bomb in the signal box; signalman later released and 75 lb bomb defused on 22 March: line closed for 24.5 hours.
		Belfast York Road	Bomb scare for 45 minutes
		Carnalea	Bomb scare for 30 minutes **NB: See Chapter Five for more details**
24.03.74	Sunday	Meigh	Bomb scare for 10.5 hours and overnight, into 25 March
09.04.74	Tuesday	Greencastle	Bomb scare at Erskine's bridge for 35 minutes
		Finaghy	Suspect object on track: line closed for 3 hours
		Belfast Great Victoria Street	Suspect car outside Europa hotel: station closed for 35 minutes
10.04.74	Wednesday	Meigh	Bomb scare for 9 hours and overnight, into 11 April
11.04.74	Thursday	Lake Street, Lurgan	Bomb hoax: line closed for 3 hours
13.04.74	Saturday	Belfast–Whiteabbey	Bomb scare for 1.5 hours
14.04.74	Sunday	Kilnasaggart bridge	Car parked under the bridge – a hoax: line closed for 9.5 hours and overnight, into 15 April
15.04.74	Monday	Lake Street, Lurgan	Armed men told the crossing keeper to get out as a keg was on the line – a hoax: line closed for 1 hour
16.04.74	Tuesday	Lake Street, Lurgan	Armed men told the crossing keeper to leave, as object on the line – a hoax: line closed for 45 minutes

17.04.74	Wednesday	Belfast–Lurgan	Reports of three bombs on the line: line closed for 1 hour
18.04.74	Thursday	Central Junction, Belfast	Suitcase found beside track: line closed for 45 minutes
26.04.74	Friday	Belfast–Dublin	Bomb scare for 5 hours from 08.56 hrs
		Belfast–Dublin	Bomb scare for 8 hours and overnight, into 27 April
29.04.74	Monday	Kilnasaggart bridge	Suspect object spotted by track walker on up line at 11.40 hrs; 40 lb gelignite bomb defused by the Army: line closed for 9 hours
		Belfast Great Victoria Street	Bomb scare for 1 hour
01.05.74	Wednesday	Belfast–Greencastle	Bomb scare for 45 minutes
		Belfast York Road	Box on the line near Ivan Street: line closed for 20 minutes
08.05.74	Wednesday	Belfast–Portadown	Bomb scare for 4 hours during two separate incidents throughout the morning, from 08.17 hrs
10.05.74	Friday	Ballymena	Bomb scare for 15 minutes
14.05.74	Tuesday	Across Northern Ireland	From 14 May to 29 May, there was an Ulster Workers' Council strike. Most of the railway incidents are recorded in detail in Chapter Five. **NB: See Chapter Five for more details**
15.05.74	Wednesday	Bangor–Belfast	Bomb scare for 1 hour; special train with police and crew on board left Bangor at 18.04 hrs to clear the line
16.05.74	Thursday	Greenisland–Carrick	Bomb scare for 1.5 hours
17.05.74	Friday	Bangor–Belfast	Bomb scare for 1 hour; special train with police and crew on board left Bangor at 08.35 hrs to clear the line
		Castlerock tunnels	Bomb scare for 6 hours.
18.05.74	Saturday	Lurgan	Signal box destroyed by explosion: line closed for 45 minutes
		Coleraine–Londonderry	Bomb scare for 1.5 hours
20.05.74	Monday	Belfast–Bangor	Bomb scare for 50 minutes, followed later in the day of a separate bomb scare for 30 minutes
		Greenisland area	Line blocked by blazing sleepers at Greenisland; obstacles on the line at Jordanstown and Whiteabbey
21.05.74	Tuesday	Carnalea	Suspicious car under the bridge: line closed for 30 minutes
		Jordanstown	Line blocked by obstacles at Jordanstown and Whiteabbey
		Kellswater–Ballymena	Bomb scare for 3.5 hours
		Tandragee	Bomb scare for 2 hours
		Central Junction, Belfast	Bomb scare for 1.5 hours
22.05.74	Wednesday	Sydenham	UDA pickets tried to stop morning rush-hour trains
		Jordanstown	Line blocked by obstacles at Jordanstown and Whiteabbey
		Coleraine	08.00 hrs special workmen's diesel from Coleraine to Londonderry was prevented from leaving by UDA pickets forming a human chain on the level crossing
23.05.74	Thursday	Victoria Park	Bomb exploded on Connswater river, Bridge No 3 at 00.20 hrs: 3-foot section of track damaged; line reopened at 12.15 hrs
		Jordanstown	Line blocked by obstacles at Jordanstown and Whiteabbey
		Ballymena–Cullybackey	Beer keg on the line: line closed for 12.5 hours and overnight, into 24 May
		Portadown	Bomb exploded in the station at 14.05 hrs: two members of staff injured, one seriously; line closed for 45 minutes
24.05.74	Friday	Crawfordsburn	Fire extinguisher on the line – a hoax: line closed for 2.5 hours
25.05.74	Saturday	Bangor–Belfast	Bomb scare for 75 minutes
		Scarva–Poyntzpass	Bomb scare for 1 hour
26.05.74	Sunday	Lake Street, Lurgan	Object on track: line closed for 2.5 hours
27.05.74	Monday	Lisburn	UDA supporters invaded the station at 18.00 hrs and told staff to close down: station closed

31.05.74	Friday	Lake Street Lurgan	Object on track: line closed for 40 minutes
03.06.74	Monday	Belfast Great Victoria Street	Bomb scare in Ulsterbus area: Platform 4 closed for 30 minutes
07.06.74	Friday	Portadown–Belfast	Bomb scare for 1 hour
		Lurgan	Bomb scare in nearby shop: line closed for 2 hours
08.06.74	Saturday	Belfast Great Victoria Street	Bomb scare in Ulsterbus area: Platforms 2, 3 and 4 closed for 30 minutes
13.06.74	Thursday	Finaghy	All three incidents closed the line for 2.5 hours
		Belfast–Portadown	
		Seagoe	
18.06.74	Tuesday	Belfast Great Victoria Street	200 lb bomb exploded outside Europa hotel at 22.00 hours: windows shattered in station and customs office
21.06.74	Friday	Belfast Great Victoria Street	Bomb scare Europa hotel: station closed for 30 minutes
22.06.74	Saturday	Londonderry line	Bomb scare for whole line: line closed for 3 hours
		Cullybackey	Bomb scare re. suspicious box on the line: line closed for 3 hours
		Belfast–Portadown	Bomb scare for 1 hour
		Bangor–Belfast	Bomb scare for 20 minutes
06.07.74	Saturday	Belfast York Road	Car outside Midland hotel; controlled explosion: line closed for 3.5 hours
		Greencastle	Suspicious box found on the line: station and line closed for 3.5 hours (as above)
11.07.74	Thursday	Belfast Great Victoria Street	Car bomb exploded adjacent to station at 16.12 hrs: windows in station and clock damaged; station closed for 1 hour
17.07.74	Wednesday	Lurgan	Bomb scare for 30 minutes
20.07.74	Saturday	Dundalk	Bomb scare for 1 hour
22.07.74	Monday	Carrickfergus	Bomb scare in nearby premises: line closed for 15 minutes
25.07.74	Thursday	Derry train	Bomb scare for 17.40 hrs Londonderry–Belfast service: train delayed 30 minutes
		Belfast Great Victoria Street	500 lb bomb exploded outside the Europa hotel at 16.30 hrs: Platforms 1, 2 and 3 out of use for 2.5 hours; Platform 4 operational
03.08.74	Saturday	Kilnasaggart bridge	03.30 hrs freight Dublin–Adelaide hijacked at the bridge; locomotive packed with explosives; 400 lb bomb defused by Army: line closed for 28 hours and overnight, into 4 August
			NB: See Chapter Five for more details
06.08.74	Tuesday	Dundalk	Telephone warning re a bomb in a mail bag on the 03.30 hrs freight Dublin–Adelaide service: Portadown–Dundalk line closed for 7.5 hours
09.08.74	Friday	Greencastle	Parcel found on the line: line closed for 1.5 hours
10.08.74	Saturday	Faughal Upper	Bomb exploded and demolished an over-line aqueduct (Bridge No 166) near the border: Portadown–Dundalk line closed for 17 hours
11.08.74	Sunday	Portadown	Parcel on the line at Annagh bridge: line closed for 25 minutes
13.08.74	Tuesday	Belfast York Road	Bomb scare for NIR offices: we just worked on!
21.08.74	Wednesday	Bangor–Belfast	Bomb scare for 9 hours and overnight, into 22 August
		Kilnasaggart bridge	03.30 hrs freight Dublin–Adelaide service hijacked on the bridge; locomotive packed with 200 lb bomb, defused by Army: line closed for 29 hours and overnight, into 22 August
29.08.74	Thursday	Bangor–Belfast	Bomb scare for 1.5 hours
30.08.74	Friday	Belfast York Road	Unattended car outside Midland hotel closed station twice during clearance operation for 2 hours; passengers gained access to trains through the diesel shed.
04.09.74	Thursday	Belfast York Road	Unattended car outside Midland hotel exploded at 12.50 hrs: glass damage to the station; service suspended for 40 minutes.
		Belfast Great Victoria Street	Unattended van in Glengall Street: train service stopped for 4 hours

09.09.74	Monday	Kingsbog Portadown–Belfast	Box found below Hart's bridge: line closed for over 4 hours. Bomb scare for 1.5 hours
12.09.74	Thursday	Belfast–Antrim Greencastle	Bomb scare for 1.5 hours Unattended lorry on motorway bridge: line closed for 2 hours
13.09.74	Friday	Whitehead	Fire extinguisher found at Kings Road bridge: line closed for 1 hour
20.09.74	Friday	Belfast Great Victoria Street	Duffle bag left beside book stall in station: station closed for 10 minutes
23.09.74	Monday	Portadown–Seagoe	Box found on the line: line closed for 30 minutes
04.10.74	Friday	Newry–Dundalk	Bomb scare for 3 hours
08.10.74	Tuesday	Meigh	50 lb bomb exploded and damaged up line: single-line working introduced; line closed for 10.5 hours and overnight, into 9 October **NB: See Chapter Five for more details**
15.10.74	Tuesday	Long Kesh fire triggering a spate of incidents	A major fire broke out in the Republican end of Long Kesh prison near Lisburn on the evening of Tuesday, 15 October 1974. This sparked major riots in various parts of Northern Ireland, and the railway of course was targeted in a number of incidents over the next four days, as follows:
16.10.74	Wednesday	Bells Row, Lurgan	Three masked men ordered the crossing keeper out and placed a parcel on the line – a hoax: line closed for 4.5 hours and overnight, into 17 October
17.10.74	Thursday	Lisburn–Lurgan	Bomb scare for 3.5 hours
18.10.74	Friday	Ballymoney	Seven buses were damaged by fire in the Ulsterbus yard at 02.00 hrs: fire damaged the railway station roof and canopy; freight trains delayed by 40 minutes
19.10.74	Saturday	Bells Row, Lurgan	Box left on the line: line closed for 1 hour
24.10.74	Thursday	Belfast Great Victoria Street	Suitcase left beside book stall: station closed for 20 minutes
25.10.74	Friday Friday	Belfast Queen's Quay Kilnasaggart bridge	Bomb scare in station for 30 minutes Army were cratering unapproved roads in the area, and amounts of rubble landed on the track: line closed for 1.5 hours, and again later on for 4 hours
30.10.74	Wednesday	Belfast–Larne	Bomb scare for 2.5 hours
31.10.74	Thursday	Belfast–Bangor	Bomb scare for 45 minutes
05.11.74	Tuesday	Dundalk–Border Belfast Great Victoria Street Balmoral	07.00 hours freight Dundalk–Adelaide service hijacked near the border (IÉ side); one rail on each side of the train removed by civil engineers in case the train ran off; objects placed on board locomotive – a hoax: line closed for 8.5 hours Hijacked lorry parked in Glengall Street – a hoax: line closed for 2.5 hours Parcel on footbridge – line closed for 1 hour
06.11.74	Wednesday	Cloghogue, Newry	Car parked under the bridge: line closed for 30 minutes
08.11.74	Friday	Bangor Whiteabbey Fortwilliam Mountpleasant and Portadown Belfast–Lisburn Central Junction, Belfast	Unattended car on the Boyne bridge: line closed for 50 minutes during morning rush-hour Canister found on the embankment; controlled explosion by Army: line closed for 4 hours Bomb scare for 1 hour 03.30 hrs freight Dublin–Adelaide service hijacked at Mountpleasant (IÉ); train sent on with no crew, and derailed in Portadown station – thought to have explosives on board – a hoax: line closed for 33.5 hours and overnight, into 9 November Bomb scare for 30 minutes Parcel on the line at Donegall Road bridge – a hoax: closed for 1 hour **NB: See Chapter Five for more details**
10.11.74	Sunday	Faughal Upper	Special freight train Adelaide–Dundalk struck two sleepers on the line near the border

14.11.74	Thursday	Belfast–Bangor	Bomb scare for 1 hour
18.11.74	Monday	Victoria Park	Canister on the line: line closed for 1 hour
		Victoria Park	Bomb scare for 30 minutes
		Jordanstown	Canister on the level crossing; controlled explosion by Army – a hoax: line closed for 1.5 hours
		Kingsbog and Kilmakee	Canister on each level crossing; controlled explosions by Army – both hoaxes: line closed for 8 hours; some glass damage to Kingsbog signal box
		Greencastle	Hijacked bus left under motorway bridge: line closed for 30 minutes.
		Whiteabbey	Bomb scare for 20 minutes
		Kilmore–Moira	Object on the line spotted by train driver: line closed for 7 hours
20.11.74	Wednesday	Whiteabbey	Parcel found on line, containing four sticks of gelignite in poor condition: line closed for 20 minutes
21.11.74	Thursday	Meigh	Milk churn found lying on the embankment; 100 lb bomb detonated by the Army on Sunday 24: line closed for 81 hours, from 23.00 hrs on 21 November to 07.30 hrs on Monday, 25 November **NB: See Chapter Five for more details**
19.12.74	Thursday	Lurgan line	Telephone warning re a bomb: line closed for 9.5 hours and overnight, into 20 December
16.01.75	Thursday	Coleraine–Portrush	Railway chairs found on facing points at Portrush, leading to bomb scare for 15 minutes
17.01.75	Friday	Faughal Upper	Car parked on Smith's occupation crossing; two bombs found in the car; one 100 lb and one 50 lb bomb detonated by the Army: line closed for 62 hours from 00.03 hrs on 17 January to 10.00 hrs on 19 January **NB: See Chapter Five for more details**
23.01.75	Thursday	Belfast Great Victoria Street	Bomb exploded in the Europa hotel at 12.10 hrs: station closed for 1.5 hrs
28.01.75	Tuesday	Bessbrook	08.30 hrs Dublin–Belfast service stopped and searched by Army; train driver alerted by railway detonators (emergency detonator devices to alert train drivers of dangers ahead) placed by Army: delay of 50 minutes
31.01.75	Friday	Bells Row, Lurgan Lake Street, Lurgan	Trains delayed by 30 minutes by crowds on both crossings, protesting about IRA prisoners in Portlaoise jail in ROI.
02.02.75	Sunday	Portadown	Box left at ticket barrier in station; controlled explosion by Army – a hoax: line closed for 4.5 hours and overnight, into 3 February
06.02.75	Thursday	Cloghogue, Newry	400 lb bomb exploded in a lorry parked near the bridge: line closed 13.5 hours overnight, into 7 February, due to debris from the blast on the track
07.02.75	Friday	Lurgan	Bomb scare for 1 hour
09.02.75	Sunday	Border	O'Rourke's bridge No 164 and both tracks damaged by an explosion at 22.44 hrs on Sunday, 9 February: line closed until 13.30 hours on Monday 10th
10.02.75	Monday	Holywood	Bomb scare for 20 minutes
17.02.75	Monday	Bells Row, Lurgan	Bomb scare for 45 minutes
		Portadown	Bomb scare for 20 minutes
18.02.75	Tuesday	Portadown	Suspicious box found in works trailer; controlled explosion – a hoax: station closed for 1.5 hours
25.02.75	Tuesday	Dublin train	Bomb scare on 17.30 hrs Belfast–Dublin train; searched at Dunmurry and mail bags removed by police for further searches: service delayed by 25 minutes
27.03.75	Thursday	Holywood	Car abandoned on REME level crossing – cleared within 1 hour
04.04.75	Friday	Dunmurry–Lisburn	Bomb scare for 20 minutes
14.04.75	Monday	Monkstown Jordanstown Carrickfergus	All three incidents were bomb scares within the same timeframe — lines closed for 2 hours

28.04.75	Monday	Belfast Central Railway	A contractor shot dead on the track at the Donegall Road bridge **NB: See Chapter Five for more details**
23.05.75	Friday	Belfast Great Victoria Street	Bomb scare for 30 minutes
26.05.75	Monday	Belfast Great Victoria Street	Bomb scare for 20 minutes
31.05.75	Saturday	Portadown	Suspicious car on Shillington bridge: line closed for 1.5 hours
06.06.75	Friday	Newry	Unattended car parked under the Egyptian Arch; Army carried out a controlled explosion – a hoax: line closed 3 hours
10.06.75	Tuesday	Bangor	Bomb scare for 15 minutes
12.06.75	Thursday	Bangor	Bomb scare for 10 minutes
13.06.75	Friday	Goodyear	Unattended car on new flyover near the station: line closed for 2.5 hours
01.07.75	Tuesday	Lurgan	Suspicious parcel delayed trains for 35 minutes
30.07.75	Wednesday	Belfast Great Victoria Street	Suitcase in station, which was closed for 1 hour
04.08.75	Monday	Dublin train	17.30 hrs Belfast–Dublin train arrived in Dublin 5.5 hours late, due to reports of a possible ambush **NB: See Chapter Five for more details**
08.08.75	Friday	Lake Street, Lurgan	After rioting in the town, a large number of unruly youths petrol-bombed the crossing keeper's hut at 03.00 hrs: hut interior destroyed
		Portadown	Duffle bag on the platform; controlled explosion by Army – a hoax: station closed for 1.5 hours
10.08.75	Sunday	Lurgan	At 02.25 hours, two bombs exploded in the station – one on either platform, causing extensive damage to all buildings and new footbridge **NB: See Chapter Five for more details**
13.08.75	Wednesday	Meigh	Suspect object on the down line on the crossing – a hoax: services delayed for 30 minutes
23.08.75	Saturday	Belfast Central	Contractors' hut destroyed by fire
24.08.75	Sunday	Goodyear	Suspect car under nearby bridge – line closed for 2 hours
29.08.75	Friday	Victoria Park	Suitcase found at station – a hoax: station closed for 1 hour
		Hilden	Suspect box 16.05 hrs – a hoax: line closed for 3.5 hours
04.09.75	Thursday	Kinnegar	Suitcase found at station – a hoax: line closed for 20 minutes
05.09.75	Friday	Belfast–Bangor	Bomb scare for 45 minutes
		Belfast–Antrim	Bomb scare for 40 minutes
		Belfast–Lisburn	Bomb scare for 15 minutes
06.09.75	Saturday	Belfast York Road	Two brown vans destroyed by incendiaries in the station yard **NB: See Chapter Five for more details**
12.09.75	Friday	Kingsbog	Bomb scare in nearby premises: line closed for 2.5 hours
16.09.75	Tuesday	Eden	Platform badly damaged by fire
18.09.75	Thursday	Lurgan	Suspect car on Convent bridge; two controlled explosions by Army: car and bridge badly damaged; line closed for 2.5 hours from 07.10 hrs
22.09.75	Monday	Kilnasaggart bridge	17.15 hrs freight Dundalk–Lisburn hijacked by armed men: locomotive badly damaged by explosions at 18.30 hrs on 22 September; line not reopened until 12.00 hrs on 25 September
		Londonderry	Duffle bag left in gents' toilets: station badly damaged by an explosion at 16.25 hrs **NB: See Chapter Five for more details**
25.09.75	Thursday	Portadown–Newry	Bomb scare for 3 hours from 12.00 hrs
26.09.75	Friday	Belfast Great Victoria Street	Bomb scare at Europa hotel: station cleared for 10 minutes
27.09.75	Saturday	Lurgan	Suspect parcel at Dougher bridge – a hoax: line closed for 40 minutes

30.09.75	Tuesday	Dunmurry	Suspect object in subway: line closed for 2.5 hours
03.10.75	Friday	Balmoral	Bomb scare for 19 minutes
03.10.75	Friday	Newry line	Bomb scare for 9 hours and overnight, into 4 October
05.10.75	Sunday	Belfast–Bangor	Bomb scare for 1.5 hours and overnight, into 6 October
07.10.75	Tuesday	Lisburn	Bomb scare for 35 minutes
09.10.75	Thursday	Belfast Great Victoria Street	Bomb scare for 30 minutes
11.10.75	Saturday	Lurgan	Suspect car adjacent to station – a hoax: line closed for 20 minutes
13.10.75	Monday	Belfast York Road	Bomb scare for 25 minutes
		Belfast Great Victoria Street	Bomb scare for 20 minutes
15.10.75	Wednesday	Kilnasaggart bridge	07.00 hrs freight Dundalk–Adelaide service hijacked by armed men; explosives placed on locomotive; two 225 lb bombs defused by Army: line closed for 87 hours, and reopened at 22.10 hrs on 18 October **NB: See Chapter Five for more details**
19.10.75	Sunday	Lurgan	Suspect object at Dougher bridge – a hoax: closed for 1 hour
26.10.75	Sunday	Dunmurry–Lisburn	Bomb scare for 2 hours
30.10.75	Thursday	Belfast York Road	Bomb scare for 50 minutes
		Londonderry–Lisahally	Bomb scare for 12 hours and overnight, into 31 October, which led to the cancellation of freight trains
31.10.75	Friday	Belfast York Road	Bomb scare for 20 minutes
08.11.75	Saturday	Lurgan	06.00 hrs Belfast–Portadown service struck a platform seat placed on the line
20.11.75	Thursday	Kilnasaggart bridge	17.15 hrs freight Dundalk–Lisburn hijacked by armed men. Train was sent on later with no crew; train derailed at Goraghwood deviation (CIÉ locomotive and 20 wagons): single-line working from 18.30 hrs on Friday 21 November, to continue over the up line for the next six days **NB: See Chapter Five for more details**
02.12.75	Tuesday	Monkstown	Bomb scare for 25 minutes.
		Whiteabbey	Unattended van – dealt with within 20 minutes
		Greenisland	Suspicious box – cleared in 40 minutes
		Bleach Green Junction	Beer keg on the line – cleared after 2.5 hours
			All these incidents started shortly after 14.00 hrs, and were linked to a protest at the treatment of loyalist prisoners at Magilligan jail.
11.12.75	Thursday	Belfast York Road	Bomb scare for 30 minutes
18.12.75	Thursday	Belfast Queen's Quay	Report of a bomb in a mail bag on board 18.15 hrs Belfast–Bangor train – a hoax: line clear by 21.15 hrs
		Lake Street, Lurgan	15 lb shrapnel bomb found by Army and defused: line closed from 15.05 hrs for 3 hours
22.12.75	Monday	Belfast York Road	Bomb scare for 30 minutes
		Belfast Great Victoria Street	Bomb scare for 25 minutes
28.12.75	Sunday	Lake Street, Lurgan	Suspect gas cylinder – a hoax: line closed from 16.00 hrs for 18.5 hours and overnight, into 29 December
29.12.75	Monday	Kilnasaggart bridge	17.15 hrs freight Dundalk–Lisburn hijacked by armed men; locomotive damaged by explosion. Crew of damaged freight train stopped the 17.30 hrs Belfast–Dublin passenger train, which returned to Poyntzpass: line closed for 88 hours, not reopened until 09.30 hrs on Friday, 2 January 1976 **NB: See Chapter Five for more details**
30.12.75	Tuesday	Belfast–Portadown	Bomb scare for 2 hours, from 18.45 hrs
02.01.76	Friday	Adelaide station	Box on platform: line closed 1 hour
06.01.76	Tuesday	Finaghy	Bomb scare for 15 minutes
		Belfast Great Victoria Street	Bomb scare at Europa hotel and station for 15 minutes

13.01.76	Tuesday	Belfast Great Victoria Street	Bomb scare at Europa hotel and station for 40 minutes
15.01.76	Thursday	Dunmurry	Suspicious package in subway – line closed for 35 minutes
23.01.76	Friday	Dublin Connolly	Unattended suitcase on 08.00 hrs Belfast–Dublin service, coach No 826; controlled explosion by Irish Army – a hoax: slight damage to train, and delays
30.01.76	Friday	Faughal (Border area)	Suspect package on track – a hoax: line closed for 4.5 hours
31.01.76	Saturday	Belfast–Jordanstown	Bomb scare for 45 minutes
		Jordanstown	Suspect bag on platform: line closed for 15 minutes
		Lake Street, Lurgan	Level crossing blocked for 45 minutes by Republicans protesting about hunger striker
05.02.76	Thursday	Kilnasaggart bridge	Three detonators set off by 07.00 hrs freight Dundalk–Adelaide – nothing untoward: services delayed by 45 minutes while line was checked
06.02.76	Friday	Scarva	5 lb bomb exploded on up line half a mile north of Scarva, as 17.30 hrs Belfast–Dublin train approached at 18.10 hrs: train derailed (CIÉ set): four passengers taken to Craigavon hospital. 17.30 hrs Dublin–Belfast service stopped at Poyntzpass; line cleared by Army on Saturday 7 February at 16.50 hrs: line not fully operational until Wednesday, 10 February at 17.20 hrs **NB: See Chapter Five for more details**
11.02.76	Wednesday	Central Junction, Belfast	Bomb in nearby shop: line closed for 50 minutes
12.02.76	Thursday	Lake Street, Lurgan	Considerable damage done to crossing keeper's hut, gates and signals by number of unruly youths Note: An IRA hunger striker died in an English jail on 12 February: a spate of incidents followed.
14.02.76	Saturday	Greencastle	Bomb scare at M2 bridge: line closed 1.5 hours
		Bells Row, Lurgan	Van placed on crossing by youths at 11.40 hours: line closed for 3.5 hours
		Lake Street, Lurgan	Crossing keeper's hut destroyed by fire started by unruly youths at 12.30 hrs
		Lake Street, Lurgan	Suspect van on main road, near crossing – a hoax: line closed for 2.5 hours from 17.00 hrs
15.02.76	Sunday	Whiteabbey	Suspect object on road bridge – a hoax: line closed for 1.5 hours
16.02.76	Monday	Crawfordsburn	Suspicious object spotted by train driver at 06.45 hrs; cleared by police
		Crawfordsburn	Bomb scare for 50 minutes from 07.40 hrs
17.02.76	Tuesday	Belfast Great Victoria Street	Bomb scare for 80 minutes, from 15.15 hrs. The author answered the phone in the office at Belfast York Road – a male caller said he was a member of the Provisional IRA and that there was a 100 lb bomb outside Great Victoria Street station, and then hung up.
19.02.76	Thursday	Cloghogue Newry	Car bomb under the railway bridge: line closed for 3 hours from 11.26 hrs
		Poyntzpass–Dundalk	Suspect object found by Army: 13.20 hrs freight Dundalk–Adelaide service stopped in the section by Army for 20 minutes
25.02.76	Wednesday	Belfast York Road	Bomb scare for 35 minutes
		Belfast Great Victoria Street	Bomb scare for 15 minutes
27.02.76	Friday	Derriaghy	Suspect bus on fire near McMaster's bridge: line closed for 2 hours from 21.20 hrs.
		Belfast York Road, Ivan Street bridge, Whiteabbey, Jordanstown	All four of these incidents were bomb scares and happened around the same time: line closed from 20.25 hrs on 27 February to 03.00 hrs on Saturday, 28 February
		Ballymena	Suspicious object in station concourse: station closed for one hour from 23.30 hrs
		Portadown–Poyntzpass	Suspicious object on Adam's accommodation crossing: line closed for 12 hours from 22.00 hrs and overnight, into 28 February **NB: See Chapter Five for more details**

28.02.76	Saturday	Portadown	Police contacted NIR to say that a newspaper had received a message stating that any train driver going past Portadown would be shot: some cross-border services affected
		Greenisland	Boulder placed on Herdman's accommodation crossing; spotted by train driver
		Larne line	Bomb scare for 1 hour
		Belfast York Road	Suspect box hanging from Ivan Street bridge – a hoax: line closed for 20 minutes
		Derriaghy	19.00 hrs Lisburn–Belfast hijacked by masked men; crew ordered off, and object placed on board coach No 84 – a hoax: line closed for 1.5 hours
		Clipperstown	Suspect object on bridge: line closed for 30 minutes
		Whiteabbey	Suspect object on line at Rush Park: line closed for 2 hours
		Sydenham	21.45 hrs Bangor–Belfast service hijacked by masked men; crew ordered off and fires started in coach No 509: train cleared by 23.50 hours
			NB: See Chapter Five for more details
29.02.76	Sunday	Belfast York Road	Signal box damaged by fire at 00.30 hours, causing considerable damage
		Glynn	Bomb scare for 1.5 hours, from 19.00 hrs
			NB: See Chapter Five for more details
01.03.76	Monday	Adelaide	Two suspicious objects on the line at Tates Avenue bridge: line closed for 1.5 hours
02.03.76	Tuesday	Goraghwood	Suspect object found at Dromantine bridge No 209: line closed for 9 hours and overnight, into 3 March
04.03.76	Thursday	Cannon Street, London	10 lb bomb exploded on an empty train, as it was being moved to a depot
			NB: See Chapter Five for more details
05.03.76	Friday	Newry area	Bomb scare for 9 hours and overnight, into 6 March. The telephone message: "Bomb on line north of Newry"
06.03.76	Saturday	Border area	Bomb scare for 10 hours and overnight, into 7 March. A telephone message: "Bombs at the Border"
07.03.76	Sunday	Kilnasaggart bridge	Bomb scare for 40 minutes
10.03.76	Wednesday	Kilnasaggart bridge	Explosion heard in the area at 15.01 hrs; line checked and in order: line closed for 1.5 hours
		Gormanstown (IÉ)	Suspect object at a signal post: line closed for 45 minutes
		Bangor line	Bomb scare for 15 minutes
11.03.76	Thursday	Belfast York Road	Bomb scare for 20 minutes
13.03.76	Saturday	Portadown–Dundalk	Bomb scare for 14.5 hours and overnight into 14 March
15.03.76	Monday	West Ham, London	Bomb exploded on a tube train; the tube driver was shot and killed following a confrontation with the terrorist
16.03.76	Tuesday	Wood Green, London	Bomb exploded on a tube train, injuring one man
24.03.76	Wednesday	Belfast Great Victoria Street	Bomb scare for 30 minutes
26.03.76	Friday	Crawfordsburn	Train driver spotted suspicious car on overhead bridge: trains delayed 30 minutes
		Belfast York Road	Bomb scare for 25 minutes
01.04.76	Thursday	Aldergrove	RAF reported wires running to the railway line: line closed for over 1 hour, from 09.40 hrs.
02.04.76	Friday	Belfast Great Victoria Street	Bomb scare for 15 minutes
		Lurgan–Portadown	Phone call to say that the 17.30 hrs Belfast–Dublin train would be blown up: delays of 1.5 hours
05.04.76	Monday	Belfast York Road	Bomb scare for 25 minutes at 15.00 hrs
06.04.76	Tuesday	Belfast York Road	Bomb scare for 35 minutes at 15.00 hrs

08.04.76	Thursday	Dunmurry	Suspect parcel at signal box: line closed for 30 minutes
12.04.76	Monday	Scarva	19.30 hrs light engine Adelaide–Dundalk struck two barrels on the line; checked by Army and cleared: line closed for 1 hour
14.04.76	Wednesday	Meigh	Beer keg on the line at Moore's bridge – a hoax: line closed for 18.5 hours and overnight, into 15 April
15.04.76	Thursday	Belfast York Road	Bomb scare for 20 minutes
19.04.76	Monday	Poyntzpass	Suspect parcel on the line at Gambles bridge at 14.10 hrs; a 10 lb bomb defused by the Army: line closed for 25 hours and overnight, into 20 April
		Bells Row, Lurgan, Lake Street, Lurgan	Both crossing keepers were ordered out at 21.00 hrs by armed men, and suspect objects left – hoaxes: line closed for 4 hours and overnight, into 20 April
20.04.76	Tuesday	Kilnasaggart bridge	Armed gangs tried to stop the 17.30 hrs Enterprise up and down services, but the drivers ignored their demands to stop, even after warning shots were fired by the terrorists.
21.04.76	Wednesday	Adavoyle	Suspect object on the line at 15.15 hrs – a hoax: line closed for 18 hours and overnight, into 22 April
22.04.76	Thursday	Border area	Suspect wires running across both lines at 15.30 hrs; 14.30 hrs Enterprise service Belfast–Dublin was stopped by the Army at Cloghogue Chapel bridge, and returned to Poyntzpass: line closed for a long period, and not reopened until Monday, 26 April at 15.20 hrs (96 hour closure)
24.04.76	Saturday	Belfast Great Victoria Street	Two unattended suitcases left: station closed for 75 minutes from 13.15 hrs
25.04.76	Sunday	Derriaghy	2 lb bomb exploded at the side of the up line at 00.15 hrs
		Adelaide	Bomb scare at Tates Avenue bridge for 1 hour from 15.30 hrs: no trains affected, due to ongoing engineering works for the transfer of services to Belfast Central on 26 April
27.04.76	Tuesday	Kilnasaggart bridge	Bomb scare for 2 hours, from 09.10 hours
03.05.76	Monday	Portadown–Dundalk	Bomb scare for 2.5 hours
08.05.76	Saturday	Belfast–Dundalk	Bomb scare for Belfast–Dublin train service: cross-border services delayed for searches for 1 hour
13.05.76	Thursday	Botanic	This was the first terrorist incident which affected the Belfast Central railway. Two bombs exploded in the adjacent Regency hotel: line between Belfast Central and Lisburn closed for 1.5 hours from 15.05 hrs
21.05.76	Friday	Botanic	Conductor of 17.40 hrs Bangor–Portadown service threw a suspicious rucksack on to the embankment; at 18.20 hrs the package exploded, causing no damage
		Broomhedge accommodation crossing (1.5 miles Moira side of Knockmore Junction)	A bomb exploded on the 17.40 hours Bangor–Portadown train at 18.40 hours. Miss Roberta Bartholomew, aged 21, was killed; ten other passengers injured, along with the conductor. The train was a five-car 80 class 81–761–732–738–88. No 81 was extensively damaged, with damage also to No 761 and No 732. Line reopened at 00.30 hrs on Saturday, 22 May. **NB: See Chapter Five for more details**
23.05.76	Sunday	Adelaide	Bomb scare for 1 hour
24.05.76	Monday	Dublin train	Bomb scare for 17.32 hrs Belfast–Dublin train, which was then searched; train left at 17.50 hrs
25.05.76	Tuesday	Dunmurry	Bomb scare for 15 minutes
02.06.76	Wednesday	Border–Belfast	Report at 08.50 hrs of three bombs on the line – nothing found: line closed for 2 hours
04.06.76	Friday	Sydenham–Victoria Park	Suspicious package on the line 07.15 hrs: line closed for 1.5 hours during morning rush-hour
06.06.76	Sunday	Botanic	Bomb scare for 45 minutes
07.06.76	Monday	Crumlin–Antrim	15.45 hrs Lisburn–Antrim train passed over a suspicious object on the track – a hoax: line closed for 4 hours

09.06.76	Wednesday	Belfast–Dublin	Bomb scare delayed cross-border services: 17.30 hrs Enterprise Dublin–Belfast arrived in Belfast 143 minutes late
12.06.76	Saturday	Kinnegar	Suspect object on the line at REME crossing – delays of 20 minutes
20.06.76	Sunday	Lurgan	Book stall damaged by fire started by youths at 03.25 hrs
23.06.76	Wednesday	Helen's Bay	Bomb scare for 45 minutes
24.06.76	Thursday	Lisburn	Bomb scare in nearby premises: line closed for 1 hour
		Border area	Bomb scare for 1.5 hours
29.06.76	Tuesday	Monkstown	Suspect parcel – a hoax: line closed for 1 hour
30.06.76	Wednesday	Belfast York Road	Bomb scare for 25 minutes
05.07.76	Monday	Bangor–Belfast Central	Bomb scare for 1 hour from 14.35 hrs; police travelled on empty train from Bangor to clear the line
		Belfast Central	Bomb scare for 45 minutes from 14.40 hrs. This was the first direct bomb scare at Belfast Central since the line opened in April 1976; we all stood out on East Bridge Street during the search.
06.07.76	Tuesday	Belfast Central–Bangor	Bomb scare for 75 minutes from 09.15 hrs; police travelled on empty train to Bangor to clear the line
		Mossley	Suspect object – a hoax: line closed for 45 minutes
07.07.76	Wednesday	Belfast Central–Bangor	Bomb scare for 50 minutes from 11.03 hrs; police travelled on empty train from Bangor to clear the line
09.07.76	Friday	Ballymoney	Suspect car parked adjacent to station at 01.30 hrs; bomb defused by the Army, and line reopened at 07.40 hrs: 01.25 hrs freight Lisburn–Londonderry running 4.5 hours late
12.07.76	Monday	Helen's Bay	Suspect parcel on track: line closed for 45 minutes from 19.48 hrs
		Seahill	Bomb scare for 45 minutes at 19.48 hrs; police travelled on empty train from Bangor to clear the line
13.07.76	Tuesday	Belfast York Road	Unattended suitcase in station – line closed for 10 minutes
15.07.76	Thursday	Dublin	Bomb scare in station: 14.30 hrs Enterprise Dublin–Belfast departed 15.02 hrs
17.07.76	Saturday	Botanic	Two suspect bags in the station: line closed for 20 minutes
22.07.76	Thursday	Londonderry	Waterside railway station badly damaged by explosion at 17.05 hrs.
23.07.76	Friday	Holywood	Suspect parcel on 15.35 hrs Bangor–Portadown train – a hoax: delays of 15 minutes
26.07.76	Monday	Holywood	Bomb scare for 40 minutes from 12.52 hours
		Holywood	Bomb scare for 25 minutes from 14.35 hours
03.08.76	Tuesday	Whiteabbey	Bomb scare for 25 minutes
07.08.76	Saturday	Botanic	Unattended suitcase found on 12.30 hours Portadown–Bangor service (coach Nos 89, 763, 737); shots fired by the Army and controlled explosion in coach No 763 – a hoax: line closed for 4 hours **NB: See Chapter Five for more details**
12.08.76	Thursday	Belfast Central	Bomb scare for 40 minutes from 16.17 hrs
23.08.76	Monday	Belfast York Road	Unattended suitcase: station closed for 10 minutes.
28.08.76	Saturday	Border area	Suspect van parked at Moore's bridge No 167 – a hoax: line closed for 29 hours and overnight, into 29 August
11.09.76	Saturday	Lurgan	Bomb exploded in nearby shop: station closed for 25 minutes
13.09.76	Monday	Whiteabbey	Barrel on up line spotted by driver of 06.15 hrs Belfast–Carrickfergus – a hoax; line cleared 08.58 hrs
		Kingsmoss	Suspect package on track: line closed for 20 minutes
		Dunmurry	Two petrol bombs thrown at new signal box at 22.00 hrs : no damage
		Belfast York Road	Suspect package at Ivan Street footbridge: line closed for 40 minutes.
		Belfast Central–Sydenham	Bomb scare for 40 minutes

14.09.76	Tuesday	Belfast York Road	Bomb scare in nearby premises; passengers left via the parcels office: station closed for 20 minutes
		Dunmurry–Derriaghy	Suspect object on line: line closed for 25 minutes
		Ballymacarrett	Suspect object on line: line closed for 1 hour
		Belfast York Road	Suspect package at Ivan Street footbridge: line closed for 40 minutes
15.09.76	Wednesday	Jordanstown	Waiting room badly damaged by malicious fire in early hours of morning
		Hilden	Suspect box under bridge: line closed for 1.5 hours
		Botanic	Bomb scare for 20 minutes
		Botanic–Lisburn	Bomb scare for 20 minutes
		Botanic–Lisburn	Bomb scare for 1.5 hours
		Jordanstown	Suspect holdall found on platform at 22.40 hrs; controlled explosion by Army: line closed for 75 minutes
		Galgorm	Unattended car left on the level crossing – a hoax: line closed 35 minutes and overnight, into 16 September
16.09.76	Thursday	Helen's Bay	Suspect box in subway: station for closed 35 minutes
17.09.76	Friday	Sydenham	20.40 hours Lisburn–Bangor hijacked by large number of youths; passengers and crew ordered off train; petrol bombs thrown into three-car MED train: coach Nos 527 and 27 slightly damaged.
		Belfast Central–Bangor	Bomb scare: line closed for 30 minutes from 21.45 hrs
18.09.76	Saturday	Clipperstown–Carrickfergus	Suspect object on the line, which was closed for 1.5 hours from 13.20 hrs
20.09.76	Monday	Donnybrewer near Eglinton	Box on the level crossing; controlled explosion by Army: line closed for 2.5 hours
23.09.76	Thursday	Border	Two suspect objects on the line – hoaxes: line closed for 1 hour
		Londonderry–Lisahally	Bomb scare for 1.5 hours
24.09.76	Friday	Central Junction, Belfast	Bomb scare in nearby premises: line closed for 15 minutes
27.09.76	Monday	Belfast York Road	Suspect bomb in Jennymount Mill: Line closed for 1 hour from 10.40 hrs
28.09.76	Tuesday	Botanic–Portadown	Bomb scare for 2.5 hours from 15.25 hrs; light engine Hunslet ran between Belfast–Portadown to clear the line.
		Belfast Central–Bangor	Bomb scare for 40 minutes from 15.50 hrs; police travelled on 16.05 hours empty train Belfast Central–Bangor to clear the line.
01.10.76	Friday	Dunmurry	Suspect box in subway: line closed for 50 minutes from 07.58 hours; services badly affected.
08.10.76	Friday	Belfast Central	Passenger boarding 20.40 hrs Lisburn–Bangor at Central handed out an unattended bag found on the train; train proceeded on its journey. A 10 lb bomb exploded on Platform 4: damage to the platform roof, also glass in ramp leading to Platforms 3 and 4.
		Holywood–Marino	Train involved in above-mentioned Belfast Central incident (20.40 hrs Lisburn–Bangor) was stopped due to the discovery of a bomb on board; army defused a 40 lb bomb on the train.
			NB: See Chapter Five for more details
14.10.76	Thursday	Dunmurry	Two bombs exploded in Moffett's factory, adjacent to up platform at 14.30 hrs: line closed for 1 hour
16.10.76	Saturday	Belfast Central	Two bombs exploded at the Gas Works at 21.25 hrs: line closed Belfast Central–Botanic for the rest of the night
23.10.76	Saturday	Border	Bomb scare for 1.5 hours
24.10.76	Sunday	Finaghy	Fire extinguisher on the line: line closed for 1.5 hours
28.10.76	Thursday	Adelaide	Car bomb at nearby premises: line closed for 4.5 hours from 12.05 hrs
08.11.76	Monday	Belfast York Road	Approx. 250 keys missing from the down line adjacent to Crusaders' football ground – noticed by the track walker at 13.15 hrs

10.11.76	Wednesday	Sydenham	Unattended briefcase found on board 08.15 hrs Lisburn–Bangor service; controlled explosion by Army: minor damage to MED coach No 29; Line closed for 3 hours **NB: See Chapter Five for more details**
13.11.76	Saturday	Botanic	Suspect car in Cameron Street – a hoax: line closed for 2.5 hours; 17.30 hrs Enterprise Dublin–Belfast arrived in Belfast at 22.00 hours (135 minutes late)
14.11.76	Sunday	Ballycarry–Glynn	Report of three bombs along the line; suspect devices found and dealt with by the Army **NB: See Chapter Five for more details**
15.11.76	Monday	Kilnasaggart bridge	Bomb scare for 13.5 hours and overnight, into Tuesday 16 November
17.11.76	Wednesday	Belfast Central–Botanic	Ammunition found in a house adjacent to railway in McClure Street; controlled explosion by Army: line closed for 1 hour from 08.19 hrs
18.11.76	Thursday	Lisburn	Suspect package in nearby premises closed the line for 1.5 hours
30.11.76	Tuesday	Dunmurry	Report of land mines in the area at 18.40 hours: line closed for extended period and not reopened until Thursday, 2 December at 15.30 hrs (45 hour closure) **NB: See Chapter Five for more details**
04.12.76	Saturday	Adelaide	Suspect car at Windsor park football ground at 06.00 hrs; controlled explosion by Army; bomb defused: Line closed for 2.5 hours
13.12.76	Monday	Cloghogue, Newry	Suspect lorry parked under the bridge: line closed at 13.49 hrs for 4 hours, but remained closed due to incident below at Ayallogue bridge
		Bells Row, Lurgan	Bus left on level crossing at 14.37 hrs; bomb on bus defused by the Army, who then dragged the bus away: line closed for 1 hour
		Bridge End	Suspect car found adjacent to station at 14.45 hrs: Bangor line closed for 1 hour
		Belfast Central	Bomb scare closed station for 45 minutes at 14.45 hrs
		Ayallogue	Suspect car under bridge near border at 14.49 hrs; 200 lb bomb defused by the Army: line closed for over 26 hours and overnight, into Tuesday, 14 December
		Central–Lisburn	Reports of land mines on track at 15.30 hrs; line cleared by inspection trains in both directions by 17.45 hrs
		Lisahally	Bomb scare at 16.08 hrs; cleared after 1.5 hours
		Belfast–Londonderry	Hoax call made and assessed: no closure of line
		Lurgan	Suspect objects found beside the track at Silverwood bridge at 21.45 hours; two bombs were defused by the Army: line does not reopen until 13.06 hrs on Wednesday, 15 December **NB: See Chapter Five for more details**
14.12.76	Tuesday	Bridge End	Suspect box on the line – a hoax: line closed for 15 minutes
		Greencastle	Suspect box at Erskine's bridge: line closed for 20 minutes
22.12.76	Wednesday	Portadown–Dundalk	Bomb scare from 22.00 hrs for 12 hours and overnight, into 23 December
23.12.76	Thursday	Dunmurry	Two bombs found in Locksley building, adjacent to railway at 15.36 hrs; bombs defused by Army: line closed for 1.5 hours
		Portadown–Dundalk	Bomb scare from 17.50 hrs for 16.5 hours and overnight, into 24 December
30.12.76	Thursday	Finaghy	Suspect box on platform – a hoax: station closed for 30 minutes
		Meigh	Bomb scare from 19.30 hrs for 13.5 hours and overnight, into 31 December
06.01.77	Thursday	Kilnasaggart bridge	Suspect object found on the line at 22.05 hrs: line closed for 18 hours and overnight, into 7 January
08.01.77	Saturday	Dunmurry	Bomb scare for 40 minutes
10.01.77	Monday	Lurgan–Dundalk	Report of land mines on track 22.00 hrs: line closed for 16.5 hours and overnight, into 11 January

17.01.77	Monday	Border area	Army advised of several explosions heard near Border at 11.29 hrs: line closed for 30 minutes
19.01.77	Wednesday	Belfast York Road	Bomb scare for 15 minutes
21.01.77	Friday	Bridge End	Suspect object found at Middlepath Street bridge at 12.10 hrs: Bangor line closed for 45 minutes
		Belfast Central–Botanic	Bomb scare for 40 minutes from 12.25 hrs
22.01.77	Saturday	Belfast Central	Bomb scare for 1.5 hours from 18.45 hrs
27.01.77	Thursday	Finaghy	Bomb scare for 15 minutes
29.01.77	Saturday	Bells Row Lurgan	Armed men advised the crossing keeper of bombs on the line at 20.15 hrs: line closed for 16 hours and overnight, into 30 January
31.01.77	Monday	Victoria Park	Suspect object at station: line closed for 1.5 hours from 22.00 hrs
03.02.77	Thursday	Larne line	Bomb scare for 20 minutes
04.02.77	Friday	Portadown	Suspect box found under a seat on the 14.30 hrs Belfast–Dublin train – a hoax: train delayed for 21 minutes
08.02.77	Tuesday	Dunmurry	Suspect bomb found in Moffett's factory, adjacent to up platform at 19.42 hrs: line closed for 17 hours and overnight into 9 February
17.02.77	Thursday	Belfast York Road	Bomb scare for 1.5 hours, from 22.45 hrs and overnight, into 18 February
22.02.77	Tuesday	Lurgan–Portadown	Bomb scare for 11.5 hours from 23.10 hrs and overnight, into 23 February. Trains ran from Bangor to Lurgan.
24.02.77	Thursday	Belfast Central–Lisburn	Bomb scare for 30 minutes from 16.00 hrs
25.02.77	Friday	Belfast Central–Bangor	Bomb scare for 1.5 hours from 12.48 hrs; police travelled on empty train to clear the line
28.02.77	Monday	Ballymena	Five buses destroyed in Ulsterbus yard at 20.20 hrs; trains stopped and station searched for 2 hours
12.03.77	Saturday	Greencastle	Suspect box on track – a hoax: line closed for 25 minutes.
28.03.77	Monday	Finaghy	Suspect van in Diamond Gardens; a 25 lb bomb defused by the Army: line closed for 3.5 hours from 11.09 hrs
		Dunmurry	Petrol tanker hijacked and left in the village; 5 lb bomb defused by the Army: line closed for 2 hours from 14.30 hrs
06.04.77	Wednesday	Central Junction, Belfast	Shrapnel bomb (1 lb) detonated by the Army beside the track: line closed for 1 hour **NB: See Chapter Five for more details**
02.05.77	Monday	Sydenham	Both up and down lines damaged by explosions at 23.50 hrs. **NB: See Chapter Five for more details**
03.05.77	Tuesday	Across Northern Ireland	An Ulster Workers Council strike ran from 3–13 May: some of the incidents involving the railway are recorded in Chapter Five **NB: See Chapter Five for more details**
03.05.77	Tuesday	Crawfordsburn	Both lines blocked by a barricade 12.15 hrs.
11.05.77	Wednesday	Bangor	Bomb exploded at the bus depot 17.20 hrs: minor damage caused
		Victoria Park	Down line damaged by explosion in evening: single-line working on the next day
11.08.77	Thursday	Kilnasaggart Lurgan Cullybackey	Bomb scares at three locations to coincide with the second day of HM The Queen's visit to Northern Ireland
21.10.77	Wednesday	Lisburn	Four incendiary devices on train in Lisburn, also one on the platform **NB: See Chapter Five for more details**
04.11.77	Friday	Bangor	One incendiary device found on train; controlled explosion by Army **NB: See Chapter Five for more details**

APPENDIX B

Selection of Terrorist Incidents on Northern Ireland Railways, 1978–2013

Date	Day	Location	Details
23.01.78	Monday	Lisburn–Dunloy	Bomb scares along the line prevented the new Londonderry service to Belfast Central via Lisburn running until mid-afternoon
21.02.78	Tuesday	Helen's Bay–Seahill	Bomb scare at 08.30 hrs; line cleared by empty diesel with volunteer crews (including the author)
02.05.78	Tuesday	Kilnasaggart	Bridge badly damaged by two bombs in the evening: services did not resume until 07.00 hrs on Friday, 5 May
		Limavady area	The Roe River bridge and the Burnfoot River bridge both damaged by bombs in the evening
			NB: See Chapter Six for more details
03.05.78	Wednesday	Dunloy Kellswater	Bomb scares at both locations during the morning up until 12.15 hrs
04.05.78	Thursday	Londonderry	Four bombs devastated the building: rolling stock stabled in the station also damaged
			NB: See Chapter Six for more details
26.05.78	Friday	Kilnasaggart	Bridge damaged again and not reopened until Monday 29 May at 16.30 hrs; Two further bombs found in the area by the Army
			NB: See Chapter Six for more details
08.06.78	Thursday	Newry	100 lb bomb found on the down line at the Egyptian Arch; defused by the Army. (The author was in the area at the time and saw the device as he approached it, partly hidden under a rail on the down line.)
27.06.78	Tuesday	Lurgan	Bomb defused at signal box at 05.00 hrs, then another bomb scare closed the line until 22.30 hrs
01.07.78	Saturday	Antrim	Four MED coaches destroyed by fire in the yard. They were en route to Magheramorne for scrapping
12.10.78	Thursday	Botanic–Belfast Central	Four bombs exploded on the 08.00 hrs Enterprise Dublin–Belfast: one passenger killed and eight passengers injured
		Dunmurry	Signal box destroyed by explosion and fire at 11.45 hrs
		Belfast–Bangor Larne Line Central Junction	Bomb scares during the day: services disrupted on all three lines
			NB: See Chapter Six for more details
20.11.78	Monday	Kilnasaggart	06.10 hrs freight Dundalk–Adelaide service hijacked and moved two miles north to Newtown bridge; objects placed on board: line not re-opened until Saturday, 25 November (six-day closure)
			NB: See Chapter Six for more details
22.11.78	Wednesday	Central Junction, Belfast	Bomb exploded under Utility Street footbridge at 17.00 hrs: no major disruption to services
28.11.78	Tuesday	Sydenham	15.55 hrs Belfast–Bangor struck an object which was later found to be a bomb: line cleared by 18.46 hrs
			NB: See Chapter Six for more details
30.11.78	Thursday	Lurgan	Signal box at William Street destroyed by an explosion and fire at 20.30 hrs.
24.12.78	Sunday	Lurgan	Station buildings extensively damaged by two explosions on Christmas Eve at 21.00 hrs
21.04.79	Saturday	Killeen bridge, near Border	Freight train stopped by armed men; locomotive destroyed by explosions: line reopened on Monday, 23 April
			NB: See Chapter Six for more details
25.05.79	Friday	Belfast York Road	Two bombs exploded on a train arriving from Larne Harbour: no injuries, but extensive damage to train
		Crumlin-Antrim	Two bombs exploded on 20.10 hrs service from Belfast to Londonderry: no injuries but extensive damage to train
			NB: See Chapter Six for more details

23.07.79	Monday	Goraghwood deviation	06.45 hrs freight Dundalk–Adelaide hijacked at the Border and sent on without the crew; the train derailed at the deviation, blocking both lines: line reopened later that day **NB: See Chapter Six for more details**
11.09.79	Tuesday	Goraghwood deviation	06.45 hrs freight Dundalk–Adelaide hijacked at the Border and sent on without the crew; the train derailed at the deviation, blocking both lines **NB: See Chapter Six for more details**
19.09.79	Wednesday	Balmoral	Bomb exploded on 22.05 hrs service Lisburn–Bangor: no injuries, but two coaches destroyed **NB: See Chapter Six for more details**
02.10.79	Tuesday	Belfast Central	Bomb exploded in an electricity generator station adjacent to the station at 12.50 hrs, starting a fierce fire: station closed from 12.14 hrs to 14.00 hrs
26.11.79	Monday	Belfast Central Adelaide Bangor line	Bomb exploded on Platforms 3 and 4; the bomb had been lifted off the 16.10 hrs Bangor–Portadown train; a second bomb was defused Two bombs exploded on 16.15 hrs Lisburn–Belfast Central train Bomb scare at 17.00 hrs: no services between Belfast and Bridge End for several hours **NB: See Chapter Six for more details**
17.01.80	Thursday	Dunmurry Belfast York Road Greenisland	Three passengers killed and a number injured when bombs exploded on the 16.55 hrs service from Ballymena–Belfast Central Bomb exploded on the platform, after being removed from the 17.35 hrs service from Belfast–Carrickfergus Bomb exploded on the platform, after being removed from the 17.35 hrs service from Carrickfergus–Belfast York Road **NB: See Chapter Six for more details**
30.04.80	Wednesday	Lisburn	Signal box damaged by an explosion, late evening
06.05.80	Tuesday	Kilnasaggart	Bridge damaged by an explosion in the late evening; nearby Grants bridge also damaged: line not reopened until Wednesday, 14 May 1980
16.10.80	Thursday	Belfast Central	Three members of NIR staff (including the author) due to be interviewed by the BBC were shot at on Platforms 3 and 4 by a gunman in Friendly Street **NB: See Chapter Six for more details**
23.11.80	Sunday	Faughalotra, near Border	Bomb destroyed an over-bridge aqueduct, which subsequently flooded the track: line reopened on Wednesday, 26 November
21.01.81	Wednesday	Border	Suspicious objects on the track closed the line for three days, until cleared by the Army (all hoaxes)
23.04.81	Thursday	Belfast Central Portadown	Inspector's hut on Platform 3 and 4 destroyed by fire at 02.20 hrs during rioting in the Markets estate 80 Class motor coach damaged by a petrol bomb; fire put out by staff
February 1982	No record	Portadown	Station badly damaged by explosions
08.03.82	Monday	Knockmore	Bombs damaged all three running lines
09.03.82	Tuesday	Meigh Bangor line, Larne line	Bomb defused by Army at level crossing Both lines closed during the day, due to bomb scares **NB: See Chapter Six for more details**
21.03.82	Sunday	Coleraine	Three stabled 80 Class carriages badly damaged by a firebomb attack in the early hours **NB: See Chapter Six for more details**
01.04.82	Thursday	Red Bridge, Newry	Bomb exploded, causing damage to the bridge (The author was on the track near the bridge shortly beforehand and spotted the bags of fertiliser there)
20.08.82	Thursday	Adelaide Freight	Police received a tip-off and found a 20 lb bomb on a freight train in the yard; defused by Army
11.09.84	Tuesday	Seahill	Suspect beer keg under down platform; controlled explosion by the Army: line closed for 2.5 hrs.

29.09.84	Saturday	Kilnasaggart	Bridge damaged by an explosion late evening: line closed for several days
03.12.84	Monday	Kilnasaggart	Freight train stopped by armed men and explosives placed on board, which detonated: line closed until Tuesday, 4 December
09.08.85	Friday	Newry	Several incendiaries ignited on board the 15.00 hrs Enterprise Dublin–Belfast Central in the station; fires put out by staff
29.08.85	Thursday	Belfast Central	Bomb exploded in the guard's van of the 11.00 hrs Enterprise Dublin–Belfast Central: Police and staff injured. **NB: See Chapter Six for more details**
31.03.86	Monday	Belfast Central	Station under siege for an hour due to 2,000 assembled passengers who had been prevented from travelling to Portadown under the Emergency Powers Act **NB: See Chapter Six for more details**
01.05.86	Thursday	Portadown	Tamping & lining machine No 07–7 badly damaged during a riot close to the station
28.05.86	Wednesday	Belfast Central	Armed robbery at booking office: £5,000 stolen
17.06.86	Tuesday	Bangor	Driver's cab of 80 Class motor coach No 83 badly damaged by a fire bomb overnight
28.07.86	Monday	Belfast Central	Hand grenade found on platform canopy (at Platforms 3 and 4) by member of staff, who threw it on to track; Security forces came to remove it
28.08.86	Thursday	Belfast Central	Bomb exploded in gent's toilets at 14.15 hrs; station re-opened 16.15 hrs and further bomb warning call closed the station from 16.45 to 17.50 hrs.
27.10.86	Monday	Kilnasaggart	Locomotive of Dundalk–Adelaide freight train blown up after being hijacked by armed men
25.11.87	Wednesday	Belfast Central	80 Class power car No 93 damaged by petrol bombs: passenger area and guard's van destroyed
04.04.88	Monday	Belfast Central	Petrol bomb attack at 00.25 hrs on Easter Monday: both platform huts destroyed and ramp No 3 and 4 badly damaged at platform end
09.09.88	Friday	Finaghy	Passenger shot dead on a Belfast-bound train at 07.40 hrs. **NB: See Chapter Six for more details**
04.10.88	Tuesday	Belfast York Road	Station and offices damaged by an explosion at 16.00 hrs: over 300 windows damaged within the station and diesel shed complex
16.12.88	Friday	Kilnasaggart	Bridge slightly damaged by explosion late evening
03.02.89	Friday	Kilnasaggart	Bridge slightly damaged by explosion late evening
17.02.89	Friday	Kilnasaggart	Bridge slightly damaged by explosion late evening
29.06.89	Thursday	Umbra	A call had been made to warn of a bomb in the vicinity of Umbra level crossing near Magilligan. Police advised NIR of all-clear but as the 06.25 hrs service Londonderry–Belfast travelled through the area, a landmine under the track went off, damaging the front bogie of the train
23.02.90	Friday	Newry	Booking office Portacabin destroyed by explosion
30.05.90	Wednesday	Derriaghy	80 Class coach No 746 gutted internally and No 95 smoke damage by an explosion and fire, had been working the 22.35 hrs Lisburn–Bangor
28.06.90	Thursday	Newry	Replacement booking office Portacabin destroyed by explosion
09.10.91	Wednesday	Belfast Central	Bomb exploded in the foyer of the station at 22.00 hrs, causing widespread glass damage
23.12.91	Monday	Belfast Central	Bomb left at front of station at 23.00 hrs; defused by the Army at 03.00 hrs
27.12.91	Friday	Newry	Replacement booking office Portacabin destroyed by explosion, which blew a portion out of a rail on the down line: line reopened Sunday, 29 December
23.01.92	Thursday	Eglinton	Explosion on the railway late evening blew out a section of rail: line closed until next day
29.01.92	Wednesday	Belfast Central	Explosion on the up line at 04.30 hrs near the Blackstaff River: line closed all morning
01.05.92	Friday	Cloghogue, Newry	A 1000 lb bomb exploded on railway adjacent to an Army checkpoint: one soldier killed; Line not reopened until Wednesday, 6 May **NB: See Chapter Six for more details**

13.07.92	Monday	Belfast Central	Army dog was killed while sniffing for a suspect device, which exploded in early evening near the Ormeau Road bridge: line still closed 14th so Royal Black Preceptory (RBP) specials from Lurgan to Bangor cancelled – went by bus
20.08.92	Thursday	Finaghy	Terrorists placed a bomb on board a train at 15.40 hrs which exploded, destroying the passenger section of 80 Class motor coach No 83. The motor coach had only been refurbished the previous month.
21.06.93	Monday	Belfast Central	Explosion on the down line during early hours towards Ormeau Road: line closed all morning
15.07.93	Thursday	Belfast Central	Bomb exploded at front of station at 02.00 hrs, causing widespread glass damage. The whole upper frontage of the station was covered in tarpaulin sheeting until the glass was replaced.
26.11.93	Friday	Kilnasaggart	Bomb exploded on bridge at 17.50 hrs: line reopened next day
12.09.94	Monday	Dublin Connolly	Small explosion on board 09.00 hrs Enterprise service Belfast–Dublin: two passengers injured.
06.07.97	Sunday	Bells Row, Lurgan	A lunchtime train from Belfast Central to Portadown was hijacked at the level crossing; passengers told to get off and train was set on fire: four carriages destroyed. **NB: See Chapter Six for more details**
14.02.00	Monday	Lake Street, Lurgan	Rioting in Lurgan; a van and a lorry hijacked, driven onto the line and set on fire at 19.00 hrs: line re-opened next day.
10.07.00	Monday	Victoria Park	16.22 hrs service Belfast Central–Bangor struck a metal obstruction on the track (a protest related to Drumcree).
09.03.01	Friday	Lurgan	A 46 lb bomb defused by the Army after a few days closure of the line.
13.07.04	Tuesday	Lurgan	Loyal Order RBP special train from Lurgan–Bangor was attacked by an unruly mob as it passed through Kilwilkie estate. **NB: See Chapter Six for more details**
12.07.10	Monday	Lake Street Lurgan	An unruly mob stopped the 16.10 hrs Enterprise service Belfast–Dublin and attempted to hijack it. **NB: See Chapter Six for more details**

INDEX